FARRAR
STRAUS
GIROUX

THE RIVER OF
LOST FOOTSTEPS

THE RIVER OF LOST FOOTSTEPS

HISTORIES OF BURMA

〜〜〜

THANT MYINT-U

FARRAR, STRAUS AND GIROUX · NEW YORK

Farrar, Straus and Giroux
19 Union Square West, New York 10003

Copyright © 2006 by Thant Myint-U
All rights reserved
Distributed in Canada by Douglas & McIntyre Ltd.
Printed in the United States of America
First edition, 2006

Library of Congress Cataloging-in-Publication Data
Thant Myint-U.
    The river of lost footsteps : histories of Burma / Thant Myint-U. — 1st ed.
        p.   cm.
    Includes bibliographical references.
    ISBN-13: 978-0-374-16342-6 (hardcover : alk. paper)
    ISBN-10: 0-374-16342-1 (hardcover : alk. paper)
    1. Burma — History — 1824–1948. 2. Burma — History — 1948–   I. Title.

    DS530.T43 2006
    959.1 — dc22

                                                            2006009199

Designed by Jonathan D. Lippincott

www.fsgbooks.com

1   3   5   7   9   10   8   6   4   2

To my son, Thurayn-Harri

CONTENTS

Map of Burma   ix
Preface   xi

1. The Fall of the Kingdom   3
2. Debating Burma   31
3. Foundations   42
4. Pirates and Princes Along the Bay of Bengal   63
5. The Consequences of Patriotism   88
6. War 107
7. Mandalay   131
8. Transitions   163
9. Studying in the Age of Extremism   198
10. Making the Battlefield   220
11. Alternative Utopias   257
12. The Tiger's Tail   290
13. Palimpsest   321

Notes   349
Acknowledgments   363

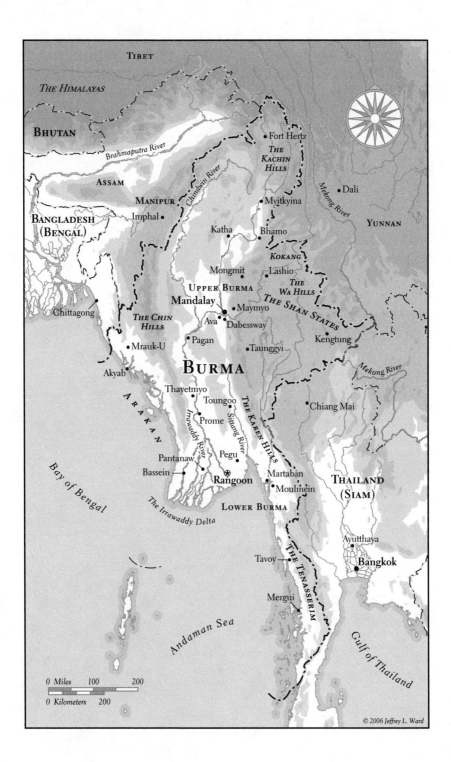

TIBET

THE HIMALAYAS

BHUTAN

Brahmaputra River

ASSAM

MANIPUR

BANGLADESH
(BENGAL)

Imphal

Chittagong

THE CHIN
HILLS

Mrauk-U

Akyab

ARAKAN

Bay of
Bengal

Fort Hertz

THE
KACHIN
HILLS

Dali

Myitkyina

Mekong River

YUNNAN

Katha

Bhamo

KOKANG

Mongmit

Lashio

THE
WA HILLS

UPPER BURMA

Mandalay

Maymyo

Ava

Dabessway

THE SHAN STATES

Pagan

Taunggyi

Kengtung

BURMA

Mekong River

Thayetmyo

Toungoo

Chiang Mai

Prome

Irrawaddy River

Sittang River

THE KAREN HILLS

Pantanaw

Pegu

Bassein

Martaban

THAILAND
(SIAM)

Rangoon

Moulmein

The Irrawaddy Delta

LOWER BURMA

Ayutthaya

Tavoy

Bangkok

THE TENASSERIM

Mergui

Andaman Sea

Gulf of Thailand

0 Miles   100   200

0 Kilometers   200

© 2006 Jeffrey L. Ward

PREFACE

～✕✕～

Just a few months after graduating from university in 1988, I found myself living uncomfortably but contentedly in a Burmese rebel base camp, a sometimes dusty and sometimes muddy sprawl of bamboo and thatch huts, the misty malarial rain forests of the Tennasserim hills in the near distance and young, determined-looking men and women in emerald-green uniforms milling all around.

The late morning hikes to lecture through the New England snow and slush, the long conversations over starchy dining hall meals, the spring garden parties, my friends off to medical school or their first jobs on Wall Street all seemed many worlds away. But at least for a little while I felt a sense of purpose, a sense that I was at the right place doing the right thing. Everything seemed exciting, the atmosphere always vibrant.

In August and September of that year, waves of antigovernment demonstrations had rocked Burma's military dictatorship to its very foundations. When the uprising was finally and violently crushed, thousands of university students, from Rangoon and elsewhere, trekked over the mountains to the jungles near the border with Thailand, attempting not to flee but to regroup and restart their abortive revolution. They hoped for American support and American arms. There were rumors that American Special Forces were on their way. Some said an American battleship was already anchored offshore in the balmy waters of the Andaman Sea.

Though I had largely grown up outside Burma, I wanted as much as anyone to see real and immediate change in a country that had been sealed off by an army dictatorship since before I was born, and I was happy to team up with others of similar conviction. But I was always against violent change, not so much on principle but because I didn't think it could work, and soon fell out with those keen on an armed revolt. I spent nearly a year in Bangkok, trying to help Burmese refugees, and then moved to Washington, where I worked with Human Rights Watch and lobbied for more effective U.S. action. I believed that maximum pressure would yield results and advocated economic sanctions.

But then I had my doubts. I came to believe that using sanctions and boycotts to isolate further an already isolated government and society was counterproductive. I was no longer sure what the most appropriate answer was. And so I stopped lobbying, removed myself from the Burma scene, and began a career with the United Nations, then in its post–cold war heyday. I served for a few years in peacekeeping operations, first in Phnom Penh and then in Sarajevo, places even worse off than Burma but where the international community would eventually take (at least in my mind) an altogether more complex and determined approach.

From Sarajevo I went back to university, this time for graduate work in modern history. I had always been interested in Burmese history, and I chose as my thesis topic the middle decades of Burma's nineteenth century, when the ancient kingdom teetered for a while on its last legs before being vanquished by the vigorous men of Victorian England. I was fascinated by this troubled period in Burma's past, when a Burmese government had tried to reform and failed, and by how this had helped determine the course of colonialism in the country. I began to think more about the ways in which Burma's past influenced the present.

This book is my account of Burma's past. It focuses on the recent past and includes stories from my own family. Though the book is roughly chronological, we start somewhere near the middle, in the autumn of 1885, when the last king at Mandalay sat nervously on the throne, when the London press relayed accounts of palace atrocities, demanding that something be done, and when British politicians plot-

ted and planned how best to remedy, once and for all, the "Burma problem." It's not meant as a book for experts or primarily as a commentary
on today's problems but as a guide to the Burmese past, an introduction
to a country whose current problems are increasingly known but whose
colorful and vibrant history is almost entirely forgotten.

Since 1988, Burma has emerged from the shadows to assume an
unenviable place in the international community, as a pariah to the
West and as a concern to almost everyone else. Once known, if at all,
as an exotic Buddhist land with few of the worries of the twentieth century, it's now become a poster child for more nightmarish twenty-first-
century ills, a failed or failing state, repressive and unable to cope with
looming humanitarian challenges, a place whose long-enduring government seems mysteriously unwilling to cede power.

But I don't think this is the only way to think about Burma.

Burma has always stood along the highways of Asia, connecting
China, India, Tibet, and the many and varied civilizations of Southeast
Asia. Her history links to the history of all these lands and beyond.
Who remembers that envoys from Rome's eastern provinces traveled
through Burma to discover the markets of Han China? That in the
sixteenth century Portuguese pirates, Japanese renegade samurai, and
Persian princes jockeyed for power at the court of Arakan? Or the First
Anglo-Burmese War of 1824–26, when the rockets and steamships of
the East India Company battled the elephants and musketeers of the
king of Ava?

And closer to today, when thinking of Burma, who remembers the
legacies of a century of British colonialism, the devastations of the Second World War, the bloody civil war of the late 1940s, or the Chinese
invasions of the early 1950s?

I wrote this book also with an eye to what the past might say about
the present. Since the 1988 uprising, Burma has been the object of
myriad good-faith efforts, by the United Nations, dozens of governments, hundreds of NGOs, and thousands of activists, all trying to promote democratic reform. But the net result has been disappointing at
best and may very well have had the unintended consequence of further entrenching the status quo and holding back positive change.
And, given that result, I think it is no coincidence that analysis of

Burma has been singularly ahistorical, with few besides scholars of the country bothering to consider the actual origins of today's predicament. We fail to consider history at our peril, not only, I suspect, in the case of Burma, but in that of many other "crisis countries" around the world.

THE RIVER OF

LOST FOOTSTEPS

ONE

THE FALL OF THE KINGDOM

⚭

The divinity most worshiped in Burma is precedence.
—Captain Henry Yule, *Mission to the Court of Ava*[1]

MANDALAY, OCTOBER 1885

He was anxious for the health of his wife and their unborn child. More than a few of the old courtiers had already advised him to flee to the villages of his ancestors. Others told him to give in. But his generals, severe in their lacquered helmets and green and magenta velvet coats, promised they would do their best to hold back the advance of the enemy; some even voiced confidence of final victory. They reminded him of the imposing fortifications that had been built up and down the valley, and of the royal steamships and smaller boats that would soon be scuttled to make the passage upriver as difficult as possible. Even the underwater explosives his young engineers had been busy developing would soon be ready for use. Too many soldiers were tied down fighting renegade princes in the eastern hills, but there were still enough men to put up a good fight.

The high crenellated walls of the royal city of Mandalay had been built in the days of his father for exactly this situation. The vermilion ramparts formed a perfect square and were each over a mile long, backed by massive earthworks and preceded by a wide and deep moat. If the invading army could be drawn into a long siege, he could direct a guerrilla operation from beyond the forests to the north.

The rains had just ended, and in the brilliant sunshine he could see his cavalry practicing in the muddy fields not far from the palace. But whatever his generals said, in his heart he knew that in the last analysis his little army was no match for the force assembling just three hundred miles to the south. But what was the alternative? Surrender? His more worldly ministers, men who had traveled to the West, told him to compromise, stall for time, open negotiations. He should avoid a military conflict at all costs and agree to all their demands if necessary. But did he trust them? There were rumors that the enemy would bring his elder half brother, now eight years in exile, and place him on the throne. The kingdom would become a protectorate. Perhaps this is what his noble advisers wanted.

His wife told him to stand firm and prepare for war.

FORT ST. GEORGE

General Sir Harry North Dalrymple Prendergast was born in India in 1834 to an Anglo-Irish family long familiar with service on the subcontinent. His father, Thomas Prendergast, had been a magistrate in Madras and after a long spell in India had retired to Cheltenham, gone blind, and then made a small fortune writing a series of trend-setting handbooks entitled *The Mastery of Languages or the Art of Speaking Foreign Tongues Idiomatically.*

Harry Prendergast himself was a distinguished soldier. During the Indian Mutiny he had fought with the Malwa Field Force. Ten years later he had taken part in the putative invasion of Abyssinia and was present when Lord Napier and his combined British and Indian army stormed and then destroyed Emperor Theodore's mountain fortress of Magdala. More recently he had become obsessed with the idea of himself commanding an invasion of Burma, personally leading reconnaissance runs near the long frontier. And now, after years of planning and bureaucratic scheming, his dream was coming true.

His Burma Field Force consisted of ten thousand troops. It included three infantry brigades, one from the Bengal Army, one from the Madras Army, and a third brigade under the command of fellow Irishman Brigadier George Stuart White.[2] Sailing from Rangoon, Prendergast arrived in Madras toward the end of October, just as the various parts of his new army were busy getting ready along the glacis of Fort St. George. It was to be a textbook operation. Plans and preparations would follow the latest thinking in military science, and nothing was to be left to chance. Torrential rains swept across the docks, and hundreds of Indian coolies labored to load big wooden crates, each neatly packed with supplies for any eventuality, onto the tall ships moored off the Coromandel coast. On 2 November, as an enormous thunderstorm broke over the south Indian city, the governor of the Madras Presidency, the Honorable Grant Duff, hosted Prendergast and his senior officers to a lavish dinner in honor of the coming campaign. Everything was set.

Within days, Prendergast's fleet was gliding swiftly over the blue-green waters of the Bay of Bengal, past the mangrove swamps and jungle hamlets of the Irrawaddy Delta, reaching the frontiers of the inland kingdom on 6 November. Anchored and waiting along the banks of the river, the flotilla stretched nearly five miles long. Forty shiny new Maxim guns, the world's first machine guns, were lifted onto the steamship *Kathleen*. A few years ago their inventor, Hiram Maxim (later Sir Hiram), visited the Paris Electrical Exhibition and was told by a man he met there: "If you want to make a lot of money, invent something that will enable these Europeans to cut each other's throats with greater facility." He relocated to London and went to work, proudly unveiling his product earlier that year.[3] The Maxim guns had a belt that could continually feed ammunition. They could fire five hundred rounds a minute. This was their debut. Not yet on the battlefields of Flanders but to be first tried and tested on the road to Mandalay.

On 13 November a steamer belonging to the Irrawaddy Flotilla Company crossed the border from Burmese territory with news that eight thousand of the king's troops were massing at the Minhla fort just to the north. The same afternoon Prendergast received a telegram from the India Office in London: The Burmese reply to a British ultimatum had been unsatisfactory. Prendergast was ordered to invade at once.

LORD RANDOLPH CHURCHILL'S WAR

Burma's watershed year, 1885, separating its past from its modern age, was also a year of considerable change and ferment around the world.

For the first time in a long while, Great Britain was facing increasing competition overseas from other imperial and rising powers: the Germans, the French, the Russians, and even the Americans. The United States, then under the bachelor president Grover Cleveland, had yet to acquire many territories overseas, but was well on the way toward unparalleled economic power. By 1885 American railways stretched westward to the beaches of California, and the relentless demand for steel and oil were creating fortunes for the Rockefellers and the Carnegies. It was in 1885 that the phonograph was invented, American Telephone and Telegraph welcomed its first customers, and all nine stories of the world's first skyscraper were built in Chicago. It was also the year that the Statue of Liberty arrived in New York, together with tens of thousands of the country's first immigrants from Central and Eastern Europe.

In February 1885 the Congress of Berlin formally parceled out the continent of Africa among half a dozen European powers in a sort of gala opening to an imperialist age that would lead to a fifth of the world's landmass falling under colonial rule over the next thirty years. But this moment of uninhibited expansionist frenzy also contained within it the first seeds of imperialism's eventual demise. In Bombay in the last few weeks of the year, seventy or so Indian lawyers, educators, and journalists came together to set up the Indian National Congress, the organization that one day, under the leadership of Mahatma Gandhi and Pandit Nehru, would help take Burma, as well as India, on the path to independence.

For England, 1885 started off quite badly. For months, the slow-motion fall of Khartoum had been reported graphically over the tabloids, and the death of General Charles "Chinese" Gordon in February had set off a wave of anger, much of it directed at the Liberal government of the country's long-standing prime minister, William Gladstone. General Gordon had won renown in the 1860s in China, where he led the multinational "Ever-Victorious Army" on behalf of the emperor against the Taiping rebels. And in 1884, having had no clear policy on the growing mess in the Sudan, the Gladstone government sent General Gordon, hoping that he could deal single-handedly with the Mahdist rebellion or at least find a way to withdraw the besieged Anglo-Egyptian garrison.

But inasmuch as distant imperial wars grabbed the headlines, the real story for many was the increasingly polarized debate over Irish home rule. Both the Liberals and the opposition Conservatives were genuinely split on the question of Ireland's future, and recent violent unrest on the island led to new coercive measures. Charles Stewart Parnell, a politician and Protestant landowner, had become the undisputed leader of the Irish nationalist movement. And because the 1884 Reform Act had extended the vote to millions of new people, including agricultural workers in Ireland, Parnell was now a major force in Westminster politics, holding the balance of power between the two main parties. When the Liberal government fell over budget issues in June 1885, it was through the combined vote of the Conservatives and Parnell's Irish members of Parliament. A new Conservative ministry, under the earl of Salisbury, was to govern until general elections could be held. And in this new Conservative "caretaker" ministry the man who would direct India policy, and thus Burma policy as well, was Lord Randolph Churchill.

Churchill was the third son of the seventh duke of Marlborough and the father of Winston Churchill (then eleven years old). He had been educated at Eton and Merton College, Oxford, where he had been a prizewinning pugilist, and was a rising star in the Conservative Party. For the past five years he had been an important member of Parliament, targeting not only the Liberal government of Gladstone but also his own Conservative front bench. By 1885 Churchill saw himself championing his own brand of "progressive conservatism," declaring his support for popular reforms and seeking to challenge the Liberals for the votes of the newly enfranchised working class. He also worked hard to win over Parnell. When Gladstone's government was defeated, many in his party credited Churchill as the "organizer of victory." As a reward, the new prime minister made him the secretary of state for India. He was thirty-six years old.

Over the summer, with elections several months away, Churchill decided to contest the radical stronghold of Birmingham. The early 1880s had seen bad economic times in many parts of Europe, and there was a growing awareness of how poor England's poor really were, in places like Birmingham, the smog-choked industrial cities of the north, and in London's own East End, where Jack the Ripper would soon enjoy his fiendish murders. Churchill needed an issue. Something that would appeal to businessmen worried about shrinking profits and workers fearful of losing their jobs. Something that would promise better times and a return to prosperity.

Earlier that year the Scottish–South African explorer Archibald Colquhoun had made himself a household name. He had traversed through the unknown lands of western China and scampered along the jungle-covered middle stretches of the Mekong River. When he returned to London, he lectured widely and wrote two best-selling books: one was *English Policy in the Far East*, and the other was *Burma and the Burmans: Or, "The Best Unopened Market in the World."*[4] He had one message: All that stood in the way of a revival of British commerce and industry, all that kept the working people of Birmingham and Leeds from a better future, was the despotic king of Burma. Remove the king, and Burma would become Britain's best friend. And from Burma, the riches of China, and all that meant for British commerce and industry, would be there for the asking. One of those impressed was Randolph Churchill.

Churchill was not unfamiliar with recent events in Burma. He had visited India over the cold weather of 1884–85 and would have read in the Indian papers stories about King Thibaw and his court at Mandalay. Thibaw received a lot of bad press. On the throne for less than seven years, he had succeeded his illustrious and much-loved father, King Mindon, in 1878. Though the truth was very different, in British eyes, or at least in the eyes of the European business community in India, he was a gin-soaked tyrant, together with his wicked wife cruelly oppressing his people, ignorant of the world, ruling through an incompetent and medieval court, oblivious of his people's need for the sort of progress only a civilized government could provide.[5]

What *was* true was that the Burmese kingdom was experiencing growing instability. In the late eighteenth and early nineteenth centuries Burma had been an aggressive imperial power itself, though on a fairly small scale. Its kings and war elephants and ancient artillery had marched from the Himalayas to the beaches of Phuket, overrunning the kingdom of Siam in the east and extending westward across Assam to the very borders of British Bengal. A long and bloody but definitive war between the Burmese and the British from 1824 to 1826 had brought a sudden halt to Burmese ambitions. A second war in 1852 led to the British occupation of the country's entire coastline, and a new British Burma was carved out of the old kingdom, with its administrative base at the port city of Rangoon.

After decades of tight British controls over the country's trade, the impact of civil war in next-door China, and the disorders generated by frantic administrative reforms, the Court of Ava* was a dim shadow of what it had been in its early-nineteenth-century heyday. The economy was in shambles, made worse by a recent drought and famine, part of worldwide climate changes related to the El Niño weather phenomena.[6] Refugees and economic migrants streamed across the frontier from the king's territory of "Upper Burma" into the relative security and prosperity of the British-held lands along the shore. The Burmese government seemed incapable of handling the multiple crises that it faced.

Years of British machinations had also produced a lively exiled opposition, and more than one of Thibaw's brothers were plotting to overthrow him from beyond the kingdom's borders. That Burma was a potentially rich country no one seemed to doubt, certainly not the increasingly vocal Scottish merchants in Rangoon, eager for unfettered access to the teak forests, oil wells, and ruby mines of the interior. What seemed even more tempting was the prospect of a back door to China's limitless markets. Perhaps Burma was the answer to Birmingham's problems.

Randolph Churchill could not simply propose war against an independent country, even a fairly inconsequential non-European one like Burma. Commercial gain could not be the only reason. There had to be a strategic interest involved, and luckily there was, supplied by the budding relationship between Paris and Mandalay. France in the mid-1880s was still smarting from its humiliating defeat at the hands of Otto von Bismarck's Prussian Empire and eager to prove its prowess abroad. Jules Ferry was premier of the Third Republic. Under his imperialist policies Paris began to expand its presence in what was to become French Indochina. Saigon was already in French hands. In June 1884, following a somewhat ignominious military campaign that featured more than one embarrassing setback, the Treaty of Hué formally established a protectorate over Annam and Tonkin and sealed French rule over all of what is today Vietnam. To those who wished direct access

---

*"The Court of Ava" was how the government of Burma had long been referred to, a reference to its old capital of Ava, near Mandalay.

between British India and the imagined markets of China, this sudden outburst of French activity in Southeast Asia could not have been welcome. A line had to be drawn somewhere. From Vietnam, the French were pushing westward into Cambodia and the Lao principalities along the Mekong. Upper Burma would be next. French rule in Indochina was bad enough; French interference in Thibaw's kingdom could not be allowed.

It was not really the French who approached the Burmese but rather the Burmese who were keen to embrace the French. The holy grail of Burmese diplomacy was recognition by the European powers as an independent and sovereign state. Attempts to gain direct ties with Britain had failed as the Court of Ava was told time and again that Anglo-Burmese relations would be handled by the India government at Calcutta and not (in the manner of a truly sovereign state) by the Foreign Office in London. What the Burmese hoped was that by becoming friends with the French, they could at least raise the diplomatic cost to Britain of any future expansion at Mandalay's expense.

At the beginning of 1884 a new treaty was agreed between the Quay d'Orsay and a Burmese mission to Paris led by the *myoza*, or lord, of Myothit. There was to be no official alliance or military agreement, nor would a French political agent be stationed at Mandalay. There was nothing in this essentially commercial agreement about which London could really complain. But this did not stop the Calcutta press or the restless trading houses of Rangoon from spreading stories of secret French clauses. As the Burmese and the French were involved, surely there was more than met the eye.

Many years later a story made the rounds that laid much of the blame for the fall of the kingdom on an unrequited love, between an up-and-coming Burmese scholar-official and a beautiful Eurasian maid of honor to the queen. The maid of honor was Mattie Calogreedy, later Mrs. Mattie Calogreedy Antram, born in Mandalay to a Greek father and Burmese mother and one of the many young women of the Western Palace.[7] As a teenager she had fallen deeply in love with a Frenchman, an engineer in the employ of the king. The affair was well known, and Mattie Calogreedy hoped they would soon be engaged. But when this man, Pierre Bonvilain, returned from a sojourn in Paris with a new French wife, she was humiliated and enraged. Not only that: she sought revenge, not just on her ex-lover but on the entire French nation.

Conveniently for her, there was someone she knew she could use, a Burmese official who had unsuccessfully tried, perhaps a few times, to seduce her. His name was Naymyo Theiddi Kyawtin. He had been a state scholar in England and had accompanied the royal embassy to Queen Victoria in 1872. Fluent in English and French and with a taste for expensive whiskey, he was in 1885 a junior secretary to the Council of State with access to privileged papers. Mattie Calogreedy agreed to sleep with him, and he agreed to share with her a secret document. And this secret document, so the story goes, quickly fell into the nimble hands of the Italian spy Giovanni Andreino.

Giovanni Andreino was a former village blacksmith and onetime organ grinder from Naples who had come to Burma at the invitation of his brother, the Roman Catholic bishop. Ambitious and unscrupulous, within a few years he had made himself the center of much palace gossip, and his seeming familiarity with the ways of the Oriental court had led to three of the biggest British firms—Finlay Flemming, the Bombay Burmah Trading Corporation, and the Irrawaddy Flotilla Company—appointing him their representative. Rome made him the Italian consul. And the British recruited him as their man in Mandalay.

The truth of the matter may never be known, but Andreino claimed to have a copy of a secret letter from Jules Ferry to the Burmese foreign minister, one that promised French arms, to be smuggled across the Mekong from Tonkin, in return for French monopolies over the king's fabled jade mines in the northern hills and much else besides. News of this "secret agreement" set off a whirlwind of Anglo-Saxon indignation. Lord Churchill had his rationale. So too did his friends on the editorial staff of the London *Times* who wrote, in September 1885, that the argument for an invasion of Burma was now "unimpeachable."

But Churchill had to be careful. The last thing he (or anyone else in the British government) wanted was a war with Burma that would lead unwittingly to a war with France. The threat of French expansion would provide the pretext for an invasion, but the British had to be sure that the French would not *actually* rally to Thibaw's defense. At this point, if the French had stood firm and said there was no secret deal or if they had intimated in any way that they sympathized with Burma's plight (and might lend Thibaw a hand), Churchill would likely have retreated. Instead, the French neither denied scheming nor suggested that they would lift a finger to save Burmese independence. The road to Mandalay was clear. Only the final piece remained: a proper casus belli.

As if on cue, the Burmese provided a timely provocation. On 12 August the Burmese Council of State imposed a large fine of over a hundred thousand rupees on the Bombay Burmah Trading Corporation. A provincial governor had charged that the Scottish company, based in Rangoon, had been illegally exporting timber from Upper Burma without paying the proper royalties. The governor had imposed a fine, the company had appealed, and Mandalay had now upheld the provincial decision. The company offered to open its books. The British commissioner in Rangoon suggested impartial arbitration. But the Court of Ava would not be moved, and the London Chamber of Commerce petitioned Lord Churchill either to annex Upper Burma or at least to establish a protectorate over the irksome kingdom. Whoever was in the right (and corrupt Burmese officials were likely to blame), the timing could not have been better for Lord Churchill.

On 22 October an ultimatum was sent by steamship to the Court of Ava, setting a deadline of 10 November with the following demands: (1) The fine should go to arbitration; (2) a British Resident should be received at Mandalay with "a proper guard of honour and a steamer" and should have full access to the king without having to submit "to any humiliating ceremony" (meaning, primarily, that he should not have to take off his shoes indoors, as was the Burmese custom); and (3) the Burmese would in the future exercise their external relations only in accordance with the advice of the government of India "as is now done by the Amir of Afghanistan." The last was effectively a demand that the country relinquish its sovereignty. For good measure, the ultimatum also called on the Burmese to open up a trade route with China for British firms.

The king and his ministers knew they had no good choices. Most knew their defenses were in a sorry state. The underwater explosives would not be laid in time. And the preparations to sink the king's steamers and create a blockade along the middle Irrawaddy were not yet complete. There were several European trainers and advisers, but they were a mixed lot, adventurers like Joseph Henri de Facieu, the son of a colonel in Napoleon's Cuirassier Regiment, who had served for an Indian prince, then for the British, before finding a home in Thibaw's army. But staring at the ultimatum, they couldn't bring themselves to surrender Burma's independence. They drafted a reply that accepted all the British demands except that one. Instead, apparently hoping for a compromise formula, they proposed that Britain, France, and Germany jointly decide Burma's status.

They understood that war was coming but canceled any moves toward a general mobilization. No one had any illusions about the outcome. They would do their best with what they had, and the rest was left to fate. Command of the kingdom's defenses was entrusted to the lord of Salay. Three columns were mustered: the Lower Irrawaddy Column, under the cavalry general Mingyi Thiri Maha Zeyya Kyawdin, recently returned from campaigning along the Chinese border; the Great Valley Column, under a colonel of the Cachar Horse Regiment, Mingyi Minkaung Mindin Raza; and the Toungoo Column, under the colonel of the Shwaylan Infantry Regiment, Mingyi Maha Minkaung Nawrata.

But this would be no grand army like the armies of the king's ancestors that had waged their own wars of aggression against Siam and Assam or had defended the country against China many decades ago. Too many battalions were far away in the Shan hills fighting to reclaim lost principalities or putting down rebellions in the border towns upriver. At best, Salay would be able to muster fifteen thousand regular soldiers to meet the English invasion.

> On the road to Mandalay,
> Where the old Flotilla lay,
> With our sick beneath the awnings when we went to Mandalay!

In the days before the war began, ordinary townspeople from nearby Thayetmyo used to come around to the riverfront to see for themselves the impressive steamships and khaki-clad soldiers of Sir Harry Prendergast's Burma Expeditionary Force. Thayetmyo (the name means "mango-town") was a small district capital of around ten thousand people and the home of a growing and profitable silverworks industry. Its citizens had lived for over thirty years under British rule, and the sight of uniformed Europeans, Sikhs, and Punjabi Muslims was nothing particularly new. But what caused considerable excitement was a sight no one expected: a Burmese prince, in full court costume, sitting in a large chair on the prow of one of the steamers. All around were attendants in the white silk jackets of the royal palace, some kneeling before him. Some thought it was the *mintha*, or prince, of Myingun, an older brother of Thibaw's who had led an abortive rebellion many years before and was rumored to be in Bangkok. Others were sure it was the prince of Nyaungyan, another exiled prince, thought to be in Calcutta. And so the speculation gained ground, and people were calmed. The British would only place a new king on the throne. Yes, Thibaw would be overthrown, but the kingdom and the monarchy would be safe. Perhaps it was all for the better.

It was that week that Maung Pein, a student at the Government School in Rangoon, was home on holiday. He was descended from a line of local chiefs, and several of his ancestors had served at the Court of Ava. Hearing about the prince, Maung Pein and his father decided to go down to the river and see what they could. They were joined in their evening stroll by a Burmese official, Naymyo Thiri Kyawtin Nawrata, who had received orders the night before not to resist the British advance.

Curious, and fluent in English, the young schoolboy talked his way past the various sentries and sauntered up to the steamship, only to find himself face-to-face not with a prince of Ava but with Maung Ba Than, a former student at his school and now a junior clerk at the chief commissioner's office in Rangoon. It was a ruse! He ran back to tell his father and the Burmese official about the impostor. They tried to send a telegram to Mandalay, but the telegraph line had been cut. And so all along the invasion route, ordinary people would be convinced that a new prince of the blood would soon be on the throne.[8]

When the first British steamships, the *Irrawaddy* and *Kathleen*, crossed the frontier at first sunlight on 14 November, there were no massed Burmese positions to meet them, only invisible rifle fire from the low hills overlooking the river. General Prendergast understood

Lord Churchill's desire to see Mandalay occupied by the beginning of polls on 25 November, but he wanted to be careful and also remembered his instructions to avoid bloody conflict. Many of his men were already lying ill from dysentery and fever even before any actual fighting had begun.

The first and only real battle of the war was at its very start, just after the flotilla had set sail and a few miles north of the frontier.[9] The Burmese garrison was under the command of the son-in-law of Thibaw's war minister, the *myoza* of Taingdar. The British were led by Brigadier George White, later to achieve considerable fame at the defense of Ladysmith during the Boer War. The first fort was overrun almost effortlessly, but the second, on the opposite bank, was taken only after fierce fighting. At least a hundred Burmese soldiers died in the battle. On the British side, the casualties were much lighter: three Indian soldiers and a young English officer, Lieutenant Dury, a promising former schoolmate of Rudyard Kipling's whom the poet later remembered: "The Crammer's boast, the Squadron's pride, Shot like a rabbit in a ride!"

The vigor of the Burmese resistance had surprised Prendergast. He was determined to proceed step by step. Fortunately for him he could now rely on detailed drawings of Burmese forts and other defensive positions left behind at the captured forts by two Italians, Captain Camotto and Captain Molinari. These two erstwhile officers had been hired by the Burmese government, in a moment of panic and apparently less than astute judgment, as military advisers. During the heat of battle the duo had ignominiously taken flight, leaving behind all their papers, including the drawings.

For the British the remainder of the war was, to use a more recent expression, a cakewalk. The Burmese had concentrated their forces about a hundred miles to the north of the frontier, just beyond the vast medieval ruins at Pagan. On 23 November two companies of the Liverpool Regiment and four companies of Bengal infantry landed along the eastern banks of the Irrawaddy and pushed toward the fort at Myingyan. But there was to be no real resistance, only a few small skirmishes. In the distance the British could see the mounted Burmese general, the lord of Salay, peering down at them from an escarpment, surrounded by his men in their red, white, and magenta coats. Many of the officers among them had vermilion umbrellas, a mark of minor nobility, held over their heads. Salay had decided not to fight, and instead he and his army withdrew, away from the river and into the low forests to the east. He telegraphed Mandalay later that day to say that Myingyan had fallen and only the great fortifications near Ava lay between the British and Mandalay.

The Kinwun Mingyi was a survivor. Now in his sixties, slight and gray-haired and with a thick, bushy mustache, he had spent the last thirty years at the Court of Ava, surviving two reigns and many rebellions. A scholar of law and jurisprudence, the Kinwun* had risen through the ranks of the palace establishment through his cunning and fine drafting skills, finally making his name as a diplomat and as the head of the Burmese king's mission to Queen Victoria in 1872. His trip was only a qualified success, but his diary of the long travel to London and back, written for the entertainment of the court ladies, was a literary hit. For the mission he was raised to the rank of secretary of state and on his return showered with new titles and noble styles.

What was difficult for him to convey in his diary was the extent to which his experiences in the world outside Burma, and especially in late Victorian England, had changed forever his assessment of what was possible and what was not in his country's relations with the greatest industrial and military power of the day. He had been taken up and down the length and breadth of the British Isles and had seen firsthand the sources of the empire's strength and skill.

When the last king, Mindon, had died, in 1878, the Kinwun formed a coalition with various factions at court and placed the twenty-one-year-old Thibaw on the throne. He hoped that Thibaw would be a weak king or at least one open to his ideas for change. The Kinwun and other reform-minded grandees, many of whom had been schooled in Europe in the 1860s and 1870s, knew that time was running against them. Only radical reform would save their kingdom. But he had not

---

*Kinwun is the best remembered of his many titles and styles and refers to a military office he held. He was also known as the lord of Legaing and his personal name was U Kaung; "U" is an honorific in Burmese, roughly equivalent to "Mister" and traditionally denoting a gentleman of some rank.

counted on the rigor of the royalist reaction, and most of their plans had come to nothing. The last few years had been ones of intense disappointment.

But what to do now that the English were almost at the gates of the palace? Military resistance seemed out of the question. For the Kinwun, that which was utterly unthinkable to many at court—accepting a British protectorate—was far from unacceptable. He had tried hard as a diplomat to win British recognition for Burma as an independent state and failed. But perhaps a protectorate would in the end bring stability and then progress, and this was all that Prendergast and his ships and his machine guns had come to do. The Kinwun knew the exiled princes well. If the British had come to place one on the throne, that was not the worst scenario. But would Thibaw give up without a fight?

When the telegram reached the palace saying that the English had sailed past Pagan, the king had begun to assume the worst. The governor of the Mandalay area, the lord of Yindaw, suggested that Thibaw retreat into the Shan hills, to the town later known as Maymyo. The minister in charge of relations with China suggested an escape by road, to the southeast and across the border into Yunnan. Thibaw weighed these options but thought that if he had to leave, he would prefer to retire to Shwebo, his ancestral home. If things went badly, he could flee even farther north and eventually reach Chinese territory through the mountain chieftainships of Wuntho and Mogaung.

He ordered his minister for war, the lord of Taingdar, to ready fifty elephants, fitted out with the king's howdahs. Everyone was told to be prepared to leave: government officials of all ranks, the ladies of the court, his elite Natshin-yway bodyguard, made up of specially chosen men over six feet in height, the hundreds of servants and retainers, royal sword bearers and umbrella carriers, as well as his two little daughters (his only son had died of smallpox as a baby) and his wife and queen, Supayalat.[10]

But others told him that running away would do no good. They reminded him of the lessons of history. As soon as he was away from the palace, they warned, his prestige would diminish, and once a king lost his prestige, "he is left with nothing but his umbrella." What about the French? They had signed a treaty of friendship. So had the Germans and the Italians. Were these good for nothing? His ambassador in Paris could not be reached, as the British had severed their communications via Rangoon. But on 23 November the Kinwun submitted a report stating that the French agent at Mandalay, M. Frédéric Haas, had come to tell him that the English would soon arrive and that His Majesty must grant them whatever they demanded. The Kinwun tried to reassure the nervous king, promising Thibaw that he would stay with him and protect him "from whatever grief or danger might come near him, not waiting in anxiety, but in brave acceptance of what was to come."

Prendergast's Field Force pushed on and within two days reached the great bend in the Irrawaddy River, here over a mile wide, where the Burmese had constructed three fortifications, one by the old royal city of Ava and two others on the opposite bank. The garrison at Ava was commanded by the lord of Myothit, a minister in the government and the diplomat who had led the embassy to France and signed a treaty at the Palais de l'Élysée only a couple of years before.

In the dark wooden halls of the palace, those who counseled surrender rather than flight or resistance finally gained the upper hand. Within a day Prendergast's guns would be within firing range of Mandalay town. A robust defense could be organized, but it seemed unlikely that anything other than a British victory was possible at this point. Perhaps the British would agree to a conditional surrender. The grandees at court must have known that their king's fate was sealed, but perhaps their own interests and the interests of their class and their country could still be protected.

By late November the weather in Upper Burma is nearly always perfect, with cool nights and warm days of cloudless blue skies. Brigadier White, standing on deck as the *Kathleen* came within sight of Ava, wrote that "the sun was pouring a flood of golden light on the last hours of Burman independence."

That afternoon the Burmese steamer *Yadana Yimun* appeared, flying the peacock flag of the Court of Ava as well as the white flag of surrender. In tow was a gilded royal barge with forty-four rowers, carrying two emissaries of the king, the lords of Kyauk-myaung and Wetmasut. The emissaries, both wearing enormous floppy sun hats, asked for an armistice and time to satisfy London's demands. Prendergast, though giving them a friendly welcome, rejected the possibility of any armistice but said that if Thibaw surrendered himself, his army, and Mandalay, and if the Europeans in Mandalay were found "unharmed in person and in property," then the king's life would be spared. No other guarantees could be given. He gave the envoys a deadline of 4:00 a.m. on 27 November, about a day and a half away.[11]

The early-morning deadline came and went, but at 10:00 a.m. the envoys finally reappeared with word of surrender from Thibaw. The British noticed that the Burmese had blocked the river just above Ava by sinking a steamer and various smaller boats, filling them with sand and stones. The Burmese forces in the area were ordered to lay down their arms, but the lord of Myothit (the fort commander) refused to accept the authenticity of Kyauk-myaung's message and insisted on a direct order from his king. Kyauk-myaung was a Sorbonne-educated reformist and known to have long advised accommodation with London. Only when a telegraph in Burmese Morse code was received at Ava, signed by Thibaw himself, did Myothit agree to stand down. His men then melted away into the surrounding villages, leaving behind piles of Martini rifles. Myothit himself stayed and wept as he saw the steamships slowly make their way the ten miles to the royal city itself.

The Burmese remember that the entire evening, from around seven o'clock until dawn the next day, the sky was filled with thousands of shooting stars and meteors, falling in all directions, appearing and disappearing as people wondered what these clear omens could mean. These were actually the Andromedids in one of the greatest meteor storms of recent times, seen all over the world. Those learned in astrology prophesied that the country and the Buddhist religion would soon meet hard times.

General Prendergast landed at Mandalay at one in the afternoon on 28 November. This was to be a day famous in Burmese history and in the Burmese calendar is remembered as the eighth day of the waning moon of Tasaungmon or Sagittarius. At three o'clock his political officer, Sir Edward Sladen, on horseback, approached the southern gates together with a small armed escort. Crowds had begun to gather along the avenues leading from the river to the city walls. Sladen was a former British Resident at Mandalay and spoke Burmese. Just then a minister came charging up on a caparisoned elephant and pleaded that troops not yet be sent into the palace precincts. Sladen left a note for Prendergast at the gate asking to give him some time and then went in alone.[12]

Edward Sladen climbed up the whitewashed stone steps and into the dark and thickly carpeted inner rooms of the palace. Escorted by the Kinwun, he walked quickly to where the king was sitting, together with his wife and his mother-in-law, the queen mother. Thibaw received him and at first spoke nervously, asking the Englishman if he remembered their earlier meetings. And then, mustering up as much courage as possible, he looked at the Englishman and said, "in a very formal and impressive manner: 'I surrender myself and my country to you.'" Thibaw asked for a day or two to prepare for leaving and said that in the meantime he would stay not in the main palace but in the summerhouse nearby. He told the political officer of his worries for Supayalat, now over seven months pregnant. But Sladen would not agree and gave him only until the morning, promising that until then the British troops would not enter the palace. With this Sladen turned and left.

Soon it was dark, and in the dark the palace descended into chaos. The old certainties of palace life and discipline dissolved with the knowledge of the coming foreign occupation. Some reacted with shock. For most the haziness of what lay ahead meant that they had to grab what they could and position themselves as best as possible for what was to come. A new king? Or rule by the English, something few could imagine? Prendergast had ordered that no men were to enter or leave the palace, but he did not mention women, and overnight dozens, perhaps hundreds of ordinary women came through the western gates and seized anything of value they could find. The king's bodyguards deserted him. And all but seventeen of the three hundred maids of honor fled, also carrying all the valuables they could.

Thibaw was by now beside himself with fear, certain that at any minute soldiers would break into his apartment and kill him on the spot. When Sladen arrived the next morning, he saw that the king and queen were practically alone and unattended and that overnight Thibaw had collected what he could of the gold vessels used by Burmese sovereigns on state occasions, the heirlooms of his family and dynasty, and these were in a little pile on one side of the room. Sladen had come with a guard of the Sixty-seventh South Hampshire Regiment. Thibaw wasn't frightened of the English soldiers, but when one of the officers' servants, a black man, came in carrying something for the officer, "Thibaw was much disturbed, and asked if he was the executioner."[13]

General Prendergast himself appeared at noon, and Sladen informed him that the king was ready to receive him. The great wooden gates flung open, and the pith-helmeted marched in, halting at the steps to the main hall and forming a line with ranks facing inward and with fixed bayonets. The Burmese ministers of state came next, led by the Kinwun and the lord of Taingdar. All walked past the teak-pillared throne rooms and the smaller salons and halls, rooms filled with French mirrors, Persian rugs, and glass mosaics, finally descending a flight of wooden stairs and into a back garden. Here under the shade of tall palm trees was the summerhouse, with a paved walkway and gas lamps in the front and a little artificial pond to the side.

Thibaw sat petrified on the verandah, the royal women behind him also clearly frightened, their eyes wandering back and forth from Sladen to Prendergast to the bayonets of the black-booted soldiers. An unseasonable drizzle had just ended, and the sun shone only intermittently through the clouds. Prendergast bowed once, and Thibaw's ministers, in their long dark velvet coats, prostrated themselves before their sovereign for the last time on the cold wet earth.

There was to be no ceremonial procession. Instead Thibaw and his young family, together with a train of servants, were led toward a few ordinary bullock carts waiting just outside the palace enclosure. They then left through the southern Kyaw Moe (Conspicuous Sky) gate, over the lily-filled moat, escorted by the men of the Sixty-seventh Foot. The captain of the king's artillery, the lord of Mabai, and the privy treasurer, the lord of Paukmyaing, followed behind, bringing with them the royal insignia. The lords of Wetmasut and Pindalay, ministers of the inner court, placed two white umbrellas, symbols of royalty, over Thibaw's ramshackle wooden carriage.

By now large crowds of ordinary people had gathered along the avenues leading from the walled city and to the Govinda wharf, some three miles away. As their king passed them by, men, women, and children instinctively knelt on the ground. Many were weeping. Some cried out at the uniformed Englishmen surrounding the captive family, and a few stones and clumps of earth were thrown as the party slowly wound its way through the progressively denser crowds. Thibaw remained silent throughout the journey, but Supayalat nervously called on the young soldiers, several of whom rushed forward to light her proffered cigar.

It was dusk by the time they reached the river. A small wooden plank connected the bank to the *Thooreah* steamer. With his attendants holding a tall white umbrella over his head, and a crush of English, Burmese, and Indian onlookers all around, the twenty-eight-year-old Thibaw walked onto the ship, never to see Mandalay or Burma again.

THE DAY AFTER

The people of this country have not, as was by some expected, welcomed us as deliverers from tyranny.
　　　　—Secretary for Upper Burma to the Chief Commissioner[14]

In the end the Burma War was neither necessary nor particularly helpful to Randolph Churchill and the Conservative Party. On 21 November, as Prendergast's fleet was sailing north toward the temples at Pagan, Charles Parnell had issued a statement denouncing Gladstone and calling on all Irishmen in England to vote for the Tories. The result was a close election, with a large Irish bloc holding the balance. The polls had opened on 25 November, when Prendergast was still moored near Ava. Mandalay's actual surrender took place not on the eve of the polls, as Churchill had hoped, but in the days of helter-skelter party politics that followed. Parnell joined a Conservative government under Salisbury and then later changed his mind and helped bring Gladstone back to power. Churchill himself became Chancellor of the Exchequer before leaving the political scene altogether a year later. No one really cared about Burma by that point. An interview with Thibaw on the morning of his departure appeared in *The Times*, and a few colorful descriptions of Burma and the war appeared in *The Illustrated London News*, but not much else. Few sensed the bloodshed that was to come.

The war had started without a plan in place for its aftermath. Much like what would happen in the Iraq War 120 years later (and several colonial ventures in between), Churchill and others who had advocated a policy of "regime change" had assumed only the best: that with the removal of the top leadership, there would remain in place an administration with which the victors could work and that it would be on the whole a cheap war, a decapitation that would lead to a new and more pliable government and little need for an elaborate strategy of occupation. But also like the Iraq War of the twenty-first century, the best-case scenario never materialized.

The most obvious plan was to place another prince of the same Konbaung dynasty on the vacant throne as a sort of British puppet. What was left of the Burmese kingdom, Upper Burma, would have become either a protectorate, like Nepal, or an Indian princely state, like Hyderabad or Kashmir. The new "prince of Upper Burma" would have lived and ruled under the guidance of a British Resident, and the ways and aesthetics of the court may have been reformed to better fit English notions of a proper Oriental monarchy. Thibaw's successors may even have become fabulously rich and joined their Indian peers at the racetracks of Ascot or the gaming tables of Monte Carlo.

The government of India had been keeping one of Thibaw's half brothers, the prince of Nyaunggyan, on standby for several years in Calcutta for just such an eventuality. Many had assumed that he was the figure seen on the prow of one of Prendergast's ships, and this may have led to the easy surrender. But he had actually died just weeks before, something kept top secret so as not to undermine the ruse. But there were other options, including the young prince of Pyinmana, a teenager who could easily have been shaped into the sort of ruler the later Victorian empire wanted and expected.

The second option was simple annexation. No more king and no more royal family. All of Thibaw's possessions would have come ultimately under the authority of a British chief commissioner or governor. Under both schemes, some or all of the old administration could have remained, both the institutions of the Court of Ava and more than a few of its turbaned and helmeted officialdom. Either way, there would have been no more external interference, from the French or anyone else, and stability and trade would have been ensured under a British Raj.

But it soon dawned on even the most optimistic empire builders that in invading Burma, the British had waded into a very messy situation. The central assumption of Whitehall's Burma policy, to the extent that there was one, was that a swift and simple change at the top would lead to quick submission and the rapid return of normal government. This was now proven horribly wrong.

Things didn't start off too badly. Heat, bugs, and unfamiliar foods took their toll, but Mandalay was far from an inhospitable place to live. There were the familiar rituals and practices of a late-nineteenth-century colonial victory. Photographs were taken of British officers and their Indian subordinates against new and exotic backgrounds. Medals and promotions were discussed. A prize committee decided which treasures and artworks to send to whom in England and Ireland and what to sell for the government of India. Queen Victoria received Thibaw's best crown, and the prince and princess of Wales two carved ivory tusks and a gold figure of the Buddha. The larger rooms of the palace were converted with little redecoration into an Anglican chapel and a somewhat makeshift Upper Burma Club, complete with billiard table and a passable bar.

There were also some early attempts to address Burmese sensitivities, to win hearts and minds, but these were often inadequate or wrongly conceived. Within days of Thibaw's departure, his white elephant, symbol of the country's sovereignty, appropriately gave up the ghost. Though a proper cremation with court Brahmins was permitted, the dead animal was then unceremoniously dragged, in full view of a shocked public, out of the palace gates. For the Burmese the elephant had been something extraordinary, bordering on the divine, and was treated with extreme respect and care. Dragging the king's own corpse along the street would probably not have provoked any greater ill feeling.

By Christmas initial luck and good cheer had turned to worry bordering on panic. Within the defunct Court of Ava the British faced growing resentment and outright hostility, while in the countryside roving bands of armed men more directly challenged the new order. Thibaw's army had scurried away, many carrying their swords and rifles. Parts of the valley had long been plagued by gangs of bandits, and these now seemed to find common cause with the ex-soldiers returning to their home villages and hamlets. British patrols were ambushed and attacked by a largely invisible army with no apparent leadership. Again, as in Iraq much later, the questions were asked: Were they remnants of the old regime? Extremists of some sort? Or criminals taking advantage of the change in government? No one had any idea.

There were a few officials of the old government willing to help the British, but only in the most cursory manner. Many gathered their belongings and left Mandalay altogether. Harry Prendergast's political officers had hoped to work with Thibaw's most senior minister, the Kinwun. But he had chosen, perhaps in part out of a guilty conscience, to accompany the former king part of the way to his exile in India. The next most senior minister was the lord of Taingdar. He was known as a committed Anglophobe, and the British eventually found reason to arrest him and pack him off to India as well. For a few weeks the royal officers who were left were reorganized and placed under the overall supervision of a British civilian, Sir Charles Bernard. But the orders they sent up and down the Irrawaddy to the king's governors and garrison commanders seemed to have little effect as a full-fledged insurgency began to take shape.

Left to deal with the growing mess was the not particularly imaginative Irishman Frederick Temple Hamilton-Temple-Blackwood, the earl of Dufferin and baron of Clandeboye, the owner of large estates in the north of County Down and more recently the viceroy of India. Educated at Eton and Christ Church, Dufferin had a long and distinguished record of imperial and diplomatic service. He was governor-general of Canada and ambassador, first to Russia and then to the Ottoman Empire. He was a Whig but also an aristocrat and landowner.[15] After his predecessor Lord Ripon's exciting and controversial tenure, the queen told Dufferin not to be too independent in his thinking, and Dufferin was happy to comply.

And Dufferin, despite any misgivings he may have had (and despite the more articulate misgivings of his senior officials), had acquiesced to Churchill's strong lead and not stood in the way of a war with Burma. But now that Churchill had moved on to bigger things, it was Lord Dufferin who was left responsible for determining Burma's postwar future.

> *No more the Royal Umbrella.*
> *No more the Royal Palace,*
> *And the Royal City, no more*
> *This is indeed an Age of Nothingness*
> *It would be better if we were dead*
> —The abbot of Zibani Monastery[16]

For the people of Mandalay the days and weeks after the king's departure would remain etched in their minds forever. Fifty years later, on the eve of the Second World War, the nationalist leader Thakin Kodaw

Hmaing remembered how as a child he had witnessed the British soldiers escorting Thibaw and his family through the dusty streets of the
city. For the ten thousand Buddhist monks who lived in and around the
capital, occupation by a non-Buddhist power was almost impossible to
comprehend. Mandalay was the center of religious life in Burma, and
the king acted as patron to dozens of monasteries and monastic colleges around the city and in nearby towns. All of a sudden their patron
was gone, and an entire system of higher education and religious training collapsed almost overnight.

For the officials of the Court of Ava, their hopes of a light occupation and the installation of a new prince were quickly fading. When it
became clear that the British had no intention of leaving and were instead inclined to abolish the monarchy altogether, many of Thibaw's
senior officials, led by the Kinwun, banded together and made a formal
request to the viceroy: establish a constitutional monarchy or relieve us
entirely of our remaining responsibilities. They wanted full authority,
under the guidance of a British political officer and with a figurehead
prince. This, they said, could work, and order could be quickly reestab-
lished. But they couldn't be expected to function as things were, with
no say over the administration of the capital and only limited authority
in the countryside. They were neither here nor there. They wanted a
decision.

Outside Mandalay the nobility and the gentry class, which had
governed the countryside for centuries, responded in different ways.
Some chose submission. They included senior military officers, like
the colonel of the Yandana Theinga cavalry, a man of much influence
in the north, who sided with the conquerors and was appointed in
charge of his township.

Others, like the lord of Yamethin, were less willing to give in. He
had been an officer in the household guards and had been posted as a
garrison commander in the Shan uplands. He now led his Kindah regiment down from the hills and into the forests around Yamethin to
harass British positions. His distant relative the *sawbwa*, or prince, of
Wuntho in the far north also decided to resist, gathering around him
the chiefs of Katha and Kyatpyin for the coming fight. Just to the south
of Mandalay, the chief of Mekkaya, head of one of the oldest aristocratic lineages in the country, organized his men against the occupiers,
ambushing the young men from Tyneside and South Wales as they

ambled through the tall elephant grass and across fields of cotton and paddy. Other rebels included notorious bandits of long standing, like Hla-U in the lower Chindwin Valley and Yan Nyun in the badlands of the middle Irrawaddy. Now wearing a patriotic guise, they enjoyed a new lease on their popularity and made common cause with their erstwhile royalist foes.[17]

Lord Dufferin arrived in Burma on 3 February aboard the SS *Clive*, accompanied by his wife, Lady Harriot Dufferin, various aides and advisers, dozens of personal servants, and a very large numbers of horses, cows, calves, chickens, sheep, and quails. After his retirement he would be created a marquess by a grateful queen (he was now an earl) and was asked to take an Indian place name to include in his title. He thought that to be the marquess of Dufferin and Delhi or Dufferin and Lucknow would excite Indian sensibilities and was best avoided. He thought about Quebec instead, having served in Canada as governor-general, but Victoria disapproved. After first dismissing most Burmese names as sounding like "something out of the Mikado," he settled on the name of the court he had just vanquished, Ava. Now he was to visit the Court of Ava for the first time.[18]

At Mandalay, in the sticky afternoon heat, the viceroy sat on Thibaw's throne, dressed in a scarlet tunic and with the white plumed helmet of empire. The now-sobered officials of the old Burmese government remained standing throughout his address, a demonstration of considerable disrespect in a country where kneeling before superiors was customary. The subsequent discussions were not particularly useful for either side. The Kinwun and the others had lost any real hope for the future, and Dufferin saw the Burmese as tiresome and hardly worth engaging any longer.

He spoke to the British military officers and heard in disappointing detail of the growing insurgency and how the ex-royal agencies were unwilling or unable to be of much use. Dufferin later wrote that "a puppet king of the Burmese type would prove a very expensive, troublesome and contumacious fiction." British troops were going to have to pacify the country in a violent campaign in any case. If the old hierarchies could not help now, they were not worth saving for the future. Lady Dufferin had an apparently successful afternoon with the women of the palace, but for Lord Dufferin any second thoughts he might have on outright annexation pure and simple were now gone. The monarchy would be abolished. And the Court of Ava would become history.

> *This is the ballad of Boh Da Thone,*
> *Erst a Pretender to Theebaw's throne . . .*
>
> *And the Peacock Banner his henchmen bore*
> *Was stiff with bullion, but stiffer with gore.*
>
> *He shot at the strong and he slashed at the weak*
> *From the Salween scrub to the Chindwin teak:*
>
> *He crucified noble, he sacrificed mean,*
> *He filled old ladies with kerosene:*
>
> *While over the water the papers cried,*
> *"The patriot fights for his countryside!"*
> —Rudyard Kipling, *Barrack-Room Ballads*

There would now be no turning back, only a big push to do whatever it took to gain control over the Burmese countryside. Sir Charles Haukes Todd Crosthwaite, a fifty-something Irish civil servant from Donnybrook, was appointed chief commissioner of all Burma, and he was determined to crush all opposition and introduce into the old royal domains an all-new administrative machine. By the end of 1886 a total of forty thousand British and Indian troops had poured into the country, three times more than was necessary for the actual invasion and more than had been deployed in either the Crimean War or in the occupation of Egypt just a few years before. The British knew they were fighting a popular guerrilla uprising and were determined to use all means to bring it to an end.[19]

The commanders on the ground also realized that no concentration of troops, on its own, would change things, certainly not overnight. Instead the function of the troops was, in the words of one brigadier general, "to produce an effect upon the imagination and moral sense of the people, to make them feel that the inevitable had overtaken them." In other words, to make clear to the Burmese that they had no choice but to accept defeat and occupation. This was no easy task. The same officer lamented that "the in-born conceit, light-heartedness, and impulsiveness of the Burmese rendered them impervious to salutary impressions of that kind" and that "neither their religion nor their temperament permit them to suspect their inferiority."

The insurgency reached a fever pitch in the searing heat of April and May 1886. During the evening of 15 April (the first day of the Burmese new year), twenty or so armed men loyal to the teenage prince of Myinzaing, a renegade half brother of Thibaw's, scaled the walls of the palace, managing to set fire to several buildings and killing two Scottish physicians before being killed themselves. The next day every single British military post up and down the Irrawaddy Valley was attacked by rebel armies, sometimes in excess of two thousand men. If there had been any doubt before, it was clear now that opposition to the new colonial regime was being organized on a national scale.

But any opposition, however well organized, would have been hard pressed to stand up against what was to come. It started with a huge military deployment throughout the Irrawaddy Valley and continued with the large-scale and forced relocation of people. Crosthwaite was determined to cut off the rebels from the bases of support. Colonial magistrates were granted wide-ranging powers to move suspected rebel sympathizers, and dozens of villages were simply burned to the ground. Summary executions, sometimes by the half dozen or more, became routine, as did the public flogging of captured guerrillas. In at least one case a suspected resistance leader was tortured in public. And the occasional beheadings of prisoners were put to a stop only through the personal intervention of Lord Dufferin himself.

There was brutality on both sides, as embattled Burmese guerrilla fighters used any tactic they could to keep their hold over the villages, and as the British counterinsurgency campaign was more than willing to match terror with terror. A widespread famine, caused in large part by the war, then hit much of the country in late 1886. Starved, worn down, and eager for relief, more and more people resigned themselves to life under the occupation.[20]

In parts of the upper Irrawaddy Valley, pockets of resistance would carry on for years. One of the longest holdouts was the guerrilla leader

Bo Cho, a onetime provincial clerk who managed to evade British capture until 1896. This was in the badlands around the extinct volcano at
Popa, and local legends credit him with killing over eighty of the enemy in the early years of the occupation. When he was finally caught,
he was taken back to his home village, where all his friends and family
were summoned by the British officer in charge to come and witness
his execution. As he walked to the gallows, he told his nephew, "[W]e
Burmese are finished and it would be better to be dead than be their
slaves." And with that he and his two sons were hanged, one of hundreds of hangings ushering in Burma's modern age.

For the old aristocracy their world had come crashing down much
faster. Intensely conservative, they had been trained to look to the past
for examples and to see their lives and their vocations as part of a seam-
less heritage going back to the very introduction of Buddhism and
monarchy well over a thousand years before. Their noble status had
rested in part on their residence within the walled city. But by the end
of 1886 the city had been turned into a military cantonment, renamed
Fort Dufferin, and the hundreds of teak houses, meticulously set according to rank and lineage, were demolished to make way for parade
grounds and a new prison. Their status had also rested on the genealog-
ical records stored in the palace archives, but these and almost all the
other papers of the Court of Ava had gone up in flames as drunken
British soldiers set fire to the king's library soon after Thibaw's surrender. It was not until Lord Curzon visited as viceroy in 1901 that the
wanton destruction of the old buildings was ended and what was left of
the Mandalay palace was preserved.

A generation of young aristocrats were among those killed in the
fighting of the late 1880s. Many others retired to the smaller towns and
villages around the onetime capital. Into the 1920s there were still wed-
dings and more often funerals at which the old members of Thibaw's
court would gather. The Kinwun died in 1908 a broken man. Some
survived much longer, and it was not until the summer of 1963, the
same week that the Beatles went on their first tour, that the prince of
Pyinmana, Thibaw's half brother and the boy Lord Dufferin had considered as a possible king, died at the age of ninety-three. By then a very
new Burma had been born.

TWO

DEBATING BURMA

≈≈≈

ELAINE: "Peterman ran off to Burma."
SEINFELD: "Isn't it Myanmar now?"
KRAMER: "Myanmar . . . isn't that the discount pharmacy?"

In the summer of 1988, before the fall of the Berlin Wall and almost exactly a hundred years after Harry Prendergast's field force had landed at Mandalay, the Burmese people took to the streets in their tens of thousands to demand an end to decades of military dictatorship and international isolation. The protests had been rumbling on for months, starting with students at the select Rangoon Institute of Technology, spreading through the sprawling capital and then up-country. In March riot police had arrested dozens of students after unrest around the Rangoon University campus. Over thirty suffocated to death in a police van on the way to detention. More protests followed. The price of food skyrocketed, and a mood of opportunity and imminent upheaval fused with long-pent-up anger and resentment against the authorities. There were rumors of strikes and rallies in different towns. Those who could listened every night for the latest (and uncensored) news on the Burmese-language broadcasts of the BBC. Even in the homes of the urban well-to-do, senior civil servants and professionals who lived in relative comfort, there was a sense that "something had to change." A revolutionary atmosphere had developed.[1]

On 23 July, not long after the monsoon rains had started in earnest, General Ne Win, the man who had seized power in 1962 and had ruled single-handedly ever since, took to the podium and addressed the hundreds of assembled delegates. Rangoon was hot and muggy, but this meeting was in a cavernous air-conditioned chamber, built next to the old racetrack, with wall-to-wall carpeting and rows of neatly dressed men (and a few women), a rare picture of modernity in a country that had seemingly turned its back on the twentieth century. General Ne Win had called an extraordinary session of his Burma Socialist Pro-gramme Party Central Committee. The party was his personal creation and the only legal political party in the country, made up almost en-tirely of ex-military men as a sort of civilian facade for the armed forces.

And there, in front of his cooled and pliant audience, and after a short speech on recent events, General Ne Win, the dictator of Burma, said something no one expected. Speaking in clear, measured tones, he called for a popular referendum on a return to democracy and out-lined a very specific process that could lead to "a multiparty system of government" within months. He said that he took responsibility for the deaths of students in police custody in March. But continued demon-strations and violence had shown that people had lost confidence in the government more generally. If the referendum opted for change, a parliament would have to be elected that would then write a new con-stitution. He himself would stand down immediately, together with his top aides.

Whether Ne Win meant what he said that day is impossible to tell. In resigning, he chose as his successor an old subordinate, General "the Lion" Sein Lwin, a man not known for his liberal ways. It was, in any event, an incredible speech. The ruling elite in front of him sat in amazed silence. Looking straight at the television cameras, he also included a less than veiled threat: "Although I said I would retire from politics, we will have to maintain control to prevent the country from falling apart, from disarray, till the future organizations can take full control. In continuing to maintain control, I want the entire nation, the people, to know that if in future there are mob disturbances, if the army shoots, it hits—there is no firing into the air to scare."

Burma's democracy movement began that day.

Rangoon was electric. Normally a sleepy city of perhaps two million people, with lush tree-lined streets, crumbling masonry, and endlessly repaired 1950s sedans, the Burmese capital was now primed for action. People did not either trust or want to wait for the process Ne Win had outlined. Underground student groups began mobilizing and busily distributed leaflets calling for a general strike. A small stream of foreign journalists slipped through the decrepit Mingaladon Airport. Outside the capital sporadic protests continued.

And then, on 8 August 1988, at eight minutes past eight in the morning, a day and time deemed auspicious by the student organizers, dockworkers along the Rangoon River walked off their jobs. When word spread, people began marching toward the city center, waving flags, banners, and placards. With no one to champion, many carried portraits of the 1940s nationalist supremo Aung San. From the northern suburbs, long columns of university and school students ambled down the leafy boulevards that led to the city center, and by noon the broad expanse around Bandoola Park was crammed with sarong-clad crowds of cheering people. Apartment balconies and rooftops across the old colonial downtown area filled with onlookers. Makeshift podiums were put up in front of City Hall, and one speaker after another pushed forward to denounce a government that had oppressed and impoverished them for more than a generation. The call was clear and echoed Ne Win's: a return to multiparty government. Thousands moved toward the Shwedagon Pagoda about a mile away, where more fiery speeches were given. Hawkers sold cigarettes and drinks, and no one doubted that the country was at a watershed.

The demonstrations were not confined to Rangoon. Across every major city in Burma that afternoon big crowds of ordinary people left work and gathered on the streets to voice their frustrations against Ne Win's regime. Nothing like this had happened in decades.

All day the military had stood around and watched. There had been no incident. The army had allowed the demonstrations to take place. But at 11:30 p.m., with thousands still milling around in front of City Hall, it decided to draw the line. Across downtown the electricity was turned off, and big mobile loudspeakers ordered the crowd to disperse. No one budged. Then, in the dark muggy night, Bren gun carriers and trucks heavy with combat-ready troops in olive-green fatigues and steel helmets wheeled out onto the main square, and the young crowd, refusing to be cowed, began singing the Burmese national anthem. The army opened fire. The firing continued until the next morning. Dozens were believed to have been killed and wounded that first night, but there was never any proper count.

The response was not what the army had in mind. Rather than curtail the demonstrations, the bloodshed incited people further, and for the next five days the death toll rose as soldiers used lethal force to break up the mounting protests. On 10 August troops opened fire on a group of exhausted doctors and nurses in front of Rangoon General Hospital who ventured out to call for an end to the violence. Many of the dead around the city were high school students or young men from the poorer neighborhoods; they had shown themselves the bravest or most foolhardy in facing the German-manufactured G-7 rifles of the Burmese army. Some placed the number of dead and wounded well into the hundreds.

Finally, on 13 August, as if the men in charge had themselves had enough of the bloodletting, the army called a halt to its actions and announced the resignation of General Sein Lwin. Everywhere the army was ordered to return to the barracks, and soldiers quietly and quickly crept out of Rangoon. A close civilian associate of the old dictator's, an English-trained jurist, was appointed president, and he gave a hearty and conciliatory speech over the radio. But the public was not impressed. Instead a feeling of imminent victory filled the air.

Over the next many days civil administration in Burma collapsed in practically every city and town in the country, as millions of people happily strolled out of their homes and did what they had not been able to do for so long: organize as they wished and speak their minds. It was no longer just the students or the workers, but people from every walk of life. Rangoon developed a carnival atmosphere. Trade unions developed overnight. And in a country where the press had been tightly controlled for a generation, dozens of newspapers and magazines, laboriously mimeographed, suddenly appeared in shops and on sidewalks. In Mandalay the army retreated behind the walls of the old palace as committees of students, workers, and Buddhist monks took over the management of Thibaw's town. When the still-government-controlled radio and television claimed that the demonstrators did not represent the silent majority of law-abiding housewives and others, the All-Burma Housewives Association was formed, and hundreds of middle-class women, happily clanging pots and pans, marched with the teeming crowds under their newly furled banners. Soon the government itself broke ranks. In ministry after ministry civil servants and clerical workers left their offices and joined the throngs in the street. At the Foreign Office top-ranking diplomats signed a letter saying that the policies of the military regime had destroyed Burma's once-proud international reputation. Eventually the staff of the Burmese Broadcasting Corporation walked off their jobs, and the official media were suddenly silenced. Even the police went on strike. The revolution seemed on the verge of success. But who would lead it?

One by one, old and new politicians came forward. First it was Aung Gyi, once Ne Win's own deputy in the armed forces. Then, on 25 August, Aung San Suu Kyi, the daughter of Aung San, spoke for the first time to a massive gathering along the western slope of the Shwedagon Pagoda. And on 28 August, U Nu, in his eighties and the last democratically elected prime minister, announced the formation of his new League for Democracy and Peace. A number of those who came into view were old leftist or Communist leaders, including several old men who had helped lead the insurrections in the 1950s. Thakin Soe, one-time Stalinist agitator and guerrilla strategist, now eighty-three, issued a rousing call to revolution from his hospital bed. General Strike Centers were set up in more than two hundred towns. But it seemed to many students (and others) that the politicians were only grandstanding. No single party or organization enjoyed the broad support needed to deal the final blow. And after the initial euphoria of revolt, many, especially in the middle classes, began to be fearful of a coming anarchy.

By late August the violence had spread to the working-class suburbs of Rangoon, and food shortages led to rioting. Rumors spread that Ne Win's spies had secretly poisoned the water supply or had infiltrated the student leadership. On 25 August, prisoners were released or broke free everywhere in the country, adding to a growing sense of insecurity. On more than one occasion suspected government agents were gruesomely beheaded or hacked to death in front of cheering crowds. What had begun as a political revolt by disaffected students was now on the verge of becoming a bloody social revolution.

Many realized that time was running out. There were hundreds of political meetings a day, in smoke-filled living rooms and corner tea shops, as men and women in cotton *longyis* engaged in passionate and sometimes ill-tempered arguments about what should happen next. On 17 September a huge mob gathered outside the Trade Ministry and disarmed the soldiers guarding the building, the first time soldiers had peacefully given up their arms. Another crowd almost stormed the War Office, the very headquarters of the armed forces, but were dissuaded from doing so by politicians who promised that the government would soon resign voluntarily. These same politicians—Aung Gyi, Aung San Suu Kyi, U Nu, and others—agreed to meet together with student leaders on 19 September to form a revolutionary transitional government. Foreign embassies in Rangoon were approached to ensure immediate recognition. But General Ne Win and his men, shocked at recent goings-on, had devised other plans.

On 18 September, after more than a month of protests, the army moved back, confidently and in force. This time the bloodshed lasted two days. But it was no use. The old constitution was formally abolished, and in place of the old regime was established the State Law and Order Restoration Council headed by army chief General Saw Maung. The army claimed to be taking power "to prevent the disintegration of the Union." Hundreds of people were believed to have been killed in Rangoon alone, with at least several dozen in other cities and towns. The protests collapsed. The country was at once outraged and exhausted. The revolutionary moment was over.

There was a muted international response. The United States, Japan, the United Kingdom, and Germany suspended bilateral aid. But there was no pronounced outcry, certainly not from the general public, in Europe or in North America. Nothing like the reaction to the massacre at Tiananmen Square a year later. There were no calls for United Nations action. No urgent transatlantic diplomacy. Part of the reason was simple: there were no television cameras present in the country at the time. There was no CNN and no nightly news stories showing the depth of popular feeling or the violence that followed. There were no pundits demanding retribution and little attention on Capitol Hill or at Westminster. Much of the uprising had been in late August and early September, just in time for the late-summer holidays.

But the lack of response wasn't just attributable to the absence of television or to the fact that important people were vacationing in Martha's

Vineyard or Tuscany. It was also because Burma was almost entirely unknown. To the extent that it was thought about at all, it had the image of an exotic and dreamy backwater, a gentle Buddhist country, lost in time and quietly isolated, hardly the sort of location for a foreign policy crisis. It was an offbeat tourist destination, unspoiled compared with neighboring Thailand, perhaps even a model of an alternative approach to life, unhurried and without the extremes of modern capitalism and communism. Prodemocracy demonstrations in Burma? It was like hearing about a coup in Shangri-La. What was to be done with a place like that?

I was then twenty-two. I had been born on a snowy January morning very far away from Burma at the Columbia-Cornell Medical Center on Manhattan's Upper East Side. At the time my maternal grandfather, U Thant, was serving as the secretary-general of the United Nations, a job he had held since 1961, since the death of his predecessor, Dag Hammarskjöld, and would continue to hold until his retirement a decade later. He was presiding over the UN during a decade of considerable change. Dozens of newly decolonized Asian and African countries had recently filled the ranks of the world body, and their concerns—mainly to reduce the inequalities between rich and poor nations—fueled much of the organization's quickly evolving agenda. There were also political challenges during this height of the cold war, from the Arab-Israeli conflict and the Cuban missile crisis to Vietnam and the Soviet invasion of Czechoslovakia. Then, as now, the UN was often marginalized and occasionally scapegoated. But perhaps more than now there was a recognized value in maintaining the secretary-general as an impartial arbitrator and neutral voice and as a backdoor channel when more public diplomacy proved impossible. Like today, there were calls for reform and many who would throw their hands up in despair at the inability of the organization to tackle this or that problem. But the 1960s were less than a generation away from the fifty million dead of the Second World War, and there remained, perhaps, in every quarter a more heartfelt desire to make the UN work.

Of course I knew none of this growing up in Riverdale, a solidly middle-class neighborhood about forty-five minutes by car or subway from midtown. My parents, both Burmese, had met and married in

New York and were living with my grandfather and grandmother in what was then the secretary-general's official residence, a rambling seven-bedroom red-brick house, partly covered in ivy and set on a grassy six-acre hillside along the Hudson River. On the map it was part of Riverdale, but in most other ways it was a small slice of Burma. In addition to my parents and grandparents (and later three younger sisters), there was always an assortment of Burmese houseguests, who stayed anywhere from an evening to many months, and a domestic staff (all Burmese as well) of nannies and maids, cooks and gardeners as one might expect in any Rangoon pukka home. Burmese dancers and musicians sometimes performed at parties on the lawn. A Buddhist shrine with fresh-cut flowers graced a special area on the first floor, and a constant smell of curries drifted out of the always busy black-and-white-tiled kitchen. The UN security guards at the gate—mainly Irish and Italian Americans—wore uniforms of light and navy blue, but inside the stone walls a Burmese sarong or *longyi*, even in the Northeast winter, was the more predictable sight.

U Thant died of cancer soon after his retirement, and my family moved not long after to Thailand, where I lived until university, first at Harvard and then at Cambridge. But many summers during those years were spent in Burma, in Rangoon, where my mother had close relatives, and in Mandalay, where my other grandfather still lived. We often traveled around, and one year—when I was fourteen—I spent a short period as a novice monk, something all Burmese Buddhist boys are meant to do. For me those trips to Burma were always a surprise, a surprise that the inside world, inside the walls in Riverdale, had become the outside world, of people on streets and in markets, in trains and in homes. What was particular to my family was suddenly public and everywhere, in a world that was at once strange and new and yet intimately familiar. I still feel that sense of surprise in Burma today when I walk outside and down the pavement in my *longyi* or talk to shop assistants or taxi drivers in my mother tongue.

When the 1988 uprising began, I was only a few weeks out of college and at the very beginning of what would later be my own career at the UN, working in Geneva as an intern for Prince Saddrudin Aga Khan, then the UN's coordinator for humanitarian assistance to Afghanistan. I listened many times a day to the BBC and read about the first wave of military violence while spending a weekend with friends in

Lausanne. Within a week I had decided to give up my internship and booked myself a plane ticket to Bangkok, determined to be part of what every Burmese believed was a turning point in the country's history. Unfortunately for me, by the time I reached Bangkok and was set to travel on to Burma, the army had closed down the Rangoon airport, sealing off the country from the rest of the world. I felt I missed entirely my chance to be a part of things and to help.

The next year was my induction into Burmese politics. When the uprising was crushed, thousands of young men and women had made their way to rebel-held areas along the Thai border, not to flee the Burmese authorities but in a desperate and ill-placed hope that the West would arm them and help them overthrow the Rangoon government. I went to see them and spent many months in their muddy makeshift camps, never thinking that an armed revolution was the answer to Burma's problems, but in every other way sharing the anger and frustration that had sent them into the malarial jungles. I could go back more or less whenever I wanted to an air-conditioned apartment in Bangkok and had a generous postgraduate scholarship waiting for me, but they, of exactly the same generation as I was and often from similar family backgrounds, were in much deeper and had risked much more.

It was a Burma I didn't really know. My Burma had been an anachronism, of retired Indian Civil Service men in well-cut suits smoking cigars on the lawn at Riverdale, and genteel and lethargic evenings in a dilapidated bungalow in Rangoon, black-and-white portraits of a long-dead district magistrate on the wall and talk always turning back to a past and better age. This was a Burma that was urgent, aggressive, and dynamic, of young people who looked only to the future.

Most of my life since that year on the border has been spent away from Burma, except for a few months here and there, most recently in 2006. But none of the questions I (and many others) asked in the late eighties have gone away: Why has Burma's military dictatorship proved so enduring, and what can possibly bring back greater political freedom and democracy? How should we think about the continuing war between Rangoon and ethnic minority–based insurgencies? Why has Burma, so rich in natural resources and seemingly once so well ahead of its Asian neighbors, fallen so far behind? More to the point, what is to be done?

To some Burma presents no mystery. The military dictatorship was the creature of General Ne Win, had impoverished the country, and had to be ousted from power. Nothing else mattered. The insurgency, the interethnic conflict, the grinding poverty, all these things stemmed from a single problem; once the military dictatorship was replaced with a new democracy, there would be a fresh beginning.

This approach has had the strength of clarity, both a moral clarity and a clarity of action. Burma was essentially a good place held hostage by a wicked government, and therefore all efforts had to be directed at the removal of the ruling establishment. But how to remove the government? For a minority, like the former university students who had camped out along the Thai border, only an armed insurrection would do the trick. For others the answer was the strongest dose possible of diplomatic and economic sanctions. People would again take to the streets. The army would buckle under.

Over the past seventeen years, interest in the country's plight has increased significantly. That the military government held, lost, and then refused to respect the results of its own elections in 1991 only highlighted its venal nature. Burma is now of celebrity and political interest as a well-entrenched second-order foreign policy matter, with a small cottage industry devoted to ensuring that Western governments hold the line against Rangoon's military regime. Norway's award of the Nobel Peace Prize to Aung San Suu Kyi in 1991 propelled the opposition leader to international acclaim. And now the cause of Burmese democracy flutters consistently on the margins of high-level attention, with dedicated albums by U2 and REM, Prime Minister Tony Blair personally lending his name to a boycott of tourism in Burma, and U.S. Secretary of State Condoleezza Rice styling the country an "outpost of tyranny."

But over these same seventeen years prophecies of the regime's imminent collapse in the wake of hardening international sanctions have proved, at least so far, fanciful. The country has changed considerably, and the government itself has transformed, only not in the way that the growing legions of Burma campaigners would wish. For a long time all Burmese assumed that the death of General Ne Win would lead suddenly to change, positive change, but then in 2002 the old man died quietly in his lakeside bungalow, and nothing happened; a fresh generation of captains and colonels had already taken charge, determined to act on their own dreams and nightmares. The mix of international policies in place—limited (American and European) trade and investment sanctions, a cutoff of most development assistance, including from the World Bank, and a steady stream of righteous condemnation, whether right or wrong—has not so far worked. Instead there is every sign that while millions remain impoverished, the regime itself has moved from strength to strength. What has had the force of clarity has not had the value of effectiveness. And so we must ask ourselves again: How did the country reach such a state?

The most striking aspect of the Burma debate today is its absence of nuance and its singularly ahistorical nature. Dictatorship and the prospects for democracy are seen within the prism of the past ten or twenty years, as if three Anglo-Burmese wars, a century of colonial rule, an immensely destructive Japanese invasion and occupation, and five decades of civil war, foreign intervention, and Communist insurgency had never happened. A country the size and population of the German Empire on the eve of the First World War is viewed through a single-dimensional lens, and then there is surprise over predictions unfulfilled and strategies that never seem to bear fruit. Burma is a place with a rich and complex history, both before the time of King Thibaw and Lord Randolph Churchill and since. Burmese nationalism and xenophobia, the ethnic insurgencies and the army dictatorship, and the failure of successive governments to keep pace with the rest of an increasingly peaceful and prosperous Asia—all these things have a history, a reason. And what emerges from these histories is not an answer to all of today's ills but at least the beginnings of an explanation. And from this explanation perhaps a richer discussion and a better intimation of what may lie ahead.

THREE

FOUNDATIONS

Burma in ancient and medieval times, when she enjoyed connections across the known world, from China to the Roman Empire, and how perceptions of her remote past influence the present

~~~

Burma is in many ways a country defined by its geography, at once isolated yet always with the possibility of connection, northward to China, westward to India, and overseas to the world, a country with a stubborn and sometimes unhelpful sense of difference and uniqueness. Much of the country (a little more than half) is the valley of the Irrawaddy River, which runs north to south, from the icy eastern curve of the Himalayas down over a thousand miles to the brackish tidal waters of the Andaman Sea. The upper portion of this valley—the heartland of successive Burmese kingdoms—is dry, almost a desert, not like the Sahara but approaching the aridity of Southern California or the Australian outback. Part of the year is intensely hot and cloudless, and the rains, when they do come in late summer, come in wild and sudden downpours, concentrated over less than fifteen days a year, drenching the sandy ground and turning gullies into raging torrents. The south, on the other hand, is entirely different. The lower portion of the valley, the Irrawaddy Delta, as well as the two adjacent coastal regions of Arakan and the Tenasserim, are warm and humid, with overcast skies and steady rains for weeks and months, lush and tropical with long stretches of picture-perfect beaches and little offshore islands.

Around this valley is a great horseshoe-shaped arc of highlands, of terrifying chasms and soaring snow-covered mountains set alongside gently sloping hills and meandering alpine streams. Taken together, the highlands prevent any easy overland access to the outside world.

This is not to say that Burma was ever sealed off, only that a constant effort was required to connect and to overcome a natural tendency to look inward and be content. And for the external world, in turn, the valley and the surrounding highlands, removed from the major highways of conquest and commerce, were readily forgotten, the rewards of association often outweighed by the risks and costs involved. There were times when Burma and the Burmese were a part of things, engaged, learning, and contributing, and there were times, like now, when the country stood nervously on the margins, looking from far away at growth and creativity elsewhere.

Burma is also, at least in the minds of many of its people, an old country, with an often vivid feeling for its own history and with the relics of the past all around. All Burmese schoolchildren are taught that their history begins at Tagaung. Tagaung is today a dusty and palm-shaded village of enterprising shopkeepers and sugar mill workers, about a half day's drive north of Mandalay, with a few seemingly old ruins and an occasional air of antiquated importance. And according to the chronicles of the Burmese kings, it was here that the Sakiyan prince Abhiraja and his followers had arrived from the Middle Country of India and founded the country's very first kingdom.[1]

The story goes that thousands of years ago, long before the Buddha preached his first sermon at the deer park in Sarnath, the king of Panchala, wanting an alliance with the neighboring king of Kosala, asked Kosala for his daughter's hand in marriage. Kosala, proud of his far-nobler lineage, refused. War ensued, and the outcome was victory for the up-and-coming Panchala and defeat and disaster for Kosala's entire royal family.

The Kosala royal family were part of the Sakiyan clan, which would later be celebrated across the Buddhist world as the clan of the Buddha himself. But that was in the future. For now the Sakiyans were in decline, and it was these bad times that led one of their princes, Abhiraja, to pack his belongings and head east, together with his personal army, across the Black Mountains and into the valley of the Irrawaddy.

Traveling to Burma from India in ancient times must have been no mean feat. Between the two countries are a series of mountain ranges with peaks over three thousand feet high and some of the wettest and most pestilential jungles anywhere. And we must imagine a land of very few people. Even in the late nineteenth century the population of all Burma was only around five million (compared with over fifty million today), and in ancient times the number was certainly much less. The land would have been covered, nearly entirely, in scrublands and thick forests of teak and ironwood, birch and rhododendron higher up, and teeming with wild and dangerous animals. Tigers and rhinoceroses and herds of elephants roamed everywhere, with leopards in the tallgrass and man-eating pythons lurking behind every bush and every tree. Even the giant panda, now no longer in Burma, may have survived near the Irrawaddy into ancient times. What people there were would have lived here and there, in small pockets, perhaps mainly alongside the rivers and streams, eking out a precarious existence.

Whatever the challenges, Abhiraja, according to the chronicles, survived and prospered. There is no suggestion that he had arrived in an empty land, only that he was the first king. The chronicles also say that he had two sons. The elder son, in the inventive spirit of his father, ventured south and founded his own kingdom at Arakan. The younger son succeeded his father and was followed by a dynasty of thirty-one kings. Centuries later scions of this dynasty founded yet another kingdom much farther down the Irrawaddy, near the modern town of Prome, and this kingdom at Prome lasted five hundred years until succeeded in turn by the medieval kingdom of Pagan. Thibaw, the last king, would trace his descent to the rulers of this medieval kingdom and thus ultimately to Abhiraja and the Sakiyan clan as well. A failed marriage, class prejudice, and a desire to start anew had, it seems, led to the beginning of Burmese civilization. As for the Burmese of more modern times, the story provided a sense of a deep continuity, right down to the fall of Mandalay.

British scholars of the colonial period were fairly skeptical of all this and of the Burmese chronicles more generally, especially of the parts covering the earlier history of the country. Some took to the notion of an Indian origin to Burmese civilization and were inclined to accept the idea of colonizers from the West bringing enlightened and long-lasting government. But they doubted the antiquity of the chronicle tradition and generally dismissed the possibility that any sort of civilization in Burma could be much older than, say, A.D. 500. Those who were not historians were sometimes more dismissive. Aldous Huxley, who traveled for a while in Burma during a leisurely round-the-world tour in 1925, wrote about the last of the royal chronicles, *The Glass Palace Chronicle*:

> It is as though a committee of Scaligers and Bentleys had assembled to edit the tales of the nursery. Perrault's chronicle of Red Riding Hood is collated with Grimm's and variants recorded, the credibility of the two several versions discussed. And when that little matter has been satisfactorily dealt with, there follows a long and incredibly learned discussion of the obscure, the complex and difficult problems raised by Puss in Boots . . .[2]

But more recent research suggests that civilization in the Irrawaddy Valley *is* in fact very old and that many of the places mentioned in the royal records have indeed been inhabited continuously for a very long time.[3] As early as thirty-five hundred years ago—the time of the Old Kingdom in Egypt—people across the region were already turning copper into bronze, growing rice, and domesticating chickens and pigs, and they were among the first people in the world to do so. By twenty-five hundred years ago ironworking settlements emerged in an area just south of what would later be Ava and Mandalay. Ironworking in turn led to more food and many other useful things, and these long-ago settlements, trading near and perhaps far in salt and glass and cowry shells as well as copper and iron, have left behind signs of their affluence, bronze-decorated coffins and burial sites filled with the earthenware remains of great feasting and drinking.

By the early centuries A.D. complex irrigation systems had begun to appear. As the climate in most of the valley was so dry and as the rains, when they came, were so sudden and short-lived, diverting and trapping rainwater were the key to expanding agriculture. Once this was possible, through elaborate systems of canals, weirs, and tanks, small and poor settlements became big and powerful. Walled cities, some of considerable size, emerged. There were kings and palaces, moats and massive wooden gates, and always twelve gates for each of the signs of the zodiac, one of the many enduring patterns that would continue until the British occupation.[4] There was yet no single kingdom, only city-states. And these city-states were already overcoming their geography and linking up with the crossroads of the ancient world. Abhiraja, if he ever really existed, was not the only ancient traveler to Burma.

A map of ancient times (say, two thousand years ago) would show four great empires, together encircling most of Europe and Asia, from the north of England to the Sea of Japan. Rome, Persia, the Mauryans in India, and the Han Empire in China ruled supreme over much of the civilized world. But there were breaks in the imperial maps, areas not controlled by any of these big states. Like the forests of Germania or the desert wastes of Arabia, a big region between Mauryan India and Han China belonged to no emperor. Part of this region was the high-up Tibetan Plateau. And below Tibet was a vast stretch of mountains and valleys, including the valley of the Irrawaddy. This was the world of the early Burmese and their cousins.[5]

It's a world that's not well known and has been little studied. It included not only all of present-day Burma but also all of what is now the northeast of India and the southwest of China, an area as big as Western Europe with many diverse peoples and places, most lost to history, not just isolated tribes and obscure mountain chieftainships but cities and kingdoms with languages and cultures entirely distinct from the Chinese and Indian civilizations to the east and west.

Near Lake Dian, just north of Burma, there have been found striking pieces of art,* figures of human sacrifice, as well as little representations of tigers, leopards, and bees, unlike any Chinese works but instead strongly reminiscent of the art of the distant Ordos Desert in Inner Mongolia. There are likely other cultures to be found. Only in 1986 did archaeologists, by chance, discover the hundreds of beautiful and mysterious bronze masks and vessels of an entirely unknown civilization, believed to have flourished more than three thousand years ago, dissimilar to anything Chinese, in what is now Sichuan. Perhaps people in Burma were already, even two or three thousand years ago, aware of the wider world, borrowing ideas and foreign styles, and buying and selling goods from far away.

Sometime in 139 B.C. a Chinese official, Zhang Qian, set off from

---

*Pinyin spellings of Chinese proper names are used throughout the book, except where a different spelling (e.g., Chiang Kai-shek, Yangtze) might be better known.

the imperial capital of Changan, then the richest and most powerful place in the entire world, accompanied by his loyal slave Kanfu and over a hundred aides and retainers. They were headed toward the unknown and seemingly endless grasslands to the west, with a mission to find allies against China's barbarian enemies beyond the Great Wall. Zhang was destined to become one of the greatest explorers of ancient times. After many grueling years of travel and barbarian captivity, he eventually found his way across the desert wastes of the Tarim Basin to what is now Afghanistan, before returning home a hero to the Han court.

He told his mesmerized compatriots about the kingdoms of the Fergana Valley and Bactria, of Persia and Mesopotamia and India, places the Chinese had known nothing about. He told them about Persian wine and the Persian merchants who traveled in ships to faraway places, about the heat and humidity of the lands along the Arabian Sea, and about the war elephants of India. And he told them something startling and unexpected: that in the markets of Bactria, he saw cloth made in the Chinese province of Shu. Shu (or modern Sichuan) is far to the south. Had other Chinese travelers gone west before him? No, he was told, the cloth and the bamboo had come from India. There existed a *southerly* route, to India and from India to the West.[6]

What Zhang Qian and the Han court had stumbled on was what merchants had long known: that there was a profitable traffic in all sorts of goods, from China down through the Irrawaddy Valley across to India and beyond. And the products of the Irrawaddy Valley and surrounding highlands were also traded: ivory and precious stones, gold and silver, the small and sturdy horses of the region, and, perhaps most desired of all, the handsome horns of the rhinoceros, endowed with magical and medicinal properties.[7]

Soon there would be more trade, more contact, as ever more urbane Burmese kingdoms profited rather than let themselves be constrained by the valley's geography. When envoys from the Roman east, perhaps Alexandria, journeyed across the Irrawaddy en route to China in A.D. 97, they were treading well-worn paths.[8] Later, when sailors were able to venture across the high seas, a different route, through the Straits of Malacca, would be the preferred way to the East. But for a brief moment Burma was on the highway of the world. And it was this already sophisticated and well-connected Burma that would reach decisively westward, to India, for inspiration.

THE MIDDLE WAY

In the time of Zhang Qian, India was ruled by the Mauryans. Two hundred years before, Alexander the Great had seen his dreams of conquering the world shattered by the mutiny of his Macedonians near the banks of the Indus River. Though Alexander soon left India permanently, his incursion into India's northwest profoundly shook existing political arrangements and allowed the prince Chandragupta Maurya to seize the throne at Magadha, then the most powerful of Indian kingdoms. Chandragupta went on to defeat Alexander's general Seleucus Nicator, and in the peace treaty that followed, the Macedonians ceded most of the occupied territory in return for five hundred elephants. A new Mauryan Empire came into being, ruling the entire north of the subcontinent. Its capital at Pataliputra (in modern Bihar) was one of the great cities of the world, if not the greatest, dazzling even Nicator's envoy Megasthenes, a man who had been to Babylon.

Emboldened, the Mauryans became avid imperialists, and their domain soon stretched from the Arabian Sea to the Bay of Bengal. Chandragupta's grandson the emperor Asoka had been a distinguished soldier in the spirit of his ancestor, leading campaigns of conquest with armies said to number in the hundreds of thousands of infantry and tens of thousands of cavalry. Then, out of the blue, in the sixteenth year of his reign, he had a change of heart. The emperor had just defeated the three Kalinga kingdoms along the steamy eastern coast, and the death and suffering he witnessed firsthand traumatized him and led him to permanently renounce war. Asoka would now take up the teachings of the Buddha. It was to be a conversion as historic as Constantine's and would transform Asia forever.[9]

Buddhism was then already a couple of centuries old. Its founder, Gautama Siddhartha, had been born heir to a minor chieftainship in the Himalayan foothills but had given up princely power and pleasures to reflect on the nature of human existence. Buddhists believe that he attained enlightenment and went on to teach what he had learned, preaching his first sermon at Sarnath and traveling around the great cities of North India until his death (from a meal of tainted pork) at age eighty in 484 B.C. Today his teachings are part of many different philosophies and schools of practice, with the Mahayana schools of Tibet, China, and Japan forming a branch distinct from the more conservative Theravada schools of Sri Lanka, Burma, and Thailand. At the core of both are his ideas on people's dissatisfaction with their lives, the origins of this dissatisfaction, and a way out of this dissatisfaction, in part through the living of an ethical and balanced life and a perspective that accepts change as integral to all things.[10]

In the third century B.C. Buddhism was only one of many contending religious schools, but the emperor Asoka's conversion was pivotal in making it the dominant faith across India and much of Asia beyond. Asoka formulated an idea of a righteous government and public policy, one that eschewed violence in all forms, including against animals, and that called for the humane and just treatment of everyone, no matter what class or caste, both inside and outside the empire. It was the first "Buddhist government" and would become the declared model for the later kings of Southeast Asia. He sent missionaries to Ceylon, Persia, and farther west, paving the way for the conversion of Afghanistan and the towns of the Silk Road. The eastern Greeks, themselves descendants of Alexander's men, would be among the most fervent of the new followers, transforming their kingdoms in Bactria and northwestern India into centers of Buddhist art and scholarship and producing the very first images of the Buddha, based on models of Apollo. Even today the Burmese word for college, *tekkatho*, is from Taxila, a long-ago center of Indo-Greek Buddhist learning just to the east of the Khyber Pass.

Burmese tradition says that two Burmese merchants named Tapussa and Ballika, natives of the area around Rangoon, were traveling in North India when they by chance met the Buddha soon after his enlightenment. They offered him rice cakes and honey and asked him for a token of their visit. He gave them eight hairs from his head, and on their return these eight hairs were enshrined deep within what became the Shwedagon Pagoda, the country's holiest shrine, and the hairs have remained there ever since. The great pagoda is today over three hundred feet high, on a hilltop that dominates the modern city of Rangoon, swathed in sixty tons of gold leaf, and surrounded by a marbled platform and sixty-four lesser pagodas and numerous shrines. But this present form is a relatively recent thing, dating back five centuries or so; beneath its exterior lie stranger and older shapes, ancient structures that might reveal its origins and earliest purposes. Entrances to four tunnels, never explored, sit tantalizingly on the pagoda platform, and though legends tell of underground rivers and miraculously guarded passage-ways, no one really knows what may lie inside the Shwedagon's base.

The Burmese legends are not impossible, and there may have been long-ago travels that introduced Buddhism very early to the Irrawaddy Valley. But it seems that Burmese Buddhism was more the product of later times and later contacts, by sea rather than land, not with the homeland of the religion in the Ganges plain of North India, but with South India, some eight or nine hundred years after the Buddha's death.

South India is a place that has always been tied to remote places. The Bible mentions that King Solomon's ships were sent there for gold, silver, peacocks, and ivory. After navigators had begun to master the intricacies of the monsoon winds, trade between India and the Mediterranean worlds grew by leaps and bounds, as ships, steering clear of the pirate-infested coastlines, were able to sail directly across the Arabian Sea. In the long-buried seaports of the Coromandel coast, archaeologists have found treasure troves of amphora containers, once filled with fine Italian wine, and hoards of Roman coins.[11]

Roman and Hellenistic traditions mixed with influences from across the Indian subcontinent in these river towns and seaports along the southeastern coast. They became important centers of international commerce as well as renowned centers of art and learning. Not only did Buddhism flourish in this cosmopolitan hub, but some of the great-est works of Buddhist learning and philosophical debate took place in the study halls and libraries of the area's abundant monasteries, debates that resonated across Asia for centuries to come. The great philosopher Nagarjuna, arguably the most important Buddhist thinker after the Gautama Buddha himself, wrote and studied here in the third century, and it was in the universities of the region that the historic divide be-tween Mahayana and Theravada Buddhism first took form.

It was part of Burma's good fortune to have established close rela-tions with such a dynamic place, its merchants and learned men going back and forth across the Bay of Bengal, absorbing Buddhist as well as Hindu art and ideas, and replanting them within the context of its al-ready long-established civilization in the Irrawaddy Valley. One imag-ines the increasingly sophisticated and prosperous Irrawaddy city-states hearing of happenings in the West and wanting to know more, bring-ing back texts and artwork, perhaps enjoying a glass of Italian wine, and adopting and adapting what they saw as the best of India and, via India, the known world.

By the middle centuries of the first millennium, this was true in much of Southeast Asia, in Java, Cambodia, Sumatra, and Siam as well as Burma. Kings took on Indian titles and names, and art and architecture bore the clear stamp of Indian inspirations. Colonial scholars tended toward the idea of Indian colonization and of Indian tradesmen braving the dark waters of the bay, building up little settlements and finally bringing light and civilization to hitherto barbarous lands. But it seems that the traffic was most likely two ways and that Burma was already enmeshed in a network of trade and contacts, even in antiquity, and that foreign ideas were imported rather than imposed.

This period of close contact with South India was when sea routes across the Bay of Bengal must have been routine.[12] In the second century A.D. the Greek mathematician Claudius Ptolemy wrote his *Geographica*, describing not only the port cities of India but also the lands of gold and silver (*Chryse* and *Argyre*) beyond the Ganges. Some of the most accomplished mariners of the ancient world were not Indians or Chinese, or Arabs or Greeks, but Malays, men (and perhaps women) of present-day Malaysia and Indonesia who sailed far to the west, colonized the island of Madagascar, and even explored the African coast, a thousand years before Vasco da Gama. The Roman historian Pliny in the first century A.D. mentions ships arriving in Africa from the eastern seas carrying cinnamon and other spices. Even today the main language of Madagascar is Malagasy, closely related to the languages of Java and Borneo, the westernmost outpost of a sailing world that took these ancient explorers and traders west to Africa and east to the farthest Polynesian islands.

By the fourth century many in the Irrawaddy Valley had converted to South India's Buddhism, the single most important development in Burma's long history. Of the many city-states flourishing at the time, the most important was at Prome, along the middle part of the Irrawaddy. Here was a city of enormous size, more than two miles across, with massive circular walls of green glazed bricks and stupas similar to those of southern India, prototypes for the great pagodas to come. Prome's rulers named themselves Vikram and Varman in imitation of Indian dynasties, and a visiting Chinese traveler remarked on the Buddhist devotion of the people:

It is their custom to love life and hate killing . . . They know how to make astronomical calculations. They are Buddhists and have hundreds of monasteries, with brick of glass embellished with gold and silver vermillion, gay colours and red kino . . . at seven years of age, the people cut their hair and enter a monastery; if at the age of twenty they have not grasped the doctrine, they return to the lay state . . . They do not wear silk because, they say, it comes from silkworms and involves injury to life.[13]

The exploits of their kings are still remembered in legend, and to the very fall of the kingdom in 1885 there would be court *ponnas*, experts in ceremony and the arcane sciences of royal life, who traced their descent unbroken to the earliest ritualists of Prome. It was a remarkably long-lasting civilization, from the early centuries B.C. to the ninth century A.D., when a new power descended from the north, bringing in its wake a new people, swift horsemen from the foothills of the Himalayas, the Myanma.[14]

LORDS OF THE SOUTH

Take the road east from Mandalay and very soon you will find yourself (nervously if on a Burmese bus) circling up two thousand feet onto the edge of the Shan plateau. The air will quickly cool, and the climate will be altogether different; the dust and the palm trees of the plains surrendering to grassy hills and forests of oak, magnolias, and pine. Go farther, perhaps for a half day, across the fearsome gorge of the Salween River, and the hills will become mountains, now eight thousand feet high, and any suggestion of the tropics will give way to thoughts of warm blankets and evenings by the fire. To the north, past fields of tea and opium and rice, will be the beginnings of the Himalayas and then the unimaginably vast and near-empty borderlands that separate China and Tibet. And just ahead will be the mountain country of Yunnan, today a part of the People's Republic. Press on for two more days (if the Chinese border guards allow you), and you will finally arrive at the tourist town of Dali, a magnet for backpackers, with charming cobblestone streets, laid-back ways, and the partly fulfilled sense of being off the beaten track. This whole area, from Mandalay through western Yunnan, is today home to many different peoples, mainly Shans (who speak a language very similar to Thai), on the Burma side, and Chinese, on the China side. But it was once very different, and a little over a thousand years ago Yunnan was the center of its own multiethnic empire.

Sometime in the early part of the eighth century A.D., around the same time that Islamic armies were completing their conquest of Spain, six principalities nestled around the limestone hills of Lake Dali, today's backpackers' mecca, were brought together for the first time into a single and unified kingdom. Both the new kingdom and its ruler were known as Nanzhao, meaning in Chinese "the Lord of the South."[15] And from the very start the kingdom was aggressive and expansionist, pushing hard in every direction, overpowering and organizing the related tribal peoples of the Tibetan borderlands, marching south into the rain forests along the Salween River and then east toward China. Success bred confidence and ambition, and over the next hundred years this kingdom, now an empire, enjoyed at times a strong friendship with the Chinese. Nanzhao's envoys were welcomed with lavish ceremony and an honor guard of war elephants and warriors in full armor at the Tang dynasty court at Changan, and the Tang in turn dispatched their own emissaries to Dali bearing luxurious and outlandish gifts.

But at other times Nanzhao allied itself with China's archenemy Tibet, then a big power in Central Asia. When in 755 a rebellion in China led by the Turkish-Sogdian governor An Lushan touched off a massive civil war, killing millions and throwing the country into chaos, Nanzhao and Tibet joined sides, sacking Chinese cities and even briefly capturing the imperial capital itself.

In the late eighth and early ninth centuries the Nanzhao empire was in full flight. It was a highly militaristic state, with all strong adult males conscripted into the imperial cavalry and those less capable mobilized as foot soldiers. At the top was the "Lord of the South" himself, dressed in tiger skin, "red and black with stripes deep and luminous, made from the finest tigers in the highest and remotest mountains," and able to look back on a century of unbridled conquest.[16]

The empire was from start to finish a multiethnic domain. But many of its people, particularly in western Yunnan, as well as the ruling class itself, spoke a language similar or ancestral to modern Burmese. The Chinese called them Wuman, "black southern barbarians," after their dark complexions. In the ninth century a gifted Chinese scholar-bureaucrat named Fan Chuo compiled a book (*Manshu: Book of the Southern Barbarians*) about Nanzhao, including a colorful ethnography of its component tribes. Many were simple folk, goatherds and shepherds, in the process of drifting southward, over the rugged mountains and into the blistering plains of central Burma.

Of a tribe known as the Loxing Man ("Man" meaning a type of barbarian), this learned study says: "They are not warlike by habit but are naturally friendly and submissive . . . Their men folk and women folk are plentiful all over the mountain wilds. And they have no princes or chiefs . . . They wear no clothes, but only take the bark of trees to conceal their bodies." Others included the Bu Man in the forests to the east of the upper Irrawaddy: "They are brave, fierce, nimble and active . . . they breed horses, white or piebald, and trained the wild mulberry to make the finest bows." Another, the Wangzhu Man, lived in the snowy ridges closest to Tibet, the home of the sand-ox with horns four feet long. Of these distant Burmese forebears, the book observes that "their women only like milk and cream. They are fat and white and fond of gadding about." The Mo Man seemed even more carefree: "Every family has a flock of sheep. Throughout their lives they never wash their hands or faces. Men and women all wear sheep-skins. Their custom is to like drinking liquor, and singing and dancing . . ."

It was these people who were marshaled into the Nanzhao war machine, trained to be fighters, and died in not inconsiderable numbers on far-flung battlefields, against Tibet and China and even farther afield. They also battled aliens closer to home. In 801, when Nanzhao was allied with China against Tibet, a combined Nanzhao-Chinese army defeated a polyglot Tibetan force, commanded by Tibetan generals but made up largely of captives from the far west. And in this way thousands of men from Samarkand and Arabs from the Abbasid caliphate of Baghdad, men from the court of Harūn ar-Rashīd and *A Thousand and One Nights*, were taken prisoner on a high Burmese mountain valley together with twenty thousand suits of armor.[17]

By this time much of the Irrawaddy Valley was also under Nanzhao authority as the warlike peoples of the north pressed down. The ancient city-states one by one surrendered or were overrun by the powerful mounted archers coming down from the north. In 832, Nanzhao destroyed the city of Halin, close to old Tagaung, returning again in 835 to carry off many captives. According to the *Manshu*, "They took prisoner over three thousand of their people. They banished them to servitude at Chetung and told them to fend for themselves. At present their children and grandchildren are still there, subsisting on fish, insects, etc. Such is the end of their people."[18]

Their cavalry are said to have swept down all the way to the Bay of Bengal despite stiff resistance. It's difficult to imagine these men of the Yunnan plateau, perhaps in the captured chain mail armor of Baghdad, on their tough little ponies, with a scent of the windswept Central Asian grasslands, riding all the way to the palm-fringed beaches along the Andaman Sea. But these were different times, when unlettered nomads and the descendants of unlettered nomads were fighting their way into all kinds of unlikely places, like the Goths and Vandals in Sicily and North Africa.

By the tenth century the Nanzhao empire had slowly faded from history. By this time Buddhism, primarily the Mahayana and Tantric variety from Bengal, had become the dominant religion at Dali, and the Nanzhao court became keen patrons of the new faith. Perhaps this had sapped their warlike vigor. Or perhaps two centuries of campaigning had drained the Yunnan heartland of the men and wherewithal to continue its policies of expansion. In 902 the entire Nanzhao ruling family was killed in an internal power struggle, and around the same time contacts with China became less frequent. But intercourse with Burma may have deepened, both culturally and politically. The old elite, who spoke the Burmese-related language of Yi, was replaced, and the new elite established a more modest kingdom, simply known as the Dali kingdom, which survived for three more centuries.*

But some of the old martial spirit must have remained, and as in all former empires, there would have been those who felt cheated from a life of invasion and plunder. They were still first-rate horsemen. And the Irrawaddy Valley, weakened from a century of invasion and subjugation, could hardly resist those tempted by the warmer weather and rich paddy fields. The tribes in the west—whose womenfolk had been enjoying their milk and cream or who wore sheepskins, and had never washed, looking forward only to drinking, singing, and dancing—these tribes under their *mang* (chiefs) began filtering south, perhaps following the course of the great river, and finally occupying the fertile rice

---

*Burmese and Yi (also known as Lolo and Norsu) are part of the same branch of the Tibeto-Burman language family, which includes Tibetan, Burmese, and dozens of other languages and dialects.

lands near present-day Mandalay. They called themselves the Myanma, or the strong horsemen.*

THE TRAMPLER OF ENEMIES

In 849, seventeen years after the Nanzhao's cavalry had last swept through the towns of the Irrawaddy Valley, Pagan[†] was founded as a fortified settlement along a bend in the Irrawaddy River.[19] The new settlement may have been designed to help the Nanzhao pacify the surrounding countryside. It was certainly a strategic spot, close to the confluence of the Irrawaddy and its main tributary, the Chindwin, and just to the west of a richly irrigated rice plain. Perhaps there was a long tradition of ironsmithing and a vibrant weapons industry.[20] Within two hundred years Pagan had become the center of a great Buddhist kingdom, and its ruins today are one of the most magnificent sites in all Southeast Asia. Its core area was this flat arid expanse (once called *tattadesa*—the "parched land"), but its imperial writ would one day cover much of present-day Burma, from Tibet to the Straits of Malacca.

The Burmese chronicles say that after the Nanzhao invasions a new dynasty arose, founded by a semimythical warrior-king named Pyusawhti. An expert archer, he came to Pagan and defeated, in the manner of St. George, a great bird, a great boar, a great tiger, and a flying squirrel, freeing the local folk from their terror. Some accounts say that he was born of the union of a prince of the sun and from the egg of a dragon; others that he was a scion of the Sakiyan lineage of Tagaung, that he lived to the age of 110 years, and that he was a giant of a man, five cubits tall.

It seems very likely that whatever his measurements and human or superhuman ancestry, he was connected in some still slightly mysterious way with the old and fallen house of Nanzhao. The ruling class of Nanzhao had a peculiar naming system, in which the last name of the father became the first name of the son. And this was the naming sys-

---

*This is not a widely accepted derivation, but a good one and from a well-respected authority in the field, U Bokay, the late director of the Pagan Museum; from a personal communication at Pagan, 1987.
†Sometimes spelled "Bagan" and with a stress on the second syllable.

tem of Pyusawhti and his descendants for seven generations. Somehow, two hundred years of the Nanzhao Empire had washed up on the banks of the Irrawaddy and would find a new life, fused with an existing and ancient culture, to produce one of the most impressive little kingdoms of the medieval world. From this fusion would result the Burmese people and the foundations of modern Burmese culture.

For two hundred years or so this new kingdom at Pagan slowly gained ground. Then in the eleventh century came a great burst of human energy in the form of Aniruddha, who seized the throne as a teenager in 1044 after killing his cousin in single combat, "his mother's milk still wet upon his lips." His name means "the ungovernable, the self-willed," and he would make Pagan the center of a new all-Burma Empire.[21]

The chronicles remember him campaigning in every direction, aided by his four captains. To Prome, enclosed by massive walls and with a proud and ancient court, Aniruddha rode with a "great company of elephants and horse," annexing the city-state and taking away its fabled Buddha relics. He also led his men to the old Nanzhao heartland and then built a line of fortified towns at the foothills of the Shan plateau to guard against any fresh incursions. It was an energetic reign, much still lost in legend, but after thirty-three years this king had done what no one had done before. He unified the Irrawaddy Valley under a single sovereign and created a kingdom that matched fairly closely the borders of today's Burma.

He did this not simply because of a love of conquest. Shipping across the warm waters of the Indian Ocean was becoming commonplace as sailors slowly mastered the monsoon currents and as economic expansion in both the East and West made long-distance trade ever more profitable. From Ceylon and South India to the South China Sea the most direct route took ships first to the Tenasserim coast and then through the Straits of Malacca. For Aniruddha and his court, capturing these seaports and profiting from global business must have been an attractive proposition. He took Thaton, a principality along the coast, and then fought his way all the way down to the Malay Peninsula. His votive tablets have been found there, near the breezy shoreline, not far from the island of Phuket and a thousand miles away from Pagan.

The society over which he presided espoused eclectic religious

beliefs, with the worship of spirits and *naga* dragons happily coexisting
with Buddhism and Hinduism and even currents of Islam. The Theravada Buddhism of Ceylon and South India competed with the ever
more fashionable Mahayana and Tantric beliefs and practices of neighboring Bengal and Tibet, including Tantric practices that would shock
and disgust the more prudish Burmese Buddhists of later generations.
Aniruddha himself, like many in medieval times, was a man of passionate religious fervor, building temples and pagodas at Pagan and elsewhere. He was also the patron of the indigenous *nat*, or spirit cults of
Burma, organizing their worship around a single national system.

By the twelfth century—the time of Saladin and the crusader kings—
Pagan was at the height of its glory and extent. Buildings of sublime
beauty soon rose up along the banks of the Irrawaddy. It was a society of
great creativity and energy, absorbing and transforming art and ideas
from across the Indian subcontinent. Its kings and nobility wrote in
Sanskrit and Pali as well as different native languages, experimenting
with various Indian alphabets. The Burmese language itself was reduced to writing (with an alphabet from South India), and new books
of Burmese grammar were enthusiastically compiled. Ideas and institutions of government, many inherited from Prome, others perhaps from
Nanzhao or imported fresh from India, were brought together to become a tradition that lasted into the nineteenth century.

Pagan's growing wealth and power did not escape notice overseas.
In 1106 an embassy was sent to the haughty Chinese imperial court at
Kaifeng. The dynastic history of the Sung records that the emperor first
ordered that the embassy be treated with the same rank and ceremony
as the Colas of South India. But the Grand Council observed that the
Colas were subordinate to the Sri Vijaya kingdom of Sumatra, whereas
Pagan was now a big and independent kingdom. In earlier times imperial decrees to the Burmese court were written on "thick-backed paper
and enclosed in box and wrapper." Now, the Grand Council recommended the same ritual should be followed toward Pagan as toward the
king of Annam and the caliph of Baghdad. All appointments and decrees should be written on "white-backed, gold-flowered, damask paper, and stored in a partly gold-gilt tube with key, and forwarded in a
brocade silk double wrapper as sealing envelope." The emperor con-
sented to this wise advice.[22]

Aniruddha was followed by a line of able kings. Together they
erected thousands of temples and hundreds of monasteries, libraries,

and colleges and repaired and constructed the dams and weirs that made middle Burma a great producer of rice. The chronicles even say that one of the Pagan kings, Aniruddha's grandson Alaungsithu, sailed around the world, to Sumatra, Bengal, and Ceylon, climbing Mount Meru at the center of the earth and then traveling to the Zambutha-byebin, the fabulous rose apple tree that grows at the World's End.[23]

The period of Pagan's greatness in the eleventh and twelfth centuries coincided with a time of unrest and upheaval throughout much of Asia, when Buddhism was in retreat nearly everywhere. In India, Mahmud of Ghazni and his Turkish and Afghan cavalry were sweeping across the Ganges plain, sacking the holy city of Benares in 1033. To the north, in China, the Sung dynasty was overseeing a gradual decline in popular support for Buddhism and the parallel rise of neo-Confucian ideas. To the south, the Colas, worshipers of the Hindu god Shiva, were extending their reach into Ceylon and Sumatra. And in Bihar, the Buddha's birthplace and very center of Buddhist learning, the ancient universities of Nalanda and Vikramasila, once home to thousands of scholars and tens of thousands of students from around Asia, were falling into decline, waiting to be overrun by the energetic Islamic armies to the west. Scholars from these universities traveled to Tibet for refuge, and others may have traveled to Pagan. The people of Pagan, as fervent practitioners of Buddhism and increasingly of Theravada Buddhism, saw themselves more and more as the defenders of a threatened faith and an island of conservative tradition in a hostile and changing world.

Once Burma had been part of a far-flung and dynamic conversation, a component of the Buddhist world that linked Afghanistan and the dusty oasis towns of the Silk Road with Cambodia, Java, and Sumatra, with scholar-officials in every Chinese province, and with students and teachers across India. Now the conversation was shrinking. Burma's Buddhism would become even more impassioned. Not part of Christendom, the Islamic world, or the cultural worlds of Hindu India and Confucian China, Burma, proud and resolutely Theravada, would be left largely to talk to itself.

Visitors to Pagan today will have a good intimation of the onetime prosperity and splendor of this medieval Buddhist kingdom. There remain a multitude of temples and pagodas, thousands by some accounts, some in ruins but many in good repair, piles of elegant masonry stretched over miles of sandy windswept plain, the reddish pink earth bordered by scrublands and the dark blue of the Irrawaddy, here over a mile across, and then the denuded mountains in the distance. But it is difficult to really imagine what Pagan was like at its height as only the religious structures remain, the rest gone or buried by earthquakes, fires, and long years of natural decay. Except for parts of a wall and the royal library, there is nothing left of the royal residences and government buildings or the streets and shops and ordinary homes of eight centuries ago. Here and there are patches of cultivated land, growing sesame, cucumbers, and groundnuts, where once were grand plazas and crowded markets, and bamboo and thatch huts, where there stood magnificent teak palaces.

The Mongol hordes in the thirteenth century brought terror and destruction to enormous swaths of Europe and Asia, and Burma was no exception. Pagan was already by then in decline, but the Mongol invasions hastened the demise of the kingdom.[24] Early in the century the warlord Genghis Khan had united the Mongol tribes in the grasslands south of Siberia, and over the next several decades he and his successors drove deep into the Islamic world, conquering Persia and Russia and China and halting, only by choice, on the very borders of Western Europe. Burma was in a way an extension of the Mongol campaign to encircle the Chinese. When Genghis's grandson Kublai Khan was a lieutenant of his elder brother Mangu, he led an invasion that put an end to the still-independent kingdom of Dali and brought Mongol arms right up to the borders of Burma. Twenty years later Kublai became emperor of all China and continued his southwesterly conquests, first demanding tribute from Pagan and then sending his infamous cavalry under the Turkish general Nasruddin of Bukhara.[25]

In 1271 under instructions from Kublai Khan, the new military governors of Yunnan sent envoys to the Burmese demanding tribute. Bad diplomacy was followed by rash actions and then by war. The Venetian traveler Marco Polo, the first European ever to mention Burma, was then a privy councillor on the emperor's staff and heard stories about what happened. According to him, the Burmese king's forces, said to number sixty thousand, included two thousand great elephants, "on each of which was set a tower of timber, well framed and strong, and carrying from twelve to sixteen well-armed fighting men." Against this, Nasruddin, "a most valiant and able soldier," had twelve thousand cavalry. They met in the hills close to the present China border, and in the early stages of the battle, the Turkish and Mongol horsemen "took such fright at the sight of the elephants that they would not be got to face the foe, but always swerved and turned back," while the Burmese pressed on. But Nasruddin was a cool soldier and didn't panic. Instead he ordered his Mongols to dismount and, from the cover of the nearby tree line, aim their bows directly at the advancing elephants, throwing the animals into such pain that they fled. The Mongols remounted and cut down the Burmese.

Nasruddin then descended into the valley of the Irrawaddy, destroying a number of stockaded positions against fierce Burmese resistance and then overrunning the ancient town of Tagaung itself, the home of the country's first kings and known in Chinese chronicles as the "nest and hole" of the Burmese. For years more there was fighting between the two sides, the Mongols eager to teach the Burmese a lesson, the Burmese battling for their own survival, a war punctuated by attempts at negotiation, including a celebrated mission in 1284 by the minister Disapramok to the court of Kublai Khan. It couldn't have been easy for the Mongols, unwashed men on horseback used to the open steppe, to face fighting elephants and a withering climate. A final invasion was headed by a grandson of the emperor himself and moved into the heartland of the kingdom. The country was soon in disorder, the king having fled in panic to Prome and there killed by his own son. Little warring principalities and rival princes emerged in place of Pagan's once-imperial writ. Burma was never integrated into the Mongol imperial administration but was nevertheless, for a few years, under the distant authority of Peking and Xanadu, and for the first and only time under the same yoke as Kiev, Moscow, and Baghdad.

In the centuries to come, no longer a capital, Pagan dwindled to a village, though always an important village, and into the 1800s the intricate local aristocracy enjoyed a symbolic importance well beyond any remaining political or economic clout. Its hereditary rulers carried the title of *mintha*, or prince, and in the nearby town of Nyaung-U the local chief claimed direct descent from Manuha, the enslaved king of Thaton, whom legend says Aniruddha brought to Pagan after a campaign of conquest in the south.

For many Burmese this history of the remote past, from the legendary rulers of Tagaung to the fall of Pagan, offers up a sense of deep-rooted tradition and of a long-lasting association among Burma, the Burmese, and the Buddhist religion. No matter that civilization in the Irrawaddy Valley long predated Buddhism or that Buddhism in its present form is a fairly new thing or that the Burmese language itself spread only with alien conquests from the north. There is a feeling of continuity and of a national and pristine past that was interrupted only with the British occupation. When the people of Mandalay mourned the exile of Thibaw, they felt they were mourning the loss of an institution that they believed stretched back across thousands of years.

But there were always other peoples, with other pasts and other traditions, as well as the slow approach of India from the west and China from the east. And in the modern world to come—with guns and gunpowder, mercenaries from as far afield as Lisbon and Nagasaki, and an emerging globalized economy that promised the adventurous untold riches—renewed Burmese attempts at empire would not go unopposed.

FOUR

PIRATES AND PRINCES
ALONG THE BAY OF BENGAL

*Burma in early modern times — when China and the Islamic world
loomed large and when the first Europeans arrived — and the Burmese
image today of an all-conquering past*

∼∾∼∾

He hath not any army or power by sea, but in the land, for people, domin-
ions, gold and silver, he farre exceeds the power of the Great Turke in treasure and strength.   — Caesar Frederick, a merchant of Venice[1]

King Bayinnaung, who lived almost five hundred years ago, is the favorite king of Burma's ruling generals. No one knows what he
looked like, but big bronze statues of him, tall and imposing, with
a broad-brimmed hat and a long ornamented sword, stare down impas-
sively at passersby in airports, museums, and public parks all around
the country. Whereas previous kings had unified the Irrawaddy Valley,
Bayinnaung proved an even more ambitious conqueror, vanquishing
an impressive array of neighboring kingdoms and even marching over
the highlands and defeating Burma's archrival Siam. At its height, his
writ ran unchallenged from parts of modern-day northeastern India
right across to the borders of Cambodia and Vietnam, an empire the
size of Charlemagne's with a striking imperial capital to match. European visitors were in awe of his wealth, the gilded palaces and jewel-
encrusted costumes, and marveled at the military might of his war
elephants and Persian and Portuguese musketeers. For today's generals,
and others of a more belligerent nationalist persuasion, Bayinnaung
represents a glorious past, something to be missed, and a sign, however
distant, that Burma was not always so lowly in the eyes of the world. Far
back enough in time not to be tainted by the colonial humiliations to

come, yet close enough that he and his heirs subjugated peoples and places still around today, he is an untarnished hero for these militaristic but lackluster times.[2]

And there is something else. For many Burmese today the stories of Bayinnaung and his contemporaries are the stories of a nation naturally inclined to fracture but which through heroic action can be welded together and made whole, of a country that will fall apart without the strong lead of soldier-kings, where greatness will only follow an iron fist. For some this was an exciting tradition, even if for others the past meant something altogether different.

In the early fourteenth century, after the last Mongol horsemen had quit the central plains, a number of little principalities and kingdoms cropped up: Ava, Prome, Mongmit, Pegu, Martaban, Toungoo, Bassein, and many others, in both the Irrawaddy Valley and the highlands toward China.[3] Most were nothing particularly impressive, just a little walled town, with a wooden palace and wooden gates, a moat and a bridge, and a few Buddhist monasteries and nearby pagodas, holding sway over dozens of surrounding villages and pretending through their ceremonies and rituals to be successors to the great kings of Pagan. It was for a while a time of inwardness as well as cultural and intellectual creativity. There were fewer connections with the outside world, especially with Bengal and South India, and a replacement of foreign influence with more confident homegrown styles. This was true in literature as well as in the arts and architecture, and the Burmese language, once a new thing, grew into a widespread vernacular and the idiom of still-classic works of poetry and jurisprudence.

The richest and most powerful of these successor states was Pegu. Pegu is about an hour's drive north of Rangoon, on the road to Mandalay. It's now far from the ocean. But in the fifteenth and sixteenth centuries it was a port of some significance, the silting up of the Sittang River in the meantime having cut off the town's access to the Andaman Sea. The people of Pegu then spoke Mon, a language related to Cambodian, which had become the mother tongue of the Irrawaddy Delta. Under a line of especially gifted kings, the Mon people at Pegu enjoyed a long golden age, profiting from foreign commerce and defending themselves ably against all challengers. Peguers traveled overseas to make money, and traders from across the Indian Ocean—Bengalis and Tamils, Greeks, Venetians and Jews, Arabs, and Armenians—all came to do business with the king of Pegu and his royal brokers, filling the city's warehouses with gold and silver, silk and spices, and all the other stuff of early modern trade.[4]

The city also became a famous center of Theravada Buddhism. Its kings and queens were great patrons of the faith and gave their weight in gold to the Shwedagon Pagoda at Rangoon, today the emblem of Burmese Buddhism, raising the ancient stupa toward its present height and form. The kingdom established strong ties with Ceylon and encouraged fundamentalist reforms that later spread throughout the country.

But Bayinnaung, the generals' favorite, didn't come from Pegu. He came instead from a poorer kingdom to the north called Toungoo, nestled in the dark teak and bamboo forests along the foothills of the Shan Plateau. Whereas the people of Pegu spoke Mon, the people of Toungoo spoke Burmese. And they were envious of Pegu's wealth and its easy access to the sea and were ready to make war and gain what they could of the outlandish luxuries hidden behind the city's heavy walls. Tabinshweti was the king of Toungoo, and Bayinnaung was the king's most trusted captain and loyal friend. Together they would bring fire and sword not only to Pegu but to every corner of Burma. And when Tabinshweti died his mysterious death, Bayinnaung went on to even greater victories and became to his people the universal monarch of legend.[5]

The empire building of Tabinshweti and Bayinnaung took place in the context of much grander empire building elsewhere. The Ottomans were then at the very peak of their vitality, reaching the gates of Vienna under Sultan Suleiman the Magnificent in the spring of 1532. Farther east, Ismail had recently become the shah of Persia and had launched the series of campaigns that would establish the formidable and elegant Shiite Safavid Empire. And closer to home, in 1526, the Central Asian warlord Babur, scion of the house of Genghis Khan and Tamerlane, had defeated the sultan of Delhi and set up Mughal domination over almost the entire Indian subcontinent. The world of imperial Islam now marched close to Burma, separated now only by the tidal swamps and malarial marshes of eastern Bengal. But perhaps most important for Burma were developments in the near north.

More than the Ottomans, the Safavids, and even the Mughals, it was Ming China that could best claim superpower status. With 150 million people, a huge military machine, and a colossal exam-based bureaucracy, there was simply nothing like it in the world, as it dwarfed neighboring Burma in population and economic size. The Ming dynasty had been founded by the tough peasant leader Zhu Yuanzhang, and he and his heirs presided over a long era of scientific progress, economic growth, and political stability. Military power was converted into an aggressive foreign policy, and the new Chinese army, the first anywhere to be equipped with firearms and cannons, was the deadliest ever seen, crushing domestic dissent and carving out huge expanses of the inner Asian steppe.[6]

The Ming also traveled overseas. A Muslim eunuch of Mongol descent named Zhang He, born in a border town not far from Burma, was one of China's most distinguished admirals. Captured and castrated as a boy for service in the Forbidden City, he later studied at the Imperial Central University and proved himself both in battle and in the intrigues of the royal court. In 1405, Zhang He, who some say inspired the story of Sinbad the Sailor in *The Thousand and One Nights*, led a fleet around the Indian Ocean that inspires awe even today. More than thirty thousand men sailed in three hundred ships on the first expedition alone (compared with a mere three ships under Christopher Columbus), and these ships were the biggest wooden vessels ever, journeying as far from China as Egypt and the Red Sea and down the African coastline to Mozambique and perhaps beyond. Over the next quarter century there were seven expeditions in all, bolstering China's political prestige while increasing the Middle Kingdom's knowledge of the world. Many of these ships were laden with porcelain, lacquer, silk, and other desired goods, and these were freely distributed as a demonstration of Sino superiority. After one voyage Zhang returned to Peking with a giraffe and other exotics for the imperial menagerie, and after another with envoys from no less than thirty countries, including a king of Ceylon, who came to render homage to the emperor in person.[7]

The Burmese were no doubt impressed by the seaborne exploits of their Chinese neighbors. But they may have been even more impressed and alarmed by a more subtle change. Land reform, advancements in technology, and sustained political stability had come together in China to produce an enormous increase in the already giant country's population. And this was no more true than in the southwest, along Burma's border, where Ming China now appeared in all its size and confidence, just on the other side of the eastern hills. The Middle Kingdom cast a huge shadow over the Irrawaddy Valley, then and ever since.

Against this backdrop of global empire building, Tabinshweti and Bayinnaung set off on their more modest dream of uniting Burma under the Toungoo banner.[8] Slowly but surely, they managed to bring all the little principalities and kingdoms of the country to heel, one by one. Pegu itself was among the first to fall, by a devious ruse rather than mere force of arms, and next to go was Martaban, a famed entrepôt of comparable riches, defended by the able and cunning but in the end failed Portuguese mercenary Paolo Seixas. At Martaban, now an overlooked and seedy village but then a place of international repute, the local prince and all his family and retainers were murdered, drowned off the gorgeous sandy beaches, despite promises of good treatment. Many other brutal triumphs followed. But then, just as all Burma lay within their grasp, the Toungoo king, now king of Burma, Tabinshweti, ran into personal trouble. It was to be his undoing.

The troubles all began with the arrival at court of a young *feringhi**—a Westerner whose name is lost to history. Nothing much is known about the *feringhi*'s past, nothing to distinguish him from the score of other rough-and-ready Iberian fortune hunters who prowled around the Bay of Bengal, looking for action and loot. He was Portuguese, and this may have meant he was born in Portugal, but it may also have meant that he was born in Asia or was of mixed Luso-Asian background.

By this time the Burmese were very familiar with the men of Lisbon and their kinsmen in the East. It was in 1494, two years after Christopher Columbus's ships landed in the Caribbean, that Pope Alexander VI issued a bull that divided the world between Iberia's most Catholic monarchs, with Brazil, Africa, and Asia, Burma included, being granted to King Emmanuel of Portugal and his heirs. It was a license to make money. In 1510, intrepid Portuguese seamen seized Goa from the Bijapur sultan, and a year later Dom Alfonso de Albuquerque overwhelmed the fabulously wealthy trading center of Malacca in Malaya, a pivot of global exchange, and thereby brought under Portuguese control the greatest sea-lane in the world.

---

*From the Arabic *firanj*, or Frank.

The Portuguese were not coming into a world with no trade; rather they were intervening to break up or circumvent already lucrative intercontinental networks, many in the pockets of Persian and other Asian Islamic businessmen. They saw Islam as their implacable foe but were content to do deals with the Buddhist and Hindu princes of the Indian Ocean world and matched commercial acumen with an unmitigated willingness to kill. Soon maritime trade in pepper from the Malabar coast, spices, cloves, and nutmeg from the Moluccas, and cinnamon from Ceylon all fell into energetic Portuguese hands, displacing the older land routes from Beirut and Alexandria to Venice and taking goods around the Cape of Good Hope. Those lucky enough to be part of this wave of globalization became wealthy beyond their wildest dreams.[9]

And this was what the young, nameless *feringhi* wanted as well, to be rich beyond his wildest dreams. But his initial plan—to attack the sultan of Aceh from the Portuguese base at Malacca—was a stupid one. He had set off in many ships and with three hundred men. But this would have been a reckless gamble even in the best of circumstances. As it was, Aceh was then under the most powerful of its sixteenth-century rulers, Ala'ad-din Ri'ayat Shah al-Kahar. The *feringhi* and his band were easily routed, and he was forced to flee to Martaban and from there was taken to the court of the new Burmese king.

Tabinshweti was at the height of his authority and decided to allow the *feringhi* to be part of his retinue, and with his charming ways, the young man soon enjoyed considerable royal favor, to no one's initial worry. He was skilled in using the most modern firearms, and this skill impressed Tabinshweti. He went hunting with the king, and the king, in friendship, gave him as his wife a lady of the court. The young man taught his new bride Portuguese cooking, and before long she was preparing dishes from Lisbon and Goa. He also introduced the king to wine and then to stronger spirits, arak, mixed with honey.

This is when the trouble began. Tabinshweti, it turned out, had a weakness for wine and spirits, and soon the Burmese ruler cared about little else but drinking, "respecting not other men's wives, listening to malicious tales, and sending men to the executioners." His actions grew increasingly violent and unrestrained. Discontent grew, and distant provinces plotted rebellion. Tabinshweti, who had achieved so much, was leading his government into chaos.

It was Bayinnaung who first warned him of his growing addiction and where it would soon lead. But it was no use. He told Bayinnaung to leave him alone. The executions continued, and the king slowly lost his mind. Ministers and courtiers pleaded with Bayinnaung to take action; Bayinnaung said that he could not be so disloyal. Instead he packed off the young Portuguese who had caused such a disaster and dispatched the king to Pantanaw, in the Irrawaddy Delta. Soon after, Tabinshweti was killed by his own courtiers some way, after he was lured into the wet jungle to search for a white elephant.[10]

With Tabinshweti dead, Bayinnaung finally came to the fore. He was made king. And just in time, as the empire he fought to create was quickly falling to pieces, every town taking the opportunity to declare its independence and shut its gates to the new monarch. Bayinnaung was left with little more than his immediate following. And so for the next twenty years Bayinnaung conquered Burma again, making relentless war, unleashing campaigns of great brutality and destruction until one day all of western mainland Southeast Asia acknowledged his sovereignty.

He depended throughout his career on his Portuguese mercenaries, with their heavy beards and baggy trousers, men who brought with them not only the latest in military hardware (the Chinese had this as well) but tested fighting ability and martial know-how. They were headed by Bayinnaung's good friend and comrade Diego Soarez de Mello, known as the Galician. Soarez de Mello had first come east many years earlier, making a name as a pirate in the waters around Mozambique in the early 1540s and then serving many different kings, from Arakan to Malaya, before becoming rich as Bayinnaung's loyal captain.

The great seaport of Pegu had first to be recaptured, and the city fell to the combined force of Bayinnaung's feared elephant corps and the tough Iberian musketeers of the Galician. The proud nobility of Pegu tried in vain to make a last stand, and in desperation the king of Pegu himself, Smim Htaw, emerged and challenged Bayinnaung to single combat, both on their war elephants. Bayinnaung, never one to pass up a fight, was victorious, charging his foe and driving him off after breaking the tusk of Smim Htaw's elephant. The Burmese say that he "paid him no more heed than a lion does to jackals." The Burmese and the Portuguese then sacked Pegu, killing men, women, and children. Smim Htaw fled into the jungle, hiding there for months until he was finally captured, paraded through the streets, and executed.

Having forced the Irrawaddy Delta for a second time to submission, Bayinnaung then headed north in a vast armada. His teak warships were crafted into the shapes of animals—horses, crocodiles, and elephants—and the king himself rode in a gilded barge shaped like a Brahminy duck, the symbol of the vanquished Pegu monarchy. The north of Burma was unprepared for the violence to come. Ava quickly gave way. And over the next four years Bayinnaung fought and defeated one by one the highland principalities, stretching from Manipur in the west (in what is now India), across to Chiangmai (in what is now Thailand) and the Lao states of the middle Mekong River.

This was a never-ending war. Month after month, year after year, Bayinnaung and his men did what they loved best, returning prisoners and loot to their new home at Pegu, the tattooed and turbaned Burmese chiefs on their ponies and elephants fighting shoulder to shoulder with their Iberian harquebusiers and musketeers, in their conquistador-style helmets. They were vicious, though perhaps no more than was the norm in those times. Against the resilient principality of Mogaung, Bayinnaung campaigned several times from 1562 to 1576. When the prince of Mogaung, heir to a long lineage, was finally defeated, he was placed for a week in chains at the gates of Pegu before being sold, together with his chiefs, in the slave markets of eastern Bengal.

Bayinnaung's was a winning team. And after a while the tide turned, and resistance ended. Tribute poured in. No one wanted to fight Bayinnaung anymore. The king of Chiangmai, one of the most formidable of the upland states, sent elephants, horses, and silks. He also sent the lacquerware for which his city was famous, and to this day the Burmese word for lacquer, *yun*, is the same as the word for the people of Chiangmai.

But this man of such relentless drive and ambition would not be satisfied with just the Irrawaddy Valley and the surrounding hills. He looked east and saw the richest and most cultured city in the region, Ayutthaya, the capital of Siam. Bayinnaung first demanded the tribute of a white elephant, and when this was denied, he prepared his invasion. The outcome was never in real doubt, as the aggressor army tramped across the plains of the Chao Phraya Valley, then laid siege to the capital itself.

The Siamese surrendered to prevent complete destruction, and the Burmese took not one but four white elephants, together with the king of Siam himself and several princes as hostages. A princess was presented to Bayinnaung as a new concubine. The entire Tenasserim coastline was permanently annexed, and a garrison of three thousand was left to ensure good behavior. Thousands of ordinary people were deported together with court entertainers, dancers, actors, and actresses. The king returned to Pegu in triumph, caparisoned elephants before him. He would soon make his capital a spectacle to rival Pagan, with golden palaces and gilded gates, each named for one of twenty subordinate kingdoms, a multiethnic city with peoples from across the country and beyond. He had established the most far-flung Burmese empire ever.

For the Burmese today the chronicles of Bayinnaung's victories read like tales of Roman conquest to schoolboys in the West. Except that the Burmese army still sees itself, in a way, as fighting the same enemies and in the same places, subjugating the Shan hills or crushing Mon resistance in the south, their soldiers slugging their way through the same thick jungle, preparing to torch a town or press-gang villagers. The past closer, more comparable, a way to justify present action. His statues are there because the ordeal of welding a nation together by force is not just history. It's as if the Italian Army were today guarding Hadrian's Wall, defending Syria against the Persians, and quelling German resistance the brutality seemingly inevitable.

Bayinnaung died in 1581 at age sixty-six, leaving behind nearly one hundred children. He had dominated a region that encompassed nearly all of today's Burma, Thailand, and Laos. His life, according to one historian, was "the greatest explosion of human energy ever seen in Burma." And he died planning an expedition to the west, to the one neighboring kingdom that never accepted his sovereignty, the kingdom of Arakan.

THE CITY OF THE MONKEY-EGG

Arakan is today a state within Burma, largely cut off from the rest of the country, the only land route being a couple of treacherous and barely paved mountain roads. Decrepit buses make the twenty-hour journey from Prome on the Irrawaddy River through thick jungle to Sandoway at Arakan's southern end. Akyab, the state capital, is sleepy and run-down, even by contemporary Burmese standards, with electricity only a few hours a day (and sometimes not at all) and no real outward signs of any kind of progress or vitality. With its ramshackle restaurants and open-air markets, it has the look of a large village, and the few Western tourists seem like the first outside visitors ever to a remote and isolated corner of a remote and isolated country.

But even the most casual observer would probably realize that this conclusion—that Arakan has always been removed from the world—was a wrong one, as Arakan is set right on the Bay of Bengal, with the bright blue waters of the Indian Ocean pressing gently up its picture-perfect beaches. For centuries it prospered on international trade and readily took in people and ideas from across the Asian continent and beyond, a flourishing civilization with the most cosmopolitan court in modern Burmese history. Arakan's isolation is a very new thing. And its lost cosmopolitanism is a part of Burma's present-day poverty.

Arakan is essentially a long and narrow slice of coastline, shut off from the Irrawaddy Valley by a long chain of mountains, some with peaks three thousand feet high, about eight hundred miles from north to south and about sixty miles from the hills to the sea. It's a luxuriant, wet landscape, everywhere clumps of mango, guava, and citrus trees, and several rivers winding across the rich alluvial plains. In the short dry season, thirsty elephants come down from the jungles to enjoy the salty waters of the mangrove swamps. The long summers are drenched in endless rain.

In ancient times, Arakan was very much an extension of northern India.[11] The Chandra dynasty that ruled over the principalities of Vesali and Dhanyawaddy claimed descent from the Hindu god Shiva while also patronizing the Mahayana schools of Tibet and Bengal. But in medieval times there was a reorientation eastward; the area fell un-der Pagan's dominance, and the Arakanese people began to speak a di-alect of Burmese, something that continues to this day. With Burmese influence came ties to Ceylon and the gradual prominence of Theravada Buddhism.

As Pagan's authority waned, Arakan quickly emerged from the shadows and became independent once again, engaging in the petty wars of the time. When in 1404 the kingdom of Ava invaded Arakan, the then king, Naramithla, fled west to the Bengali royal city of Gaur. He lived there for many years, absorbing the polished world of eastern Islam, before going home and retaking his throne. It was to be a fateful exile.

Here the history of Arakan intersects with the history of India and especially with Bengal. Two hundred years before, the first Islamic armies—bands of Turkish and Afghan cavalry—had galloped their way across the rich Ganges plain. They were led by Muhammad Bakhtiyar, and they were merciless as they overran the towns and Buddhist universities of Bihar and sacked the holy city of Benares. When they reached Nudiya in Bengal, they disguised themselves as horse traders and sneaked their way inside the city walls. Once safely in, they cut down the unsuspecting garrison and then fought their way to the king himself, who was about to sit down to dinner. The king took flight, managing to escape through a back door but then disappearing forever into the jungles of the eastern delta. This was the beginning of Islamic Turkish-Afghan rule in Bengal, and it continued for over five hundred years.

Naramithla, the fateful Arakanese king, had thus fled to Bengal when the Turkish-Afghan sultanate in Bengal was already two centuries old. In 1430, after nearly three decades in exile, he returned at the head of a formidable force, largely made up of Afghan adventurers, who swiftly overcame local opposition. This was the start of a new golden age for this country—a period of power and prosperity—and the creation of a remarkably hybrid Buddhist-Islamic court, fusing traditions from Persia and India as well as the Buddhist worlds to the east. He abandoned his old capital and established a new one, which he called Mrauk-U, or the Monkey-Egg (no one knows why). His astrologers had warned him that although all the omens for Mrauk-U were good, he himself would die if he moved there. But he was willing to tempt fate. The capital was moved with lavish ceremony in 1433. The king died the following year.

Mrauk-U grew to be an international center of over 160,000 people. Its inhabitants were a mix of Arakanese, Bengalis, Afghans, Burmese, Dutch, Portuguese, Abyssinians, Persians, even Japanese Christians from

Nagasaki escaping the persecution of the dictator Hideyoshi Toyotomi. Some of these Japanese Christians were *ronin*, masterless samurai, and they formed a special bodyguard to the Arakanese king. This cosmopolitan court became great patrons of Bengali as well as Arakanese literature. Courtiers like Daulat Qazi, author of the first Bengali romance, composed distinguished and original works in verse, while others like Alaol, considered the greatest of seventeenth-century Bengali poets, also translated works from Persian and Hindi. Several of the kings took Islamic as well as Pali titles, patronizing Buddhist monasteries and erecting Buddhist pagodas while also appearing in Persian-inspired dress and the conical hats of Isfahan and Mughal Delhi, and minting coins with the *kalima*, Islamic declaration of faith.

The city was set inland, and a massive defense system of earthen ramparts, moats, and citadels supplemented the ring of hills and rivers nearby. The Portuguese Jesuit Father A. Farinha, S.J., called the city, with its numerous intersecting rivers, "a second Venice,"[12] and other writers of the time compared Mrauk-U with Amsterdam and London. The ruins of this city, abandoned when the British annexed Arakan in 1826, are still there, the smoke of village fires rising from where there once stood the genteel homes of soldiers, scholars, and merchants from across Eurasia.

For a hundred years or so Arakan existed in a sort of tributary relationship with the much more powerful Bengal sultanate next door. But then the Bengal sultanate landed on hard times, and the Arakanese began to spread their wings. They built up a strong navy with hundreds of ships. They occupied the island of Ramu and in 1578 took the big port city of Chittagong, today in Bangladesh. Teaming up with newly arrived Portuguese pirates and mercenaries, they soon captured most of eastern Bengal. The Arakanese then also pushed eastward, temporarily holding Pegu and deporting from there three thousand people, including members of the royal family.[13] Arakan was soon at the height of its powers, and for a brief moment its dominion extended across more than a thousand miles of prime beachfront property from Dacca to Martaban.

Scientists today say that human sexual attraction may be based, at least in part, on the influence of pheromones, a personal cocktail of chemicals that signals suitability (or not) to a potential mate. This was apparently old knowledge to the kings of Arakan. According to the Portuguese merchant and travel writer Duarte Barbosa, who visited in 1610, twelve of the most attractive young women from every part of the realm were sent to the palace on a regular basis, not in the first instance to meet the king but to stand, fully dressed in the heat, on a "terrace in the sun." They would then take off their clothes, and the "damp cloth" they had been wearing (with their names scribbled on them) would be sent for His Majesty to sniff. Only those who passed this scent test would be invited into the royal apartments. The rest would be proffered to lesser lords.[14]

Over the years Mrauk-U grew rich from loot and the settling of captives into the fertile river valleys nearby. It also grew rich from trade, including trade in slaves. The slave trade was an important part of business in the Bay of Bengal. And this was the seventeenth century, when not only were tens of thousands of Africans from Gambia, Angola, and elsewhere being trafficked to the plantations of the West Indies and Virginia, but Barbary pirates were raiding the coasts of Western Europe, Ireland, and even Iceland (in 1627) in search of captives for the king of Morocco and the markets of Constantinople. Portuguese and other freebooters were happy to help fill the slave markets and, together with the Arakanese king's men, ravaged the coasts of Bengal, capturing tens of thousands of people a year. Places once thickly peopled became deserted, "the desolate lair of tigers and other wild beasts."[15] But for Mrauk-U this only meant more riches and an ever more splendid city.

The Dutch were also eager to gain a piece of the action.[16] By the early 1600s Portuguese energy was dissipating, and in its place new Europeans were working hard to make their presence felt. The Verenigde Oostindische Compagnie, or Dutch East India Company, was founded in 1602, when the Netherlands States-General granted it exclusive rights to carry out commerce in the East. A regional headquarters was set up at Batavia (now Jakarta), and other outposts were soon scattered across Asia, in Japan, Persia, Bengal, Ceylon, Siam, and China as well as in Burma and the Spice Islands. The Dutch began to dominate the immensely lucrative trade back to Europe in nutmeg and mace. By the middle 1600s, the Dutch East India Company, or VOC, had become the single richest company the world had ever seen, with 150 merchant ships, 40 warships, 50,000 employees, a sizable private army, and a handsome dividend to its shareholders of no less than 40 percent a year. In Arakan the Dutch interest was primarily in slaves, and schemes were drawn up to transport tens of thousands of Arakanese-captured slaves to populate new Dutch colonies in the East Indies.[17] But too many died, of disease and abuse, before ever reaching the shores of Java.

There was also a Dutch trade with Pegu and other Burmese ports, and the new commerce brought new luxuries and new trends. In the early 1700s well-to-do Burmese had even acquired an exotic taste for North American beaver hats, all the way from the St. Lawrence Valley, which fetched extravagant prices, and one imagines the fashionably correct at Pegu and Ava, and perhaps Mrauk-U as well, setting off their multicolored silks with the black broad-brimmed hats of a Rembrandt or a Vermeer.[18]

FROM THE RIO TEJO

Around the time of the first Elizabethan settlements in Virginia, Filipe de Brito e Nicote escaped poverty in Lisbon and sought to make himself a Burmese king. He had come east as a teenage cabin boy on the lofty three-masted sailing ships of the day, working his way down the coast of Angola, around the Cape of Good Hope, to Goa and finally to the calm waters of the Bay of Bengal. By the time he reached Arakan, many years later, he was already an experienced fighter, and he was recruited as a musketeer in the local army. Before long he was an officer and led royal Arakanese troops in battle. The Portuguese were well experienced at making money from Goa and Malacca. But now some sought even greater power. Ceylon had just been taken over, and this whetted the appetite of many men like de Brito for the treasures that would come with actual dominion over an Asian land. In 1599, Portuguese and Spanish mercenaries nearly succeeded in taking over Cambodia. It was now de Brito's turn to see how well he could play his hand.[19]

His business plan was a simple one: The Estado da India did not possess a single customshouse or fortress on the long eastern coast of the Bay of Bengal, with the sole and important exception of Malacca. A port in southern Burma was well placed to be Malacca's northern counterpart, and from a Burma-based fleet, the Portuguese would be able to control all the trade from Bengal to Malaya as well as the inland trade of Burma itself. Bayinnaung was dead, and his heirs, though princes of considerable strength, could be handled. Much of the country had fallen apart yet again, with Bayinnaung's successors, now based at Ava, only holding part of the Irrawaddy Valley.

This was also when Arakan was in full flight and in temporary possession of nearly the entire Burmese coastline. De Brito's nominal master, the king of Arakan, had granted him the port of Syriam, very close to modern Rangoon. De Brito quickly went to work, building up the settlement as best he could, encouraging men from all around the region to settle there under his protection. He had with him his lieutenant, Salvador Ribeyro. They constructed a wall and a moat and recruited an impressive militia around a steel core of hardened Iberian fighters. They included many men of mixed European and Asian descent as well as Burmese, Africans, and Malabaris from South India. The Burmese called him Nga Zinga, meaning, in the patois of the Indian Ocean, "The Good Man."

His next step was to circumvent the Arakanese entirely and appeal directly to the viceroy at Goa, Dom Aires de Saldanha, for money and men, and the viceroy, seeing a good proposition, gave de Brito what he wanted. With resources pouring in, Syriam became a power in its own right, though in theory it was still under the sovereignty of Arakan. Most of de Brito's riches came from forcing ships to use only his Syriam as a port and from looting and pillaging the towns of the Burmese interior. He even pillaged pagodas, melting down the bronze bells of many Buddhist establishments to make cannons for his army.

De Brito also sought alliances and married his son, Simon, to one of the daughters of the prince of Martaban. He took as his own wife Doña Luisa de Saldaña, a niece of the viceroy himself, born to a Javanese mother, "neither tall nor slender" but "with that dash of beauty which is so dangerous in women."[20] It was now the early years of the seventeenth century. Portuguese power in the East was waning, but things seemed to be going very well for the onetime cabin boy from Lisbon. De Brito lived extravagantly and took on the airs of an Oriental monarch.

In addition to his Portuguese captains, de Brito had as his good friend a Burmese nobleman named Natshinnaung, remembered as a champion polo player and an accomplished poet and scholar. In 1593 this nobleman had been present at a battle in which the Burmese crown prince was killed on elephant back by the crown prince of Siam. He was fifteen at the time and was handed the task of riding to Pegu and informing the widow of the dead prince of her husband's fate. She was Raza Datu Kalayani, many years older and a famous beauty. He fell in love with her, and she eventually fell in love with him. From that day on, Natshinnaung dreamed of becoming king and making Kalayani his queen.[21] In Filipe de Brito he found a kindred spirit.

The man who would destroy both de Brito and Natshinnaung's heady plans was Bayinnaung's grandson Anaukpetlun, the king of Burma. Not quite the world conqueror his ancestor was, he was nonetheless a serious prince with a serious army. He wanted at least to rule over the entire Irrawaddy Valley, and de Brito was in the way. No one was happy with de Brito's Syriam, not the Persian merchants of Masulipatnam in South India who were losing trade and money, not the Arakanese whose nominal rule he was discarding, and certainly not the Burmese whose territory he had annexed. Encouraged by many, the king of Burma decided to put an end to de Brito once and for all, sailing down the Irrawaddy with a huge force including more than four hundred war boats. Six thousand of his men were Muslim mercenaries from the Indian Deccan, Persia, and elsewhere in the Islamic world. Slowly but surely, the towns and villages under de Brito fell to the Burmese until only Syriam was left. De Brito was surrounded.

De Brito had roughly three thousand soldiers with him, including about a hundred Portuguese. But he was running low on gunpowder for his cannons as well as food and other provisions. He sent a messenger with money to Bengal for help, but the messenger just pocketed the money and ran away. When the gunpowder ran out, the Syriam defenders poured boiling oil on the Burmese to stop them from scaling the walls. Ships were dispatched to break the siege, but these were forced back. After more than a month de Brito, reading the writing on the wall, asked for terms, but the Burmese king replied that he would accept only unconditional surrender. For three days and three nights the Burmese attacked, and hundreds lay dead by the time the fighting was over. De Brito was finally captured, betrayed by a Mon officer within his own ranks.

Filipe de Brito was set up on a hill above his would-be royal capital and impaled on a wooden spike. He survived two days in agony. His wife, Luisa, was seized and cleaned by the river and then brought to the Burmese king, who intended to keep her for himself. But when "she turned on him with such scorn and courage that his desire for her beauty was turned to anger," he sent her to Ava to be sold together with the common slaves. Senior Portuguese officers like Francis Mandez were also impaled. Others like Sebastian Rodriguez were taken first to Ava and then to villages north of Ava to be settled as hereditary members of the king's bodyguard and artillery. King Anaukpetlun, before returning himself to the north, donated gold and diamonds and two thousand rubies to the Shwedagon Pagoda.[22]

Natshinnaung remained loyal to the end. The Burmese king had tried to divide the two friends and told de Brito that he would receive good treatment only if he turned over the renegade Burmese. The messenger who carried the letter was brought blindfolded to where the two were sitting. De Brito, who most likely could not read Burmese, asked Natshinnaung to read it. When he heard the offer, he said, "Tell your master that we Portuguese keep faith. I have given my word to Natshinnaung and cannot break it." During the last days of the siege Natshinnaung converted to Roman Catholicism and was baptized by a priest from Goa.

Nothing remains of de Brito's legacy at Syriam today, only the scattered bricks of the old wall and Catholic church. But at Henzada in the Irrawaddy Delta, not far away, there is a small pagoda with an inscription that it was built by "Nanda Baya and his sister Supaba Devi," children of an Arakanese lady Saw Thida and "the Feringhee Nga Zinga, king of Syriam."

Under a cloudless blue sky in early January 1997, I rented an old Nissan and drove about two hours to the valley of the Mu River, just to the northwest of Mandalay. Here and there scattered among the seemingly endless fields of rice, cotton, and tobacco, the clumps of banana trees, and the occasional shiny pagoda on a hill were the so-called *bayingyi*, or *feringhi*, villages—Roman Catholic villages in a sea of Buddhist Burma. The people of these villages were all descendants of earlier generations of Europeans who had come to the country, including descendants of de Brito's Portuguese officers and other immigrants and

captives from the West. It had been the habit of Burmese kings to settle
newcomers in specific places, so that they could police their own communities and so that the Court of Ava could keep a better account and
press them as needed into the king's service. Muslims and Christians
each had their own towns and villages. And here near the Mu River was
the home first of Iberian and later of Dutch and French mercenaries
and war captives, their wives, and their children for generations down
to the fall of Mandalay.

The little wooden and thatch huts, shaded under palm trees and
huddled together on sandy ground, were no different from any other
settlement in Upper Burma, except for the powder blue and white
church off to the side and a flooded cemetery, set low against a nearby
canal, with dozens of half-submerged crosses peering out from beneath
the brackish water. There had been no signs, and I had to ask directions
many times; but once there, seeing the faces of the people, it was hard
to mistake the villages' *feringhi* past.

I spoke to a local schoolteacher and to a nun, who had only recently
returned from Rome, both very aware and proud of their unique inheritance. They said that no one in the village any longer spoke a language
other than Burmese and some English, but that as recently as their
grandfathers' time (both women were in their thirties or forties), there
were some who knew a bit of Portuguese. The schoolteacher said that
her great-grandfather had served in Thibaw's palace as part of a Royal
Fifty regiment, and other ancestors had been translators at the royal
court. Nearby, a crowd of children, many with brown hair and green
eyes, were playing football. There was a sadness that things were at a
turning point and that a community that had maintained its identity for
so long would very soon lose its difference. They didn't have the money
to rescue their cemetery, its tombstones inscribed with the names of
Galicians, Bretons, and Walloons, and no encouragement from the
government to celebrate their heritage.

In 1861 Bishop Bigandet of the Roman Catholic mission in Mandalay made a pastoral visit to these same villages and wrote:

> It is a remarkable fact that despite the great effect that must have
> been produced by the accession of the predominating Burmese
> element, the Christians of Burma exhibit unmistakable signs of
> their primitive origin in the features of their face. They have

all[,] without exception, lost their family names, which would at once reveal the origin of their ancestors, but on a close examination of their personal appearance, particularly of the face, we can, with perfect ease, trace up their origin. At Monhla, for example, the writer remarked an old man with green eyes, and a face of the Dutch type. With other people, the French features could not be mistaken, whilst with most of the people dwelling in the village of Khiaonio, an observer could not fail to remark the striking resemblance between them and the descendants of the Portuguese as we see them, on the Western coast of the Indian peninsula and the Straits of Malacca.[23]

There would soon be other additions to the Burmese melting pot.

MUGHAL FUGITIVES

Shah Shuja, the Mughal viceroy of Bengal and Orissa in the middle years of the seventeenth century, was the second son of the emperor Shah Jehan and the empress Mumtaj Mahal.[24] The Mughals were the new overlords of a vast Indian empire that stretched across nearly the entire subcontinent. Originally Central Asians, they claimed descent from Genghis Khan through Tamerlane, the great conquering warrior of Samarkand (and the Tamburlaine of Christopher Marlowe). The first Mughal emperor, Babur, had taken Delhi in 1526. From there he and his successors expanded east, soon establishing their authority over the entire Ganges Basin and by 1612 crushing the last remaining pockets of Afghan and Hindu resistance in eastern Bengal, stopping only at the swampy frontiers of Arakan. The Bengal sultanate was gone, and Mughal Bengal was Mrauk-U's new neighbor.

Shah Shuja was a first-rate soldier. As a young prince he had taken part in many military campaigns, and even as viceroy he twice broke his tenure to travel to the northwest, where he led the fighting against Afghan rebels along the Khyber Pass. A typical Mughal aristocrat, Shah Shuja was also a man of considerable learning, cultured and polished, and his court was soon filled with appropriately refined Persian poets and scholars. There were minor border wars, against the kingdom of Kamarupa in the north and the small dependency of Cooch Behar, but otherwise Bengal was largely at peace, and the local zamindars seemed overawed by the presence of a member of the imperial family as their immediate overlord. Grand buildings were built at Dacca, and the English and Dutch traders eager for a share of Bengal's riches were welcomed.

In the autumn of 1657 the emperor fell ill. Rumors spread that the emperor had in fact died but that his death was being kept secret by his eldest son, Prince Dara Shikoh, to give him time to secure his position on the throne. The other three senior princes—Shuja included—then began their march on Delhi. In the end, and after many bloody battles, it was Prince Aurangzeb who emerged victorious. Dara was captured and killed, and Shuja, pursued by an imperial army under Mir Jumla, decided to flee to the east.

On 6 May 1658 Shah Shuja boarded at Dacca a Portuguese ship headed for Arakan and eight days later made contact with representatives of the Arakanese king. His plan was to stay in Arakan for only a short while and then to proceed to Mecca and ultimately to Persia or Constantinople. But the monsoon rains were just beginning, and the seas were rough. He asked for asylum in Arakan and help in later making his way to the west.

Shah Shuja was at first warmly received by the king of Arakan, Sanda Thudamma, and a house was built for the princely guest on the outskirts of the city. Mrauk-U, even in its heyday, must have seemed like a provincial backwater to the scion of one of the greatest imperial families in the world. He is said to have remained aloof from the Arakanese court, and this did little to enamor him to Sanda Thudamma, who presently cast an envious eye over the enormous treasure Shuja had brought with him. Even greater treasure was soon offered by Aurangzeb's envoys for the new emperor's fugitive brother. Weeks went by, and then months, eight months altogether. Sanda Thudamma did not hand over Shah Shuja to the Mughals. But neither did he allow him to leave. Instead the love-struck Arakanese monarch (even without advantage of a "damp cloth") asked for the hand of Shah Shuja's eldest daughter, the beautiful princess Ameena.[25]

The thought of his daughter marrying this half-barbarian chief drove the hapless prince over the top. He couldn't escape, and in his desperation Shah Shuja decided to try to seize power. He had two hundred good men with him and the support of at least some of the local

Muslim community. But the plot could not be kept secret, and the king heard of it in time. Shuja's followers were quickly rounded up. There was fighting, and parts of the city were set on fire, but Sanda Thudamma's position was never in peril. Shuja managed to escape into the interior, hiding in the jungle for weeks before he was found and executed. The great treasure he had brought was melted down and brought into the palace. Ameena and the other princesses were taken into the king's harem. Within a year the king suspected a plot against him and killed all the surviving members of the imperial family, including Ameena, who was said to be in an advanced stage of pregnancy. Her brothers were beheaded.

When the news reached Delhi, Aurangzeb was incensed. He would have killed Shuja and the rest himself, but he couldn't tolerate the idea of some distant foreign monarch's spilling the blood of his kinsmen. He also wanted to teach the Arakanese a more general lesson and check their still formidable military power. In 1665 Shayista Khan, the new Mughal viceroy of Bengal, sailed east at the head of a huge fleet of nearly three hundred warships, driving the Arakanese out of their fortress on Sandwip Island, while another force of sixty-five hundred under Buzurg Umid Khan hacked its way down the coast. The following year, after a long siege, Chittagong fell to the Mughals, marking the end of Arakan's century-long hold over eastern Bengal. Two thousand Arakanese were sold into slavery, and over a hundred ships were taken. Many of the Portuguese mercenaries at Mrauk-U had changed sides and were permitted to settle in Mughal territory; their descendants still live at a place called Feringhi Bazaar, twelve miles south of Dacca.

Some of Shah Shuja's followers also survived. After his abortive takeover attempt, those who were not killed were retained by the Arakanese king as archers and formed a special palace guard, eventually growing in strength and helped by fresh arrivals from Indian lands. They were finally disbanded in 1692 and then deported to the island of Ramree. Their descendants are known to this day as Kaman (the Persian word for "bow") and live both in Ramree and elsewhere in Arakan. They speak Arakanese but often retain the Afghan or Persian features of their forebears. The present military government has categorized them as a distinct ethnic group and one of the 303 nationalities of the Union of Myanmar, surely the only one able to claim descent from the fleeing soldiers of an imperial prince.

Arakan as a kingdom did not fare very well after this onslaught of Mughal power. There was now no longer any possibility of raiding Bengal for slaves, and the Mughals made sure that Dutch ships steered clear of Arakanese ports. And on the kingdom's other side more secure Burmese kings, rid of de Brito and other challenges, prevented any Arakanese aggression. The authority of Mrauk-U gradually shrunk, and by the early eighteenth century much of the countryside had lapsed into anarchy and conflict. Earthquakes regularly shook the land for decades, confirming in people's minds the onset of bad times. And in 1761 an enormous earthquake raised the entire coastline by five feet. The end of the kingdom was near.

THE FLIGHT OF THE MING PRINCE

From the west it was the Mughals, moving in against the borders of a fast-shrinking Arakan. But to the north and east, it was an ever more vigorous China, pressing down hard, right into the heart of Burma. In China in 1646, after the fall of the Yangtze Valley and the eastern coast to the invading Manchu armies, the twenty-three-year-old prince of Gui, the last surviving grandson of the Wanli emperor, became the last and desperate hope of the Ming imperial cause. For years China had been at war. The Manchus under their leader, Nurhaci, had unified the Tungusic-speaking normads along the Amur River valley, first threatening the northern border regions and then taking Peking in 1644. Their new dynasty, the Qing, then moved down into China proper, scattering the loyalists of the old regime. Until the republican revolution of 1911, China would be ruled by these milk-drinking, cheese-eating onetime nomads of the far north.[26]

The prince of Gui's father was the seventh son of the Wanli emperor, and the young prince had been brought up among the sybaritic pleasures and strict hierarchies of the Imperial City. He was now on the run, fleeing first to his ancestral estates in Hunan, central China, and then to the southwest near present-day Hong Kong. It was there, among the limestone cliffs of the Pearl River delta, that his fugitive court named him the Yongle emperor and rightful heir to the three-hundred-year-old Ming throne.

He became a lightning rod for the growing resistance to the Manchu occupation. For the next year and a half the prince of Gui and his men trekked across the far south of China, along the borders of Vietnam, and then southwest into the tribal regions of Guangxi. The long flight from Peking meant that the self-styled imperial court was far from what a proper Ming court should be, and one contemporary observer described it as being filled with "all manner of betel-nut chewers, brine-well workers and aborigine whorehouse owners."[27] But it did rally the die-hards and for a while kept the advancing Qing rulers at bay.

By early 1650 Qing forces had managed a breakthrough, crushing opposition in areas that had declared their support for the prince of Gui and launching a direct attack on his southern bases. In this offensive the Manchus relied on Ming Chinese generals who had defected more than a decade before, and these generals pursued the loyalists farther and farther southwest until, in 1658, they made their last stand at the little border town of Tengyue and then slipped over the hills into the kingdom of Burma.

The prince of Gui entered Burmese territory in the hills of the northeast, part of a great arc of upland areas only indirectly under Ava's rule. Here the the vast majority of the local people were not Burmese at all but spoke instead a variant of Thai or Siamese, known in Burmese as Shan. Some of these principalities were of considerable size. Chiangmai and Kengtung, for example, were the size of modern Belgium or Wales, while others were little more than a collection of impoverished mountain tracts. In the early years of the Ming dynasty many of these principalities, perhaps the first in Southeast Asia to acquire knowledge of guns and gunpowder from the Chinese, had expanded aggressively to the south, overrunning Ava and the Burmese plains. But more recently they had adopted a more modest posture; in varying degrees their rulers, or *sawbwas*, maintained a tributary relationship with the Court of Ava, providing daughters for the royal harem and gifts of silver and horses for the king.[28]

When the prince of Gui arrived with over seven hundred followers at the border post of Momein, he met first with a local Shan chief, requesting refuge in Burma and offering his sovereign a not inconsequential treasure in gold. The king at the time was Pindalay, who agreed, welcoming the prince and constructing for him a residence at Sagaing, just across the Irrawaddy River from Ava. But it turned out that the prince of Gui was only the first of many thousands of Chinese now streaming across the border, some refugees, others bandits and freebooters who had taken advantage of the anarchy in southwestern

China and now sought to terrorize the Burmese countryside. These marauding bands declared their allegiance to the prince of Gui and asked their leader to leave Sagaing and join them. They seized the towns of Mongnai and Yawnghwe in the east and routed the army Pindalay sent to try to stop them. Monasteries were burned. Whole villages were looted, and men and women taken captive and carried off. Soon they were at Tada-u, just outside the gates of Ava itself, where only the tough resistance of the king's Portuguese artillery managed to stave off their advance.[29]

The prince of Gui was deeply apologetic. He insisted that he had nothing to do with what was going on in his name. Blame fell first on the Burmese king. Pindalay was a weak ruler, the son of a concubine rather than a queen and thus enjoying less than normal legitimacy. He had all along been manipulated by an increasingly powerful noble class, and this nobility now turned against him, making him the scapegoat for the troubles and replacing him with his younger brother the prince of Prome. It was the hereditary officer corps in the army that had first agitated for his removal. They had seen the devastation in the countryside firsthand. Many had families in the irrigated lands to the south of Ava, and when food became scarce in these lands as a result of the invading Chinese, they had appealed for their king's help. Instead Pindalay had allowed his favorites and concubines to sell rice to the hungry at exorbitant prices. The army men then appealed to the royal ministers, who were quick to replace Pindalay with his half brother Prome.

Prome was a stronger monarch, and he soon turned his attention to the increasingly nervous prince of Gui. He suspected the refugee emperor of conspiring with the Chinese bands all around them and summoned the prince's followers, all seven hundred of them, to the Tupayon Pagoda at Sagaing. Prome said he wanted them to take an oath of allegiance. They refused until the lord, or *sawbwa*, of Mongsi, whom they trusted, agreed to be there as well. But it was a trick. At the pagoda the lord of Mongsi was taken away. And royal troops moved in to encircle the Chinese. The Chinese reached for their swords and then were shot down by the king's musketeers. Those who survived the shooting were beheaded. The prince of Gui became even more nervous.

In 1662, four years after the prince had first entered Burma, the

great Chinese general and viceroy Wu Sangui marched into the kingdom at the head of an enormous imperial force, twenty thousand
strong, coming straight down the mountains and halting only a few
miles from Ava, and demanding the surrender of the Ming prince. Wu
Sangui was then fifty years old. He had been a senior Ming commander but had switched sides and had opened the gates of the Great
Wall of China to the Manchu armies of the north. In 1673 he would
switch sides again and rebel against the new Qing dynasty. But for now
he was on the side of the Manchus and had taken as his wife the sister
of the new Manchu emperor.

It was said that Prome wanted to fight but that his ministers told him
to get rid of their troublesome guest once and for all. And so the prince
of Gui and his family were handed over as prisoners. The prince was
now thirty-eight. His son was fourteen. They were taken to Kunming in
Yunnan and strangled to death in the marketplace with a bowstring.
Another son apparently died in Burma and is buried at Bhamo near the
Chinese border. His wife and daughters were taken to Peking. During
their days in Burma the whole family had converted to Roman Catholicism, under the influence of a Jesuit priest at Ava, and had taken the
Christian names of the fallen Byzantine house: The prince of Gui's son
had become Constantine, his mother, the empress, was named Anne,
and the other princesses were named Helen and Mary.

The upheavals weakened the now nearly two-centuries-old dynasty.
But the kingdom stayed together, absorbing the blows of the Chinese
incursions without breakup or revolt. This was in large part due to the
reforms that had taken place. Like all societies in Southeast Asia at the
time, the key to economic power was not so much land as people; there
was always a dearth of people. Wars were waged to capture people as
well as loot, and government was about the proper management of the
king's men. All this was improved and systematized.[30] And the image of
empire, of Bayinnaung's exploits, and of more distant memories of
Pagan and Prome remained. When the dynasty finally fell, the new
royal clan would accept the old traditions, turning only later toward radical reform when confronted with disaster at the hands of an entirely
new foe, the English East India Company.

FIVE

THE CONSEQUENCES
OF PATRIOTISM

*Burma's last dynasty comes to power during the Seven Years' War
and then goes on to build an empire, fighting the Siamese and
the Manchus and inspiring a new martial spirit*

～≫≪～

Aung Zeyya was an unlikely savior of his people. For decades fierce Manipuri horsemen had been raiding up and down the valley of the nearby Mu River, torching villages all around, ransacking pagodas, and stealing away captives. Led by their rajas Jai Singh and Gharib Newaz and riding the stylish little ponies for which they would later be renowned, the Manipuris defeated again and again the soldiers dispatched to stop them. The Burmese court seemed powerless against the rising menace, and its frailty lost it support at home and even the nominal allegiance of its eastern tributaries. In the summer of 1739 Gharib Newaz's cavalry reached the Irrawaddy itself, burning the monastic libraries on the north shore and halting, the Burmese believe, to bathe in the holy waters of the river. In 1743 the famed Manipuri teacher Maha Tharaphu arrived in person at Ava, intending to instruct the Burmese king in the ways of the Hindu faith. The dynasty founded two hundred years before by Bayinnaung was on its last legs. For Aung Zeyya, the *kyedaing*, or hereditary chief, of Moksobo, it would soon be time to take matters in his own hands.

The source of the immediate trouble was Manipur, a fertile and compact plain, about the size of Connecticut, enclosed by pine-clad mountains and set today along the Burmese-Indian border, a few hundred miles to the northwest of Aung Zeyya's hometown. The area had once been the site of innumerable warring clans, but more recently Manipur had been united under a passionately neo-Hindu regime. Brahmin priests from Bengal, devotees of the god Vishnu, had converted the Manipuri ruling class, encouraging new ceremonies and caste rules. A fresh energy was instilled that was then channeled into a southward military advance. The first raids into Burma had taken place in the middle and late seventeenth century, but they were now increasing in frequency and destructiveness.

With the king's authority crumbling in the north, the southern provinces—around Pegu and the delta—seized the opportunity and declared their independence. Dissatisfaction had been fermenting for years in the south as taxes increased and people felt the weight of a harsh but ever more ineffectual government. The rebellion began at Pegu in 1740, led by a local Mon nobleman, Bannya Dala, who crowned himself king in 1747 and promised to restore the greatness of the one-time imperial capital. Many in the area were speakers of Mon, the language of the Pegu kingdom in the fifteenth century, and dreams of a Mon kingship had never disappeared.

Within a few years all the key towns of the south—Henzada, Prome, Martaban, as well as Pegu—were in the hands of the popular rebel regime, and Bannya Dala's army then moved slowly northward to complete its victory. A bright future seemed guaranteed. The once-great fortress of Ava itself fell without much of a fight. The old royal family had surrendered and was led away into captivity. All that seemed left was a mopping-up operation, and small military detachments were sent out from Ava to secure the loyalty of the local chiefs to the new Pegu-based king. This was 1753, and on the other side of the world, a Virginia militia under Major George Washington was trudging west, through blinding snowstorms and freezing cold, toward Fort Le Boeuf, to check the French advance in the Ohio Valley. Few then could have imagined the connection between these two events or how the tables would soon turn in Burma, changing not only Burma but the course of European imperial history.

THE GENTLEMEN OF THE MU VALLEY

When Bannya Dala's cavalry careered past Ava into the valley of the Mu River, they had hoped to win the easy submission of the hereditary gentry class that governed the area. Through periods of strong and weak kings, the same gentry chiefs had managed the affairs of the countryside, not just in the Mu Valley but everywhere in Burma, administering justice, collecting taxes, and presiding over the many ceremonies and Buddhist festivals at the heart of rural life. Traditional gentlemen and part-time soldiers, they were the all-important intermediaries linking ordinary villagers to the world of princes and courtiers.

The most important of these chiefs held the hereditary office called *myothugyi*, and these were powerful men, sometimes ruling over hundreds of towns and villages. But there was a confusing plethora of other offices, depending on local custom and history. As a class the gentry were an exceptionally proud group of men and women, marrying among themselves and wearing clothes and living in houses that set them apart from the common people. They were customarily descended from the founding lineages of their home area and valued their special role of providing the officers and officials of the Court of Ava. This was no more true than in the Mu Valley, where Burma's very first kingdom at Tagaung was located and which was the home of its best fighters.

At the time Ava fell to the southern army, Aung Zeyya was thirty-six years old and married, with teenage sons. A tall man for the times (just under six feet), he was solidly built and had the dark, sunburned complexion of many Upper Burmans. His village was Moksobo, a not particularly important place with perhaps a few hundred households, about sixty miles north of Ava, set in the middle of fields of rice, millet, and cotton, a ridge of low teak-covered mountains to the east and Indaing forests and hills to the west.[1] Aung Zeyya came from a large family and was related by blood and marriage to many other gentry families throughout the valley; for generations his ancestors had held important local offices, and he claimed descent from a fifteenth-century cavalry commander and ultimately from the Pagan royal line.

Some of Aung Zeyya's fellow chiefs had sensed the way the wind was blowing and had meekly submitted to the new overlords at Pegu. But not Aung Zeyya. When he heard that Bannya Dala was sending an armed force to Moksobo to administer the new oath of loyalty, he immediately swung into action, organizing the nearby villages, chopping down palm trees and using the trunks to fortify the walls, sharpening his swords, collecting a few old muskets, and ambushing the unsuspecting Mon soldiers as they came through the thorny scrub jungle.

The Mons then sent a larger force to punish the recalcitrant chief.

But they too were met by Aung Zeyya and were quickly defeated. News spread. And soon the *kyedaing* of Moksobo was mustering a proper army from across the Mu Valley and beyond, using his family connections and appointing fellow gentry leaders as his key lieutenants. Fresh levies were sent from Pegu, but all were routed, and their allies among the local leadership were crushed. Success drew fresh recruits every day. There were other centers of resistance, at Salin along the middle Irrawaddy and at Mogaung in the far north, but it was Aung Zeyya who had emerged as the unexpected and exciting champion of the Burmese north against the Mon south.

On a frosty morning at the beginning of 1754 Aung Zeyya left his little village and made his formal entry into the smoldering ruins of Ava to worship at the old city's royal pagodas. Tributary princes from the eastern hills came and knelt before him and made their submission. Their dreams of problem-free conquest crumbling quickly, Pegu then sent their entire army upriver, only to have the whole force beaten back by the man who now called himself king.[2]

MONSIEUR DUPLEIX AND THE DREAM
OF A BIRMANIE FRANÇAISE

Joseph François Dupleix had already lived in the East for nearly thirty years, as a successful merchant and as a colonial administrator, when he became governor-general of French India in 1742. This was before England's East India Company had established its mastery of the subcontinent and when the French, with their own bases and own Indian armies, could still pose a threat to English designs. Ambitious and imaginative, Dupleix, like many Europeans in the East, had come to affect the dress and style of an Oriental prince and sought alliances with native rulers as a way of increasing French power. His appointment as governor-general was during the War of the Austrian Succession. When the war ended in 1748, without much satisfaction for the French or the English, Dupleix looked for the right chance to strengthen his country's position against his Anglo-Saxon enemies, including across the bay in Burma.

Dupleix knew that Bannya Dala had recently seized power at Pegu. He also knew that Pegu was already running into problems in the north and that Bannya Dala would need help if he were to keep his brand-new throne. Dupleix's strategy in India had often been to support the weaker side with the aim of ensuring a future dependent relationship. And though Bannya Dala seemed to be doing reasonably well, his was still an upstart regime that would likely need all the help it could get. When an embassy from Bannya Dala arrived at Pondicherry, the principal French town in India, in 1750, it was welcomed with great pomp and enthusiasm. In return, Dupleix sent as his representative Sieur de Bruno, a man of some charm who proved a big hit and quickly won over Pegu's Mon leaders. A treaty of friendship was signed, promising French military aid in return for lucrative trading concessions. It looked as if Pegu would soon be in France's pocket. Dupleix wrote home to the directors of the Compagnie Royale about a new French empire on the shores of the Irrawaddy.

The English at Fort St. George were alarmed. The English East India Company had been involved in Burma since the seventeenth century. It too was looking for opportunities, not so much to expand its influence in Burma as to offset any French initiatives. In 1746 Madras had been taken by a naval force under Bertrand François, Comte Mahé de La Bourdonnais, the governor of the isle of Bourbon,* and French power was still formidable in the Carnatic. The Company was aware that in a future war, England's Indian ports could again be lost, and reckoned that a safe harbor not too far away in Burma was a good fallback. Burma's shipbuilding industry was world class, and in the 1730s and 1740s the French had commissioned there many of their best warships. Hearing of the French concessions, the English quickly sent their own mission to Pegu, asking Bannya Dala for permission to open an office at Negrais, a small island off Burma's extreme southwestern coast. But they were met with studied hostility. French muskets and cannons were making their way into the Mon arsenal, and Pegu was moving decisively into the French camp. Soon Bruno was appointed resident at Bannya Dala's hopeful new court. Dupleix's dreams seemed to be coming true.

Panicked, the English decided to take a gamble and occupy Negrais by force. This was a mistake. By then Paris had actually rejected Dupleix's plans. In normal times he might have disregarded this, but his hands were full in South India. The English didn't really need to do

---

*Modern Réunion, a department of France in the southern Indian Ocean.

anything. But now they had taken Negrais, and the little colony there was paralyzed from the very beginning by all manner of tropical diseases, food shortages, and the occasional mutiny. For better or for worse, the Company was now involved in Burma's civil war.

Both the English and the French were of course still keen to back the winning horse. And it was beginning to look as though the tide were turning against Bannya Dala and that Dupleix had miscalculated. Not only had Aung Zeyya, whom neither side had ever heard of before, cleared Upper Burma of the Pegu army, but this unknown village chief was now proceeding in strength down the Irrawaddy. A master tactician, and perhaps one of the greatest military leaders of his time, Aung Zeyya was outmaneuvering any opposition and winning submission from gentry leaders and influential officeholders all along the way. In early 1755 he took the strategic river city of Prome, honoring there the lords of Salay and Pakhannge, both of whom had led local risings in support of his campaign.

Three more years of bitter fighting were to follow, but few now doubted the eventual outcome. The delta stronghold of Danubyu was captured in a brilliant victory, and in May 1755 the old pagoda town of Dagon fell into Aung Zeyya's hands. In all his new possessions, the new king enforced a harsh but effective system of justice and proved himself a capable administrator as well as general. Hoping the civil war would soon be over, he renamed Dagon Rangoon, meaning "the end of the enemy." Some of his followers began to call him Alaungpaya, "the future Buddha."

A nervous Dupleix now tried to increase his hold over the Pegu government by threatening to switch sides and help the Burmese under Aung Zeyya, now Alaungpaya. Both to make good on his threat and to cover his bases, Dupleix then sent a gift of arms to Alaungpaya, who accepted the weapons while still clearly regarding the French as his enemy. Alaungpaya's strong preference was for an alliance with the English. He protested the unilateral occupation of Negrais, but he also offered to cede the island to England in return for military help. Alaungpaya was winning, and both Dupleix and Fort St. George knew this. The problem for both was that they had few arms to spare. In Europe, England had just declared war on France in the beginning of the Seven Years' War. Prussia under Frederick the Great was fighting an array of nations from Spain to Sweden, and the English would soon be battling Louis XV's armies and navies across North America, the

Caribbean, and India. Burma might be an important sideshow, but it was still a sideshow in this critical test of global supremacy.

SYRIAM AND THE SEVEN YEARS' WAR

> The King said that if all the Powers of The World was to come, he could drive them out of His Country. He then asked me if we were afraid of the French; I told him that the English and the French had no great liking for each other but there never was that Englishman born, that was afraid of a Frenchman . . .[3]
>
> —English envoy Ensign Robert Lester at his audience with Alaungpaya[4]

For the Burmese under Alaungpaya, two places remained to be taken: Syriam and Pegu itself. The first attempt to take Syriam in 1755 was a failure. Bruno and a number of French officers had reinforced the garrison already there, and the sturdy walls and modern cannon made difficult any attempt to simply storm the fortress. Around this time an English ship, the *Arcot*, had somewhat clumsily, and apparently without instruction, joined a combined French and Mon attack on Rangoon. The attack was unsuccessful, but the English, now justifiably fearing reprisals from the Burmese, sent an envoy, Captain George Baker, to Alaungpaya with presents of cannons and muskets and with orders to speedily conclude a treaty of friendship.

Alaungpaya was then back in his home village, which was not a village anymore. Thousands of people from the nearby countryside had been moved to Moksobo, and new walls and buildings were quickly transforming the little settlement into a proper national capital. *Moksobo* means "the hunter chief." Alaungpaya decided this wasn't good enough and renamed it Shwebo, the "golden chief." *Shwebo-tha* ("sons of Shwebo") became the war cry of his followers, with more than a hint of Upper Burma (and Burmese ethnic) patriotism against the Mon-speaking culture of the south.[5] He was temporarily in Shwebo directing an expedition into Manipur, turning the tables on that once-aggressive little principality, in the first Burmese invasion involving firearms and the first of several devastating invasions of Manipur to come. He also sent the captain of his musketeers, Minhla Mingaung Kyaw, into the Shan hills to secure the submission of the highland chiefs.

Though Syriam and Pegu had not yet fallen, Alaungpaya was already master of a huge territory stretching from the Himalayas down to the border with Siam. The young English envoy George Baker got more than a dose of bravado. "See these arms and this thigh," Alaungpaya said to Baker as he drew up the sleeves of his shirt and tucked up his *paso*. "Amongst 1,000 you won't see my match. I myself can crush 100 such as the King of Pegu." He agreed that the English could stay at their pestilential colony at Negrais but postponed signing any immediate treaty with the Company. Instead he sent a letter on gold leaf ornamented with precious stones to King George II:

> The King, Despotick, of great Merit, of great Power, Lord of the Countries Thonahprondah, Tomp Devah and Camboja, Sovereign of the Kingdom of the Burmars, the Kingdom of Siam and Hughen and the Kingdom of Cassey; Lord of the Mines of Rubies, Gold, Silver, Copper, Iron and Amber, Lord of the White Elephant, Red Elephant and Spotted Elephant, Lord of the Vital Golden Lance, of many Golden Palaces and of all those Kingdoms, Grandours and Wealth whose royal person is descended of the Nation of the Sun, Salutes the King of England, of Madras, of Bengal, of Fort St. David and of Deve Cotah, and let our Compliments be presented to His Majesty and acquaint him that from the time of Our Ancestors to Our Time, there has been a great Commerce and Trade carry'd on by the English and Burmars, with all possible Liberties, Affection, Advantage and Success . . .[6]

The letter goes on to suggest a firm alliance between the two countries. But months would go by, and there would be no reply from the Hanoverian king or his secretaries at Hampton Court. And despite what Alaungpaya regarded as a magnanimous gesture over Negrais (against the advice of his Anglophobe Armenian advisers), no military help of any kind materialized. Had he been tricked? He wasn't sure. But the idea that the English could not be trusted was planted early in the hearts of the new dynasty and in the imagination of early Burmese patriots.[7]

Meanwhile, Bruno and his fellow Frenchmen, trapped in sweltering Syriam, were growing desperate for reinforcements from Pondicherry. Alaungpaya had recently arrived from the north together with some of his best men to finish the job. It seemed only a matter of time.

Food was running out. At this point Bruno decided to do the less than honorable thing and tried secretly to negotiate with the Burmese. He was found out and placed in shackles.

For Alaungpaya, the worry was that French reinforcements would indeed soon arrive. He decided that the time had come for the fortress to be stormed, now. He knew that the French and the Mons, expecting no quarter, would resist fiercely and that hundreds of his men would die in any attempt to breach the walls. He called for volunteers and then selected ninety-three, whom he named the Golden Company of Syriam, a name that would find pride of place in Burmese nationalist mythology. They included guards, officers, and princes of the blood, descendants of Bayinnaung. The afternoon before, as the early monsoon rains poured down in torrents outside the makeshift huts, they ate together in their new king's presence. Alaungpaya gave each a leather helmet and lacquer armor.

That evening, as the Burmese banged their drums and played loud music to encourage Syriam's defenders into thinking festivities were under way and to relax their watch, the Golden Company scaled the walls. After bloody hand-to-hand fighting they managed to pry open the great wooden gates, and in the darkness, amid the war cries of the Burmese ("Shwebo-tha!") and the screams of the women and children inside, the city was overrun. For the men of the northern villages, the wealth of Syriam, crammed with luxury goods from around the world, could hardly be imagined. The next morning Alaungpaya stacked up the captured gold and silver and presented the combined loot as a reward to the twenty men of the Golden Company who survived and to the families of the seventy-three who died.[8]

A few days later and a few days too late, two French relief ships, the *Galatee* and the *Fleury*, arrived, crammed with troops as well as arms, ammunition, and food from Pondicherry. As they approached the river (Syriam was several miles from the sea), they sent a small boat to ask for a pilot. The boat was captured by Alaungpaya's men, who then forced the captive Bruno to write a letter in French decoying them up the river. The trick worked. The ships ran aground and were quickly surrounded by Burmese war boats. On board were two hundred French officers and soldiers. They were now press-ganged into Alaungpaya's army. Also on board were thirty-five ship's guns, five field guns, and over a thousand muskets. It was a considerable haul. Bruno was executed, some say impaled and left to die in the searing heat, together with his senior aides.

The newly arrived Frenchmen were, however, generally well treated. Many of the gunners were given Burmese wives and were recruited into the royal service, some rising to become officers of the Household Guard. They were settled in the *feringhi* villages, Bretons and Normans adding to the Portuguese and other Catholic subjects of the king already there. One, the chevalier Pierre de Millard, lived for nearly twenty more years, becoming a captain of the king's artillery and serving his new master in the field against Pegu, Ayutthaya, and Manipur.

By this point Pegu's fate was no longer in question. The great city fell to Alaungpaya in May 1757. Bannya Dala had sent his only daughter on a gorgeous palanquin as a peace offering, but there would be no mercy for the starving city. Pegu was taken at moonrise, and the assembled Burmese horde massacred men, women, and children without distinction. Alaungpaya entered through the Mohnyin Gate on his best elephant, surrounded by a crowd of his guardsmen and French gunners, and prostrated himself before the Shwemawdaw Pagoda. The city walls and the twenty gates, built by Tabinshweti and Bayinnaung two centuries before, were then razed to the ground.

For the Mon-speaking people of Pegu and the nearby countryside, this was the end of their dream of independence. For a long time they would remember the utter devastation that accompanied the final collapse of their short-lived kingdom. Thousands fled across the border into Siam. Many others were sold into slavery. Wrote one Mon monk of the time: "Sons could not find their mothers, nor mothers their sons, and there was weeping throughout the land."[9] Soon entire communities of ethnic Burmese from the north began settling in the delta as centuries of Mon ascendancy along the coast came to an end.

And by now the Seven Years' War was over as well, and England's global mastery over the French well ensured. The East India Company under Robert Clive had chased the French across the Carnatic, and in September 1759 General James Wolfe defeated the marquis of Montcalm on the Plains of Abraham in Quebec, gaining for Britain all of New France. More important for the Burmese, Clive had also routed the forces of Siraj-ud-Daula, the nawab of Bengal, and entrenched

British power throughout the Indian east. Without Alaungpaya, Pegu would likely have ruled over a new Burmese kingdom, backed by the Dupleix and Pondicherry and influenced from Paris, but now only English power held sway all around the Bay of Bengal.

THE SACKING OF AYUTTHAYA

For the next half century Alaungpaya would be followed on the Konbaung throne ("Konbaung" for the area around Shwebo) by three of his sons and one of his grandsons, in one of the most militarily ambitious and expansionist periods in Burmese history. The destruction of Mon-speaking society in the south had removed the possibility of southern revolt and laid the basis for a more compact ethnic nationalism throughout the Irrawaddy Valley. And in the years before Britain was viewed as the number one threat, all eyes at Ava looked eastward, to dominion over Siam.

It was Alaungpaya himself, energized with the blood of his conquests from Manipur to Mergui, who first ventured across the Tenasserim hills. In the cold weather of 1759–60, he personally led the attack on Ayutthaya, calling on the besieged city to submit to him as the new *chakravartin*, or universal emperor. The king of Siam refused, despite the thinness of his defenses; luckily for them, Alaungpaya suddenly took ill, and his army felt forced to retreat. But the Burmese would soon be back, and the results this time for the Siamese would be catastrophic.

Two of the country's most distinguished soldiers, Naymyo Thihapati and Maha Nawrata, were given joint command. Naymyo Thihapati invaded from the north, heading an army made up mainly of highland Shans under their own chiefs. The northern city of Chiangmai was taken in 1763, and within months all of the old kingdom of Lanna (now northern Thailand) was in Thihapati's hands. As the Burmese chronicles put it: "having mopped up all the people in the towns of the fifty-seven provinces of Chiang Mai who insolently were unsubmissive, there was no trouble and everything was as smooth as the surface of water."[10] The Lao king of Vientiane had already offered to become a vassal of Ava and his rival the king of Luang Prabang would be crushed in March 1765, thus giving the Burmese complete control of Siam's entire northern border. Naymyo Thihapati moved down the

Chao Phraya Valley, taking the towns of central Siam along the way and meeting with the main Burmese invasion force, led by Maha Nawrata, which had crossed the Dawna Range from Martaban and Tavoy. The Burmese-led armies, swelled by local levies, were joined on the outskirts of Ayutthaya at the end of the January 1766, the gold-covered palaces and temple spires shining in the near distance.

Against this massive threat, the Siamese response was belated and uncoordinated. King Suriyamarin had sent out several of his best legions some months before, but these had been chopped to pieces by Maha Nawrata. The Siamese hoped that if they could only hold out until the summer monsoon rains, the Burmese would be forced to retreat. But then the rains came, the city held out, and the Burmese refused to be disheartened, concentrating their men on newly fortified high ground, and building or commandeering boats to keep their forces in action. A few attempts were made to break the siege toward the end of the year, but to no avail. A year into the encirclement the great city was starving, and disease began to take a severe toll. As if this were not enough, a fire at the very start of 1767 then destroyed thousands of homes. Facing imminent defeat, Suriyamarin offered his submission, but Ava's generals, now haughty with the smell of success, would agree only to an unconditional surrender.

On 7 April 1767 the Burmese breached the defenses. Everything in sight was put to the torch, and tens of thousands were led away to Burma in captivity. Virtually nothing was left of the fourteenth-century Grand Palace, home to kings—thirty-three in all—of five dynasties, or the glittering Sanphet Prasat, used to welcome foreign envoys and state visitors, including an ambassador of Louis XIV in 1695. The last king of Ayutthaya was believed to have slipped away in a small boat, only to starve to death days later. A former king, hundreds of ministers, noblemen, and members of the royal family were resettled in Burma. Romantically named after the capital of the Rama of legend, the city of Ayutthaya, far greater than any in Burma, with a population said to rival contemporary London and Paris, was reduced to ashes by the seemingly unstoppable Burmese military machine.

Myedu, Alaungpaya's second son and now king, had planned to leave behind a substantial garrison at Ayutthaya, either placing a protected Siamese prince on the throne or appointing senior Burmese officials to rule the country directly. But an unexpected threat was now looming: a huge Manchu invasion from the north.

CREATING BORDERS

The Qianlong emperor Aishin Gioro was the fifth emperor of the Manchu Qing dynasty. He was a successful military leader and presided over a period of enormous territorial expansion, made possible by the strength of his armies and by the weakness and disunity of the Mongol and Turkish peoples to the west. In 1759 the Qing conquered Kashgar and Yarkand and slaughtered the last of the Dzungar forces with great cruelty, extending Peking's control to the heart of Central Asia. And in 1793 it was Qianlong, then in his eighties, comfortable and complacent, who was to tell Britain's envoy, Sir George McCartney, that the Middle Kingdom had no use for things foreign, as it was entirely self-sufficient. His reign, from 1736 to 1799, was the longest in the history of China.[11] But amid all these victories and the arrogance they brought was one fantastic and largely secret failure: the Burma campaigns of 1767–70, the most disastrous ever waged by the Qing.[12]

For much of the preceding Ming dynasty, the southwestern region of Yunnan, next to Burma, was only somewhat integrated into the imperial administration. In the late seventeenth and eighteenth centuries the region became a sort of freewheeling frontier province, with tens of thousands of fortune-hunting migrants from elsewhere in China attracted to its vast and lucrative silver mines. There were few, if any, remnants of the old Dali kingdom, and instead Kunming and the other big towns took on a sort of pan-China character, with Mandarin Chinese acting as a lingua franca between the patchwork of peoples who now called Yunnan home.

In the southwest of the province many small chieftainships and principalities were keen to preserve at least a de facto independence, both from Kunming and from the Burmese kingdom to their other side. With Alaungpaya's rise to power and his determination to assert his control as far into the Shan uplands as possible, many of these chiefs and princes reckoned that a closer relationship with China was their best strategy. In the 1760s Myedu continued his father's aggressive policies and quickly became embroiled in several conflicts along the eastern border.

The Burmese chronicles say that the war began when a Chinese merchant was killed in a barroom brawl in Kengtung, a semiautonomous principality not far from the Mekong. Burmese and Chinese troops had already clashed in the Pu'er Prefecture (famous for its tea), and the Chinese had been utterly defeated. The governor of Yunnan at the time, Liu Zao, was known as an upright and honest man, but in his embarrassment first tried to conceal what had happened. When the emperor became suspicious, he ordered Liu's immediate recall and demotion, but instead of complying, the humiliated Liu committed suicide by slicing his throat with a stationery knife, writing as the blood was pouring from his neck: "[T]here is no way to pay back the emperor's favour; I deserve death with my crime."[13] This sort of suicide in the face of bureaucratic failure was apparently no unusual thing in Manchu China, but it enraged Qianlong nonetheless. Sorting out the Mien (the Chinese word for "Burmese") was now a matter of imperial prestige, and the new man to address the Burma problem knew that he would be closely watched and expected to deliver. And so the real war began.

The new man was Yang Yingju, an experienced border satrap with long service in the northwest as well as in Canton. When he arrived in the summer of 1766, he confidently launched a sizable offensive into the Shan hills, only to find his army decimated and chased back into Chinese territory. Unknown to him, Myedu had laid a trap: Bala Mindin, the Burmese commander in the field, had been ordered to give up the town of Bhamo near the border without much of a fight so as to lure in the Chinese and then surround them with two other Burmese armies. What Yang did realize, as would many others after him (including the British a few decades later), was that there were two enemies in Burma, the troops of the Burmese king and disease, and of these two enemies, disease was far the more terrible foe. There are no clear statistics, but there is no doubt that cholera and dysentery and malaria struck down the Chinese soldiers by the thousands. Qianlong was skeptical and dismissed as "unbelievable" a report from the field stating that eight hundred out of a thousand soldiers in one garrison had died of disease and that another hundred were ill. Yang also began resorting to lies. But rather than wait this time for Yang to commit suicide, the emperor dismissed him from command, brought him back to Peking, and ordered him to kill himself.

THE BANNERMEN TAKE CHARGE

For the emperor, it was now time for the Manchus themselves to come into the picture. He had always doubted the battle-worthiness of his

Chinese Green Standard armies. The Manchus saw themselves as a warlike and conquering race and the Chinese as an occupied people. It was surprising that the Burmese were able to resist the Green Standard troops, but they would surely be outclassed by his elite Manchu Bannermen. He appointed the veteran Manchu commander Mingrui as governor-general of Yunnan and Guizhou and head of the Burma campaign. Mingrui had seen battle against the Turks in the northwest and was in command of the strategically key post of Ili (in present-day Kazakhstan); his appointment meant that this was no longer a border dispute but a full-fledged imperial war. Troops were rushed down from North China and Manchuria. Provinces throughout China were mobilized to provide supplies. As a precaution against illness (which Peking now took seriously) the campaign was planned for the winter months, when diseases were believed to be less prevalent. The Burmese now had the world's biggest empire mobilized against them.

At first, everything went according to plan, and Mingrui led a victorious Manchu force down into the Irrawaddy Valley, throwing Ava into panic as he crossed the Gokteik Gorge and seized the town of Singu, only thirty miles or a three-day march from the capital. But Myedu himself didn't panic and led his men personally toward the front line, saying that he and his brother princes, sons of Alaungpaya, would fight the Chinese single-handed if they had to. He then sent a second army to Hsenwi in the hills, despite the threat to the capital, overpowering the Manchu garrison there after fierce fighting and effectively blocking the advance of a second invasion force under the Manchu general E'er-deng'e. Battle-hardened Burmese reinforcements from Siam also soon arrived, led by Maha Thiha Thura.

Mingrui had overstretched himself, and the Burmese under their overall commander Maha Sithu took every advantage, cutting his supply and communications lines and surrounding and pummeling his forces from several directions. Before long, thousands of the elite Bannermen, felt-booted nomadic tribesmen from the freezing grasslands along the Russian border, began dying of malaria, as well as Burmese attacks, in the furnacelike hot weather of central Burma, with temperatures soaring to over a hundred degrees. Mingrui gave up all hope of proceeding toward Ava and instead tried to break the Burmese encirclement and make it back to Yunnan with as many of his soldiers as possible. In early 1768, after months of grueling combat, and just as he was about to cross the border, Mingrui was himself severely wounded in battle. He cut off his queue and hanged himself on a tree. Of the army of more than ten thousand Manchu troops that had first entered Burma, only a few dozen returned.

The Qianlong emperor had sent Mingrui and his Bannermen assuming an easy victory. Indeed, he had begun dreaming about how he would administer his newest territory. For weeks Peking had heard nothing, and then the news finally came. The emperor was shocked and ordered an immediate halt to all military actions until he could decide what next to do. Generals returning from the front cautioned that there was no way Burma could be conquered. But there was no real choice but to press on. Imperial prestige was at stake.

At this point the emperor turned to one of his most trusted advisers, the chief grand councillor Fuheng. He had a reputation for steeling the emperor's will at times like these. Back in the 1750s he had been one of the very few senior officials who had fully backed Qianlong's decision to eliminate the Dzungars at a time when most believed war was too risky. And so, on 14 April 1768, the imperial court announced the death of Mingrui and the appointment of Fuheng as the new chief commander of the Burma campaign. Manchu generals Agui, Aligun, and Suhede were appointed as his deputies; the top rung of the Qing military establishment prepared for a final showdown with the Burmese.

Even before any fighting resumed, some on the Chinese side were beginning to send out peace feelers to the Court of Ava. The Burmese also sent signals that they would like to give diplomacy a chance, given their preoccupations in Siam. But the emperor, with Fuheng's encouragement, made it more than clear that no compromise with the Mien could be made. The dignity of the state demanded a full surrender.

Fuheng arrived in Yunnan in the late spring of 1769. His aim was no less than to establish direct Qing rule over all of Myedu's possessions. Emissaries were sent to Siam and the Lao states informing them of the Chinese ambition and seeking an alliance. He wanted to proceed by three routes from Yunnan to Ava and sought advice on the passages taken a century before by the great Ming general Wu Sangui. Taking another page from history, Fuheng also sought to copy the thirteenth-century Mongol army that apparently used the Irrawaddy River to good effect; thousands of sailors from the Fujian Navy were brought to the front lines, and hundreds of boats were built. An enormous fortress was constructed at the little border village of Nyaungshwebin. The emperor was pleased: "[O]nly Fuheng is moving forward courageously," he said. More ominously, he also decided to ignore the pleadings of his officers and began the campaign at the height of the rainy season, to the surprise of the Burmese, hoping that the "miasma would not be everywhere."[14]

The king of Burma also prepared. One army was sent north to Mogaung on the upper Irrawaddy in the last week of September under Thihathu. A second army under Maha Thiha Thura moved upriver by boat toward Bhamo. And a final army, including elephants and cavalry and French musketeers under Pierre de Millard, now the *myoza* of Tabe, marched up the east bank of the Irrawaddy under the command of the prince of Mongmit. An enormous earthquake had recently shaken much of the country, and many at Ava took this as a bad omen. And so great treasures—hundreds of gold and silver images—were lavished on the Shwezigon Pagoda at Pagan and the Shwedagon Pagoda at Rangoon in the hope of propitiating the spirits on the eve of the threatened devastation.

The Manchu invasion began in October 1769 at the height of the monsoons. And predictably, the Manchu soldiers and Chinese sailors fell ill and began to die in huge numbers. Fuheng himself was struck down by fever. At the Burmese fortress of Kaungton, not far from the border, the Burmese put up a remarkably tough defense, and even after four weeks the Qing emperor's best troops were not able to break the spirited Burmese line. More died of disease as well as fighting, and finally both sides had had enough. Fuheng was probably too ill to protest the negotiations that followed. Maha Thiha Thura knew that peace was Burma's best option. And so on a frosty 22 December 1769, against the blue green mountains of Yunnan, fourteen Burmese and thirteen Manchu officers signed a peace treaty. The Manchus were required to withdraw north of the Shweli Valley near the present frontier, prisoners of war were to be released, trade resumed, and an embassy between the two countries was to be sent every ten years. The Qing burned all their boats and melted their cannon and left Burma forever.

Not long after, the prince of Badon, the fourth son of Alaungpaya and then thirty-six years of age, ascended the throne in a river of blood. In addition to his nephew the ex-king, any possible challengers, including dozens of kinsmen and officials, were put to death. He assumed the somewhat lengthy title Sri Pawara Vijaya Nandayastri Bhuwanaditya Adipati Pandita Maha Dhama Rajadhiraja, but is better known to Burmese history as Bodawpaya, the "Grandfather King." Like all but the last Burmese monarch, he would take many wives, but even by the standards of the Court of Ava he was particularly prolific, with no fewer than 207 queens and concubines, 62 sons, and 58 daughters, a little more than half of whom would survive the scourges of infancy and childhood. No one knows how many grandchildren the Grandfather King had but they included two future kings. They also included my own great-great-great-grandmother, descended from him (as were countless others in the early nineteenth century) through a minor concubine, the daughter of the border chief of Mwayyin.

Bodawpaya's reign marked the end of the early dynasty, when his father and elder brothers soldiered to create the kingdom, leading their men personally in distant campaigns, and the later dynasty, when the kings stayed at home, enjoying the softer trappings of monarchy, and busied themselves in the intramural, if no less vicious, affairs of the Court of Ava. This is not to say that Bodawpaya was a pacific man, only that he himself never took the field, and left it to his generals to wage wars of aggression against Arakan and Siam. He was keenly interested in religion, debating with monks and scholars, intervening in monastic disputes and at times tolerating and other times persecuting new and heretical sects. He was a man of great appetite as well as grand vision and personally supervised for a time (until he got bored and gave the job to his son) the construction of what would have been the largest pagoda in the world, five hundred feet high and rivaling the Pyramids of Giza. It was never finished, though the ruins of the enormous base are still there at Mingun, a day's boat trip from Mandalay.[15]

Under him the Court of Ava became fancier and perhaps more ostentatious, royal and noble titles longer and more impressive. It also became a more active patron of the arts and learning. The presence of captive princes, scholars, artists, and musicians from the extinguished and older courts of Mrauk-U and Ayutthaya enlivened the intellectual life of the still-young dynasty, prompting new debates on history and law and making possible a rebirth of Burmese theater and dance. Pundits from Arakan whetted royal interest in Sanskrit learning, and hurried efforts were made to bring court practice into line with proper Brahmanical standards.

Burma and Burmese patriotism were now in full flight. Siam had been humiliated, and the entire might of imperial China had been repelled. The Burmese saw themselves now as an all-conquering race, destined to hold neighboring peoples in subjugation, an emerging equal of great powers everywhere. For the Mons and the Arakanese, this would be the end of centuries of independence and their own proud and in many ways more cosmopolitan traditions.

As the dynasty settled in for what would be a hundred more years of rule, royal administration was tightened, as was supervision of the towns and villages of the countryside. Surveys reviewed, revised, and reinforced hereditary rights and obligations. Even a new capital was built nearby and named Amarapura, the "Immortal City," and missions were sent west, sometimes only to bring more sacred water from the Ganges but also to see, a little nervously, just how far the flag of St. George was now flying over the middle kingdoms of India.

SIX

WAR

The Burmese kingdom and the East India Company
fight an epic war for two years, with devastating consequences
for the Court of Ava

~~~❦~~~

In the early years of the nineteenth century the generals and grandees of the Court of Ava, brimming with confidence and expectation from years of martial conquest, became convinced that the English and their East India Company were their principal adversaries. They dreamed of alliances against the English and worried about the English upsetting their own increasingly belligerent ambitions. They tried to learn more about the Company and assess their chances in an actual war. Few harbored illusions about the extent of English power. But the Court of Ava was riding a wave of military victories, and those factions that advised audacity gained the upper hand.

These were new feelings. Ralph Fitch, a merchant of Elizabethan London, was the very first Englishman to arrive in Burmese lands (in the mid-sixteenth century), and he was followed, at varying intervals, by several other traders and fortune seekers, all hoping that the eastern shores of the Bay of Bengal, so close to bases in India, would somehow prove as lucrative as the Spice Islands, farther away. But the prospects for trade never really materialized, and the effort of developing a Burmese market seemed little worth the cost of dealing with a new and outlandish court and all manner of tropical disease. The Company had set up small stations at Syriam and Ava in the 1600s, but these were later closed for no reason other than being unprofitable. To the Burmese, though, these were all peripheral matters, and the English and English trade were not viewed as particularly significant.

The English, to the extent that they were considered, were seen initially as just another group of people from the West. And for Burma the West began in Bengal. All the many and varied visitors and immigrants—Bengalis, Tamils, Singhalese, Afghans, Persians, Arabs, Armenians, Jews, Greeks, and Portuguese—were classified together under the single ethnic category of *kala,* an old word of no clear derivation. The newer *kala* from Europe were sometimes referred to as the *bayingyi kala. Bayingyi* was a Burmese corruption of the Arab *feringhi* or "Frank," a term with wide circulation (and many different pronunciations) throughout the Indian Ocean world, a legacy of the Crusades in a country that had no knowledge of the Christian-Islamic wars of medieval times.

The English were a newer breed of *feringhi* and had an early reputation as a commercial race, less interested in war making and less useful as mercenaries than their Spanish and Portuguese predecessors. Sometimes they were called the *tho-saung kala,* the "sheep-wearing *kala,*" no doubt a reference to the wool outfits they wore and that they encouraged the comfortably cotton-clad Burmese to buy and wear as well.

But slowly the rising power of the English in India became apparent, even to the somewhat isolated Court of Ava, and during the civil war of the 1750s friendship with either the English or the French became a natural aim of both sides. Alaungpaya wanted cannons and muskets, but he also wanted a more lasting partnership. Through some oversight, his letter to King George II never received a reply. Muslim and Armenian courtiers whispered in his ear that the British could never be trusted.

Apprehension over the Raj then worsened for two reasons. The first was knowledge of British expansion. By the turn of the century the Court of Ava had become increasingly aware of the mushrooming of British control across India. Spies were sent deep into British territory; many masqueraded (or doubled) as pilgrims visiting Buddhist holy sites. To better understand the enemy, an Englishman, known to posterity only as George, was employed to teach some of the royal family the rudiments of the English language. "Only the East India Company flag flies along the Coromandel coast," warned one intelligence report. Another compared the British to a banyan tree, which first leans on others to grow and then drains the life out of them when it is stronger.

The fate of numerous Indian princes and potentates was worryingly plain to see.

Between the 1750s, when Alaungpaya made his offers of friendship, and the early nineteenth century, the Company's army had grown more than six times, from just around eighteen thousand men to well over one hundred thousand. And they had proved themselves more than a match for any force in the subcontinent, defeating rivals, including the nawab of Bengal and the Tipu Sultan. The Burmese king had attempted to engineer some kind of alliance with the Tipu (and with many other Indian courts), but he and his determinedly Anglophobic state were now long gone. By the 1820s the kingdom of Nepal had been reduced to a protectorate, and even the once-undefeatable Marathas had been wiped off the map by the most powerful commercial firm in the world.

The second reason was Burma's own imperial ambitions, which were, within its own modest world, in many ways no less belligerent than the Company's. The road east was largely shut. Despite the devastating 1767 sack of Ayutthaya, the Siamese were able to regroup farther downriver at the new port city of Bangkok and from there, under a vigorous new leadership, quickly developed the wherewithal to resist further Burmese attacks. The Qing invasions of northern Burma had given the Siamese the respite they needed, and this had proved decisive. By 1800 any Burmese occupation of Siam seemed unlikely. Instead it was Siam that was growing stronger, annexing bits of Cambodia and Malaya and asserting its authority over the middle Mekong states once under the king of Burma's thumb. And no Burmese moves to the northeast seemed possible either. China was now right on the country's doorstep, and with the resumption of trade in the late eighteenth century the Court of Ava had no desire to rekindle hostilities with the Qing. That left the smaller fry to the west.

In 1784, a dissident member of the Arakanese royal family, Naga Sandi, formally requested Bodawpaya to intervene, and the king was more than willing to accept. The campaign, placed under the command of the crown prince, Thado Minsaw, was ordered to defeat and occupy the kingdom and seize the ancient and much revered Maha Muni image, the very emblem of Arakanese sovereignty. The main army, totaling over thirty thousand men, arrived at Prome just after the end of the rainy season and marched in stages over the mountains, joining up with a smaller force that had come up along the coastline from Bassein. Their objective was not an easy one. The beleaguered city, enclosed by rugged hills and once considered impregnable, had formidable defense works running over nineteen miles and moats with giant sluice gates. Some say that the attacking force was helped from the inside. In any case, on the last day of the year, the great fortress of Mrauk-U fell. Twenty thousand people were deported to populate the king's new capital, Amarapura, "the Immortal City." In the looting and destruction that followed, much of Arakan's cultural and intellectual heritage was lost. The royal library was burned to the ground. The country was to be annexed and ruled through four governorships, each supported by a garrison.[1]

The Burmese occupation was bloody and repressive. Huge numbers of Arakanese began fleeing north and west into Company territory. The Court of Ava had been hungry for labor and rounded up thousands of Arakanese men for building and irrigation projects in the center of the country. In 1795 a levy of twenty thousand men to expand a lake south of the capital set off a wave of desperate refugees into British Bengal. It also began a strong Arakanese resistance movement, led by a local hereditary chief, Chin Byan. In 1811 a new levy, this time for forty thousand men, led to another exodus toward Chittagong. The resistance strengthened, overwhelming the local Burmese garrison and momentarily holding Mrauk-U. Chin Byan offered to rule Arakan as a vassal of the East India Company, and this aroused Ava's suspicions of the British, especially as the Arakanese rebels were staging many of their attacks from bases inside Company territory. Soon the first clashes between British and Burmese forces took place as Burmese soldiers attempted to pursue Chin Byan's men across the Naaf River border.

Manipur was another target of aggression. Alaungpaya had already ravaged that kingdom in 1758, and this brutal invasion was followed up by another in 1764. Thousands of people were deported, and the valley was left nearly empty for years. Many of the captives were smiths, weavers, and craftsmen of all sorts. They were formed into hereditary groups owing special service to the crown, and for generations they and their descendants labored as servants and agricultural workers for the Burmese nobility. They also formed the new Cassay Horse, an elite cavalry regiment that supplied some of Ava's best polo players. Two more invasions followed together, and a Burmese-educated puppet prince was installed.

Even farther to the north and west, from their most northern forts along the Hukawng River, the army pushed farther west to Assam. The kings of Assam had ruled over the Brahmaputra Valley from the descent of the great river in southeastern Tibet to its turn into the rice plains of Bengal. A narrow valley hemmed in by high mountains, Assam had for centuries been under the rule of the Ahoms, a Hindu royal house. The Ahoms had fought in a series of plucky defensive wars against the Mughal Empire, but by the late 1700s their power was on the wane. Intradynastic disputes came together with a widespread uprising to create more and more instability. Rival groups appealed to both Ava and Calcutta for assistance. In the winter of 1792–93 the East India Company moved in with a small force to help the king, or *swagadeo*, of Assam quell a popular rebellion. But the Burmese were also interested.[2]

In 1817 a representative of a rival court faction appealed to the Burmese to intervene against the *swagadeo* Chandrakanta Singh. Bodawpaya had already been looking to send a force in support of the rebels and now decided to send a well-equipped army eight thousand strong. They began their march at Mogaung, marshaling along the way thousands of tribal levies. In an amazing logistical feat, they then crossed nine-thousand-foot-high Himalayan passes and entered the valley at its northern end, near Tibet. It was a punishing, many-week-long march past scenery unlike anything the men had ever seen. The officers rode horses and elephants; the ordinary foot soldiers hiked alongside in thick quilted cotton jackets, hardly enough to keep them warm in the sub-freezing nighttime temperatures. They passed for weeks through dark leech-infested jungle, so dense that sunlight never touched the ground, and waded through frigid mountain streams in nothing but bare feet. In the higher elevations, oak trees and rhododendrons would suddenly give way to sheets of ice and snow leopards on the distant cliffs.

With the army still amazingly intact, the Assamese were decisively defeated at the battle of Kathalguri, and a pro-Burmese minister was placed in power. But several years of local princely intrigue followed, and in 1821 the Court of Ava became convinced of the need for tighter control. A new expedition crossed the snowy mountains and extinguished the Ahom court once and for all. Assam would become a Burmese province under a military governor-general. The Burmese then turned their guns to the little hill principality of Cachar to the south, and early in November 1823 assembled a sizable force of about five thousand troops on the Cachar frontier. An alarmed Calcutta sent its own troops in defense of the raja of Cachar, and bloody encounters with the Burmese almost immediately followed.

Early in January 1824 the governor-general warned the East India Company's Court of Directors at Leadenhall in London that war might very soon be inevitable, in order "to humble the overweening pride and arrogance of the Burmese monarch."[3]

The king at the time was Bagyidaw, grandson of Bodawpaya (the "Grandfather King") and a great-grandson of the dynasty's founder, Alaungpaya. He had inherited the empire at its very height. Described by the British as a "mild, amiable, good-natured and obliging" man, said to be "fond of shews, theatrical exhibitions, elephant catching and boat-racing," he was in 1824 very much under the influence of the war party, those pressing for confrontation.[4] Part of the war party was his senior queen, Me Nu, and her power-hungry brother, the lord of Salin.

Another member of the war party was the Burmese commander in the theater, the lord of Alon, Thado Maha Bandula, stalwart idol of the modern Burmese armed forces and an ambitious soldier then in his early forties. He was the firstborn son of a minor gentry family who had taken on early responsibilities after the death of his father. A stocky man of medium height and blunt demeanor, Bandula was as well known for his outspokenness as for his successes on the battlefield. He had risen through the ranks of the royal service, first through special assignments for the crown prince and later as the governor of the Dabayin. His later promotions were rapid, and he had become the spokesman of a faction at court bent on an aggressive westward policy.

Bandula was supported by twelve of the country's best battalions, including one under his personal command, all totaling ten thousand men and five hundred horses. His general staff included some of the country's most decorated soldiers, men like the lord of Salay and the governors of Danyawaddy, Wuntho, and Toungoo. In those days, as today, many senior officials held both administrative and military offices.

In Jaintia and Cachar, Burmese forces were led by one of Bandula's top lieutenants, the lord of Pahkan, Thado Thiri Maha Uzana.

On 5 March 1824 Lord William Amherst, governor-general of Fort William and best known until then for leading a failed diplomatic mission to Peking, formally declared war on the kingdom of Ava. For the next two years the armies of the Burmese king and the English East India Company would fight the longest and most expensive war in British Indian history. Fifteen thousand European and Indian soldiers died, together with an unknown (but almost certainly higher) number of Burmese. The campaign cost the British exchequer five million pounds, or about ten billion pounds (roughly eighteen and a half billion U.S. dollars) today if measured as a percentage of the country's economy.[5]

Leading the British side was Sir Archibald Campbell, born at Glen Lyon in the Scottish highlands to an old army family, an experienced East India Company soldier who had devoted more than thirty years to the service, mainly in South India and the war against the Tipu Sultan. He had also taken an active part in the Peninsular War, under the future duke of Wellington, and had firsthand knowledge of the latest in European warfare.

A combined force of over ten thousand men soon set sail from Fort William in Bengal and Fort St. George in Madras. The initial objective was to seize the port city of Rangoon.

At Amarapura the king's men knew from their spies at Calcutta or Madras that the English were coming by sea. How should they respond? Should Bandula and the army along the Bengal border be recalled? This would lead to a collapse of the western front and the certain loss of Arakan and Assam. How big would the English force be? No one could say for sure. But the strategic choice seemed clear: either admit defeat in the west now and throw everything against the English once they landed, or hope for the best and maintain a two-front strategy. The Burmese liked to hope for the best. With some luck, the English would land and be defeated, and Bandula's army would push forward and take eastern Bengal. The key was to destroy the English force as soon as it landed, most likely at Rangoon. And to do this, the Burmese would employ tactics the English had never seen.

ALL WAS MYSTERY OR VAGUE CONJECTURE

Rangoon was a not particularly attractive and sometimes fishy-smelling town of about twenty thousand people, a good half day's sail upriver from the sea, with a strong wooden wall, about eighteen feet high, which cut off the town from the river and prevented any view of the water. It occupied a small fraction of today's Rangoon and was centered just east of where the Strand Hotel and British embassy are today. A handsome teak palace served as the home and court of the king's governor. But there were few brick structures, other than a big customshouse and the Armenian and Portuguese churches; most of the buildings were made of wood and bamboo, giving the place a sort of ramshackle look, except for the glittering Sule Pagoda just to the west. And beyond the town walls was a scattering of villages, today all neighborhoods within Rangoon, but then separated from the main settlement by forests and gardens and grasslands crowded with tigers (especially in the area near where Prome Road is today, which was well into the nineteenth century known as Tiger Alley). A map of greater Rangoon is a little like a map of lower Manhattan, with the old town at the very bottom and rivers to both sides. Rangoon was a commercial port. But to ordinary Burmese what was much more important was what lay sitting on a great hill just five miles north: the Shwedagon Pagoda, the country's most important place of pilgrimage and the pride of Buddhists across the region.

British military planners hoped that the Burmese court would sue for peace as soon as Rangoon was captured. They expected a fight, perhaps a tough fight, but fully expected that this second city of Burma would before long be theirs. Perhaps the ordinary people themselves, believed to be cruelly oppressed, would rise up and help. At best the king's envoys would then open negotiations, and after some give-and-take, a peace treaty favorable to the Company would be signed. At worst the Burmese wouldn't give in so easily. Rangoon would be used as a base. Boats and boatmen would be requisitioned, food supplies would be restocked, and the invading army would quickly make its way northward to the capital itself. The campaign would still be over in a matter of months, if not weeks.

But the British had no plan for what actually happened. As the tall wooden ships approached the shore on 11 May, they noticed only an intermittent row of fires, apparently burning at observation posts in and around Rangoon. The HMS *Liffey* was the first to sail into the King's Wharf, and soon the first Company troops landed on Burmese soil. But there was no fight. No artillery fire. No gunfire. Moreover, there were no people, soldiers or civilians. The town was entirely deserted, a ghost town. The Burmese had begun a policy of scorched earth. There would be no boats to be had or boatmen and certainly not any food. No crowds of oppressed peoples would welcome Sir Archibald or his men.

The withdrawal must have been harsh; it was also alarmingly total, for not only were no supplies or collaboration to be found, but the British were unable even to gather any sort of intelligence.[6] The native state and society had simply been rolled back like a giant carpet before the invaders, leaving nothing useful behind, not even a scrap of information. There were certainly no white flags to be seen or offers for immediate negotiations.

There were also no boats, and boats were key to moving beyond the Rangoon area. There were few real roads, only some dusty and seldom used footpaths. Other than waterways, only malaria-infested jungle separated the villages and towns of the delta. What British planners back at Fort St. David had not known was that all the boatmen of the Irrawaddy were crown servants, organized into close-knit regiments under their own hereditary chiefs. In peacetime they made their livelihoods ferrying people and goods. But in wartime they were the king's men, and all had disappeared without a trace.

Over the next several days, as he conferred with his red-coated officers about next steps, Sir Archibald did his best to establish defensive positions in and around Rangoon. Against little or no resistance, the British and Indian soldiers moved north and took the Shwedagon Pagoda and the Singuttara Hill, on which it stood, as well as several nearby hamlets. But they had no idea what lay beyond the marshlands and small lakes they could see. As one officer remembered, "Neither rumour nor intelligence of what was passing within [the enemy's] posts ever reached us. Beyond the invisible line which circumscribed our position, all was mystery or vague conjecture."[7]

Unknown to Campbell, and just beyond the last Company outpost, the king's generals had assembled a huge force of over twenty thousand

men. The pullout from Rangoon complete, the Burmese had focused
their energies on building fortified positions along an east-west ten-
mile arc. Here and there they massed their musketeers and cannons,
on little hillocks and at strategic points leading away from the city. They
were led by an experienced military man and a half brother of the
king's, the prince of Dwarawaddy, until then the commander of the
royal garrison in the Shan hills. There were several other princes of the
blood, including the future king Tharawaddy, each on his decorated
elephant, and the broader aristocracy was also well represented.
Among the commanders waiting for battle in the forests north of Rangoon were the lords of Zayun and Yaw and even the *sawbwa* of Kan-
myaing, a remote upland principality near the Chinese border.

Thado Mingyi Min Maha, the master of the royal fleet, had come
down in person at the head of dozens of boats and over a thousand rowers. And the king had dispatched many of the remaining top echelon in
his Household Guards, including the captain of the Left Brigade,
Mingyi Maha Minkaung, and the distinguished cavalry general Thiri
Maha Zeyya Thura.

Bandula and the cream of the military corps were on the western
front, but Burma was itself a martial state, and there was no shortage of
men raring for a fight. The upper classes had prided themselves on a
generation of relentless conquest. Only by retaking Rangoon could
that pride be restored. By late May, as fierce electrical storms heralded
the start of the southwest monsoon, the Burmese were more than prepared for war.

On 28 May, with fresh reinforcements on the way from Madras, Sir
Archibald Campbell ordered a few frontal assaults on some of the nearest enemy posts, all carried out after cannon fire had first weakened the
Burmese line. And then a much bigger attack, by four regiments of Indian as well as European infantry, was made a couple of weeks later at
Kemmendine, close to the river, where the sizable Burmese stockade
was first pummeled by artillery fire from the British warships nearby.
Two hundred Burmese were killed before the stockade was taken, and
among the dead and dying left behind was the royal governor of a
nearby province, lying close to his gilt umbrella. Soon the Burmese
were forced to retreat toward Kamayut, five miles from the Shwedagon,

abandoning their major fortresses. At another big battle, on 8 July, a convincing British victory left another eight hundred Burmese casualties on the battlefield, including one of the king's chief ministers and other senior officials of the court. Behind the front lines Burmese villages were crowded with wounded soldiers.

Despite these initial successes, the picture was rapidly turning grim for the British, as they, like the Manchu armies of the 1760s, encountered their most deadly foe in Burma, disease. The soldiers, living and sleeping in soaking rain, with little fresh food, quickly succumbed by the thousands to malaria, dysentery, and other tropical illnesses. By September sickness had decimated Campbell's force, and it was only with difficulty that they were able to resist a spirited midnight Burmese attack on their main positions around Singuttara Hill. Luckily, this was around the same time that the Company managed to seize the Burmese provinces of Tavoy and Mergui along the Tenasserim coastline, and these places, with their nice beachfront towns and cool evening breezes, became important convalescent stations for the growing numbers of British sick.

The Burmese side had also received reinforcements as a jittery Court of Ava began to realize the full gravity of the situation. The armies in Cachar and Jaintia were immediately pulled back, and Bandula himself was ordered to wheel his forces around and return home. Even in good weather, moving tens of thousands of men over the Arakan hills, with peaks more than three thousand feet high, heavily forested and with only narrow footpaths, open to attack by tigers and leopards, would be difficult, but to do this at the height of the drenching rains, through clouds of flying insects, was no easy task. And yet Bandula and his deputy, Uzana, in a testament to their generalship and logistical skill, managed to do just that and were soon rewarded by a grateful king with impressive promotions. Both were granted the title Agga Maha Thénapati Wungyi, the highest possible military rank. Others who had survived the recent slaughter were also decorated and promoted. Bandula was made *myoza* of Sittang. The king was nervous, and he had reason to be. Unknown to him, not only were fresh Indian and European battalions arriving from Madras, but also an entirely new military weapon, never before used on the battlefield.

AND THE ROCKETS' RED GLARE

The modern war rocket started its life not in the West, as one might expect, but in India. In 1799, as the British laid siege to Seringapatam, Colonel Arthur Wellesley (the future duke of Wellington) advanced with his men toward a small hill nearby, only to be attacked by a tremendous barrage of rocket fire and forced to flee in complete disarray. When the fortress finally fell, among the enormous loot sent away to England were two specimens of Mysorean rockets.

Rockets were of course long familiar to Europeans, but these were different. The technology was much advanced, using iron instead of wooden tubes, and this allowed for much greater range, stability, and explosive power. Most important, the rockets had no recoil, meaning that they could be fired from ships. Tipu Sultan's father, Hyder Ali, had a rocket corps of twelve hundred men. Tipu Sultan himself had over five thousand. Three or four rockets were sometimes placed on a single cart, acting as a sort of launchpad, and the resulting flash and noise when fired en masse often had a devastating effect on both the enemy's men and war animals. The British were much impressed. A vigorous research and development program followed at the Royal Woolwich Arsenal. The resulting weapons, a new and improved version of the South Indian prototype, were known as the Congreve rocket after their designer. In 1807, as part of an assault on the Danish fleet, the British were able to fire forty thousand of these Congreve rockets at hapless Copenhagen, setting off big fires and causing panic throughout the city. By 1812 they formed an important part of the British attack on Washington when the White House was burned to the ground.

In November 1824, just as Bandula was heading south with the main Burmese army, the first shipment of Congreve rockets were unloaded at Rangoon.

The arrival of Bandula and the armies from Arakan and Assam must have cheered the demoralized Rangoon front line. Bandula immediately prepared for confrontation. To the east, at Pazundaung, he placed the governor of Myolat with three thousand men. To the north he placed his brother Mindin Minkaung with another three thousand. To the west he placed a captain of the royal guards, Mingyi Maha Minhla

Zeyyathu, with four thousand, and in the forests just in front of Sin-guttara Hill, where Sir Archibald Campbell was encamped, he sent Mingyi Maha Minhla Raza, a minister of state, with a fourth brigade of four thousand.

With Bandula the tactics of the Burmese army changed. Rather than fighting defensively, he believed he could take the British head-on and win. He convinced the court that this was possible, and in turn the court gave him everything it could in the way of supplies to support him. At Ava he was able to mobilize men who were otherwise reluctant to fight. The British were impressed and believed that actually a much larger force, estimated at sixty thousand, including seven hundred Cassay Horse and thirty-five thousand musketeers, were now arrayed against them. They later remembered that the "spearman were of great physical strength," and Sir Archibald himself wrote: "If I may trust the information I receive . . . I may conclude that the united strength of the Burmhan empire is now collecting on my front . . . The Bundoola, all prisoners say, has arrived in Donoobew, with unlimited powers, and is to make a general attack on our positions early in the ensuing moon."

Bandula had established his rear base at Danubyu, and on 30 November his armies quietly assembled in the forests and open fields north of the enemy's positions. All day the British could hear the blows of axes and the crash of trees. The next morning the Burmese let loose their best artillery, and under the fire of their musketeers, they attacked, only to be repulsed in hand-to-hand fighting around the Shwedagon Pagoda. At midday, four Burmese regiments, led by their captains on horseback, moved from the southwest across Dalla toward Rangoon. To the northwest of the city the Burmese closed in toward the Shwedagon while the main force stood just to the north, near what is now Inya Lake. By the early afternoon the British found themselves entirely surrounded.

What happened next took the British by surprise. The Burmese began digging trenches as "the whole line disappeared beneath the earth." Less than a hundred years later the British would themselves employ the same tactics on the fields of northern France, but for now this was a novel thing and not well understood:

> The moving masses, which had so very lately attracted our anxious attention, had sunk into the ground; and to any one who

had not witnessed the whole scene, the existence of these sub-terranean legions would not have been credited: the occasional movement of a chief, with his gilt chattah (umbrella), from place to place, superintending the progress of their labour, was the only thing that now attracted notice. By a distant observer, the hills, covered with mounds of earth, would have been taken for anything rather than the approaches of an attacking army; but to us who had watched the whole strange proceeding, it seemed the work of magic or enchantment.[8]

Over the next several days the Burmese moved forward as best they could, digging themselves in, trying to get within firing range of the two main British positions—on Singuttara Hill and at Rangoon town itself. Every step of the way the British blocked their way, and in dozens of clashes each side wore the other down, until by 7 December Camp-bell's troops, often supported by intense rocket fire, had begun to gain the upper hand. Hundreds of Burmese dead lay on the battlefields. Bandula and his strategy had been defeated, and Sir Archibald fol-lowed up with an offensive on 15 December that drove the Burmese from the last remaining stronghold along the river at Kokine.

Bandula now fell back on his rear base at Danubyu, a small town not far to the west of Rangoon, in the Irrawaddy Delta. The king sent down his remaining guards officers, and all the south was mobilized under the governor of Bassein. Added to this a special levy, commanded by the prince of Dwarawaddy, was dispatched from the Shan hills and hundreds of new boatmen were mustered. There were about ten thou-sand troops in all, of mixed quality, including some of the king's best fighting men but also many untrained and barely armed conscripts. The stockade itself stretched a mile along the riverbank and was made up of solid teak beams no less than fifteen feet high. Behind the stock-ade were brick ramparts from the old town wall, and a complex mix of ditches and spikes was laid out against attack.

When the British, about four thousand strong, arrived nearby, a messenger was first sent with a call to surrender. Bandula replied: "We are each fighting for his country, and you will find me as steady in de-fending mine, as you in maintaining the honour of yours. If you wish to see Donabew come as friends and I will shew [*sic*] it to you. If you come as enemies, Land!"

The first British attack failed, and Bandula attempted a counter-charge, with foot soldiers, cavalry, and seventeen fighting elephants. But it was no good. The elephants were stopped by a hail of rockets, and the cavalry found it impossible to move against the sustained fire of British artillery. Hundreds more lay dead. On the river itself the British steamer routed the war boats sent against it.

Bandula was growing anxious. Around this time two Burmese soldiers, after their officer had been shot down by a rocket, abandoned their post. Bandula led them back to the spot and, standing exactly where the rockets had landed, instantly severed their heads. He knew the end was coming. On 31 March he met with all his war chiefs and decided to push one last time, knowing full well the likely result and unable, to the end, to consider different tactics. That night he sent a letter to Campbell on a dirty canvas: "In war we find each other's force; the two countries are at war for nothing, and we know not each other's minds!"

The next morning the British let loose their forces, pounding down on the town with their heavy guns and raining their rockets on every part of the Burmese line. At first there was no response. And then a small group of Burmese stragglers emerged with the news that Danubyu had been evacuated. Bandula had been killed by a mortar shell, and the Burmese forces had evacuated shortly afterward, first to Prome and then farther upriver. Bandula had walked around the fort, to boost the morale of his men, in his full insignia under a glittering golden umbrella, unwilling to heed the warnings of his generals that he would prove an easy target for the enemy's guns.

The Burmese remember Bandula's last words in this way:

> We may lose this battle. This is our destiny. We fight our best and we pay our lives. However, I cannot suffer indignity and disgrace for losing the battle for the lack of courage and fighting prowess. Let them realize that the Burmese lost the battle because of the loss of their Supreme Commander. This will prove to be an everlasting example of the Burmese fighting spirit and enhance the honor and glory of our nation and the people amongst the neighbouring states.[9]

For the British the prizes of battle included a pair of Bandula's Rajastani armored boots, which were taken by Campbell and today are showcased in London's Royal Armouries.

EMPTY YOUR HANDS OF WHAT YOU HAVE WON . . .

Storm clouds turned the intense heat of recent weeks into a steady downpour of rain. For five months the British rested at Prome. The Company's forces now totaled around five thousand, including three thousand European troops and a troop of dragoons and artillery.

Some at Ava, including the prince of Tharawaddy, advised the king to open negotiations. A military man who had been by Bandula's side at Rangoon, Tharawaddy had witnessed firsthand the enemy's superiority in battle. Others argued that the kingdom's strength was far from spent and that victory could still be theirs. But there was no apparent discussion of an alternative strategy, only an attempt to mobilize more men and meet the British again in the open field or behind a well-fortified stockade. For all his present and future fame, Bandula had not been able to imagine the use of guerrilla tactics or any innovative strategy whatsoever.

Later in the summer Sir Archibald Campbell received instructions to contact the Burmese government and begin peace talks. He immediately received a reply, and a temporary armistice was arranged for one month beginning 17 September. The two sides then met halfway between British-held Prome and the Burmese lines at Myeday. The Burmese delegation included both ministers of the Council of State and Bandula's senior lieutenants from Arakan, and all were said to have "heartily enjoyed" the lunch of cooked ham and claret that Campbell had prepared. The British then presented their terms: the government of Burma recognize the "independence of Manipur" and "desist from interference with Assam and Cachar," "cede Arakan and its dependencies," receive a British Resident at the Court of Ava, and pay two crores of rupees as an indemnity. Rangoon, Martaban, and the Tenasserim, all now in British hands, would be held until the indemnity was paid.

These were conditions the Burmese were not prepared to accept. They first played for time and then said:

If you sincerely want peace, and our former friendship re-established; according to Burmah custom, empty your hands of what you have, and then, if you ask it, we will be on friendly terms with you . . . however, after the termination of the armistice between us, if you shew any inclination to renew your demands for money for your expenses, or any territory from us, you are to consider our friendship at an end.

But the Burmese really had little choice. They were not willing or able to think of a new strategy and had little at hand that could really stanch the British advance. All they could do, they reckoned, was throw thousands more ill-trained and ill-equipped men at the front lines, pause for new negotiations, and try again. The king and court had been annoyed by the proposed terms. Perhaps they expected much lighter conditions than the full dismemberment of their western empire and the crushing financial penalty demanded. They described to the British their treaty with China in the 1770s, forgetting to add that this had been a treaty agreed to after a run of Burmese victories rather than after as many unqualified defeats.

In later talks, the Burmese envoy, the lord of Kawlin, said that the royal treasury had been depleted by the war and the court was in no position to pay the indemnity. He said his government would be willing to give up any claim to Assam and Manipur but that it objected to the British choice for a future Manipuri raja. He said the Burmese were even willing to cede the Tenasserim coastline but not Arakan. Arakan was special and should now be an integral part of the Burmese kingdom. The British were unimpressed: "The question is not how much you will cede to us, but how much we shall return to you."

There were a few more moments of determined resistance. In November, forces under Maha Naymyo had threatened Prome in a daring circular movement that had almost surrounded the town and cut off communications lines to Rangoon. The British noted the "great boldness" of the troops arrayed against them as well as their "well-directed and destructive" artillery fire. Much of the new army was drawn from the Shan hills, and the Shans were led by their own *sawbwas*. Several were gray-haired old chieftains, men from the China borderlands, and they died with their swords in their hands, sometimes in close combat. Sir Archibald's men even found themselves attacked by three "young and handsome" Shan women, who rode on horseback, encouraging their compatriots and leading them into battle.

But the British won this and other engagements. Over the next many weeks the Burmese suffered thousands more casualties under the withering fire of British guns and missiles. The commander himself, Maha Naymyo, died in early December as Campbell's forces went on the offensive and attacked every part of the Burmese line. The Burmese had one hope left, the huge teak war boats, over a hundred feet long, each with up to sixty oarsmen and thirty musketeers and fitted with six- or twelve-pounder guns. They readied all the boats they had and hoped, as a final gamble, that the effect of these boats would win them better conditions.

In 1823 the British had built a new ship, the *Diana*, at the Indian port of Kidderpore, the first steamship ever to be deployed in wartime. Commanded by Captain Marryat, who was sick most of the time with malaria, the *Diana* was not very large, but she had a sixty-horsepower steam engine and a few small cannons and rockets. She could navigate up the rivers faster than a rowed boat, and she could tow a line of boats carrying troops or supplies. She sped up the Irrawaddy just in time. When the giant war boats attacked her, she simply steamed away from them until their rowers were exhausted. Then she could steam up to them one by one and sink them with her small cannons, drowning their crews of warriors and rowers. Time after time she and her small crew chased and destroyed larger war boats or even fleets of war boats and sank them all with virtually no damage to the *Diana*. The king's navy was gone. Virtually nothing was left.

Two prisoners of the Burmese king, one English and one American, were released and sent as envoys to the British camp. They were told that the terms still held good. But the king objected to the money payments, and yet another levy was raised and placed under Minkyaw Zeya Thura. This new army had no chance. It was made up almost entirely of peasant conscripts, armed with little more than their own personal swords and with no real fighting experience, officered not by experienced army men, all of whom were now dead or wounded, but by courtiers and palace staff. All that was left was brought together and marshaled under the shadow of the Lokananda ("the Joy of the World") Pagoda near Pagan for a final and desperate defense, but it was no good, and this army of last resort was soon swept away.

A confident Sir Archibald Campbell advanced on to Yandabo, four days' march from Ava. There he was met by the same two Anglo-American envoys together with two Burmese ministers and all the British prisoners. The Burmese were authorized to sign a treaty meeting all British demands. The delegation then and there paid twenty-five lakhs of rupees in gold and silver bullion as the first installment of the indemnity.

Under the Treaty of Yandabo, the Court of Ava agreed to cease interference in the affairs of Jaintia, Cachar, and Assam and to cede to the British their provinces of Manipur, Arakan, and the Tenasserim. They also agreed to allow for an exchange of diplomatic representatives between Amarapura and Calcutta and to pay an indemnity, in installments, of ten million rupees or one million pounds sterling (then about 5 million U.S. dollars), an incredible sum for the time. The British would withdraw to Rangoon after the payment of the first installment and from Rangoon after the second. The Burmese Empire, for a brief moment the terror of Calcutta, was effectively undone, crippled and no longer a threat to the eastern frontier of British India. Success would bring Campbell fame and fortune and a governorship at New Brunswick in Canada. For the Burmese it was to be the very beginning of the end of their independence.

THE GLASS PALACE CHRONICLE

The *Lonely Planet* guide tells visitors to Mandalay that the surrounding countryside "has a number of attractions well worth visiting" and that four "ancient cities" are all within "easy day-tripping distance."[10] One of these cities is Ava, the oldest of the four, built in the fourteenth century and the capital (apart from a few brief periods) for nearly four hundred years. Ava is an island. To the north the Lesser River (the Myit-ngè in Burmese) winds its way into the Irrawaddy, and a deep canal cuts the city off from the south. It was a place meant to be defended and once had high walls and moats, only traces of which remain.

The proper name in Burmese for Ava is Ratanapura, or the City of Gems, and Ava (meaning "the mouth of the fish pond") was an older name. When General Campbell's army reached Yandabo, it was within the city's lacquered and antique walls that the king listened to the counsel of his generals and ministers and wives and decided to accept a defeat unthinkable only a few years before. A despondent mood followed as the foreigners occupied the western and southernmost provinces, and nearly all the royal treasure, perhaps the equivalent of two billion dollars today, was emptied into the coffers of the English ships. Generations of success and celebration were at an end, and only bad fortune seemed to lie ahead.

Tourists are normally taken down a busy highway from Mandalay and then on a ferry, often together with a local farmer and his cow, across the river where a dozen or so oxcart drivers vie for their business. They will insist that Ava is much too big to explore on foot, and they are right (not to mention the danger of snakes lurking along the dusty roads). There are now only the ruins of brick buildings, and all that remains of the palace is a hundred-foot-high watchtower, shattered by a great earthquake in 1839 and now leaning precipitously to one side. There are long avenues of tamarinds and huge bombax trees with herds of cattle grazing nearby. There is also a gorgeous and happily unrenovated teak monastery, still in use, called the Bagaya Monastery. It's now a private school for orphaned children, run mainly from funds donated by the occasional Western tourist and by Burmese villagers nearby. In the eighteenth century it was one of the great monastic colleges in the land and the training ground—in law, history, literature, and science—of generations of ministers and princes. Now it is set in what seems like a jungle clearing but what was once the center of the city of Ava.

Ava was a cosmopolitan city with a sizable Islamic community, both Sunni and Shia. Many were believed or believed themselves to be of Arab, Persian, or Turkish origin, but most had come directly from various parts of India, Arakan, and Manipur. English visitors had found them largely indistinguishable from other Burmese, remarking that "their women of all ranks go unveiled, and clothe as scantily as the rest of their countrywomen, they marry for love and women even pray in the same mosques as men."[11] In the middle years of the nineteenth century Muslims held high positions in government. The mayor of the royal city itself was a Muslim, as was the governor of Pagan. British visiting diplomat Sir Henry Yule noted the large number of Muslim eunuchs, courtiers, and members of the royal bodyguard.

In the years after the defeat at the hands of the English, the king himself faded far into the background. He had been shocked by the immense bloodshed of the recent war and the fatal blow to the prestige of his family and his throne and stayed very much to himself, seeing few friends other than the Spanish merchant Don González de Lanciego. For others in the court, the war and the defeat had been no less traumatic. A whole generation of men had been wiped out on the battlefield. And the world the Burmese knew, of conquest and martial pride, had come crashing down. Patriotism at the Court of Ava had grown for more than half a century on the back of impressive military success; now to see the English in occupation of Arakan and the Tenasserim, and to have to hand over nearly the entire royal treasury, was something difficult to accept. This trauma, and what was to come over the next half century, would take Burmese nationalism in new directions.

From the southern gate of the city there is a long and spacious causeway, a beautifully weathered gray, now leading across fields surrounded by tamarinds, a low carved wall on either side. There is a little inscription, barely readable, which records that this bridge, called the Maha Zeya Pata ("the Great Victorious Path") was built by "The Prince of Singu and his wife and two daughters," and that "It was not for the love of praise and worldly fame that the Prince erected this grand bridge but simply to acquire merit towards the attainment of Nirvana."[12]

On the other side of the causeway is the very dusty town of Tada-U ("Head of the Bridge"), in colonial times the quiet administrative center of the area, with a wooden courthouse and bungalow and police post, but today the site of a huge concrete and glass (and barely used) international airport, a Thai-Italian joint venture and much-publicized showpiece for the military government. It was here that in 1656 Chinese soldiers loyal to the last Ming emperor, having plundered their way down from the eastern hills, were met by the king of Burma's Muslim and Portuguese gunners. These days Air Mandalay and other private carriers swoop down and disgorge planeloads of well-heeled tourists from Rangoon, air-conditioned coaches and taxis waiting to whisk them away to their hotels in Mandalay.

My father's family was originally from the area, from a collection of seven hamlets known as Dabessway just next to Tada-U, spread out over miles along the meandering Lesser River, a parched landscape of eucalyptus and toddy palms, low denuded hills, and the white-painted masonary of crumbling pagodas. My ancestors must have lived there for centuries, living in little bamboo and thatch huts like many of the people there today, before making some money and emerging from the shadows of anonymous village life. My great-great-great-great-grand-father, named U Kyaw Zan, was born in Dabessway sometime in the mid-eighteenth century, was educated in a local monastery, and managed to find his way to Ava, where he made a fortune as a private banker to the king.

Though he was of fairly humble origins, his newfound wealth allowed him to marry a younger daughter of the lord of Mekkaya, a person of long pedigree and considerable station, who governed by hereditary right an old fortified town about half a day's journey away. Kyaw Zan was a typical merchant-banker of his day, first making money from local and long-distance trade to China, in cotton, ivory, and precious stones, and then making more money by lending silver to the poor cash-strapped farmers of the rice- and cotton-growing lands east of Ava.

As his business prospered, he was invited to join the private court of Prince Singu, and when Singu became king in 1780, Kyaw Zan was appointed one of his several *thutays*, or royal brokers. This meant that he handled the king's financial dealings. The Burmese kings in those days stood at the apex of a financial pyramid. At the very bottom were the ordinary farmers, who often needed to borrow money, in the form of silver, to pay their taxes, to pay for important celebrations, or to pay interest on old loans. They might borrow from a local moneylender but might also borrow from their local lord or village chief. At the very top was the king himself, who lent silver to his lords and tributary princes, and for this he depended upon his private bankers.

In January 2004 I traveled by car over bumpy roads, past bullock carts and bicycles, from Ava to Dabessway. In the dry weather several small canals had turned into billowing rivers of sand. There was a small but well-maintained Buddhist monastery and a local primary school, where the little children in white shirts and green sarongs were learning English by rote. A few very basic shops sold soap, plastic cups, and T-shirts, and a bamboo shack offered fresh-made toddy wine. Little groups of men and women sat around on wicker chairs in the shade of the tamarinds, smoking cheroots or local Duya cigarettes, and every now and then a man and his oxcart ambled back from the fields. I had been there many times before and in the past had been content with visiting the center of the village, but this time I walked away from the center to the village's Muslim neighborhood.

The Dabessway Muslims were preparing for a special celebration in honor of a Sufi saint associated with the place, and there was much activity. A big platform was being constructed, and there was a lot of painting and general cleaning. The head of the community was a man named Omar, dressed neatly in a stylish polo shirt and cotton *longyi*. He explained that Muslims, traders and soldiers of the king, had settled in Dabessway more than two hundred years ago, he didn't know exactly when, from somewhere in India. He said he had studied, recently, for two years in Cairo and spoke some English as well as Burmese and Arabic. Omar seemed a confident man and a worldly man, and he was bigger than all the rest, with a Middle Eastern cast to his features. There are perhaps as many as two or three million Muslims in Burma, and almost every city and town has at least one mosque; but they are a largely hidden minority, not included in official government lists of minorities and seen always as something foreign in otherwise overwhelmingly Buddhist Burma.

Though my ancestor Kyaw Zan became rich and worked his way into the inner sanctuaries of the Court of Ava, he still retained his connections to his home village. It was where he wanted to leave his mark. Near where the mosque is today and close to a bend in the river on a small grassy knoll, he built a little eggshell-colored pagoda, as a work of merit to help him in his future incarnations. He wanted to be remembered as the *dayaka*, or donor, of the Dabessway Pagoda, and this must have been true for a long time, though now there is no trace of his memory or of any of the old ruling group (though the pagoda is still there). It seemed that the traditional distinctions of class and hereditary status had been washed entirely away and replaced only with a religious divide between the area's Buddhists and Muslims. When I had visited a couple of years before, I had met the oldest person in Dabessway, ninety-five at the time, but this man pleaded ignorance of any history, saying that he was merely an unlettered woodcutter and had in any case moved to Dabessway from his own faraway village only in 1919. History was something very distant.

U Kyaw Zan fathered several children, some quite late in life, and his second son, Mya Yit, joined government service around the time of the First Anglo-Burmese War in the 1820s, rising up through the ranks and becoming a senior secretary to the Council of State in the 1850s. He was a poet and late in life was granted the noble style Maha Mindin Thinkaya. He was also made the *myoza*, or lord, of the seven villages of Dabessway, the pundits and those adept in matters of royal appointment taking into proper account the family origins of this banker's son.

My family was doing well. But these were the gloomy years after the war, when memories of Burmese imperial conquest met up against ever-fresher memories of humiliation at the hands of the English. The aristocracy and the grandees of the court were largely paralyzed, unwilling to accept the country's new place in the world and move in fresh directions. Some turned to history. In the late 1820s, as the British were counting the boxes of silver being unloaded for them in Rangoon, a new royal commission, of scholars and Buddhist monks, met in the Glass Palace (named for the walls covered in glass mosaics) to pore over old palm-leaf manuscripts and even older inscriptions and arrive at a new rendering of Burma's history, *The Glass Palace Chronicle of the Kings of Burma*. It was a fitting thing to do, when the future seemed unclear, the present had become so painful, and the lessons of the past needed a more proper accounting.

Then one day a new king took the throne in a bloody coup, and soon U Mya Yit and his sons and their families and indeed the entire Court of Ava, in their white and pink silk headdresses and velvet slippers, were told to gather their belongings and with tens of thousands of others, on oxcarts, ponies, and elephant back, journey upriver, to a brand-new capital, Mandalay.

SEVEN

MANDALAY

*Burma's last kings in the middle decades of the nineteenth century
design ambitious plans to reform their governments and
preserve the country's independence*

∾∿∾

Like Sarmarkand or Zanzibar, Mandalay is one of those names that evoke a sense of far-flung exoticism, of a climate different from Europe, outlandish dress, strange smells, and unchanging customs. Most people are then surprised to learn that Mandalay is not very old, that it is in fact quite young, having been built in the same year that Macy's department store first opened its doors to customers in downtown Manhattan.

In a way the connection of Mandalay with something old is not altogether wrong. Mandalay conformed to a pattern, and that pattern was set a long time ago. The descriptions we have of cities in the Irrawaddy Valley from early medieval times would have seemed remarkably familiar to visitors to Mandalay in the later part of the nineteenth century: the high square walls, the Buddhist monasteries, the palace buildings at the very center. Recent aerial photography[1] shows evidence of dozens of little walled cities like this—some with names recognizable in Burmese legend—now lost underground or in thick jungle but once the domain of elaborately costumed chiefs aspiring to conform to a certain type and live in the prescribed style.

By the time the first Europeans arrived in Burma, the model had been cast, and in this way Mandalay was a replica or at least a subtle variant of past royal citadels, the same twelve gates, the same nine-tiered roofs of the principal throne hall. When there was a change, like the oblong rather than square shape of Pegu, it was a conscious attempt to veer from the norm rather than a misunderstanding of what was expected.

Even the buildings and building materials were the same, meaning that they were not only the same type or design, but the actual same thing, moved from capital to new capital. One imagines that the same incredibly long and straight teak beams today at Mandalay once served the same function at Amarapura and even at Ava long ago. The British saw a nomadic spirit in all this; this was an exaggeration, but the taking apart of the dark wooden palaces, moving them by men and animals over dusty roads, and setting them back up just as they were before, is perhaps not altogether unlike the folding and unfolding of the great tent cities of desert khans.

In another way it is the newness of Mandalay that is important to note. The Burmese like new things. One can travel the length and breadth of the country and be hard pressed to find a single nonreligious structure more than a hundred years old. To a large extent this is of course the result of war and weather. But there is also no special value in living in an old house with some history or aristocratic connections; the pukka house is a brand-new house and not a refurbished one. Most dwellings are (and were) simple constructions. They are generally made of some wood, bamboo, and thatch, and people would tear down their homes and reconstruct them every few years so that they looked as recently made as possible. This inclination, deeply held, extended later on to more solid structures as well. Whereas in the West shop owners will take pride in a sign proclaiming the age of their building (BUILT IN 1791), in Burma the opposite is often true. The original dates on a colonial-era building (BUILT IN 1921) will be hidden under coats of white paint, and a new sign might instead proclaim the year of the most recent repair.

And so Mandalay was also an attempt at freshness. It was in many respects a very modern project, an attempt to fit new ideas and new concepts into a purposely old form, in order to achieve a new beginning. It tried to say that custom and tradition were important but could be remade to serve in a new environment and that Burma's past would help it engage with a very troubling future. When, on the muggy day of 16 July 1858, King Mindon was carried in a gem-encrusted palanquin by retainers, men of known blood and exact rank, in a grand procession clockwise around his new domain, then seated himself on his Lion

Throne to the sound of a distant orchestra, he was hoping that traditional Burma would find itself a place in the modern world.[2]

When the idea of Mandalay was first coming to light in the middle
years of the 1850s, the world was going through a period of far-reaching
change and political restlessness. The decade saw considerable advances
in science and technology. The production of steel was revolutionized
by the Bessemer process, the first transatlantic cables were laid, and
Charles Darwin published his *Origin of Species* to instant acclaim.
Much of America was enjoying an era of sustained economic prosperity, as trains pulled west to the gold rush in California and as millions
of hopeful Irish and German immigrants disembarked from famine
and unrest in Europe.

For the British, long decades of Indian expansion were only momentarily checked by the Great Mutiny of 1857, a passionate rebellion
across the northern plains that led first to the collapse of the Raj in Lucknow and Kanpur and then to a bloody and vengeful reconquest, the
overthrow of the last Mughal king, and the replacement of the East India Company with direct administration from London. Atrocities on
both sides were to leave lasting scars and new thinking about colonial
relationships.

Earlier in the decade, in 1852, a second Anglo-Burmese War, briefer
than the first, had led again to an unambiguous British victory and the
loss of more Burmese territory. Whereas the first was the result of aggression by the Burmese as well as British expansion, in this one the
blame was entirely with Calcutta. It started with an incident: The governor of Rangoon fined the captains of two British ships for alleged customs violations. And then there was an ultimatum in which Lord
Dalhousie, the governor-general of India, demanded that the Burmese
rescind the fine and sack the offending governor. The Burmese government, aware of what might be in store, quickly accepted. But then the
British naval officer on the scene, Commodore George Lambert (the
"Combustible Commodore"), went ahead and blockaded the entire
coastline anyway, without any additional provocation.[3] Dalhousie,
though furious with Lambert, then surmised that war was inevitable and
decided to demand one million rupees, with the justification that this
was the amount the British had already spent preparing for war. And fi-

nally, without even waiting for a Burmese response, the British seized Rangoon and other port towns in the south.

The Burmese were drawn into a war they neither wanted nor were ready for. The army was led by the lord of Dabayin, son of the Maha Bandula and a career military man. But despite an energetic resistance at Pegu, thirty years of technological advance on the British side and few improvements on the Burmese side meant that the defenders had little hope.

The fighting dragged on and effectively ended only when a revolution at the Court of Ava overthrew the incumbent king and placed the prince of Mindon, a half brother of the king's and the future builder of Mandalay, on the Konbaung throne. In the dark days of the second war, when defeat was again staring them in the face, those inclined to face reality banded together around the thirty-nine-year-old prince, earning him the animosity of the more conservative and militant faction then in charge. Rumors circulated, and as British troops pushed north, Mindon fled north to his ancestral home at Shwebo and raised the standard of revolt.

He was accompanied by his brother the prince of Kanaung as well as many armed retainers. More men were recruited and organized, and before long, along the banks of the Irrawaddy, they were able to smash the loyalist troops sent out against them. When they then appeared on the outskirts of Ava, at the head of their new army, their pennants flying against the low blue green hills in the clear November light, the nobility, not wishing for more bloodshed, changed sides. Two of the court's most powerful ministers, the lords of Kyaukmaw and Yenangyaung, convinced the Household Guards to stand down. The gates were thrown open, and Mindon and Kanaung entered the great teak ramparts unopposed. It was more a coup than anything else, and now a new generation was in charge.

By 1853 the old men of the once sprawling Burmese empire had finally retired from the chambers of government and were being replaced by a younger generation that had grown up under the shadow of English power. The older men included military men like the accomplished general Mingyi Maha Minhla Mingkaung, a cavalry officer who had commanded all Burmese forces in Manipur and Assam in the 1810s and had gone on to be a deputy of Bandula's during the first English war. However much they may have tried, it would have been difficult for these men, fueled by memories of earlier conquests and martial pride, to grasp Burma's new position.

But there were also others who did try to learn new things and who made possible the burst of reformist activity that would soon follow. The lord of Myawaddy, for example, best known in Burma today as a man of letters, was also famous in his own time for his beautiful works of music and drama and especially his translations of the Javanese epic *Enao*. He was a soldier as well and an all-around scholar-administrator, and he came from a line of courtiers more than two hundred years old. Schooled at the Parama Monastery near Ava, he rose to the rank of minister while at the same time making a name as both a distinguished artist and musician and a brave soldier. In the war against the English he had been the commander of the left on the Arakan frontier and had seen firsthand the destructive power and discipline of the East India Company's army.

While this turned some men to simply hate the enemy, Myawaddy instead became curious and more eager to learn about the outside world. He taught himself some Hindi and learned a few lines of a Latin hymn that he happily sang for visiting British envoys.[4] He encouraged new ideas and new thinking. He too died just after Mindon's takeover at the old age of ninety-two.

The real doyen of European learning in the interwar years was a member of the royal family, the new king's great-uncle, the prince of Mekkaya. The American Baptist missionary Adoniram Judson described him as "a great metaphysician, theologian and meddler in ecclesiastical affairs." Born in 1792, he had learned to read and understand spoken English, taught by a mysterious English member of the court known only as Rodgers, and had obtained a copy of Dr. Abraham Rees's recent *Cyclopaedia*, a massive multivolume work, keenly poring over thousands of articles on the recent Industrial and Scientific Revolution. Later he helped compile the very first English-Burmese dictionary, and at numerous meetings with the British envoy, Sir Henry Burney, Mekkaya would question him relentlessly on matters of geography, science, and mathematics. Burney noted that the prince had both a barometer and a thermometer hanging in his apartment and that his personal library included Dr. Samuel Johnson's *Dictionary*, the Holy Bible, and recently translated papers on the calculation of eclipses and the formation of hailstones. He concluded that "he had never met an individual with as great a thirst for knowledge as this Prince."[5] Ahead of Siam, Japan, Korea, and Vietnam, the Burmese court was opening itself up to the West, and with Mindon's coming to power, the stage seemed set for reform.

THE PENULTIMATE KING

Mindon is remembered by many Burmese as their last great king and among the most devout patrons of Buddhism ever. He is remembered for his innumerable works of merit, the monasteries and pagodas he built, the thousands of monks he sponsored, and his convening of the Fifth Great Buddhist Synod in 1871. The synod was billed as the first of its kind in twenty centuries, bringing together twenty-four hundred monks, including several from overseas, in a grand attempt to review and purify the scriptures. The monks recited the new edition day and night for six months under the shadow of Mandalay Hill, while over seven hundred enormous stone slabs, each engraved with a page of the revised canon, were being chiseled away by master craftsmen, there to be read for all time.[6]

That Mindon was a passionately religious man who took his religious beliefs to heart is not in doubt. He was passionate but not a fanatic in the sense of being intolerant of other faiths. He patronized the Islamic community in Mandalay, building a mosque and even a guesthouse at Mecca for the convenience of Burmese Muslim pilgrims. He was also happy to see the Anglican mission set up a new school just outside the palace walls, agreeing to send a number of his own sons there to be educated by the head of the mission, Dr. Marks.

But what is nearly never appreciated nor even remembered at all are Mindon's political reforms, his attempt to refashion government and help his country modernize in the face of continuing British Indian expansion. They are not remembered largely because they failed in the end, lost with the conquest of General Prendergast and the titanic political and social changes that followed. But they were important nonetheless, deeply affecting the very fabric of Burmese society in the late nineteenth century and creating the context within which British colonial rule developed.

He worked closely with his half brother the Kanaung prince, and the two divided up between them the main areas of government, with Kanaung specializing in areas of military and administrative reform. It was almost a joint kingship, and Kanaung was designated heir apparent, to the deep chagrin of Mindon's elder sons, with a lavish personal court rivaling that of the king himself. Mindon's chief queen was also an important influence. She was his cousin, from a more senior branch of the royal family, and was well known for both her interest in science and astrology—learning to use an English nautical almanac for her calculations—and for her uncontested dominance over the hundreds of other royal women.

Burma was not alone in its realization that it had to adapt to an increasingly European-dominated and fast-changing world. In Egypt, Mehmet Ali and his successors had already set in motion a series of reforms, encouraging the learning of Western science and technology, modernizing the armed forces, overhauling administration, and making possible the development of a huge cotton export industry. Similar reforms would be enacted in Siam under Mindon's contemporary, King Mongkut (the king from *The King and I*), and in Japan sweeping social and political changes would begin in 1868 with the end of the Tokugawa shogunate and the Meiji restoration. Other countries in North Africa and Asia that had survived colonization into the late nineteenth century followed suit. Burma was not at the very head of the pack, but it was certainly not behind.

As an important part of their reform drive, Mindon and Kanaung arranged for dozens of young Burmese men, mainly sons of court officials, to be sent abroad for their education. Some went nearby to schools and universities in India, but a good number went farther afield, to Italy, France, and Germany. By the late 1870s several in the upper echelons of the Court of Ava were foreign-trained, and they would all become part of the final and ill-fated push for modernization.[7]

The army was also strengthened and reorganized.[8] Factories were set up and began producing rifles and ammunition to replace the antiquated muskets still in use. Steamships were also imported, ten in all, and though they were meant for regular transportation, they came to play a critical role in maintaining internal security. Much more important, the system by which families provided men and officers on a hereditary basis into the army was dismantled, and instead a proper standing force was set up. For centuries the same families, proud of their martial tradition, had supplied Ava's troops, and this connection to the crown had been a pivotal source of their status in their own rural communities. This was now undone.

In 1870 a telegraph line was laid linking Mandalay to Rangoon as well as to other towns in Upper Burma, and a system of Burmese Morse code was invented. Western books on chemistry, physics, and biology were eagerly sought, and plans were made to translate the entire *Encyclopaedia Britannica*. Ambitious schemes and generous amounts of silver were poured into new industries, with factories producing everything from glassware to textiles, and though these were never economically viable, they were meant to show that a new Burma was being born just outside the ocher-colored ramparts of Mandalay.

At the same time, the business of government itself was refashioned, changing the workings of political power and, in the process, undermining (as with the ending of the crown service system) the very basis of social organization in the Irrawaddy Valley that had existed for hundreds of years. Administration was centralized and made more systematic, old royal agencies were abolished and new ones created, and an entirely new system for financing government was devised and implemented, replacing the traditional and often haphazard arrangements that had grown up organically over the centuries. The idea was that to be modern, there had to be uniformity, definite lines of authority, and clear boundaries of jurisdiction. These were things that had never existed before. The power of the hereditary gentry, the old clans whose influence over their townships had held sway since long before the present dynasty, was now diminished against the influence of Mandalay and its appointed agents. For as long as anyone could remember, members of the royal family and nobility had received towns or villages as their appanage, drawing their income from the income of these places (and thus known as the town's *myozas*, or "eaters"). Now they would receive a salary instead, severing their links with the countryside. And a new tax was set up, meant to replace all existing (and again haphazard) taxes and fees. It was a revolution in the system of government and soon threw Upper Burma's society into disarray.

Like Egypt's, much of Burma's modernization was to be financed by the cotton trade. Now without the fertile delta, the areas that made up Mandalay's reduced kingdom rarely had a rice surplus, and Mindon realized early on that cotton was the one cash crop that could be encouraged and sold abroad, both to China and overseas, and that this could keep his coffers full. For a while it worked, and in the 1860s as the American Civil War and the Union blockade of Confederate ports drove up world cotton prices, Mindon's brokers were able to make a handsome profit. For a while times were good.

DIPLOMATS

For Mindon war with England was not an option. Unlike his father, who had tried saber rattling and may have entertained on more optimistic days dreams of driving the infidels into the sea; and unlike his great-grandfather, who actually believed that conquest in India was possible, Mindon had no similar illusions. But he did have an illusion of sorts, which was that friendship on equal terms was possible and that the British, convinced of his pacific intentions, might one day return to him the southern half of his kingdom.

Shortly after taking the throne, he had dispatched the lord of Magwe to Calcutta in a bid to negotiate a British withdrawal from Rangoon, but this had ended in total failure, temporarily strengthening the hand of hard-liners who wanted to fight on. But both the new king and Sir Arthur Phayre, recently appointed chief commissioner of British Burma, were committed to a peaceful resolution of relations, and their diplomacy, ably supported by the informal British agent at Amarapura, Sir Thomas Spears, slowly eased tensions. Through Spears, a Scottish merchant, Phayre even arranged for 250 durians, the foul-smelling "king of fruits," native to the lost southern territories and a favorite of Mindon's, to be shipped specially to the Burmese king as a gesture of goodwill.

Sir Arthur made a formal visit to the Court of Ava at the end of the rains in 1855. In the manner of the mid-Victorian imperialist-explorer, he was accompanied by geographers and scientists as well as an escort of over four hundred Indian infantry and cavalry, all traveling on two top-of-the-line steamships. But the Burmese had no desire to be outshone in the test of diplomatic wills, and Mindon ordered that the embassy be met at the frontier by his Armenian minister and confidant,

T. M. Makertich, a scion of a local Armenian trading family, and a flotilla of over a thousand teak war boats and gilded barges.

When Phayre and Mindon first met, Mindon began the interview by asking in the traditional Burmese manner, whether "in the English country . . . the rain and air were propitious so that all living creatures were happy." They spoke amiably about such diverse topics as sailing and steamships, the size of the Russian Empire, America's republican system of government, Anglo-American relations, recent developments in Persia, Egypt, and the Ottoman Empire, and the relationship between the (soon-to-be-last) Mughal emperor and the British Empire.[9]

The last topic was more than a passing interest. Mindon did not care as much about the substance of his relationship with Calcutta and London as about the form. It was a matter of personal and national pride that Burma be treated as a sovereign country even if in every way its actions were to be circumscribed by British power. Mindon was conscious of history. On the Burmese *Glass Palace Chronicle*, he said: "Read it carefully and let it enter your heart. The advantage will be two-fold. First, you will learn the events which have passed, and the kings who have succeeded each other; and secondly, as regards the future, you will fathom from them the instability of human affairs and the uselessness of strife and anger."[10]

They were wise words. He also said: "Our race once reigned in all the countries you hold in India. Now the *kala* have come close up to us."[11] By this he meant that the Burmese and kindred peoples were the original peoples of the subcontinent, pushed aside over the centuries by men from the West, Muslims and now Europeans. It hinted of better times long past and that history was not on the side of the Burmese.

All the same, for now the Civil War in America was keeping cotton prices high. But soon three things would come together to undercut the king's reforms: The first was Britian's insistence on liberal trade, something that would cripple the royal treasury. The second was the gathering crisis in China. The third was rebellion at home.

THE PRINCELY REBELLIONS OF 1866

At around noon on 2 August 1866 the princes of Myingun and Myin-hkondaing, elder sons of the king, set fire to buildings within the palace walls as a signal that their rebellion had begun. They had been unhappy with their father's appointment of Kanaung as heir apparent, and relations between uncle and nephews had worsened over time. The two princes had once been caught stealing into the palace in the middle of the night after an evening of frolicking outside (and, according to one story, killing the sacred royal cow for some late-night steaks), and on this and other occasions the king had, perhaps unwisely, left it to Kanaung to discipline the youths. Now they would have their revenge.

Kanaung had been chairing a meeting to examine recent changes in the tax system. About halfway through, Myingun and Myinhkondaing together with several dozen followers entered the small pavilion where the meeting was taking place, drew their machete-like *dahs*, and cut down the heir apparent as well as a number of other ministers and royal secretaries. My own great-great-great-grandfather Maha Mindin Thinkaya, the lord of Dabessway, who was at the time a royal secretary, would have normally been in the pavilion. But then in his seventies and complaining in the morning of a cold (caught, he believed, from washing his hair too late the night before), he had decided to take the day off and stay at home.

Kanaung was not so lucky, and his head was cut off and paraded about. The conspirators had also sent messages to several other princes, pretending they were from the king, and then killed the unsuspecting royals when they rushed to the scene. Soon general fighting broke out between the rival sides, and several high-ranking military officers were killed while personally leading efforts to contain the rebellion.

Mindon himself was about a mile away, at a temporary summer residence at the foot of Mandalay Hill. Together with another son, the Mekkaya prince, and his royal bodyguard, he managed to reenter the royal city unopposed. Two of the king's senior ministers were now dead, one was captured, and only one, his old tutor, the lord of Pakhan, remained with him. Only after fierce fighting through the afternoon did loyalist forces manage to reorganize and throw the two princes on the defensive. Realizing they would not be able to get to the king, the conspirators retreated through the Red Gate, commandeered the king's ship the *Yenan Setkya*, and regrouped near British territory.

The shocked king sent a column against them under an experienced general, the lord of Yenangyaung, who mustered the royal troops under the shadows of the medieval ruins at Pagan and then headed south under drenching rain.

But the rebellion was now evolving in an entirely different direction, for the attempted putsch at Mandalay had set off another princely revolt, this one by the son of the murdered Kanaung Prince. With other members of Kanaung's family, the son, the prince of Padein, had left the city and decamped north at the ancestral home at Shwebo. Traumatized by his father's gruesome end, he had feared for his own life and was uncertain of the king's position. Mindon offered him amnesty and complete protection. But he was now encouraged by a growing crew of supporters and decided to raise his own flag of rebellion. The powerful local governor joined him and cobbled together a sizable force, which quickly marched on the capital.

It was now mid-September, and the British Resident at Mandalay, Colonel Sladen, guessed that Mindon's days on the throne were numbered. He therefore refused the king's request to make use of the residency steamer, and officials in Rangoon likewise refused to release the two royal steamers docked in Rangoon. There is no evidence for British complicity in the actual assassination of Kanaung and half the government, but neither did the British choose to lend a hand to Mindon at his hour of greatest need.

Padein was approaching from the north, east, and west, and Myingun in the south attracted an even larger following. Mindon considered abdication. But his chief queen, a respected astrologer, consulted her charts and predicted victory. Mindon carried on, and finally, after repeated appeals, the British released two Rangoon steamers. Together with two hundred war boats and ten thousand men, they then closed in on Mindon's wayward sons. By October the sons had fled into British Burma and surrendered.

Padein was next. Another even bigger force, under the king's loyal son, the prince of Nyaunggyan, including a division from the Shan hills under the *sawbwa* of Yawnghwe, was assembled at Mandalay. A delegation of Buddhist monks attempted a last-ditch negotiation, but this failed, and on a cloud-covered autumn morning, royalist forces under the prince of Nyaunggyan forded the Irrawaddy River with artillery, sixteen war elephants, and six hundred handpicked cavalry. Padein was routed by his cousin in a series of battles. He was eventually captured, confined for some time in the privy treasury, and finally executed for treason.

Mindon never really recovered from the affair. He had lost his closest colleague and friend, and his own eldest sons had turned against him. Reform efforts continued, but the king was increasingly drawn to matters of religion and left the business of government and diplomacy to a new generation of scholar-officials. And they had to deal with yet another set of problems, to the north, in China.

THE LAST STAND OF THE PANTHAY

On 19 May 1856, Qing officials in Kunming, the capital of the southwestern province of Yunnan, methodically oversaw a three-day massacre of the city's Muslim community. Ethnic Chinese townspeople, the local militia, and imperial officials joined together and slaughtered between four and seven thousand Yunnan Panthay—men, women, and children—burned the city's mosques to the ground, and posted orders to exterminate Muslims in every prefecture, department, and district in Yunnan. This was genocide, and the widespread attacks that followed triggered the beginning of the eighteen-year Panthay Rebellion, one that had devastating consequences for the Burmese kingdom next door.

In the latter part of the eighteenth century Yunnan experienced a dramatic transformation. The interior of China was already incredibly densely populated, and the pressures of continuing demographic growth coupled with generous government incentives convinced large numbers of people to migrate in ever-increasing numbers to Yunnan. These were the years after the Qing invasions of the 1760s and after trade had begun to resume between southwestern China and Burma. The migration led to an increase in the province's total population from around four million in 1775 to ten million in 1850, larger than all of Burma at the time.[12]

Yunnan had a mixed society, Chinese as well as many other peoples, including many who spoke languages very similar to Burmese and who had lived in the area since at least the days of the medieval Nanzhao and Dali kingdoms. It also had a sizable Muslim minority, descendants of long-ago Mongol and Turkish soldiers and settlers as well as local converts. These were the Panthay. The new Chinese arrivals were different from the older Chinese inhabitants who had been there for generations. They were brash and aggressive, illegally occupying land, forcefully taking over silver and other mines, and enjoying a close relationship with the Qing government. Through them, Yunnan's basic economic and cultural orientation took a decisive turn away from Tibet and Southeast Asia and toward China proper.

But for Burma, Yunnan remained important. In the nineteenth century, overland trade—cotton, silk, tea, silver—with the Chinese province was very important, especially after the British seized the coastline. And to the extent that this trade was in the hands of the king's brokers and was taxed, financing for Mindon's reforms relied on the steady progress of commerce. This would now change.

With the huge influx of Chinese settlers into Yunnan, animosity between the various ethnic groups, especially between the Chinese and the Panthay, flared into violence. In 1839 a local official organized a militia that with government consent slaughtered seventeen hundred Panthay in the border town of Mianning. Six years later in the early hours of 2 October 1845, local Qing officials, aided by bands from Chinese secret societies, barred the city gates of Baoshan and unleashed three days of frenzied violence on the Panthay population.[13]

But now, as Chinese repression moved into high gear, the Panthay were determined to fight back. Within four months of the Kunming massacre, Panthay forces captured Dali, where they declared the establishment of a new and independent kingdom. In the southern and eastern regions of Yunnan, fierce battles erupted as panicked provincial officials struggled to maintain lines of supplies and communications between Kunming and central China.

On 23 October 1856, in a ceremony marking the founding of the new state, the Panthay leader Du Wenxiu was formally declared Generalissimo and Sultan of All the Faithful. He had been born in the western Yunnan city of Baoshan in 1823, was educated in the Chinese classics, and studied for the Chinese Civil Service exams, a practice not uncommon among elite Panthay families. Though multiethnic in its support base and many of its policies, the new Panthay government also sought to revitalize Islamic teaching, establishing madrassas and printing the first Koran in China and encouraging the use of Arabic.

For Mandalay, this was not good news. Mindon sympathized with the Panthay, whom he saw as oppressed and as descended from the original inhabitants of the Yunnan. But he could ill afford the censure of Peking. Peking demanded sanctions against the renegade province, and Mindon was forced to comply; all trade to the north was stopped, crippling the royal treasury.

All this was happening against the backdrop of a much greater drama across China, the Taiping Rebellion, a civil war that consumed the lives of at least twenty million people between 1851 and 1864.

Qing power was already being challenged, both from internal uprisings and from outside imperialist powers, when the self-proclaimed mystic and little brother of Jesus Christ Hong Xiuquan launched his massive revolt. At its height the Taiping (the "Heavenly Kingdom of Great Peace") controlled much of southern and central China. But by 1864 the tide had turned, partly with the help of Western forces, and the theocratic army was crushed.[14]

Once the main Taiping revolt was over, Qing forces mercilessly bore down on the Panthay and other more minor rebellions that had spread around the country. On 26 December 1872 imperial troops surrounded Dali. Du Wenxiu, in a move that he hoped would spare the lives of the city's residents, decided to hand himself over to the Qing general. Swallowing a fatal dose of opium as his palanquin carried him to the Qing camp, Du was already dead by the time that he was delivered. But not to be robbed of the gratification of killing him, Qing officials hastily dragged Du's body before the waiting troops to be decapitated. His head was encased in honey and sent to the emperor.

Three days later imperial troops began a massacre that, according to the government's own conservative estimates, took ten thousand lives, including four thousand women, children, and old people. Hundreds drowned trying to swim across the near freezing waters of Erhai Lake. Others attempted to flee through the narrow passes at either end of the valley. All were chased down and killed by the Manchu cavalry. An ear was cut from each of the dead, and these filled twenty-four baskets, which, together with Du's severed head, were sent to Peking. Thousands fled to Burma, where they still form a unique minority at Mandalay and in the hills closer to home.

By the time the rebellion was finally crushed and the first tentative mule caravans again began winding their way up and down the Shan hills, Burma's finances were in growing disarray, and British and Burmese attempts to place their relationship on a steady keel were coming to a head.

AN EMBASSY TO VICTORIA

On a hot and sticky March morning, the SS *Tenasserim*, flying the peacock flag of the Burmese kingdom as well as the Union Jack, steamed down the Rangoon River and into the salty waters of the Indian Ocean.

It was a new state-of-the-art ship, built in Glasgow for the Henderson passenger line, and came with no less than twenty well-appointed first-class cabins. On board was a delegation from the Court of Ava, led by the scholarly Kinwun Mingyi, a minister of the king's, destined for England and for what he and his companions knew was their country's last best chance at preserving its centuries-old independence.[15]

It wasn't just a short trip in the manner of today's diplomatic missions. The Kinwun and his team would remain in Europe for more than a year, mainly in England but with side trips to other parts of the British Isles as well as to Rome and Paris. Their hope was for a direct treaty between their king and Queen Victoria, which in their minds and those of the Burmese government would elevate them above the princely states of India and would serve as a guarantee against future aggression. But in visiting the West, the Kinwun also saw for himself the great gulf that had grown up between his country and contemporary Europe, not just in science and technology but in so many other things as well. What he saw and heard influenced him deeply and, through his writings, influenced others at Mandalay as well and would ultimately lead to change and tragedy.

The Kinwun was then fifty years old, having been born just before the First Anglo-Burmese War in a small town appropriately called Mintainbin ("The King's Advice") along the Chindwin River, not far to the northwest of Ava. He had followed a classical education, studying at the Bagaya Monastery at Amarapura, and developed a reputation as a first-rate scholar and poet. He was from the military caste, but he was destined for a softer career, entering first the establishment of the prince of Kanaung and then Mindon's own service as a gentleman of the household and later as a chamberlain. When Mindon came to the throne, he appointed the Kinwun his privy treasurer and raised him to the nobility. From then on his ascent up the court ladder was assured. He rose to become the governor of Alon, the chief secretary to the Council of State, and finally a minister in his own right. Along the way he had been charged with studying the designs of ancient capitals and submitted detailed plans for the creation of Mandalay.

He had been of significant help to Mindon during the 1866 rebellion, and a grateful king had now asked him to take on this most important of tasks. Accompanying him were three other royal envoys. The first was Maha Minhla Kyawhtin, a junior minister, selected for his

American mission school education and his knowledge of English. The second was Maha Minkyaw Raza, an aristocrat of partly Portuguese or Armenian background, educated at Calcutta and then in Paris at the École Centrale des Arts et Manufactures. Europeans who knew him praised his polished and winning manner; he was perhaps the most Westernized of all the Burmese at court, often wearing French dress; he was even the subject of a brief poem by the Kinwun (such was the literary bent in those days of the Burmese ruling class), admonishing him for giving up his Burmese habits and for having taken a wife in Paris.

The last envoy was Naymyo Mindin Thurayn, a scion of an old aristocratic lineage that traced its ancestry back to courtiers of the old Ava dynasty, a graduate of the French military academy L'École Saint-Cyr and destined for a short career in the Cassay Horse regiment of the soon-to-be-extinct Burmese cavalry. And rounding out the team was a Mr. Edmund Jones, a "merchant of Rangoon" and king's consul.[16]

Their ship sailed over the dark blue waters of the Indian Ocean, around Ceylon, and then through the Suez Canal and on to Cairo, where they marveled at the Pyramids. They also approved of what they saw as the Western-style administration of Egypt. In Italy, their first stop on the European continent, they were treated to a grand parade and an audience with King Victor Emmanuel before venturing on as tourists to Pompeii. The Kinwun described the ruined ancient city in detail and noted that through such excavations "people of modern times can learn how wise and advanced their ancestors were." He said: "This is the habit of all Europeans—to endeavor always to discover and preserve ancient towns and buildings." In general the Burmese envoys were impressed with newly unified Italy and saw in the Italian progress of the time something that Burma might usefully copy.

It was onward through Florence and the south of France and Paris (where they stopped to have a look at Napoleon's tomb) and arriving, on 4 June, at Dover. There the envoys received a very pleasant welcome from British officials ("we can never forget Dover until the end of our days") and left in special carriages to a nineteen-gun salute as ordinary people waved and cheered from the sidewalks and their houses. Finally in London, they took up rooms at the Grosvenor Hotel, and Jones set about hiring the appropriate carriages and outriders, footmen, waiters, and messengers, all in special livery, for the new embassy of Burma.

The next few weeks were a whirlwind tour of late Victorian society. First it was Ascot on a bright and sunny June day, where the Kinwun and his compatriots noticed that the Prince of Wales "was wearing an ordinary suit and moved about the crowd, speaking freely with everybody, without assuming the airs of a prince, as if he were an ordinary lord or a commoner." All along the way people had cheered them on, and they had bowed and nodded in return. The envoys were warned such bright and sunny days were rare in England. They visited "a school where 700 young boys were not only taught, but also clothed, lodged and fed," and they went with the lord mayor of London to the Tower of London, "where we saw the dungeon and the place where traitors were executed," and then to a reception at the Kensington Museum. On another day they went to see the country home of the duke of Devonshire, listened to a concert, and enjoyed a five-course meal at Westminster with various members of Parliament.

The Kinwun and his colleagues also visited Madame Tussaud's, where they saw figures of people they had seen in real life, such as the Prince of Wales. As the Kinwun looked into a hall full of wax figures and visitors, he noted in his diary that he "found it difficult to differentiate between the lifeless wax figures and the human beings." They were given a book about the museum, which they looked through together back at the hotel. When they visited a charity bazaar at the home of the earl of Essex, the earl took them inside and showed them "a painting of a monkey which had been bought by his parents for 40,000 rupees." They attended that year's Eton and Harrow cricket match, toured Middlesex Prison, spent an afternoon at the Crystal Palace, and walked around the "clean and tidy" casualty ward at St. George's Hospital. Then it was Bethlehem Mental Asylum, where "patients were cared for in very pleasant surrounding." Over the next week the team visited Westminster Abbey, went on a boat trip up to Hampton Court, and gazed at the exhibits at the British Museum. On a hot July evening, "as hot as any October day in Burma," the envoys had a chance to repay some of the hospitality shown by throwing a reception on board the royal ship.

For the Kinwun (less so for the others who had already spent time in the West) all this was eye-opening. If he had any doubts before that Burma could resist future Western aggression, he would only have more now. The gap, not only in science and technology but in so many aspects of society and political life, was plain to see. Until the fall of the kingdom the Kinwun would counsel restraint and compromise with the British; he would also be on the side of those pushing for ever more radical reforms within the palace walls. But for now he still had his mission, a treaty with the queen.

On 21 June the mission was received by the queen herself at Windsor Castle. Dressed in their most gorgeous silk and velvet robes, they traveled in excited anticipation on the royal train and were met at the little station outside London by the queen's lord chamberlain, Viscount Sydney, and three state coaches. In the castle they noted that the queen stood up to receive them ("the European way of showing the deepest respect"), and the Kinwun handed the queen a casket containing the royal letter of greeting and the boxes of gifts.

"Is His Burmese Majesty, the King of the Sunrise, well?"

"His Majesty is well, Your Majesty."

"Did Your Excellencies have a pleasant journey to England?"

"We had a pleasant journey, Your Majesty."

It wasn't much more than that, and the envoys were disappointed that they had been presented to Victoria not by the foreign secretary but by the duke of Argyll, the secretary of state for India. But they hoped this was a start, and after a final walk around the castle, it was back to the Great Western Station and the Grosvenor Hotel for a rest. That evening the Kinwun and his aides were invited to a state ball at Buckingham Palace, "where members of the royal family, their friends, ambassadors of foreign countries and their ladies, lords and dames, high officials and their wives romped, danced and made merry."

A big part of their time in Britain was also spent meeting with the various chambers of commerce, whose real interest was not so much Burma as Burma as a back door to the fabled markets of China. A China–Burma railway seemed to hold the key to untold fortunes. The Kinwun visited Manchester, Birmingham, Leeds, and several other industrial cities, touring factories and meeting with local businessmen, and at each place the interest in China loomed large. Crowds of curious people followed the envoys everywhere, and at the Lime Street Station in Liverpool nearly two thousand men, women, and children greeted the embassy as they arrived on the six o'clock train from Birmingham.

The Kinwun tried to impress the Liverpool Chamber of Commerce with Burma's potential. It was a way of describing the country that was to be often repeated over the next century.

> [O]ur land is fertile and richly endowed with minerals and raw materials. We have great mines of rubies and other precious stones. Our teak has no equal in the whole world. European visitors marvel at our gushing oil wells. We have also iron and coal. We produce gold and silver. Our land produces enormous amounts of sesame, tobacco, tea, indigo, all kinds of paddy, all kinds of wheat, and all kinds of cutch. We are glad to note that western nations agree with us that the time has now come to develop this rich country.[17]

By this time the notion that the Burmese king was somehow a hindrance to opening a backdoor trade to China was gaining currency, and at Halifax the Kinwun took pains to make clear that Mandalay was not at all opposed to a railway to China but that the routes suggested thus far were impossible to follow as they would pass wild and desolate areas where the terrain would challenge even the most modern engineering.

At Glasgow, after a visit to the stock exchange, they were hosted to a lunch at the town hall with three hundred merchants. This was the home of many of Rangoon's primarily Scottish business community. The president of the Chamber of Commerce said: "[W]e must be truthful and say that the commerce of the Burmese kingdom of the past few years has not progressed at all, because of many difficulties and hindrances, and only when the Burmese King is prepared to remove those difficulties and hindrances, will the two kingdoms really benefit."

The tour continued. On 26 September they crossed the Irish Channel, and took the train to Dublin, where they stayed at the Shelburne Hotel and visited St. Patrick's Cathedral as well as the "great teaching school of Dublin" (Trinity College). For evening entertainment, their Irish hosts organized a show that included a pair of Siamese twins and dances by a couple of dwarfs. As heavy rains fell, they traveled through the countryside; the Kinwun noted that there was very little cultivation and that the soil in Ireland seemed much less fertile than in England, consisting only of "marshy lands, dark brown in colour."

At a private observatory in Newcastle, the Kinwun was interested to learn that the moon was covered by deep valleys, that its water boiled,

then froze during alternate weeks, and that there were no living creatures. And at Holyrood, in Edinburgh, the Kinwun and his colleagues
gazed at the portraits of the Scottish rulers, and the Kinwun expressed
particular interest in the "tragic history of the beautiful Mary Queen of
Scots."

All this was wonderful, but after months of traveling around, there
had been only the one audience with the queen and no sign that the
British were at all interested in a treaty. Back home Mindon was fast
losing patience, and in November he ordered the Kinwun and the others to Paris, a veiled warning to London that Burma had other friends
and in the hope of finalizing a new commercial treaty with the new
French republic. But here there were sights to be seen as well, even
amid the destruction of the recent Franco-Prussian War, including at
the Louvre, where they marveled at the collection of weapons, the Japanese silks, and the Egyptian mummies, and at the National Library,
where the Kinwun was startled to find an old map that included Burma
and was apparently drawn by Marco Polo at the time of Pagan. This, he
said, made him realize "that Europeans had been visiting Burma for so
many centuries." Then, as Christmas approached and under their very
first snowfall, the team trekked up to Versailles, where they met the
French president and signed a commercial treaty. It was the beginning
of a Franco-Burmese relationship that in practice came to little but that
would soon encourage the British to imagine the worst and decide to
end the Kinwun's kingdom.

THE LAST GAMBLE

Ever since the princely rebellions of 1866 the king had been reluctant
to create a new heir. The murder of his half brother Kanaung by his
own sons and the bloodbath that followed had sickened him. He knew
that a smooth succession required that he choose among his sons, but
he also knew that in choosing one, he could be condemning others to
imprisonment, exile, or worse. There had been peaceful transfers of
power in the past, most recently in 1819, but these were different times,
and often reckless British intrigue only encouraged rivalry and distrust
within the royal clan. And so he had chosen to ignore the issue, though
every year the future cost of this willful neglect must have weighed

increasingly heavy on his conscience. His favorite son was the Mekkaya prince, intelligent and capable but also ambitious. He had for a while been given charge of the new factories being built outside the city walls and had considerable experience in government. But when he was discovered conspiring with a particular ministerial clique, a new edict had to be issued to end all private communications between officials and royals.

Mindon's death, when it came during overcast days of late 1878, was sudden. The king was struck down with dysentery, and the best efforts of his German physician had little effect on his fast-worsening health. His Majesty was confined to his gilded *thalun* bed in his private apartments and was looked after night and day by his wives and daughters and the retainers of his innermost court.

A few hundred yards to the northeast, the power brokers of Mandalay were gathered to decide what would happen next. Present were all the senior ministers—the *wungyis* and the *atwinwuns*—together with the captains of the Household Guards, men whose very titles (Master of Gate) suggested their value in any palace coup. They all were members of the nobility, and several were closely related by blood and marriage. Together they represented a political establishment that reached back over 130 years to the founding of the dynasty. More than a few were descended from lineages even older than the royal family itself.

Their first desire was to avoid civil war. If the king wouldn't appoint a successor, then the responsibility, by tradition, fell to them. The obvious choices were the eldest princes: the prince of Mekkaya, already mentioned; the prince of Nyaunggyan; and the prince of Thonze. They had stood by Mindon in the darkest days of 1866, and their mothers were high-ranking queens, each with considerable following and influence. But few wanted any of these three princes. Theirs would be a radical choice.

By the time they met, some dressed in snow white silk jackets and others in long cherry-colored velvet robes, they already knew what they wanted: a pliant prince, pliant, they said, as "soft bamboo," someone they could collectively control.[18] The world was much too dangerous for an irresponsible or a headstrong royal to be placed in charge. They all were deeply devoted to monarchy but were more than willing to assert themselves over the actual descendants of Alaungpaya, now doubtless scheming themselves, in other gardens and behind other teak walls, for power at the Court of Ava. Beyond the few mature princes, there were many more in their teens or even younger available for election.

A minority added another element for consideration. These were the men around the Kinwun, the erstwhile ambassador to Queen Victoria. He was the most experienced minister in government, and he and his protégés were inspired by what they knew of European government and the idea of constitutional monarchy. The Kinwun was a former holder of high military office and had a certain backing within the army. He had also served as governor of Alon, the principal recruiting grounds for the Household Guards, and had married into the family of the hereditary chief of that province. The old man added muscle to the younger scholar-officials attracted to his leadership.

The old lord of Yenangyaung was one of those who met that damp September day. A member of the *twinzayo* gentry, from the rich oil-producing area to the south, he was allied by marriage with a number of important ministerial and military office-holding families. Tough and resourceful, he had fought the English in 1852 and enjoyed showing off his battle scars as well as his most recent twenty-something mistress. One of his many daughters was married to the king, and her son, the eight-year-old prince of Pyinmana, was his natural candidate. But many princes were related by blood to the aristocratic clans represented that day, and other suggestions were also put forward.

The deciding influence was that of the Middle Palace queen. Mindon's chief queen had died some years before, and the Middle Palace queen was the highest-ranking of all the royal women. She was ambitious but had no sons, and so her ambition was to ensure that one of her daughters be the most senior wife of whoever next ascended the Konbaung throne. She too wanted a pliant prince, and her choice was the prince of Thibaw, the son of Mindon by a relatively inconsequential queen. Unknown to some, Thibaw was then already in love with the Middle Palace queen's eighteen-year-old daughter, slight and with luminous brown eyes, the princess Supayalat. In the end it was a coalition between the Kinwun and his reformists, on the one hand, and the dying king's ranking wife, on the other, that sealed the election. On 19 September 1878 the Council of State appointed Prince Thibaw as heir.[19]

This was only phase one of the Kinwun's plans. He and the Middle

Palace queen secured control over the palace complex with the help of the Household Guards and then ordered the arrest of many prominent members of the royal family, including all the elder princes, Mekkaya, Thonze, and the rest. Mindon on his deathbed heard what had happened and, after listening to the desperate pleas of the princes' mothers and wives, had them released. But the old man knew that his days were numbered, and as his last edict he named each of the eldest princes viceroy of a distant region, a way of getting them to leave Mandalay and out of harm's way at once. But it was no good. No one was afraid of the ailing king anymore, and his orders were rescinded by the Council of State and the princes rearrested. Soon Mindon was dead, believing to the last that his sons were safe.

On 8 October, Thibaw appeared at the Glass Palace and was proclaimed king of Burma.

REFORMERS IN CHARGE

Thibaw was then all of twenty years old, shy and little known even within the palace walls. For a few years he had been sent to school at Dr. Marks' Anglican mission, just across the street from the southern ramparts, where he arrived every morning with three other princes on elephant back, with a retinue of gaily dressed attendants and golden parasols overhead.[20] On occasion he was made to stand in the corner for bad behavior. He had also learned to play cricket and was remembered as tolerably good with a bat, "being something of a slogger" as well as using unprincely language when he bowled. On leaving he entered the prestigious Bagaya monastic college, busying himself during his teenage years with his Pali grammar and arcane Burmese legal treatises and becoming an accomplished classical scholar. Just a year before, he had passed the next to highest *Patama-gyi* examination and had been feted by his proud father in a grand ceremony. It was around then that he fell under the spell of Supayalat, his strong-willed half sister, who was no scholar but was already adept at understanding how power really worked at the Court of Ava.

A month after Thibaw was formally appointed king, the Kinwun and the other senior officials met at a newly built pavilion in the South Royal Gardens and set in motion a series of sweeping reforms. Dozens of princes and other members of the royal family were still in prison. To ensure that others in the conservative establishment could do no harm, they dismissed from office the heads of powerful ministerial factions, together with a host of other courtiers. In their place, ministers and army officers who had supported their coup were rewarded with new posts and attractive titles.[21]

Government was reorganized around fourteen ministries, the old system of audiences with the king was abolished, and a cabinet-style regime was set up. A proper salary scale was also instituted with bureaucratic ranks, and even the new king and queen were now required to apply to the treasury secretary for funds. All this was done in deliberate imitation of Western administrations, and for a short while it looked as if there would be a fresh start. In an interview with the London *Times* in November 1885, Thibaw remarked that he had been, for his first year as king, virtually a prisoner of his own ministers.

On specific policy issues there was also quick action. A tentative agreement was reached with a British firm for the construction of a railway through Upper Burma (something the merchants of Glasgow had been impatiently demanding), restrictions on trade were relaxed, and as a friendly gesture, an armed guard was permitted to be stationed outside the British Residency. More traditionally, and reflecting the literary inclinations of many of the court's grandees, the new king was also presented with thirty-six new works of orthography.

All this time the young king was practically powerless, but he was still the king, and the hopeful lord of Yaw took it upon himself to bring his new monarch into the reformist fold.[22] Yaw, like nearly all others in the top echelons at court, came from a long line of courtiers and Guard officers, his father having been a chief minister in the 1830s and his father-in-law having been Mindon's first foreign minister. He was also brilliant, authoring numerous and learned works on everything from law to chemistry and even becoming an accomplished architect. A beautiful brick monastery he helped design, called Itakarama, based on Italian Renaissance designs he had studied, still stands, abandoned, just behind the Mandalay Golf Club.

For Thibaw, the lord of Yaw wrote a collection of essays, including his now-famous *Rajadhammasangaha*, or "Treatise on Righteous Government." Deriving his ideas from classical Burmese and Pali sources, the minister argued for limits to royal authority and for the king to rule, through his cabinet, in the interest of all his subjects. It was an essay on constitutional monarchy and Yaw emerged as perhaps the most radical of the government's thinkers. The treatise was also to be the very last of this scholar-administrator's nearly two dozen books; he would not long survive the events to come.

LOVE, MARRIAGE, AND THE PRINCE OF YANAUNG

All the while, as the reformers energetically pressed ahead in the outer pavilions, within the dark and thickly carpeted inner apartments of the palace, very different patterns of influence and power were taking shape. Thibaw was after all a coalition candidate, of the Kinwun and his scholar-officials, on the one side, and the Middle Palace queen, her daughter, and their cohorts, on the other. In the final weeks of 1878 and in early 1879 both the Household Division and the royal suite were purged, and many high-level posts were handed out to childhood playmates and hangers-on of Thibaw. The most important of these was Maung Toke, the lord of Yanaung, who was an old companion of Thibaw's from school. He now saw his quiet and malleable friend's rise to the throne as a heaven-sent opportunity for personal aggrandizement.[23]

Yanaung came from an old military family, and his father was still a senior army officer. Yanaung himself was appointed colonel of the Tavoy Guards; more scandalously, he talked Thibaw into raising him to the status of prince, or *mintha*, even though he was not of royal blood. He would soon make his newfound influence known, using the king's name and extending his tentacles all around the stuffy little halls of the inner palace. He had read his history books, and his favorite hero was the sixteenth-century king Bayinnaung, also a man of nonroyal blood, who first became the king's chief lieutenant and then took the throne himself. Quite the ladies' man, Yanaung enjoyed only one modernization. He had many wives and more concubines and was said to have installed an electric buzzer system through which he could call one to his bed without the knowledge of the others. The sound of the buzzer would be heard, but only the chosen wife or concubine would know exactly who had been summoned. Yanaung liked to believe this lessened jealousies.

Yanaung found a useful ally in the lord of Taingdar, a man later reviled in the British press. An army man and from a family that had long held office in the Arakanese occupation, he was forceful and quick-witted and was determined not to lose power to the group around the Kinwun. Ironically (or perhaps to cover his bases), he had married his daughter to one of the leading Sorbonne-educated reformers.

The first clash between the two sides came early on. A decade before, the Siamese king Mongkut had died and been succeeded by his eldest son, Chulalongkorn. The new king, destined to revolutionize Siamese government and society, was then only fifteen years old, and the chief minister acted as regent for several years. Like Thibaw, Chulalongkorn had a partly Western education, from Dr. Marks in Thibaw's case and in Chulalongkorn's from different European tutors, including most famously Anna Leonowens, of *The King and I* fame. The regent, seeing his opportunity to push through wide-ranging changes, had Chulalongkorn travel abroad for some time, to have him out of the way but also to open his eyes so he would see for himself how desperate was the need for modernization. The young king went to Singapore, Java, and India and later visited Europe twice.

The Kinwun may have had this example in mind when he proposed that Thibaw too take a trip around the world. Thibaw was at first enthusiastic, and in early 1879 a detailed plan was presented to the young king to visit London. Arrangements were made, and a list of accompanying courtiers and retainers was drawn up.[24]

But Yanaung and Supayalat were no fools and understood that with the king away, they would fall easy prey to the ministers in power. They worked to change Thibaw's mind, telling him that this all was a ploy to undermine the king's position and that once in London, he would be abandoned there, "like a dog left on a sandbank," unable to get home and without anyone to help. Thibaw was scared and agreed to cancel the journey. The ministers were dismayed. Yanaung and Supayalat decided they were on a roll.

Up until this point dozens of princes and princesses, half brothers and sisters of Thibaw's, as well as children of the assassinated Kanaung Prince, languished in a fetid prison north of the main palace complex. Only the prince of Nyaunggyan had escaped. Disguised as an ordinary laborer, he had sneaked into the British Residency and then, with British help, traveled on an armed steamship to Rangoon. He was now

in Calcutta, waiting for his chance. But the others were in the hands of
the new regime. The Kinwun and the reformists were happy to keep
them under lock and key, remembering the rebellion of 1866 and how
troublesome the royals could be. But Yanaung and Supayalat wanted to
go a step further. What if another escaped? Better to be safe than sorry.

On 13 February several top officials, including a number of ministers, were dismissed and imprisoned under Yanaung's direction. Among
those arrested was the lord of Yaw, the distinguished scholar and master who had written the treatise for Thibaw on constitutional government. Beginning the next day, Valentine's Day 1879, the executions
began. The North and South Tavoy Guards, under Yanaung's command, herded the royals, many weakened from poor food and some in
rags, in batches out of the royal city and to a dusty field about half a
mile toward the Irrawaddy. There they were strangled or trampled by
elephants (the accounts differ), and all together, over the next several
days, no fewer than thirty-one of Mindon's forty-eight sons and nine of
his sixty-two daughters were killed. Others who opposed Supayalat and
Yanaung, officials and rivals in the army, also met the same fate. At the
end of it all, the so-called fourteen-department government was ended.
Yanaung and Supayalat would be free to do and spend as they pleased.

Only now, months after the death of his father, did Thibaw formally
mount the throne. He was consecrated king, with Supayalat by his side,
in a ceremony modeled on that of his great-great-grandfather Bodawpaya. The pundits of the court also drew deep into their archives and
gathered ideas from even older ceremonies, in particular the consecra-
tion of King Thalun in 1629 and King Dasaraja of Arakan in 1123.
With this reaffirmation of tradition, the reformist movement was dead.

The British were shocked and appalled by the goings-on in Mandalay,
and the British press in Rangoon, Calcutta, and even London reported
gruesome accounts of massacres and demanded what we would today
call a humanitarian intervention. Thibaw was depicted as a blood-
soaked ogre, and there was talk of war. Additional troops were placed
along the frontier near Prome, and preparations were made to place
the escaped prince of Nyaunggyan on the Konbaung throne. If this had
happened, Burma would have been turned into a protectorate of
British India's, the Burmese monarchy would have been retained, and

the entire history of Burma in the twentieth century would have been different. But it didn't happen.

Just a few weeks before, Zulu *impis* had overwhelmed and annihilated an entire battalion of the South Wales Borderers at the battle of Isandhlwana, a disastrous start to what would be Lord Chelmsford's four-month South African campaign against King Cetshwayo. The same winter forty thousand British and Indian troops marched into the Afghan kingdom of Sher Ali and occupied much of that country with little problem until September, when the British Resident in Kabul, Sir Louis Cavagnari, and his staff were massacred by a huge mob. A new expeditionary force had to trudge back over the high mountain passes only to be bogged down for months fighting an unwinnable war against resolute Afghan tribesmen. Invading Burma because Thibaw had killed some of his relatives no longer seemed like a good idea.

Supayalat loved clowns and comedians. Dance troupes and traveling theater groups would perform for her in the Western Court, and the clever and go-getting among them would declare, "[T]here is only room for one drum in the orchestra."[25] This was what she liked to hear. For unlike every other king in Burmese history (and unlike most princes, noblemen, and chiefs), her husband, Thibaw, had decided to have only one wife. This was a sharp departure from precedence, unthinkable really, not simply because a king was meant to have many wives, but because many, if not all, of these marriages represented a connection with a tributary prince, chief, or high official, whose daughters or sisters were taken into the palace. The king was meant to be at the apex of a broad network of kinsmen, loyal by marriage as well as by blood. But Thibaw had only Supayalat and his mother-in-law.

No one was happy with the situation, including Yanaung, and he encouraged his old school friend to do the royal thing and take on more wives and concubines. Thibaw equivocated, and Yanaung decided to take matters into his own hands, and introduced the king to Mi Hkin-gyi. She was the daughter of the lord of Kanni (a minister in the government), the niece of the lord of Pagan (a privy councillor), and the granddaughter of the lord of Kampat (a former foreign minister under Mindon). Thibaw would become related to at least one important family. And she was tall and young and beautiful.

Thibaw fell in love with her, but he was afraid of Supayalat. For a while the young girl was secretly brought into the palace in the short white jacket and silk *paso* of a page boy and hidden in the king's servant quarters. Then Supayalat became pregnant and was confined for several weeks in her own apartments, and the relationship became more open. Eventually—after the birth of a daughter—Thibaw summoned the courage to tell Supayalat the truth and about his intention of installing Mi Hkin-gyi as a queen. Supayalat became hysterical with anger. The quarrel between the two even made the overseas gossip columns, the *Calcutta Statesman* in November 1881 alleging that Supayalat had demanded a divorce and that Thibaw was considering retiring to the quiet of the monastery. In the end Thibaw either did not stand up for Mi Hkin-gyi or tried and failed. Within a few months she was detained and then executed, some say drowned in the Irrawaddy. Thibaw never looked at another woman again.

Yanaung was next. No one liked his influence over the king, not the Kinwun, who saw him as a reactionary thug, and not Supayalat, not after what had just happened. Around that time heavy teak boxes in which ordinary townspeople could deposit petitions had been placed around the royal city. Hundreds of petitions were received, and among these were dozens complaining about Yanaung, listing and detailing a number of offenses, including capital offenses, like using the king's peacock seal. Egged on by others, Thibaw tossed his friend into jail but then, being a naturally kind man as well as a man of weak disposition, began questioning his decision. Supayalat, though, was more action-oriented and had Yanaung executed on 17 March, together with other members of his gang. A few days later, in a bid to underline her new power, a number of grandees who had challenged her, including Mi Hkin-gyi's uncles and grandfathers, were sacked and imprisoned.

GHOSTS OF DUPLEIX

Government in the last few years of independent Burma was an uncomfortable partnership, with Supayalat reigning supreme in the inner palace and the Kinwun leading a mixed group of reformists and conservatives in the affairs of state. In some areas, efforts to modernize continued, but these were increasingly hampered by a growing financial and administrative crisis. From 1883 onward there was a huge fall in Mandalay's tax collection in large part because of mounting disorder in the countryside. For nearly thirty years now the Court of Ava had worked to strengthen central control, to systematize its relationship with the towns and villages that made up most of the country, and to rein in the power of the hereditary service chiefs and *myothugyis*. But the net result in many parts of the Irrawaddy Valley was to undermine the position of the old gentry class while not being able to replace their authority with anything new.

Bandits and dacoits filled the vacuum, and in areas very close to Mandalay law and order began to break down completely. Even the best efforts of the most elite regiments could not stop the collapse in royal authority. Famine threatened after two consecutive years of bad harvests, and all this, combined with the pull of peaceful and increasingly prosperous Lower Burma, led tens of thousands of families to cross the frontier into British territory in search of new beginnings.

Mandalay's reach in the Shan hills also withered away. There had long been signs of unrest, ever since Mindon's attempts to collect new taxes and British machinations to make secret contact with the local princes. Thibaw's decision not to take additional wives meant that he had not married any of the daughters or sisters of the tributary Shan rulers, as had always been done. This was seen as an insult, and the *sawbwa* of Mongnai, among others, refused to attend Thibaw's first durbar. Soon revenues from the Shan principalities, never great, fell to nothing, and from Mongnai rebellion spread eastward across the highlands. For six years thousands of Mandalay's best troops would be sent to put down the revolt, dying in the malarial forests, trying in vain to resurrect a long-dead empire. Meanwhile the British, having routed the Zulus and washed their hands of Afghanistan, were waiting in the wings.

Burma's very last opportunity to secure an independent future came and went in 1882. The government of William Gladstone had recently appointed the marquess of Ripon as viceroy of India, and Ripon was a man keen on repairing relations with Mandalay and seeking a just accord between the two countries. A convert to Catholicism, he was a man of liberal instinct who used his four years in office to include more Indians in the administration of the country. He had visited Rangoon the year before and told the mainly Scottish chamber of commerce that he was uninterested in war for profits and instead would seek to negotiate a new trade arrangement with Thibaw's court. A few months later Mandalay dispatched the lord of Kyaukmyaung to meet with the viceroy at the hill station of Simla, and in the cool, pine-scented air the Burmese envoy presented a long list of demands. This was not a good tactic by the Burmese, but Ripon was generous and understood the importance to the Court of Ava of a direct relationship with the British crown. He suggested two separate treaties, one a commercial treaty between Calcutta and Mandalay and another a treaty of friendship between Thibaw and Queen Victoria. There would also be agreements on the British Residency, the importation of arms, and the status of Burmese refugees. Accounts of what we today call human rights abuses were very much in the public eye, and Ripon also wanted a clause prohibiting further political executions, but Kyaukmyaung refused, saying this would amount to interference in the country's internal affairs.[26]

Finally, in August, the two sides agreed, and the envoy returned with the two treaties in hand, ready for signature. This was the very first opportunity the Burmese had for a relationship with London since Alaungpaya's missive to King George more than a hundred years before. It was what they had always sought. But Thibaw's government apparently thought it could do even better and did not realize how far Ripon had managed to shift official policy. Months passed, and there was no word. Then at Christmas a Burmese embassy arrived with two slightly amended treaties, one that included a clause on the extradition of Burmese refugees. Ripon refused. Mandalay's chance for survival was gone.

What followed was invasion, occupation, and the collapse of centuries of tradition. Burma without a king would be a Burma entirely different from anything before, a break with the ideas and institutions that had underpinned society in the Irrawaddy Valley since before medieval times. The new Burma, British Burma, would be adrift, suddenly pushed into the modern world without an anchor to the past, rummaging around for new inspirations, sustained by a more sour nationalist sentiment, and finally finding voice in the extremist years of the 1930s.

EIGHT

TRANSITIONS

In the late nineteenth and early twentieth centuries, British soldiers,
merchants, and officials create a colonial Burmese society
(and a story of my family during this time)

~~~~

PANTANAW

Sometime during the cold weather of 1909–1910 a young man in a small town not far from Mandalay came to acquire a reputation for feats of magic. It was rumored that he could disappear at will or become invulnerable to bullets and bayonets. He soon developed a spirited following, and this, together with his newfound fame and the encouragement of others, emboldened him to raise a standard of rebellion against the English occupiers and lay claim to the vacant Konbaung throne.

His rebellion was not to last long or to have much impact, except perhaps in the imagination of some of his countrymen. It came nearly a generation after the guerrilla campaigns of the post-Thibaw years and so seemed anachronistic, a throwback to an unsettling past. He and his little gang of coconspirators first attacked a nearby British police post, killing a couple of Sikh constables, and then rampaged for a while up and down a narrow strip on both sides of the Mu River. The predictable response was quick in coming. The rebellion was crushed, the royalist band was rounded up, and the magical young man himself, his powers having evidently left him, was sentenced to death and hanged in the courtyard of a British jail.[1]

Around the same time, and many hundreds of miles to the south, at the little town of Pantanaw, a well-to-do couple decided to name their first son Thant, the name of the erstwhile pretender. It was not an obvious choice. The new father, U Po Hnit, then in his late thirties, was the very picture of a loyal subject and part and parcel of the up-and-coming class of Anglophone professionals and businessmen benefiting most from British rule. As a teenager he had been sent to university in Calcutta and had returned some years later to take up a coveted job with the provincial civil service. This was in the early 1890s, only a few years after Thibaw's overthrow and the violent suppression of Upper Burma resistance. What role he played, if any, in support of the colonial authorities is not known. But he was posted at Yamethin, well within the boundaries of the old kingdom, and he would have been part of the new and unloved British Raj.[2]

U Po Hnit was my great-grandfather (on my mother's side), and he left the service only two years after joining. Perhaps he didn't like the work or perhaps he had qualms about serving the foreign occupation so directly. Either way, his decision had been made easier by the helping hand of his rich uncle U Shwe Khin, Pantanaw's leading businessman and landowner. Po Hnit's father had died fairly young, and his uncle had looked after him, paying for his expensive Calcutta education. Whatever disappointment the older man might have had about his adopted son's leaving the prestigious ranks of the colonial administration, he was now happy to bring him into the family firm.

Pantanaw stands at the heart of the delta, where the great river slowly branches out into hundreds of tributaries, a vast level expanse of light green paddy fields, just inland from the warm and salty air of the Indian Ocean. It is all new land, created over the past few centuries from the silting of the Irrawaddy, and covered in an incredibly rich stiff yellow clay, so rich that rice was grown broadcast without any need for transplantation. Tobacco and chilies are planted along the many little waterways. In the summertime, monstrous downpours drench everything in sight, and the weather is almost unrelentingly hot and humid. It was a place of some distinction. The town had once been very rich from fishing and trading in fish, and though this industry was now in decline (because of the silting up of the Pantanaw canal), it was still prosperous and growing fast. And it was in the jungles nearby that the king Tabinshweti had met his death while pursuing a white elephant, having lost his mind to drink during the heyday of the Portuguese adventurers.

For several hundred years the people of Pantanaw spoke Mon, the language of Pegu, until sometime after the civil wars of the eighteenth century. This had been the language of most of the delta until revolt and repression drove tens of thousands of people from their homes, many to the east toward Siam. It was then that new settlers, Burmese speakers, came from the north, and these were largely royal servicemen looking for a better life. They were hereditary rowers of the king's boats and were led by their chiefs. According to local tradition, they came from the riverbanks around Pagan and Nyaung-U and arrived shortly after Alaungpaya's conquest of the area in 1757. They came in great teak vessels of forty oarsmen each and settled not only in Pantanaw but in many of the surrounding towns as well.

They brought with them their *sandala* slaves, outcasts who dealt in death and burial. Within living memory there was a cluster of bamboo huts on the road leading to the main monastery, and all the people living there were believed to have descended from these original slaves of Pagan. Several hundred yards farther on, just to the north of the monastery itself, there is a wasteland, today overgrown with weeds, with a small cleared area around a huge fallen tree. It was here, say the townspeople, that an infamous dacoit in the earliest days of settlement was finally captured and tied to the tree before being stabbed to death. There are no Mon-speaking people left, though many who claim some Mon ancestry remain. But the pagoda of the town is seven hundred years old, long predating the Burmese conquest, and was built, according to folklore, by a visiting Singhalese prince, heartbroken after an ill-fated love affair with the daughter of a local Mon lord. They say his treasure, in gold, silver, amber, and jade, is still buried in the *tabana* within.

Though there were few, if any, Mon speakers left in the area, the Burmese at the turn of the last century were far from the only inhabitants of Pantanaw and the surrounding country. The majority of people in the surrounding villages were Karens, who spoke an entirely different language from Burmese and who had begun converting to Christianity in large numbers under the influence of American Baptist missionaries. Many had arrived recently as well, from the hill areas farther east in Burma. And there were also new arrivals of Indian descent, both Hindu and Muslim, including the first big wave of Chettyar moneylenders from the Coromandel coast.[3] Overall, the population had increased dramatically, and the town itself was then home to more than five thousand people.

This was true in much of the Irrawaddy Delta, which was transformed during these years.[4] Hundreds of thousands of acres of jungle, swamps, and marshes with pythons and crocodiles and wild elephants were cleared to create the world's number one rice-growing region. In the old days there was no export market for rice as the Burmese kings, worried about famine, had expressly forbidden any external trade; instead any surplus from the delta was shipped north up the river to the more arid parts of the country, where rice was often scarce. But the British had no such concerns. Rangoon's port facilities were rapidly expanded, and by the late 1850s rice production in the delta was expanding at an already phenomenal pace, made possible in part by waves of immigrants, like the boatmen from Pagan, coming down from the old kingdom to the north.

In the fifteen years up to 1860 the amount of land devoted to rice cultivation more than tripled to 1,350,000 acres. The American Civil War of 1861–65, which cut off the supply of rice to Europe from the Carolinas, fueled yet more demand for the Burmese crop. In 1869 the Suez Canal linked the Indian Ocean directly with the Mediterranean, drastically cutting the travel time between India and Europe and creating a permanent European market for Burmese rice. Rice was now the country's cash crop and by far the most important source of Burma's foreign earnings, replacing nearly all other important industry in the Irrawaddy Delta and in much of the rest of the province as well. In the twentieth century it fed the growing population of Calcutta as well as Indian plantation workers in the Straits Settlements. By 1930 no less than twelve million acres of land in Burma were devoted to rice, and out of a total production of nearly five million tons, two and a half million—worth over half a billion U.S. dollars today—were sold abroad. The Irrawaddy Delta had become a colonial society, with few links to the past, new immigrants, and, for a while at least, an air of economic optimism.

Po Hnit's own family was very much one of these colonial families, with almost no ties to the old kingdom, and from a mixed background, with both Muslim and Buddhist forebears. His grandfather had come to Pantanaw from Akyab in Arakan. A merchant who had done well in the early years of British rule, he had decided to seek his fortune in the delta. Though the town was prosperous, it was prosperous by the standards of the time. It had no electricity in 1909, and the only means of transport to neighboring towns or to Rangoon was by steamer or on land (in dry weather only) by bullock cart.

Po Hnit must have been something of an oddity as the only English speaker in Pantanaw. He had seen something of the rest of the world and now tried to keep a part of it. He built up a library of several hundred English books, no mean feat in a place as humid and moldy as the Irrawaddy Delta, and subscribed to no less than three English newspapers as well as weekly journals, sent down through the steamer service from Calcutta. He also received a copy of the Burmese-language newspaper *The Sun*, a politically influential paper of which he was an early backer and shareholder. In those days it was possible in a small isolated Burmese town to feel part of international learning and discussions in a way that wouldn't be possible later, perhaps not even with the advent of satellite TV (which Pantanaw still doesn't have).

He remained a bachelor for quite some time, settling down only in 1906, after he met and married Nan Thaung, a much younger woman (he was thirty-five and she was twenty-three), and together they had four sons in rapid succession. He traveled often to Rangoon and even took his beautiful young bride on a sort of belated honeymoon to India in 1907. They lived in a big two-story teak house set in a garden of jasmine, mango, and guava trees and under the shade of a giant tamarind. Grown fat and prosperous-looking, Po Hnit was doing well, helping manage his uncle Shwe Khin's diverse businesses and owning over a hundred acres of his own farmland as well as five houses around Pantanaw. He came to be seen not only as the rich and now-aging Shwe Khin's adopted son but as his natural successor. But others were making other arrangements.

In June 1922, just as the first of the monsoon rains came pouring down, the uncle, U Shwe Khin, died suddenly, apparently of a heart attack. Po Hnit's eldest son, Thant (my grandfather), was thirteen at the time, and years later he remembered the old man's gatekeeper knocking on the door at four in the morning with the news of Shwe Khin's death. Po Hnit rushed over to Shwe Khin's house, just a few doors down, only to find, to his great surprise, that his uncle had been dead since eleven the night before. Shwe Khin's wife had stashed away somewhere all the valuables in the house, including a fortune in diamonds as well as thousands of British pound sterling notes stuffed into empty tins of Huntley & Palmer's Golden Puff biscuits, a teatime favorite throughout the country. The diamonds and the cash alone were said to be worth at least a million rupees, the equivalent of perhaps ten million pounds today (about eighteen and a half million U.S. dollars).[5] The old lady had no children of her own. She did, however, have relatives.

The next day old Shwe Khin's unexpected death and the strange and suspicious behavior of his widow were the talk of the town. Friends of my great-grandfather began asking him why she waited so long to send him word of the heart attack and why she had removed all the valuables from the house. She of course denied that any valuables were missing. But when Po Hnit opened the two fireproof safes in the house (to which he had the keys), they were empty. A close friend of Po Hnit's had told him that just the week before he had sold some emeralds and diamonds to Shwe Khin.

The truth was not long in coming. Everyone in town (at least in my family's telling of the story) had seen Po Hnit as Shwe Khin's adopted son. In Burma, though, even under British rule, there was no practice of legal adoption or of leaving behind a will, and there were no legal documents to substantiate Po Hnit's relationship with his uncle or his rights to any of the family money or business. A few days later my great-grandfather was told that all the valuables and money had been given to a nephew of the widow. She was determined to keep everything and make sure that Po Hnit received not a rupee of the estate.

Po Hnit went to his solicitors in Rangoon at once and on their advice formally requested a part of Shwe Khin's estate. The lawyers told him that his chances were good and that he should be able to inherit at least some of his uncle's wealth. A strong legal case was prepared. Weeks and months passed, and eventually the matter was brought up before a district magistrate the following April. There was confidence it would be settled soon and fairly.

Then, just as the court proceedings were starting, and things looked as if they would go Po Hnit's way, he was suddenly stricken with a mysterious illness. My grandfather remembered his perspiring profusely. There was no proper hospital nearby, only a small ten-bed clinic, and the resident Indian doctor had no diagnosis. Within days Po Hnit was dead.

My great-grandmother Nan Thaung was left with no husband and four sons, aged four to fourteen, and a messy legal case on her hands. Her lawyers told her to press on. She wasn't sure; after all, she still had the houses and land her husband had owned himself. But Shwe Khin's widow now upped the stakes and served my great-grandmother notice for recovery of a huge sum of money allegedly lent to Po Hnit by Shwe Khin the year before. Nan Thaung felt compelled to continue.

At the district court my great-grandmother won hands down, both the original case and the new one for the alleged loan. She was set to receive a sizable amount of money. But Shwe Khin's widow appealed to the High Court in Rangoon and there, apparently by the bribing of a corrupt judge, everything was lost. My great-grandmother was left with almost nothing and with the expensive legal fees coming on top of the rest. She was forced to sell the land and all but one of the houses, the gardens with the mango trees, and even some personal possessions.

Up until this time Thant had lived a happy and comfortable life. He was an avid swimmer and in the past couple of years had taken a strong interest in English books and magazines, enlivening his classmates after school with tales of Stanley's search for Livingstone in the remote African jungle. When his father died, he was fourteen, and he made his first journey to Rangoon the following year (to go with his mother to the High Court), the very same time the Prince of Wales (the future King Edward VIII) was visiting as well; Thant saw the royal party making its way down one of the main thoroughfares of the colonial city. Edward was then accompanied by his cousin Lord Louis Mountbatten, later the viceroy of India. Few could have then imagined that Lord Mountbatten and the boy on the street from Pantanaw would meet decades later, both as international statesmen, in a skyscraper along New York's East River.

Thant's dream, what he talked to his father about, had been to become a civil servant in the British Burma administration. He wanted nothing more than to graduate from university and sit for the elite Indian Civil Service exams. But now there was no way. He had his little brothers and his mother to think about and four years at university was too long to be away; it was important that he find a job more quickly to support them. He decided to go only for a two-year intermediate course at Rangoon University. It wouldn't meet the requirements for senior government service, but it would be enough to pursue his new ambition, to become a journalist. He thought it was the right thing to do.

Thant was a serious student at university. His classmates remember him as "studious, quiet, tidy and neat but not expensively dressed." He had few very close friends but was generally outgoing and well liked; he was elected secretary of the University Philosophical Association and the Literary and Debating Society. He also began to write many articles and letters to local newspapers, including nineteen on the Simon Commission then investigating India's constitutional future. Influenced by his father, he was critical of colonialism but was equally critical of mindless anticolonial rhetoric, reserving his harshest judgment for those self-styled nationalists who he thought shied away from any real debate and were instead happy simply to blame the British for all of the country's ills.[6]

It was at university that Thant first met John Sydenham Furnivall, a onetime colonial officer turned anthropologist, who had left government to teach and write and encourage a generation of young Burmese students. He was to write seminal books on colonial Burma and Indonesia and introduced to the world the concept of a plural society (with Burma as the archetype), a society where different communities with different religions, cultures, and languages live side by side, but separately and in the same political unit.[7] He had a modernizing vision of Burma and knew the country intimately, being fluent in Burmese and having served long years touring hundreds of villages as a district officer in the 1890s and 1900s. He was probably considered an oddball by many of the other Europeans in Rangoon, being as interested as he was in the country and its history; in the late 1920s, in addition to lecturing at the university, he had set up his Burma Book Club. Thant was one of the club's main patrons and contributed often to the bimonthly magazine *The World of Books*, founded by Furnivall with one of Thant's younger brothers. Another of Furnivall's students was Thant's good friend Nu, who was to become the first prime minister of independent Burma.

Furnivall encouraged Thant to continue at university and compete in the civil service exams and said he would help make sure he received a good posting. Thant may have been tempted, but felt too strongly his responsibilities at home. He was also increasingly interested in pursuing writing as a career and thought he could do this from anywhere. And so, at the ripe old age of nineteen, Thant returned home and landed a position as senior master at the local national school.

The next many years were spent back at Pantanaw, in his family's old teak house under the shade of the big tamarind tree. New books were added to his father's library—Sidney and Beatrice Webb, Harold Laski and H. G. Wells, Bertrand Russell—and evenings were spent reading by candlelight, usually after a postprandial game of billiards at a house nearby. At age twenty-four, Thant won a nationwide Secondary Teachership Exam, and was made the youngest headmaster in the country. In second place was another denizen of Pantanaw, his own former English teacher K. Battacharya, a Bengali with a strong passion for Russian literature. He had introduced Thant and his other prize students to Tolstoy, Chekhov, and Gogol and was delighted to hear of his protégé's success. By chance, Thant's best friend, Nu, a few years older, was appointed the school's superintendent.

As a young writer in his twenties, my grandfather chose the pen name Thilawa, after a fourteenth-century swashbuckling nobleman best remembered for having laughed only three times in his life,[8] perhaps not for Thilawa's violent successes but for his reputation as a man of few words and calm disposition. Thant was apparently attracted to serious and somber men as opposed to the rowdy and colorful Burmese politicians who were making their names in those days. While some young Burmese looked up to Mussolini or Chiang Kai-shek, Thant's personal favorite was Sir Stafford Cripps, the severe and humorless Socialist lawyer and safe pair of hands, the man who would one day head last-minute diplomatic efforts leading up to Indian independence. It was an interesting choice of role model for a small-town Burmese headmaster.

He worked diligently to be a good teacher and taught history and English, his two subjects at university. His school was a so-called national school. It was different from the few government schools paid for by the British Burma administration and the private schools run by missionaries. The national schools were an outgrowth of protests in the early 1920s against colonial education policies; they received only minimal official funding and depended heavily on voluntary support. Their aim was to provide boys and girls with well-rounded educations and to instill in them a sense of pride in Burma and being Burmese. The Pantanaw National School was one of the few still surviving in the early 1930s, with about three hundred students in all, many of whom were too poor to pay any fees. Thant started out with a very modest salary of 175 rupees a month, and from this would routinely donate at least 40 or 50 rupees toward the upkeep of the school.

His wish to be a good teacher was more than matched by his desire to follow a career as a journalist. He wrote for his father's old paper *The Sun* and an English-language journal titled *New Burma* as well as a number of Burmese-language magazines. In Furnivall's *The World of Books*, he wrote a monthly editorial as well as an occasional column entitled "From My School Window." From the verandah of his wooden house, with wild orchids all around, set a few yards back from a wide dirt road and surrounded by the smells and sounds of the Irrawaddy Delta, he tried to connect to the wider world. He became the first Burmese member of the British Left Book Club and was proud of owning all the published works of Cripps as well as John Strachey, the Webbs, and George Orwell. He also wrote several books, the first being a translation of *The Story of the League of Nations—Told for Young People*.

It was a happy time, and in November 1934 he married my grandmother, Thein Tin, whom he had met two years before. The only daughter of a small-town lawyer, she was originally from Tada-U, near Mandalay. When her father died, she and her mother moved to Pantanaw, where they had relatives, and her mother became quite the successful businesswoman, owning and managing a very profitable cigarmaking firm. It had been a long and formal courtship, with my grandfather spending countless evenings with his future mother-in-law in a sort of yearlong interview. It was then that he picked up his cigar-smoking habit, becoming a chain-smoker until he was diagnosed with cancer at New York's Presbyterian Hospital in 1973. His first son died in infancy (child mortality rates were and still are shockingly high), but he and his wife had two more children in the 1930s, a son (who also died, but much later in a traffic accident) and a daughter, my mother.

The year my grandfather was appointed headmaster was the same year that the Reichstag made Adolf Hitler dictator of Germany and the year that Japan withdrew from the League of Nations and launched its ferocious campaigns on the mainland of China. In America, Franklin D. Roosevelt had just succeeded Herbert Hoover and was launching his New Deal to end the Great Depression. There were many signs of the instability to come, but few would have guessed that the violence and upheaval would soon devastate Burma as well. The Depression was already wreaking havoc on the lives of farmers across the Irrawaddy Delta. Within a few years the little town of Pantanaw itself would be burned to the ground and its people forced out as refugees, many never to return. Burma was ill prepared for what lay ahead.

NO MORE ROADS TO MANDALAY

The house was not difficult to find. It was a very large, rambling brick house in the pukka English style of the 1920s and 1930s, and the lawn was overgrown, the small side entrance to the compound almost entirely covered by long grass and weeds. A woman was bathing near a well in the back, a darkly colored sarong wrapped around her shoulders. A few big geese were feeding nearby. Just on the pavement outside, an old vendor sold bananas, and across the street a brand-new Chinese temple in bright yellow was being built, bamboo scaffolding propped up against the newly painted walls. It was the house of His Royal Highness Hteiktin Taw Hpaya, the eldest grandson of King Thibaw and Queen Supayalat and heir to the Konbaung throne, and I had come up from Mandalay to visit on Boxing Day 1997. Dressed comfortably for home in a pair of gray trousers and a red and black lumberjack flannel shirt, the prince warmly ushered me to a reception area just inside. A young, neatly dressed woman silently appeared with a tray of tea and biscuits.

We spoke for much of the afternoon. The prince was very charming and friendly, with a ready smile and a cheerfulness that made him seem much younger than his seventy-two years. He spoke with an old-fashioned British India accent and had been living here in Maymyo for much of his life at this house on Forest Road. Maymyo is a former British hill station, about a two-and-a-half-hour drive up a winding road from Mandalay, the place where European officials and their wives retreated during the hot months of March and April and tried to re-create what they could of home. It's named after a Colonel May of the Fifth Bengal Infantry (*myo* means "town" in Burmese). It was always cool, even cold at night, and in this pretend facsimile of English summer weather (without the clouds or the rain) the British had built mock Tu-

dor homes and a beautifully landscaped botanical garden, in large part
the handiwork of Turkish prisoners during the First World War. There
were (and are) fields of strawberries and gardens of larkspur, hollyhock,
and petunia and houses with names like Fairview and Primrose Cottage. The old chummery, or bachelor residence, of the Bombay
Burmah Trading Corporation is today a hotel, still with a huge fire-
place and hot baths and less than tempting roast beef and Yorkshire
pudding. The main street is like something out of a Wild West film except for all the people in sarongs, with horse-drawn carriages and
wooden shopfronts and the big Purcell Clock Tower at the very center.
Though the British have all left, many others who came in their wake
remain, including a strong Gurkha community, descendants of old Indian Army soldiers who decided to make this their new home.

The prince was familiar with people calling on him to discuss his
grandparents, the events of the 1880s, and the fate of the royal family.
He didn't seem at all displeased to talk about these things and instead
energetically waded into different topics. He said that his family had
wanted to repatriate Thibaw's remains from India to Burma after independence, but the British embassy had intervened and made sure it did
not happen. They were afraid, he said, that it would inflame anti-
British feeling.

The prince was keen in his relaxed way to explain how important
the royal family still was in the hearts of the Burmese people. He recounted a story from the 1960s or 1970s when he had been asked by the
army to appear at an anti-Communist rally in Shwebo, the capital of his
ancestor Alaungpaya, only never to be asked again to appear in public
after the strength of popular feeling that had been shown that day. He
was a man strangely dislocated, in his own country yet from an entirely
different Burma, both the Burma of royal times and the British Burma
of his boarding school years. When he saw how interested I was to talk
about the old dynasty and court, he gained an energy, a brightness.

He said that over the years many people, claiming to be doing research or writing a book, both Burmese and foreigners, had come to
visit him and he had lent them pictures and other mementos, but they
had never been returned. He mentioned an Australian man who had
come a few years back, taken some papers, promising to come back a
week later, but never did.

It was a way of explaining why he had very little to show. Still, he went into a back room and proudly brought out what he did have, a huge paper, all rolled up, with the genealogy of his entire family. He also brought out the few photographs he had left, including one of a wedding in 1922 that he said was the very last occasion which brought together members of the royal family and the surviving members of the court. The prince was most animated when talking about the restrictions on his life and the unfair way in which his family had been treated over the past century.

"You know, the British wouldn't even allow us to travel to Mandalay. We all had to live in Rangoon or places farther south. When I was a student in Moulmein, I was on the football team and my team was invited to play against St. Paul's in Mandalay. But you know what? The Brits told me I couldn't go!" He laughed but was bitter.

He said he had never really had a profession. For all his seventy-two years, he was, first and foremost, a prince of the deposed royal family. The short war of 1885, Randolph Churchill's hope that a Burma victory would help the Conservatives win the elections, Lord Dufferin's decision to abolish the monarchy altogether—these things had defined his entire life. I asked him what he had done earlier, say, in his twenties and thirties. Had he been able to work at all? "Well, I was quite into bodybuilding," he said, and laughed again. He still had a stocky frame. "This was my big thing. And so when U Nu was prime minister, he made me the head of the Council on Physical Fitness!"

My host's grandfather had arrived in India in early 1886, first at Madras and then at the muggy seaside town of Ratnagiri on the Konkan coast, just south of Goa. Thibaw was given a substantial house, and he and Supayalat had brought with them a number of servants, mainly young girls from the Kachin hills. Later he was allowed to build his own small palace, which still stands today, set on twenty-three acres of land on a promontory overlooking the green Arabian Sea, with teak finishings and Italian colored glass placed against the setting sun. They had also brought Supayalat's mother, but relations between the ex-king and the ex-Mistress of the White Elephant were not good, and the British presumably thought that after taking away his country and abolishing his throne, the least they could do was let him live apart from his mother-in-law. The old woman, once a formidable power at the Court of Ava, was eventually allowed to sail back to Burma, and she lived the rest of her days in seclusion on the beach at Tavoy.[9]

By all accounts Thibaw and his family lived a life of intense boredom. He seemed never to have accepted his fate and, hoping for some sort of improvement in his status, wrote several memorials to the viceroy. At the very beginning this amounted to a request to return to Mandalay and rule as a British puppet. This would of course have been more than acceptable back in 1880 but was now out of the question. In later times Thibaw's requests became more modest, asking, for example, to attend the 1905 durbar with King George together with the other Indian princes.

Money was a constant problem. Thibaw and Supayalat had brought with them precious stones as well as other valuables, which over the 1890s were almost all sold to local merchants. Their pensions were small. Again and again Thibaw petitioned his captors for more funds. They in turn worried that he was being irresponsible, and a number of tiresome attempts were made to better supervise Thibaw's spending, as if the former king were a young child with an allowance.

Thibaw led an immobile life. He wasn't, however, a prisoner in any normal sense. He had, by anything other than kingly standards, an impressive residence and staff and extensive grounds and even a car, a Model T Ford, which he could send on errands into town. His daughters and other members of his household were allowed to wander in the neighborhood, but apparently Thibaw and Supayalat did not or were not allowed to leave the immediate area around the house. But from the records of his British minders, he never asked to venture out and see things. He appeared singularly without intellectual curiosity or an interest in sports or other hobbies of any kind. His monastic training and early achievements as a Buddhist scholar were not borne out by any later requests for religious books (though Buddhist monks were often on hand for private ceremonies), and his physical activity was seemingly limited to his movements around the house. He also seemed to have few vices. Despite antebellum British propaganda to the contrary, he did not drink alcohol. His only soft spot was for fried pork, which he ate in generous amounts.

The royal couple had arrived at Ratnagiri with three young daughters (one had just been born en route in Madras), and Supayalat gave birth to another in their new home. In the early years of the century all

East India Company forces under General Sir Archibald Campbell land at Rangoon in 1824.
(The British Library)

A Burmese minister of state in military dress, together with attendants, during the First Anglo-Burmese War (1824–26). (The British Library)

The lord of Magwe arrives in Calcutta to discuss peace with the marquess of Dalhousie in 1854. (© CORBIS)

Thibaw and Supayalat, Burma's last king and queen, at Mandalay in the early 1880s.

The lord of Kyaukmyaung and other officials visiting the viceroy Lord Ripon at Simla in 1882.
(Picture Collection, The Branch Libraries, The New York Public Library, Astor, Lenox and Tilden Foundations)

British troops under General Sir Harry Prendergast at Christmas service in front of Thibaw's palace, soon after the capture of Mandalay in 1885. (© Hulton-Deutsch Collection/CORBIS)

My great-grandparents on my father's side, both children of court officials, after the fall of the kingdom.

My maternal grandfather, U Thant, at Rangoon University in 1927.

General Aung San in London for talks with Clement Attlee's government in 1947. (© Hulton-Deutsch Collection/CORBIS)

Burma's first post-independence prime minister, U Nu, in 1948. (© Hulton-Deutsch Collection/CORBIS)

Army chief General Ne Win (far left) and Burmese diplomats at the War Office in London in 1948.
(© Hulton-Deutsch Collection/CORBIS)

Aung San Suu Kyi (right) with my mother, Aye Aye Thant, at a party at our house in New York in 1970.

Burmese troops parading past the statues of long-dead kings in 2006. (AFP/Getty Images)

four were young women. In Burma, and at the royal court, an unmarried woman in her late teens or twenties or even older was not a strange thing. Spinsters were not uncommon, and many princesses never married by choice or for want of a suitable husband. But the late Victorian officials whose job it was to tend to the Burmese royals did worry. A list was produced with the names of unmarried Burmese princes. Thibaw dismissed everyone on the list, saying he knew them and they were all a bunch of good-for-nothings. Eventually the matter was taken up by the viceroy himself. Though the Burmese royal family was generally endogamous, it would have been in the contemporary Indian tradition to marry into another family of similar rank. As the Burmese were Buddhist, one possibility was the royal family of Sikkim, the tiny Himalayan state sandwiched between Nepal and Bhutan. The people were allied to the Tibetans and were Mahayana Buddhists. Close enough, the British must have thought. The crown prince of Sikkim, the future Chogyal, was approached. He agreed to meet with the two elder daughters. In the end he found them unsuitable, saying that their English was not fluent.

And then there was a scandal during the hot weather of 1906. The first princess became pregnant with the child of the Indian *durwan*, the gatekeeper. He was already married and with a family of his own. Everyone was shocked. But in the end it seems the British were more shocked than the Burmese. Thibaw and Supayalat soon reconciled themselves to the situation, and their first granddaughter became their new focus of attention. She was nicknamed Baisu.

Then something happened that the royal couple could not accept. The second princess, always known for being strong-willed, fell in love with a man named Khin Maung Gyi. He was Burmese and had served as a minor official at Mandalay. Here Thibaw drew the line. The father and daughter had a row. The second princess then left, to the house of Mrs. Head, the wife of the British district collector. When Thibaw heard what had happened, he ordered his car and driver to fetch the wayward princess. When the driver and the Model T Ford returned a while later, with no princess, the erstwhile king of Burma had a heart attack. Within weeks the last of the Konbaung monarchs was dead.

Thibaw was only fifty-six years old when he died in 1916. His death was barely noted at home, except within ever-shrinking aristocratic cir-

cles at Mandalay. One wonders what would have happened if Thibaw
had led a healthier life. At the start of the Second World War he would
have been eighty-one. Would he have become a king under the Japanese? Would he have outlasted the British and become the first head of
state of a newly independent Burma in 1948, sending his permanent
representative to the new United Nations at New York?

What did happen was that with the end of the Great War the British
relaxed their grip and allowed the various Burmese royals in India to return to Burma, though not to Mandalay itself. The first princess stayed
behind with her little daughter, Baisu, and slowly fell into poverty.
Baisu herself married and had a sizable family, with several children
and grandchildren, moved to the city, and merged into the great urban
poor of Bombay's slums. She was still alive at the beginning of the
twenty-first century, then in her late nineties, and journalists who went
to visit her spoke of her generosity and kind manners, a little picture of
Thibaw and Supayalat tacked onto the wall of her shack and a hint of
Upper Burman features being the only thing to distinguish her from
her neighbors.

The fate of the second princess is something of a mystery. Her sib-
lings (with whom she had no contact after her elopement) say that she
and Khin Maung Gyi had no children. Apparently, the couple wound
up at the hill station of Kalimpong, near Darjeeling, and bought a
dairy farm, where they lived out the rest of their lives in the cool pine-
scented air of the Himalayan foothills.

Supayalat returned with her two younger daughters and took a
house on Churchill Road, a winding, tree-lined road in one of the better residential areas in Rangoon, named for Lord Randolph Churchill,
the man who had overthrown her husband thirty years before.

Other royals were also exiled. British policy was to uproot the monarchy entirely and to ensure that the clan of Alaungpaya would never
again be a political force in Burma. Dozens were sent far to the south,
to Tavoy and Moulmein, and dozens of others were forced to go to India, where they were scattered in different cities and towns.

The prince of Limbin, for example, was exiled to Calcutta in 1887
and then to Allahabad along the Ganges River, a big bustling city and
the birthplace of Jawaharlal Nehru, the future prime minister of India.

Rudyard Kipling was then a traveling correspondent for the *Allahabad Pioneer*. Limbin was one of thirty-five children of Mindon's brother the prince of Kanaung. For a short while he had led his own rebellion in Burma, heading an alliance of dissident Shan chiefs; but he hadn't played his cards very well and ended up in India, like his cousin the ex-king, together with his wife and ten children.

His youngest daughter, Princess Ma Lat, was born in Allahabad in October 1894. She was sent to a good school there, learned to speak English fluently, and grew up to be by all accounts a beautiful and well-educated woman. When she was sixteen, she was introduced to the crown prince of Prussia, Wilhelm, who had stopped in Allahabad as part of his grand tour of India. As a close relative of King George's he was treated to many glitzy receptions, beginning in Ceylon and carrying on through much of the subcontinent. They had met at the Allahabad Club, where Limbin was a member. Afterward the crown prince (and future lover of Mata Hari) said that Ma Lat was the most striking woman he had met on his Eastern tour. With her charm and good looks, it was perhaps no surprise that another royal fell desperately in love with her—the heir apparent of Nepal, Prithvi Bir Bikram Shah Devand—and the two planned for possible marriage. But the story goes that the oligarchy of Nepal was set against the marriage from the start because Ma Lat was Buddhist, and soon the Nepalese prince died, aged thirty-six, some say by poison.

Only after independence were the royals allowed back to Mandalay. And there many of their descendants still live, in their own little society, often only their neighbors and close friends and descendants of some of the old aristocratic families aware at all of their ancestry. Thibaw's grandson told me that they had formed two organizations, a royal council for the immediate royal family (Thibaw's family), which he chaired, and a broader association for all those of royal lineage. But by the 1950s few actual princes and princesses were left, only their children and grandchildren, who, without special pensions or legal status, had become indistinguishable from the general population.

Some survived for a long time. The prince of Pyinmana, a son of Mindon's and half brother of Thibaw's, lived in Mandalay until his death in 1956, with his wife, a princess and a descendant of captured Siamese royalty. They had been fourteen when Prendergast's troops had marched into their homes, and they remembered going out onto the balcony to watch the British soldiers in their shining helmets and plumes. But both were resigned that the days of their family were long gone by. To the writer Norman Lewis, who visited them in the 1950s, the prince complained only about the lack of reading material and asked for a volume of Thomas Hood's poems from England.[10]

The prince of Pyinmana had been considered by the Japanese as a possible puppet during their occupation of the country during the Second World War; Pyinmana would have become like Henry "The Last Emperor" Pu Yi, for whom the Japanese created a new state in Manchuria. But it never happened, and the royal family sunk into oblivion. There was never a strong monarchist movement, and the nationalists were keen to look elsewhere for their inspiration, abroad and not to the defeated and somewhat sad House of Alaungpaya. There would be no turning back. But where to look for inspiration? The break with centuries of tradition had been so stark. How should the future be imagined?

FROM KINGDOM TO COLONY

Within fifty years of Thibaw's overthrow, not only were memories of royal government fading fast, but the society that had grown up over hundreds of years under kingly authority had been aggressively transformed. In Upper Burma, in the old royal domains, the traditional order had crumbled altogether with the capture of the king and the dismantling of his court. Mindon's reforms had begun the process, and in the countryside the gentry chiefs had steadily lost influence to new moneymen and court appointees. Many, especially those from the old crown service class, had seen their special status fading away and had headed south to British territory. Altogether hundreds of thousands of people in the late 1800s had packed up to make new lives in the Irrawaddy Delta, in the greatest single migration in Burmese history.

My father's family, from Mandalay, was not among those who headed south. At the time of annexation my great-great-grandfather Maha Mindin Kyawthu was a privy treasurer to King Thibaw, in charge of court records and valuables, one of many in the family whose entire lives were bound up in the inner world of the palace and the last of three generations of retainers and minor nobility that had served the Konbaung family since the 1760s. He was in his fifties when Prendergast entered the city, and had achieved the special designation of *pyinnya-shi*, or pundit, meaning that he was learned in the Burmese and Pali classics and advised on matters of court ceremony and precedence. Like many others, he was traumatized by the abolition of the monarchy and the violent imposition of English rule. All the things he had studied and lived for no longer existed. His brother Maha Mindin Minkyaw Raza, in charge of the now-defunct royal armory, was in a similar position and in no mood to stay on at Fort Dufferin or anywhere else in the old capital. Seeking employment in the new Raj was out of the question. Instead the two brothers and their families moved back to their ancestral home, about a day's carriage ride south, to the little sand-covered hamlets of Dabessway, to spend the rest of their days nostalgic for the old court and still dreaming of restoration.

This was a change of life and lifestyle repeated hundreds of times in those days, as the aristocracy and courtiers of Ava simply faded away into the dusty hinterland, a few court costumes never to be worn again and perhaps a photograph or two taken behind palace walls their only mementos of a vanished time.

Village life itself was also transformed. The old categories of *ahmudan* and *athi*, of who belonged to a founding family and who did not, of chiefs and their retainers, of the myriad regiments of royal servicemen and the many types of outcasts and slaves all dissolved into a new and undifferentiated pool of Burmese peasants. Salaried clerks and village headmen replaced the proud little courts of the hereditary gentry with their vermilion-painted gates and red and gold umbrellas. It had been a long time since the men of Upper Burma had been called away to distant wars, in Assam and Siam, but now families with generations of martial tradition were not even called up for guard duty at the palace. Buddhist monks also saw their role and status overturned. They had been the teachers of the country, and their monastic colleges had trained all the scholars of the royal court. The new government and Christian missionary schools had replaced them, undercutting for better or for worse the age-old tie between the Buddhist religion and education.[11]

Even things like ordinary dress and pastimes changed dramatically. Today some remark on how the Burmese maintain their native dress, in comparison, say, with their neighbors in Thailand. But today's dress,

a unisex sarong or *longyi* for both men and women, worn formally with
a white collarless shirt and short jacket for men and with a blouse for
women, is a fairly new thing and a product of British times. No self-
respecting man, at least in Upper Burma in the nineteenth century,
would have been caught in public wearing a *longyi*. Then men wore
long checkered *pasos* wrapped around their waists and then tucked under their legs, something like a dhoti in India, together with close-fitting
white upper garments, or long coats. And women wore *tameins*, slit up
the front to well above the knee, together with shoulderless and sleeve-
less bodices wrapped around the middle and short, tight jackets over.

All men also tattooed their bodies from their waists to their knees in
an indigo dye, the intricate tattoos set closely together so that from a
distance it seemed as if they were wearing tight blue trousers. This was
now quickly becoming a thing of the past, though in some rural areas
one could find old men tattooed in the traditional fashion until quite
recently. Men in the old days also kept their hair uncut and tied up in
a knot on the top of their heads, with white or colored pieces of cloth
wrapped around. By the turn of the century hair was cut short, in the
English way, and many (like my own great-grandfathers) sported mus-
taches in the European fashion of the times.

Old pastimes also disappeared. The pony races and boat races that
had enlivened village life, not to mention the much more elaborate festivals and equestrian events of Ava and Mandalay, were gone, as were
many (though not all) of the touring drama troupes once patronized by
the great aristocrats of the land. In their place came Hollywood and
later Bollywood films, football, and golf, the latter because of the large
number of Scots who were making Burma their home. A good golf
club remains de rigueur for any worthy Burmese town.

But the biggest change of all was the influx of new people, not just
the British, who were never more than a tiny fraction of the population,
but the Indians, who soon arrived by the millions.

THE LAST MUGHAL
(AND OTHER NEWCOMERS FROM INDIA)

In a mirror of Thibaw's exile to India's Konkan coast, the last emperor
of India, Bahadur Shah Zafar, was forced to live out his final years as
a British prisoner in Burma. The Mutiny of 1857–58 had ended with

the destruction of the three-hundred-year-old Mughal court at Delhi. Though the rebellion had first begun among the native soldiers of the East India Company, it had spread across the northern plains, drawing in others unhappy with British rule. The rebels had appealed to the octogenarian Mughal Emperor Bahadur Shah Zafar to lead them. When the tables turned and resistance to the British was crushed, the emperor and his family were taken away.

The old man had asked to be sent to Mecca. This was rejected. Many of the rebels had been sent to the sun-drenched Andaman Islands, but it was thought too dangerous to place him in close proximity to his erstwhile followers, and instead the ex-emperor was packed off to newly conquered Lower Burma, with the rest of the imperial family, including his son Prince Mirza Jawan Bakht, his grandson Prince Mirza Jamshed Bakht, Begum Zeenat Mahal, some ladies of the zenana, the Taj Mahal Begum (a second wife of the emperor's), and dozens of attendants, including the young princes' tutor, Hafiz Mohammed Ibrahim, traveling to Rangoon unceremoniously on a Mackinnon Mackenzie ship. Thus ended the career of the last monarch of the race of Timur and Genghis Khan.

In Rangoon, Bahadur Shah Zafar had few visitors. He was quite frail as well as sad, and his British captors had no interest in tempting him out of his isolation. Instead the ex-emperor, an accomplished Urdu poet and calligrapher, sat in his little house just to the south of the Shwedagon Pagoda, reflecting on the fate of his family and what he had heard about British reprisals in Delhi and elsewhere. Four years after arriving in Burma he was dead at age eighty-nine, having scribbled his own epitaph in the form of a ghazel: "How unlucky Zafar is! For his burial, he couldn't get even two yards of earth, in my beloved country." He was quickly interred in the same compound and in extreme secrecy in the hope that the exact location of his grave would never be known.

His descendants fared poorly, living on a meager government pension and otherwise ignored by the British Indian government. Prince Jawan Bahkt, the ex-emperor's son, was banished to Moulmein, though he was sometimes allowed to come to Rangoon to visit his family and was a celebrity at the Rahim Baksh kebab shop downtown. When Allied forces retook Moulmein in August 1945, a very old Mughal prince, presumably one of Jawan Bahkt's sons, came down from a hilltop house to collect his pension of twelve and a half annas.

Two other grandsons (from another of Bahadur Shah Zafar's forty-nine children), Princes Jamshed Bakht and Sikander Bakht, were born and grew up in Rangoon, becoming friends with members of the large and prosperous Muslim families from Delhi and Surat who were living in the city at the time. Jamshed Bakht went on to study at the American Baptist–run Judson College. He married a Burmese woman, and their son Mirza Muhammad Bedar Bakht was among the many refugees who fled to Calcutta at the beginning of the Japanese occupation in 1942. He never returned, remaining there to work in a bread factory and dying in poverty; his widow is still there today, selling tea on the pavement at Calcutta's Howrah Station.

The most unusual fate was perhaps that of the ex-emperor's grand-daughter Princess Ranauq Zamani Begum, who married an exiled Panthay prince (exiled after the failed Panthay Rebellion in Yunnan in the 1860s), mixing the lineages of Babur and Du Wenxiu, the erstwhile sultan of Dali. Others in the original entourage also settled in Rangoon, and in the heavily Muslim neighborhoods around the Surati Bazaar remain those who proudly claim descent from the retainers of the last Mughal.

The British hoped the emperor would be quickly forgotten. But today, nearly a century and a half later, Bahadur Shah Zafar is perhaps more celebrated than at any time since his capture by Captain Hodson at Humayun's tomb. In 1991 the Burmese and Indian governments agreed to build a grand memorial for him at the site of his confinement, and as workmen were laying the foundations, they stumbled on the emperor's hidden grave. A grand stairway now leads underground to his untouched tomb, covered in a green satin embroidered with gold peacock feathers. He is worshiped as a saint by many of the local Muslim community and the prime ministers of India and Pakistan come to pay their respects.

Bahadur Shah Zafar was not the first, and was certainly not the last, Indian to make his way to Burma during the years of the British occupation. He was perhaps the least willing. Millions of others made the passage voluntarily and often with great hopes for easy money or a better life. There had of course always been people moving between Burma and places across the Bay of Bengal. The country's foundation story, as we have seen, was of an Indian prince, forced into exile, who established Burma's first kingdom at Tagaung. Long before the

British conquest scholars and merchants from India had settled at Rangoon, Mandalay, and elsewhere. But by the early twentieth century Indian migration had become a flood, changing the smaller country forever.[12]

For many Indian families, Burma was the first America. It was the land of opportunity and new beginnings. Thousands of young men journeyed from Surat, Bombay, Lucknow, Karachi, Calcutta, Madras, and elsewhere to Akyab, Moulmein, and Rangoon to seek their fortune. Burma then offered more jobs and higher incomes, a dynamic economy, and a sort of frontier where anything was possible and lives could be remade.

Many were Nattukottai Chettyars from South India, Hindus well known (not just in Burma) for their financial dealings and business acumen. They were clever and hardworking. Their original home is a fairly dry and bleak area, not far from Madras, where poor agricultural conditions long ago forced the Chettyars to look to moneylending for a living. By the turn of the last century they had made their way out of India and had spread overseas to Ceylon, Java, and Malaya. And thousands had come to Burma, setting up shop all across the Tenasserim and the Irrawaddy Delta. In those days there was a wild scramble for land, and the task of clearing the land required a capital investment. Hardly any Burmese had money to spare, and the Chettyars stepped into the breach. They became the village moneylenders. In less than a generation many became rich.[13]

Many also came from nearby Bengal. Muslim families from Chittagong, once the port of the Mrauk-U kings, moved en masse into the western townships of Arakan, and in the rest of the province Bengalis, both Hindus and Muslims, arrived as doctors, clerks, schoolteachers, and lawyers, forming an essential part of the new urban class.

Other Indians arrived under less favorable circumstances as coolies and seasonal workers, many from Orissa, a very poor province of India just opposite the bay from Arakan, as well as Tamils from the Madras Presidency. At the beginning of the last century Indians were arriving in Burma at the rate of no less than a quarter million people a year. The numbers rose steadily until, in the peak year of 1927, immigration reached 480,000 people, with Rangoon exceeding New York City as the greatest immigrant port in the world. This was out of a total population of only 13 million, the equivalent of the United Kingdom today taking 2 million people a year. Some came only for a short time and returned home after making some money. But enough stayed so that each ten-year census showed a marked rise in the Indian-born proportion of the population.

In the early twentieth century Rangoon also became home to a vibrant Jewish community. Arabic-speaking Jews had been trading along the Burmese shore for centuries, but under British rule there was a much greater immigration of families, most ultimately from Baghdad and Isfahan, who had been living for a generation or more in India. The very first Jew known to settle in Burma was an officer in Alaungpaya's army in the 1750s called Solomon Gabriel. By 1898 there was a big enough Jewish population in Rangoon to build the Musmeah Yeshua Synagogue. A second synagogue was built in 1932, and by that time Rangoon had its own Zionist organization and even, briefly, a Jewish mayor, David Sophaer.

The Indian presence transformed daily life. In Rangoon, Indians made up over half the population, and nearly every city and town in the country became home to a significant pan-Indian minority, Tamils and Malwaris, Bengalis and Pathans, from street sweepers to big businessmen and government officials. Friendships and marriages between Burmese and Indians, both Hindu and Muslim, were common. By the early twentieth century Indian food (especially street fare like samosas), clothes (like today's ubiquitous *longyi*), and entertainment (both music and films) were part and parcel of urban life for all Burmese.

Immigration is always contentious, in any country. And for a country as small as Burma, taking on board so many new people would have been difficult in the best of times. But for it to happen under alien rule was bound to lead to ill feeling and hostility. It led to a break, which had never existed before, between Burmese and Indians, and a Burmese racism that combined feelings of superiority with fear. Superiority because many of the Indians whom Burmese people came across were unskilled workers, menials and house servants, wretchedly poor and willing to do any job. Fear because of the sheer numbers but also the business acumen and success of so many.

It also did something else. With the fall of the kingdom the number of people living in Mandalay declined considerably, and Rangoon became the preeminent city and the only really modern city in the country. And in Rangoon as well as in many of the larger towns—Akyab,

Bassein, Moulmein—the Indian immigrants became a majority of the population. More important, they constituted what was new in society. They occupied most professional jobs and formed the urban working class. The Burmese no longer had their kings and princes, soldiers and officials. And now they would not be the commissioners and judges, the businessmen and bankers, or even the shopkeepers and factory workers. What had been urban and cosmopolitan in old Burma had vanished. And what was modern in the new Burma was alien. When the British quit and the Indians were forced to go, only village Burma would remain.

THE CINDERELLA PROVINCE

Personally I love the Burman with the blind favouritism born of first impression. When I die I will be a Burman, with twenty yards of real King's silk, that has been made in Mandalay, about my body, and a succession of cigarettes between my lips. I will wave the cigarette to emphasise my conversation, which shall be full of jest and repartee, and I will always walk about with a pretty almond-coloured girl who shall laugh and jest too, as a young maiden ought. She shall not pull a sari over her head when a man looks at her and glare suggestively from behind it, nor shall she tramp behind me when I walk: for these are the customs of India. She shall look all the world between the eyes, in honesty and good fellowship, and I will teach her not to defile her pretty mouth with chopped tobacco in a cabbage leaf, but to inhale good cigarettes of Egypt's best brand.

—Rudyard Kipling[14]

For the British, Burma was always a backwater. There was really no plan for annexation or for what should happen after annexation, and once the 1885 general elections were done and over and Randolph Churchill moved on to other things, Burma faded as quickly from public view as it had emerged, a few more articles in *The Illustrated London News*, an occasional report of the continuing insurgency, and then little more until the Japanese took Singapore, and Burma lay on Tojo's march to Delhi.

It was never a place where great family fortunes or political careers were made. No one really remembers Fytche, Pharye, Sladen, Butler, or Dorman-Smith, not in Burma or in Britain. With changes in street names (Fytche Square is now Bandula Square), no one is even curious about who these men might have been. The only English person connected with Burma who is well known and whose connection with Burma is well known is Eric Blair (later George Orwell). While India evokes names like Hastings and Clive and images of bejeweled maharajas and Merchant Ivory costumes, Burma, through Orwell, is most poignantly remembered as a bad experience.

Burma was first and foremost a province of India. It was governed in the normal British Indian way, with a governor at the top and then a hierarchy of divisional commissioners, district deputy commissioners, and subdivisional officers running the countryside, in their pith helmets and sand-colored suits, dispensing justice and administering taxes from the verandahs of their teak bungalows or from little foldout tables under the shade of a big banyan tree. The British Indian legal system was grafted onto Burmese law, and at the secretariat in Rangoon, British officials and their Bengali clerks ensured that the rules and regulations of the empire were met and that a correct and steady flow of paper reached their superiors in Calcutta and at the India Office in Westminster.[15]

Many of the men who came out to fill official positions came out for an Indian career and often wound up in Burma accidentally or as a second choice. One of the few who chose Burma was George Orwell, who signed up for the Indian Imperial Police in 1922 and placed Burma as the top of his preferred places to serve. He said it was because he had relatives there (his family had a long history in Burma, and his grandmother and an aunt were still living in Moulmein).[16] But in general Burma was quite low on the pecking order, and a career begun in Burma never led to the senior echelons of the Writers Building or a seat on the Viceroy's Council in Calcutta. One imagines disappointed young men fresh out of public school and then Cambridge or Oxford, having chosen a life in India (or having tried for the Diplomatic Service or Home Civil Service and failed) being told that no, they wouldn't be going to the India of their imagination, to the North-West Frontier or the little villages along the Ganges, but to Burma, an entirely different country really and one hardly known back home.[17]

The exception were the merchants, mainly Scots, for whom Burma became a sort of home over several generations. By the 1880s the Scots were settling in for a comfortable stay and quickly built up a number of very successful firms. William Wallace of Edinburgh set up the Bombay Burmah Trading Corporation in 1863 and employed nearly two thousand elephants in the late nineteenth century as part of the company's very profitable logging business. George James Swan of Perthshire established the Irrawaddy Flotilla Company, which dominated inland Burmese transport, and William Strang Steel of Glasgow's Steel Brothers made a fortune from the country's rice trade. The similarly Scottish-owned Burmah Oil Company had its headquarters in Glasgow and around the turn of the century had monopolized the fast-growing oil production in Upper Burma. From their profits Burmah Oil later went on to create the Anglo-Persian Oil Company, better known under its present name, British Petroleum.[18]

By the early twentieth century the mix of British officials and businessmen and the growing tide of professionals, merchants, and ordinary workers from across the Indian Empire (including Burma) had made Rangoon a fairly vibrant and cosmopolitan, if workmanlike, city, surely not with the intellectual or cultural flair of contemporary Bombay or Calcutta, but a city that could still compare well with most others in the Far East.[19] There were hotels like the Strand, considered one of the best in Asia, banks like Lloyds, travel agents like Thomas Cook, department stores like Rowe and Co., offering the most up-to-date goods straight from London, and nightclubs like the Silver Grill, owned by the American restaurateur Peter Artoon, complete with 1940s crooners and black-tied waitstaff, and destined to be a favorite of American airmen in the months before the war.

Rangoon even became connected by air. In 1933 Imperial Airways began flying its new Armstrong Whitworth AW15 Atalanta planes directly from London to Akyab as well as to Rangoon, as part of a much longer route all the way to Sydney. Described as "the fastest and most luxurious aircraft designed and produced for the tropics, with ample room for passengers to walk about and chat and to enjoy refreshments," the little propeller planes dramatically cut travel time from the U.K. to Burma by more than two weeks. It still took ten days (!) with all the stops (London, Paris, Basel, Genoa . . . Baghdad, Basra . . .), but at least Rangoon was firmly on the map.

Rangoon society, meaning Rangoon European society, centered, as everywhere in the empire, on the clubs. And "European" was a term used in colonial settings in a racial sense and used in contrast with

"Indian" or "Burmese." There were several clubs, and the three most exclusive were the Pegu Club, the Rangoon Gymkhana, and the Rangoon Boat Club, all in leafy surrondings, with manicured lawns and liveried Indian servants. The Pegu Club even gave the world one of its favorite cocktails in the 1920s and 1930s, made with gin, Cointreau, lime juice, and bitters on crushed ice. The membership was confined almost entirely to senior officials, army officers, and leading businessmen, and the Pegu Club at least never allowed a single Burmese to join.

> *When I was young and had no sense*
> *In far-off Mandalay*
> *I lost my heart to a Burmese girl*
> *As lovely as the day.*
> *Her skin was gold, her hair was jet,*
> *Her teeth were ivory;*
> *I said, "For twenty silver pieces,*
> *Maiden, sleep with me."*
> *She looked at me, so pure, so sad,*
> *The loveliest thing alive,*
> *And in her lisping, virgin voice,*
> *Stood out for twenty-five.*
> —George Orwell, 1925

And there was the issue of Burmese women. Burma had a reputation for "rest and recreation," and the preponderance of British Residents there kept Burmese mistresses. In 1890 there was a halfhearted attempt to end this practice, and the chief commissioner, Sir Charles Crosthwaite, sent out a confidential circular calling for an end to these relationships. That weekend at the Rangoon Turf Club, one horse was named CCCC (for the Chief Commissioner's Confidential Circular), and another Physiological Necessity. Sir Charles later admitted that "what cannot be done in England ought to be equally impossible in Burma."[20]

The habit of taking mistresses became a sore point in relations between the British and the Burmese. It also gave rise to a quite substantial number of people of mixed ancestry; by some accounts the Eurasian or "Anglo-Burmese" population in British Burma was equal in size to the "Anglo-Indian" population in all the other Indian provinces put together. Many went into government service, in particular the police, and Anglo-Burmans largely ran the railways. The end of the British rule led also to their sudden demise, like so many other communities, with thousands migrating to Australia and elsewhere in the Commonwealth, though some stayed on, taking Burmese names and largely assimilating into the majority community.

Another sore point was simple racism and the day-to-day treatment of Burmese (and other non-Europeans) by the British Resident in the country. There were never that many British people in Burma, many less than, say, in Malaya, as a portion of the population, and the ordinary person would probably live his or her life without ever coming across an authentic representative of the Raj. For some who did, the experience was pleasant enough, and there were indeed friendships and marriages across the racial divide. But what seems much more common was at least the sense of ill-treatment and humiliation, not simply from the fact of living under foreign occupation but through everything from perceived slights to outright brutality.

It could be a small thing. For my grandfather U Thant, a person who grew up with a deep admiration for English culture, one incident stood out in his memory. He was in his early twenties and sitting on a bench in Rangoon waiting for a ferry to take him back to Pantanaw. Neatly dressed and minding his own business, he felt the tap of a cane on his shoulder. He turned around and saw an elderly Englishman and his wife. The man said nothing, though the wife seemed a little embarrassed. My grandfather got up and left. He didn't say a word, not then and not to anyone for decades. But it stuck in his mind. For U Tin Tut, a graduate of Cambridge, a senior civil servant, and an officer in the First World War, it was an episode at the Gymkhana Club in 1924. The club was unable to field fifteen for a rugby match. Knowing that Tin Tut was a good player and under pressure from the governor to open its doors a little wider, the team asked if he would mind playing. He was happy to and played well. But afterward he was told in no uncertain terms that he was not allowed to shower with the rest of the team.[21] Twenty years later Tin Tut happily threw in his lot with the young nationalists determined to end colonial rule.

All of the profit making and the comfortable expat careers relied on a modicum of law and order, and for this the British rulers created an ironfisted web of police, surveillance systems, courts, jails, beatings and whippings, and, as a last resort, the British and Indian armies. Despite this, even in the heyday of the Raj, say, in the 1910s and 1920s, the country was never really settled. There were dacoits, or armed gangs of men, attacking villages and robbing travelers, and the province was notorious for danger and lawlessness. By the 1930s its rate for thefts alone was nearly four times that of the average for India. In 1940, of a population of around ten million, there were over seven hundred murders, comparable to the homicide rate of a major American city in the 1990s. There were differing interpretations for why this happened. Some Burmese believed it had to do with the decline of monastic education and related ethical training. Others blamed the sudden breakdown of traditional social structures, the lack of colonial legitimacy, or the effects of the sudden immigration of hundreds of thousands of people, including those with criminal backgrounds. For most British it all meant that the Burmese really were in no position, at least for now, to govern themselves. British rule might have its problems, but to paraphrase Monty Python, "Who else could run a place like this?"

There was also always a clear distinction between the Burmese and peoples in other parts of the Indian Empire, the Indians. Kipling, who actually only spent part of one day in Burma and never went anywhere near Mandalay, was far from the only one to emphasize a difference. H. Fielding Hall, a onetime civil servant, wrote in his tellingly titled A People at School:

> In India, I think the most pervading impression that one receives is of its immense sadness. The people seem always to be fighting against starvation, which is very near. The thin cattle, the starved dogs, the skinny fowls, the whole hard landscape is imbued with the same tragedy of life . . . There is an oppression, a weight, as if life were a weariness and a disillusion terribly spent trying to hold at arm's length disease and want and death . . . In Burma all is different. The people seem young. They are never old. Life comes to them always as a pleasant thing. It is worth living. It is to be passed through with a laugh and jest, not to be taken too seriously. The people seem all happy, all well to do, as if the wants of life were easily fulfilled.[22]

Other Europeans picked up the same theme. Said the visiting Frenchman Joseph Dautremer:

> The Burman neither flatters nor cringes. He is usually very lively and overflowing with high spirits, full of banter and quizzicality. He is never cast down by bad luck and never overcome by abundant riches; sometimes he heaps together a fortune, but it is not a common occurrence, for he lives from day to day and takes very little care for the future. He has no idea either of discipline or perseverance, but he is very whimsical and very independent. His character does not fit him for regular and permanent work, and he will even give up the wages which are due to him if he gets tired of his place and thinks he would like to take up something else.[23]

By the early twentieth century past images of Burma, of a corrupt and brutal Oriental tyranny, bound up in ageless custom, had given way to a lighter, less serious picture of a childlike and happy people, not particularly hardworking or well disciplined but with many attractive qualities and a welcome sense of individuality and independence. There was not really a counterpart to the hated Bengali babu or to the romanticized virile fighters of the Khyber Pass. To some extent the British looked backward for the sort of Burman they liked, someone like Maung Hlwa, Thibaw's governor of Ava—"an official of the good old Upper Burma type. Not overeducated, without delicate scruples, of proven courage, with boundless personal influence"—someone they could work with and who wouldn't make much of a fuss. But these kind of men, they thought, were now few to be found.[24]

All these interpretations of the Burmese character are important because they've proved long-lasting and have deeply influenced Burmese self-perceptions. For the British it meant that Burma was not a very important place and that there were few serious policy choices to be made. A benign neglect was no bad thing. More than half a century after they were made, General Ne Win and his Revolutionary Council used the same characterizations to make the argument that the Burmese were not suited for democratic government and that for all the good things about them, they needed to learn discipline and teamwork. Life came too easily to the Burmese, and they had to work harder, learn to do things for themselves; they didn't need to be too educated but had to be tough. Though there may be other, more local roots of this thinking, the colonial influence is the most obvious. Some British observers called Burma the Cinderella Province, beautiful and ignored compared with its sisters, Madras, Bengal, and Bombay, a Cinderella perhaps for whom the shoe never fitted.

The British did not have only the Burmese to think about. The borders of the province were drawn without clear criteria and were more or less accidents of Anglo-Burmese history and the three wars of the nineteenth century. More or less all of the old kingdom was incorporated into the new province of British Burma. But British Burma also included other areas that had never been part of royal administration. These were mainly the highlands that surrounded the Irrawaddy Valley, one of the most linguistically diverse places in the world, home to hundreds of languages and mutually unintelligible dialects and to an array of often proudly independent cultures, each nestled in its own little mountain niche. Not surprisingly, it's these very areas that have been the primary site of the country's armed conflict for the past forty years.

The various parts of the country were administered separately, less of a divide-and-rule policy and more of a cheap and easy policy. After Thibaw's overthrow the men on the spot found that the low country (the Burmese areas) was traditionally ruled by hereditary chiefs, but that the authority of these chiefs had weakened in recent times and that in any case many were actively leading the resistance against them. They would be of little use, and their power and position were broken within a generation. In the highlands, though, and in particular in the Shan hills to the east, there were hereditary chiefs of a different nature—the *sawbwas*—who were much less directly ruled from the Court of Ava and were still very much in charge of their own domains. The cheap and easy thing to do was to keep them in place, organize them properly, and simply let them carry on as before, provided they accepted British suzerainty and the occasional guidance of the superintendent of the Shan States, based at a little hill station nearby.

Different still were the various peoples of the mountain regions. The Kachins, for example, were a medley of people who lived in the far north, just below the Himalayan range. They were never part of the Burmese government system and in the late nineteenth century had taken to raiding and looting frontier towns like Bhamo along the China border. They eventually accepted British overlordship, and American missionaries converted nearly all to one form of Christianity or another.

The few British army men and officials who spent time in the hills liked the people they found, perhaps not surprisingly as they were usually outdoor types happy not to have desk-bound jobs. They decided that the Kachins and others were "martial races" along the lines of the Gurkhas in Nepal or the Pathans of the North-West Frontier and good soldier material. Though the Kachins and other upland groups were only a tiny fraction of the population (perhaps 2 percent), they became the majority of the army in Burma. In this scheme the Burmese themselves, the people who had actually conquered by fire and sword half the Southeast Asian mainland, were seen as not martial enough and left out. It was a policy choice that rankled deeply in the Burmese imagination, eating away at their sense of pride and turning the idea of a Burmese army into a central element of the nationalist dream.

It was the British also who began to think carefully about where the Burmese "came from" and how they were related to other peoples. The late nineteenth and early twentieth centuries were the heyday of race theory. Ethnology was born as a colonial enterprise, and there were energetic attempts to categorize the peoples of the empire and understand how ancient migrations and more recent history might have led to their current conditions and characteristics. Though there were genuine attempts at science, much was also a way to show how the English were on top. Some ideas did not seem to have much supportive evidence at all. In the 1901 Census, for example, an essay by one Dr. McNamara, entitled "Origins and Character of the Burmese People," proposed a common ethnic origin of the Irish and Burmese, through Cornish tin miners who had sailed east.[25]

Other ideas, more long-lasting, were based on existing Burmese notions of race and caste. The scholars and pundits of the Court of Ava had over time produced numerous systems for classifying the people of the world, with five overarching classes, each with its own subclasses: the Burmese themselves; the Chinese; the Mons; the Shans or Thais; and the *kalas*. The *kala* traditionally referred to all the peoples to the west—the Indians, Persians, Arabs, Europeans, and so forth. The

British picked up some of these ideas and merged them with the new study of comparative languages.

By the turn of the century the idea of language families had become well known and well accepted. The eighteenth-century Calcutta judge and polymath Sir William Jones, who had mastered thirteen languages and knew twenty-seven others "reasonably well," had long ago proposed an Indo-European language family, one that connected many living Indian and European languages, including English, with Sanskrit, Latin, and Greek and traced them all to a common, now dead, source. Now all the languages of the world were being clumped together into families, with the idea that they derived from a single proto-language that had become fractured and dispersed through ancient and modern migrations. Burmese and Arakanese were placed within the Tibeto-Burman family, whereas Mon, the language of Pegu, was considered entirely separate and related to Cambodian. Shan and its near relatives Thai and Lao were also set apart, and in this way the notion developed that all the various peoples of Burma were of different origins and came to the country at different times. Language and ethnicity became closely linked.

The British also liked the idea of chaotic and sweeping migrations, in the manner of the barbarian hordes of the Dark Ages, having peopled Burma in aeons past. According to Sir James Scott, in his authoritative *Burma: A Handbook of Practical Information*, "there poured swarm after swarm of Indo-Chinese invaders, crowding down from North-western China, from Tibet, the Pamirs, and from Mongolia, following the course of the great rivers . . . the first invading horde was that of the Mon-Hkmer [sic] sub-family. These were followed by the Tibeto-Burmans who drove their predecessors before them — many up into the hills . . . Upon these warring bands there came down finally the peoples of the Siamese-Chinese sub-family — the Karens and the Tai, or Shans — who crushed and thrust and wedged themselves in where they might." The practical handbook continued: under British rule "bands are still poured from the teeming loins of the frozen north," but "they are marshaled like the orderly queue entering a public meeting."[26]

These are ideas now firmly rooted in people's imaginations; I remember visiting in 1989 a rebel camp belonging to the Mon National Liberation Army and being told how the Mons were a "Mon-Khmer" people, entirely different from the Burmese. For the Burmese it tended to increase their sense of difference from other groups in the country and perhaps make harder the emergence of a single national identity.

So what did all this mean? Thibaw's court had vanished, and there was no going back to the old ways. The old aristocracy had quit government service, content for now to harbor quietly its resentments and frustrations while merging every day into ordinary village life. In places like Pantanaw, many benefited from the peace and prosperity of early colonial times, anxious only to enter the new and dynamic modernity showcased for them in Rangoon. But the new and dynamic modernity was resolutely alien, uncompromisingly British at the top and with an assortment of Indian communities, energetic and entrepreneurial, creating the country's new urban class. Soon a powerful ethnic nationalism, based narrowly on the idea of a Buddhist and Burmese-speaking people, one that saw little need to accommodate minority peoples, took root. At the center of this nationalism would be a desire for a new martial spirit.

NINE

STUDYING IN THE AGE
OF EXTREMISM

*Modern Burmese politics and Burmese nationalism come of age
in the 1930s and a generation of anticolonial leaders are
seduced by the militant ideologies of the time*

~~~~~

S oon after the Great Mutiny was crushed in 1858, the British government decided to establish direct rule over its Indian possessions. The East India Company, which had governed the expanding empire since its earliest beginnings in Surat and Madras more than two hundred years before, amassing fortunes and making war, was dissolved, and Company territory from Rawalpindi to Moulmein and seven hundred princely states from Kashmir to Cochin were transferred to the sovereign rule of Victoria as the new empress of India.

It was in the decade that followed that there emerged new Indian leadership, later with names like Gandhi and Nehru, that would eventually challenge colonial rule and show the way to independence. On a cool December day in 1885, just as the Burmese kingdom was about to be annexed to British India, seventy-three lawyers and educators and other professional men met in Bombay to found the Indian National Congress. They all were part of an up-and-coming well-to-do middle class and desired a better future for themselves in a new and modern India. The congress had no special ideology and no base of popular support and in the early years met simply to express support for the Raj and pass fairly harmless resolutions on nonthreatening issues, like civil service reform.

But things began heating up in the early years of the twentieth century. In 1905 the viceroy, Sir George Nathaniel Curzon, divided the province of Bengal for what he said were reasons of administrative efficiency, but this inflamed Bengali opinion makers, the most vocal and politically articulate in the empire, who suspected a clear-cut divide-and-rule tactic. A cycle of unrest and repression followed. After a long period of relative quiet, Indian politics had lurched toward violence and less patient desires for self-government.

The British reacted in part with limited reform, reuniting Bengal and including more moderate Indians into the workings of the colonial administration, but also with what they regarded as a proper Oriental spectacle. At the end of 1911 the king-emperor, George V, visited the country for a grand durbar in the old Mughal seat of Delhi, appearing before a vast, gorgeously costumed and impeccably choreographed audience of eighty thousand princes and virtually every person of note in the Indian Empire, all there to pay obeisance to their sovereign in person. With a background of bespoke music by Sir Edward Elgar, Victoria's grandson bestowed honors and titles on the assembled maharajas and nawabs, wearing a specially designed crown and acting his role as the heir to the House of Babur.

It was an opportune time to try to cement a degree of loyalty from the empire's Indian subjects, for in three years the Indian Army, all voluntary, would be sent out to fight in every major theater of the First World War, suffering over forty thousand dead and sixty thousand wounded on battlefields from Flanders to Mesopotamia. This was an immense sacrifice and naturally made Indian politicians more confident in their demands for self-government. In December 1916, just after the battle of the Somme had left a million casualties and in the months before the Russian Revolution, a joint session of the Congress Party and its eventual foe, the Muslim League, met at Lucknow to demand constitutional change. A formal pact was agreed upon. The British felt compelled to respond, and the following summer the government in London announced a new policy of eventual home rule within the British Empire.

In 1919 Secretary of State for India Edwin Montagu and the viceroy, Viscount Chelmsford, introduced legislation that gave considerable authority to partly elected provincial councils. It was a system called dyarchy. Some government departments like agriculture and education were placed under ministers responsible to these new councils. But others, including the really important ones like finance and home affairs (which controlled the police), were kept under officials appointed by the (usually British) governor.

For some in India this was far from satisfactory. But at least there was some change and some discussion of further reform. But one part of the Indian Empire was to be deliberately left out of the change process altogether: Burma. In British eyes Burma was "the most placid province in India,"[1] and no political reform there was expected or required. The British Parliament's joint committee on Indian constitutional reform said: "Burma is not India. Its people belong to another race in another stage of political development, and its problems are altogether different . . . The desire for elective institutions has not developed in Burma . . . the problems of political evolution of Burma must be left for separate and future consideration."[2] It was to be a rude shock.

CAMBRIDGE, 1905

By the First World War a new generation of English-educated Burmese had grown up, uncertain of their place in the world and far less politically experienced than the professional classes in Bombay and Calcutta, but increasingly anxious not to be left behind. One of them was a young lawyer named Ba U, who would one day become president of independent Burma.[3]

In 1905 Ba U, two of his cousins, and a friend were on their way to a new life as university students in England. They traveled on the SS *Herefordshire*, a plush passenger ship of the Bibby Line, which took them from Rangoon to Liverpool via Colombo, the Suez Canal, and Marseilles. But as soon as the big ship set sail and they left Burma for the first time, they were not happy; they felt they were being discriminated against. Alone among all the passengers, their cabins were at the aft of the steamer, next to the ship's surgeon's rooms and close to the lavatories. They protested to the chief steward, who laughed. At dinner they were given a little table in the corner and were served by a steward from Goa, while they noticed that all the white passengers were waited on by white stewards. They had tried to live up to English standards and had gone out of their way to find the best European tailor in Rangoon. But when the ship's surgeon saw them for the first time in their new suits, he snickered as well. Their coats were too short, their trousers were too tight, and they had put on caps that were too small for their heads. "We looked liked dressed-up monkeys." The tailor knew they were just Burmese students and hadn't bothered to do a proper job. It was the start of a difficult few years.

Ba U was a young man proud of his family background. He was descended from a princess of the old royal house through her son the lord of Henzada. Henzada had run afoul of court intrigues around the middle of the nineteenth century and had run away to British territory. Like many other aristocratic families at the time, Henzada and his children made the transition from grandees at Ava to members of a small but increasingly prosperous middle class. Ba U's grandfather joined a Scottish rice-trading firm and married the daughter of another displaced nobleman. His father became a deputy commissioner, one of very few Burmese at the time to make it into the ranks of the official elite; his uncle was to be one of only four Burmese granted a king's commission after the First World War. On his mother's side, Ba U was part of an important local family that had, for generations, supplied magistrates and governors for the towns of the Irrawaddy Delta. He had gone to school in Maubin, next to Pantanaw, and then to University College, Rangoon, where he studied hard and won a place at Cambridge. It was his dream and his parents' dream. To the extent that there was an Anglicized class expected to be loyal to the empire, Ba U was part of it.

He was an undergraduate at Trinity Hall and found lodgings at Portugal Place, a tiny lane of white brick houses very close to the center of town. The other lodgers were English, and Ba U was the only Asian, and at first he excused the disdain they showed toward him as they were "members of the well-known ancient families of England." But he grew increasingly agitated. He was made fun of in the hall. "A senior student, named Seymour, came toward me, fixed a monocle in his right eye, and stared at me as if I were a being from another planet. The students who were standing nearby burst out laughing. I felt so insulted and humiliated that I wished I could have been swallowed up by the earth." After continued provocations, he eventually confronted Seymour, grabbing him by his lapels and physically threatening him, and Seymour, apparently unused to having a colonial protest, quickly backed down. But Ba U was to have other problems.

He was invited to dinner at the home of an English family and brought with him little gifts from home. But he was, in his own words, "flabbergasted" when the young daughter of the host asked him, "Do you all eat human flesh?" "My spirits fell. I could not answer the question straight away. I simply stared at the girl. What made me feel sad was that we should be placed in the same category as the African." The mother tried to save the evening. "No, they are civilized, just like us, you're thinking of the Africans." Cheered by that clarification, Ba U then took the offensive, describing Burma's conquests of Siam and telling the Cambridgeshire family that the Shwedagon Pagoda had been built twenty-four hundred years ago, "when some Europeans were still roaming about the forests."

Sensitive to discrimination and rejected by the mainstream of Cambridge student life, Ba U hoped that the Burma of his imagination was at least superior to what he knew of Africa and prehistoric Europe. He began to be political as well. There were other Burmese students in Cambridge in those days, actually more in those years than there would be at any time before or after, and they decided to form a group, the Burma-Cambridge University Club, one of the very first modern Burmese associations.

In a room at King's College, Ba U and about two dozen others met once a week or so, to debate topics like "The republican form of government is better than the monarchical form" and "Traffic in opium in Burma is harmful on both the morale and health of the people." They spoke in English, rather than Burmese. Some of the club members also began debating a growing circle of other Asian students, from India, Ceylon, Siam, and Japan; but many were unhappy with their lives and what they understood as their prospects. One of them was Chan Tha, a young man from a well-known and very wealthy family who was reading law at Downing College. Over time the stresses and strains of living in England, the perceived slights and discrimination unnerved him. He began pacing up and down the corridor at his hall and muttering to himself. He said to Ba U, "I hate these damned white men. They treat us colored people like dirt and vermin." Ba U told him that they needed to return to Burma and to lead their country to freedom; only then would the Burmese be treated with respect. But for the would-be Downing College lawyer, it was too late. One summer day Chan Tha went out to the seaside near New Forest, sat down on the beach, and put a bullet through his head. The law student left behind a note: "I am very unhappy because I shall never in this life reach the woolsack."*

---

*The "woolsack" refers to the seat of the Lord Speaker in the UK House of Lords.

Even for the Burmese of this class, with the money and position to attend university in England, who had the best chance of securing a good life under the colonial sun, British rule still seemed like a dead end, the choicest jobs within sight but beyond their grasp. For others the frustration was much greater.

At about eleven in the morning on Easter Monday 1916, in the middle of the Great War, hundreds of armed and determined men and women belonging to the Irish Volunteers and the Irish Citizen Army set out to occupy key buildings in the middle of Dublin: the General Post Office, Boland's Bakery, the Four Courts, Jacob's Factory, the South Dublin Union, St. Stephen's Green, and the College of Surgeons. Though their initial actions met with virtually no resistance (British intelligence having failed), the uprising was to last only a few days. The Post Office was the center of their resistance and was briefly declared the headquarters of the Irish provisional government.

But Dublin Castle remained in British hands throughout, and over the coming days the British gathered reinforcements as well as intelligence about Irish strength and strategic positions. By 28 April the rebels, never numbering more than sixteen hundred, were facing upward of twenty thousand soldiers. The Post Office was cut off and then came under an enormous artillery barrage that left much of the city center in ruins. The uprising collapsed. It had not enjoyed any widespread popularity, but the British reprisals that followed, in particular the executions of Patrick Pearse and other nationalist leaders, increased sympathy for the militant cause. Three years later Sinn Fein declared an independent Irish government at Dublin. Sinn Fein was backed by the new Irish Republican Army, convinced that only violence would lead to change and led for a while by the youthful and charismatic Michael Collins. It was a guerrilla war this time, not an all-out insurrection like that in 1916, and included targeted assassinations against police and intelligence officers. By the end of 1920 London was ready to compromise. An Irish Free State was created in the southern part of the island, fully self-governing and with the status of a dominion, like Canada or Australia. Only the six counties in the north stayed part of the United Kingdom.

The Burmese, for one, were fascinated. They, like many others, believed that Sinn Fein had masterminded the action from the start, and from then till today Sinn Fein and the cause of Irish Republicanism remain high in the pantheon of Burmese nationalist thinking. The Burmese were looking in all directions for inspiration and guides to future action. The short-lived revolt of the pretender Maung Thant in 1909 was the next-to-last anti-British effort that looked backward for models and a restoration of monarchy as a goal.

Around the same time that the Burma-Cambridge University Club was being formed, men of similar background and thinking were setting up political associations back home. In 1906 a Young Men's Buddhist Association, mimicking the YMCA movement, was created and was led by the Arakanese Cambridge graduate and onetime London barrister U May Oung.[4] But in general the Burmese were bored with lawyerly associations and polite petitions and wanted action, like the IRA. There was a pent-up hostility, waiting to boil over.[5]

As the Bengal partition had helped give rise in India to more radical sentiments, for Burma the catalyst was the country's exclusion from the Montagu-Chelmsford reforms, coming as it did at the same time as the Irish uprising, the end of the First World War, and the beginnings of mass political mobilization in India under the leadership of the South Africa–returned lawyer Mohandas K. Gandhi. At a time when many Burmese were still hoping for the baby steps to self-government held out by the 1919 India Act, the Irish example seemed to hold the promise of a much quicker return to independence. This was a period of revolutionary change and rising expectations. In October 1917 the Bolshevik Revolution installed the new Soviet government, and everywhere in Europe the old order was falling to pieces. On 18 January 1918 President Woodrow Wilson of the United States had delivered his speech to Congress outlining his Fourteen Points for reconstructing Europe after the war. He called for the abolition of secret agreements, disarmament, and the right of national self-determination, and he championed the establishment of a League of Nations. The Burmese, for the first time since 1885, began to think that history was on their side.

Virtually overnight politics went from placid to passionate. Monk-politicians soon came to the fore: men like U Ottama, another Arakanese, who had traveled widely in Asia and came back to Burma after becoming intimately familiar with the work of Gandhi's Congress Party. Mass meetings were held in Rangoon with fiery speeches glorifying Burma's past and calling for home rule. Monks and others vigorously began to protest the long-standing British habit of walking on pagoda platforms in their shoes and boots, something deeply inimical to Burmese custom, and for the first time the British gave way, not by taking off their shoes but by not going at all. Visitors from home were warned to boycott the pagodas.[6] And most Western visitors complied, a notable exception being the aviatrix Amelia Earhart, who was on what was to be her final trip in 1937 and who was more than happy to take off her shoes and flout colonial convention.[7]

In April 1919, at Amritsar in the Punjab, fifty soldiers under General Reginald Dyer fired 1,650 rounds of ammunition into a defenseless and trapped Indian crowd, leaving hundreds dead and unleashing a wave of protests, including a campaign of noncooperation with the new dyarchy constitution. It was Congress's efforts to bring Burma into these protests that heralded the first cooperation between Indian and Burmese nationalists. Strikes were organized around the country, culminating in the university strike of December 1920, timed just days before the official opening of Rangoon University. Schoolteachers and students then also went on strike, and hundreds camped out at the base of the Shwedagon Pagoda, the very place where their grandchildren seven decades later would call for an end to military dictatorship.

Rangoon also became a haven for Bengali radicals who had fled to the province in the wake of increasingly tight surveillance and repressive measures at home. Many had found work as clerks in government offices, and in Burma they founded branches of radical political parties willing to employ terrorist tactics to gain independence. Known to the British as "gentlemanly terrorists," they were often from respectable middle- and upper-middle-class backgrounds. By 1926 more than two dozen senior terrorist organizers had arrived and set up cells in Rangoon, Mandalay, and elsewhere, mixing with the young Burmese around them and providing another set of ideas to the nascent Burmese nationalist movement.[8]

The men on the spot for the British Raj were neither particularly empathetic nor inspired in their response. Sir Harcourt Spencer Butler, who was governor until 1917, was an archetypical Indian civil servant, educated at Harrow and Balliol, Oxford, who began his career as an assistant collector and magistrate in the villages of North India. He had more than twenty-five years of India experience behind him but hardly knew Burma. His successor, Sir Charles Craddock, also had little Burma knowledge, being a former chief commissioner of the Central Provinces and having spent many formative years as a district officer in that part of the empire. They recommended only very limited changes in Burma's constitutional setup. But the mass meetings continued, and in July 1919 a delegation of Burmese politicians went to London, to meet with journalists and Labour MPs and finally with Secretary of State for India Lord Montagu. Another delegation traveled the following year, with great fanfare and local media attention. All this coincided with the birth of the Burmese film industry. When one of the key delegates to London died soon after his return (of the Spanish flu), his funeral was beamed to jam-packed cinema audiences in every city and town.

London's own attention was elsewhere, with hundreds of thousands dead from the war and influenza, with labor strikes at home, and with Gandhi's mammoth protests providing a much bigger headache than anything the Burmese could muster. In the end London gave in for want of alternative and little energy to deal creatively with the problem. By this time the political atmosphere in Burma had shifted amazingly quickly in the direction of violent revolutionary protest.

What the Burmese eventually got in the early 1920s by way of political reform was more than anyone would have expected or even dreamed of just a few years before, but it already fell far short of rising nationalist aspirations. There was a new dyarchy constitution very much along the lines of that of other Indian provinces, general elections (with voting rights for women as well), and a new Legislative Council. Roughly half the seats in the new council were elected from general constituencies, and the others were either appointed directly by the governor or elected by communal and business groups. But there wasn't much enthusiasm, and only 7 percent chose to vote at all in a system that was largely discredited even before it started.

All this applied only to the lowlands of the Irrawaddy Valley, together with Arakan and the Tenasserim. The governor continued to exercise direct rule over the Shan States as well as the Kachin and Chin hill areas, with more than 40 percent of the total area and about 15 percent of the population, where there were to be no reforms at all, no preparation for self-government. They were officially called the Excluded Areas or the Scheduled Areas and less generously as the Primitive Areas.

In "Burma proper," political mobilization continued, and new politicians, all hammering home on vague and patriotic themes, emerged to wow the crowds and attract ever-greater popular followings. Like Aung San Suu Kyi seventy years later, the debonair U Chit Hlaing, "the uncrowned king of Burma," toured the country, as did many other political heroes now long forgotten. Some took seats in the Legislative Council while others shunned any cooperation with the authorities. But the rhetoric was the same: of independence and a restoration of a proud past, of a great army that was vanquished but would rise again, and a once conquering people that should reestablish its place among the nations of the East. Some politicians called on colonial authorities to recruit an ethnic Burmese army (led by British officers). Others demanded that Burma become a "unit among other races within the great British empire."[9]

It was this last demand that would become a hot topic. The British had viewed dyarchy as a ten-year experiment for India and had long planned for a commission to propose the next steps. In 1927 a commission was appointed a bit ahead of schedule under the chairmanship of the Liberal member of Parliament Sir John Simon. The commission traveled around India and visited Burma in 1929. This was when a much bigger drama was playing out across the Indian subcontinent. The Indian National Congress under Mahatma Gandhi had launched a new round of civil disobedience campaigns in the early 1930s, and Gandhi himself had been arrested. Under pressure, the British government convened all-party talks in London; Burma was included as an afterthought. U May Oung, the London barrister who had founded the YMBA, had already passed away but was ably succeeded as one of the province's chief representatives by his daughter Daw Mya Sein, who gave speeches all around the British Isles and did much to raise the profile of a fairly unknown and exotic corner of the empire. Battle lines were being drawn up between the Congress Party under Gandhi and Pandit Jawaharlal Nehru and the Muslim League under Mohammed Ali Jinnah, later the founder of Pakistan. But for the Burmese, there was one overarching question: whether or not to remain part of India.

Very few Burmese wanted anything other than separation from India and for Burma to become its own country. But could they trust the British? India was speeding ahead toward home rule. Wouldn't separation from India mean only that Burma would become a colony like

Ceylon or Hong Kong with little hope of future freedom? Wasn't it worth it to stay on the Indian bandwagon? Burmese politicians were deeply divided, and for years, like today, differences over tactics preempted or postponed any real debate on the substantive and often pressing issues of public policy.

In 1935 a Government of India and Burma Act, which devolved considerable autonomy to the provincial level, was approved by the British Parliament. All subjects were in the hands of ministers who were individually and collectively responsible to their almost entirely elected legislative assemblies. Chief ministers headed the governments of each province, though the appointed governors retained "emergency powers." At the center in Delhi, British control remained more obvious. The hereditary princes and their sometimes extensive domains remained outside the system. India would become a dominion within the British Empire—like Canada, Australia, South Africa, New Zealand, and Newfoundland—and was even given a seat at the League of Nations. Burma was at the same time formally separated from India, ending years of debate, and given a comparable or even slightly more advanced constitution. Not everyone was pleased. This was still far from self-government. And ambitions were running far ahead of anything the British were ready to offer.

THE ROAD TO POVERTY

The Wall Street stock market crash of October 1929 sent an economic tidal wave around the world, decimating international commodity prices and sending the Burmese economy into a tailspin. For decades rice exports had grown by leaps and bounds, fueled by easy credit. It was the foundation on which Burma's modern economy had been built. When U.S. imports declined precipitously, the American Depression was exported overseas. The price of rice plummeted while bank collapses in America and Europe raised the cost of money. Over the next three years the value of Burmese exports plunged by more than 50 percent. For many years government officials had fretted about the increasing indebtedness of farmers but had done little to address the problem. Now it was too late. As in many parts of the world, the coming Depression hit hardest those least able to cope. Hundreds of thousands of rural families became landless across the Irrawaddy Delta, the Tenas-serim coastline, and elsewhere.[10]

On 5 May 1930, just after eight o'clock in the morning, a great earthquake centered in the far north shook much of the country, kill-ing as many as six thousand people and destroying the onetime capital of Pegu. The great pagoda there, housing relics of the Buddha himself, crumpled to the ground. A few months later another quake, this one followed by a tsunami, caused extensive damage to coastal areas. For many Burmese this was an omen that the end of British rule was near. But no one knew what would come next.

On 22 December that same year a traveling mendicant named Saya San declared himself king of Burma in a jungle clearing in the Thar-rawaddy District not far from Rangoon, launching his rebellion at the specially chosen and auspicious time of 11:33 p.m. He styled himself the Thupannaka Galon Raja, and a broad white umbrella was held over his head as he took possession of the various marks of royalty in a ceremony modeled exactly on those of the extinguished Court of Ava. The day before, the acting governor, the innovatively named Sir Joseph Augustus Maung Gyi, had refused even to consider a petition from impoverished farmers in the area who had been pleading for a re-duction in the year's taxes. The rebel army, originally several hundred strong with about thirty firearms among them, eventually grew to up-ward of three thousand men. It was a passionate, desperate revolt and was not put down until the spring of 1932. In the United States, *Buck Rogers in the 25th Century* was playing four times a week on radios across the country while in Burma magicians egged on the tattooed supporters of this kingly pretender. By June 1931 the government had to deploy over eight thousand troops, and by that summer, seven new battalions, six Indian and one British, had been added. Saya San was eventually forced to flee north of Mandalay, where he hid for a while in a monastery. He was captured while making his way to the Shan hills, convicted of treason, and hanged sometime after the rains.

Old-style revolt wasn't the only product of hard times. Earlier that year Burma's pluralistic society had taken a disturbing turn toward long-

term ethnic conflict. A labor dispute between striking Indian dockworkers and Burmese strikebreakers, with taunts about race and
women, had turned bloody, escalating quickly into an all-out assault by
mobs of Burmese against any and all Indians in the poorer quarters of
downtown Rangoon. It was a massacre, and hundreds, perhaps more,
of ethnic Indian civilians were killed. Worse might have followed, from
renewed Burmese attacks or from Indian reprisals, had it not been for
the deployment of the Cameron Highlanders of the Rangoon garrison,
their machine guns mounted and made ready along Fraser and Dalhousie streets. These were the first but not the last Burmese-Indian riots. In 1938 another round of attacks left up to two hundred people
dead and over a thousand wounded. This time the spark was set by a
Muslim-authored book allegedly hostile to Buddhism. *The Sun* newspaper, once respectable, was now taken over by the firebrand politician
U Saw, who used the daily to inflame local opinion. For two weeks law
and order broke down in parts of the capital city.

An anti-Indian character was now deeply etched into ethnic Burmese nationalism, with disastrous consequences in the years to come.
But there was another local and rival nationalism that developed during these years as well, the nationalism of the Karens.

Many of the Karens, one of the country's largest minority peoples,
had converted to Christianity as a result of the efforts of American Baptist missionaries in the nineteenth century. The first missionary was
Adoniram Judson of Malden, Massachusetts, who arrived by ship from
New York in 1812. A man of hardy constitution, he spent most of the
next four decades in Burma, surviving two successive wives (and marrying a third), two children, and a brutal eighteen-month imprisonment at the hands of the Burmese king during the First Anglo-Burmese
War. Other eager and earnest Americans soon followed, and Judson
later wrote the first English-Burmese dictionary, still in use. There was
never much success with the Burmese. The first convert was in 1819, a
full six years after Judson's arrival. His attempts to influence the court
were even less successful. On his first trip to Amarapura he had taken a
beautifully bound and wrapped Bible together with a brief summary of
Christianity in Burmese; the king, Bagyidaw, a somewhat doctrinaire
Buddhist, read the first couple of lines of the summary and then tossed
it back.

But the Karens were much more open to Christian conversion.

They had their own stories of a great flood and of a woman being created from the rib of a man. They also apparently had a tradition that messengers from across the seas would one day bring them "the lost book," about as good an opening for European missionaries as one can imagine. By the late 1820s a number of Karens had joined the Baptist Church, and their numbers continued to grow, in particular in the Tenasserim and parts of the Irrawaddy Delta. The majority of Karen speakers were never Christian. Most were animists, practicing their own rituals and maintaining their old beliefs, and many, especially those who lived in the lowlands near the Burmese, had become Buddhists. But it was the Christian Karens who became the leaders of the community, including several who had been to university in America. Today about 6 percent of Burma is Christian, out of whom about half a million people are Karen Christians belonging to the Baptist Convention. In America, Judson's work as the first Baptist missionary excited fellow church members and led to the formation of the first General Convention of Baptist Denominations in 1814.[11]

Over the following century many Karens came to associate British rule and their cooperation with the British with a better life and future. In the months after Thibaw's downfall, a special levy of Karen soldiers helped patrol the newly won territories, and it was Christian Karens who helped crush a sympathetic uprising in Lower Burma. From then on, large numbers of Karens were recruited into the army and military police. Karens had been instrumental in hunting down Saya San and his followers.

Once Burmese nationalists began pushing for home rule, Karens (about 7 percent of the total population of the province) countered with their own demands for separate electorates and reserved seats in the new Legislative Council. The leader of the Karen National Association in the 1920s was the Albany Medical College–educated Dr. San C. Po, and he insisted that his people would never receive a fair deal under Burmese rule. Even before the Muslim League began its call for a separate Pakistan, San C. Po was calling on London to set aside all of the Tenasserim as a Karen state. As between Burmese and Indians, relations between Burmese and Karens, however confrontational at times, was tempered by many personal connections and friendships. Day to day there was as much interaction as ever, and mixed marriages were (and are) common. But the seeds of later conflict were being laid, with a militant ethnic Burmese nationalism taking center stage, nearly half the country excluded from ongoing constitutional reforms, a rival Karen nationalism calling for a separate state, the Indians seen increasingly as foreigners, and the minds of British policy makers, as usual, focused elsewhere.

"THE IRISH OF THE EAST"

As one looks back from the beginning of the twenty-first century, it is remarkable how Burmese politics has been the preserve of a handful of men who grew up in the 1920s and 1930s. In a way, the history of Burma in the twentieth century can be told as the history of this group of men (and a very few women), many of them friends or at least at university at the same time in the dark years before the Pacific war. My grandfather U Thant, the first and longtime postindependence prime minister U Nu, the Burma Army commander and later dictator general Ne Win, the martyred hero of the independence movement Aung San, the leader of the Communist insurrection Than Tun, and many others—government ministers and opposition politicians, army officers and their guerrilla counterparts—nearly all were at Rangoon University at the same time.

They were not the only ones at the university in those days. They were not even the better students. The better students had come from the more expensive boarding schools like St. John's in Rangoon and gone on to become barristers, magistrates, university lecturers, and civil servants. It was the boys from what were called the Anglo-vernacular schools and the nationalist schools that found their way into the history books, boys from small-town middle-class families, the sons of successful shopkeepers and rice mill owners, who rejected the high-status and well-paid careers ahead of them and instead chose the path of politics.

Or as some might say, the high-status and well-paid careers rejected them. Few of the future politicians were destined for the highest marks and the best jobs. In the 1930s at Rangoon University, 40 percent of those who qualified for the B.A. examinations regularly failed to pass. Their school training did little to stimulate a sense of loyalty to the Raj and yet at the same time disconnected them from their families and backgrounds. Rangoon University had opened their eyes to the bigger world, given them the time and place to read and think and debate, and then made them realize that in this British Burma only a few doors led to success.

Many were also swept up into the political world around them. Sinn Fein was a perennial favorite, but Irish republicanism was hardly going to offer an answer to all of Burma's woes. India was the obvious place to look, and the Indian National Congress would prove a great influence. But its pacifist tendencies and Hindu religious overtones did not excite the young students in the way that Michael Collins and the Irish Republican Army had excited an earlier generation. Excitement led in other directions. In the 1930s almost all Europe was moving toward authoritarian government. The Fascists had been in power in Italy for a decade, and on 30 January 1933 Adolf Hitler was officially sworn into office as Germany's new chancellor. By 1939 Spanish republicans were defeated after a long and hard-fought war against General Francisco Franco. And communism, as personified by Joseph Stalin, seemed a genuine blueprint of what was to come and one that could be adopted in the non-Western world. For the Burmese students it was hard to see parliamentary democracy and slow constitutional reform as the wave of the future.

Like many of the others, Aung San, the man who would later lead the country to independence, came from a small-town and a middle-class family background.[12] His grandfather was from a prominent gentry family in Upper Burma, with kinsmen in the royal service, including a minister under King Mindon. His father was a lawyer. Slight and unprepossessing, he had a hard-to-explain charisma that drew a loyal following even in his earliest days at university. His all-consuming passion was politics, and he was soon elected to the Executive Commission of the Student Union, then housed in a roomy whitewashed building on the edge of the campus. He said his heroes were Abraham Lincoln and the nineteenth-century Mexican nationalist leader Benito Juárez, and he spent hours memorizing the parliamentary speeches of Edmund Burke. He also became editor of the Student Union's magazine. In February 1936 he had his first direct conflict with British authorities for refusing to reveal the name of the student who had written an inflammatory article about the university principal entitled "Hellhound at Large." He was expelled, but this led to a university-wide student strike and the authorities backing down.

Aung San struck many as an oddball, if a strangely attractive one. As a child he didn't speak until he was eight, and as a teenager he often spent hours on his own, thinking and not responding at all to those around him. He seemed unconcerned about his appearance or dress, and his room at university was always a mess. For someone later known as a man of action, he also placed a great store on reading. He was a voracious reader.[13] Through his reading he was drawn toward the extremist rhetoric of the day. One of his first battles, on the opinion pages of *The World of Books*, was with the up-and-coming political commentator U Thant, and the subject was school uniforms. The older man, then all of twenty-six, argued for fostering in children a sense of individuality, while Aung San wrote that the "standardization of human life" was both "inevitable and desirable" and questioned Thant's sense of nationalism. With U Nu as an intermediary, they later became friends.[14] But Aung San's views soon carried the day.

The Do Bama (We Burmans) Society, mainly a group of youngsters and a few off-mainstream politicians, was founded in 1935.[15] Its members took the ironic style "Thakin," meaning "lord" or "master" and generally used to address Europeans, in the same way as sahib in Hindi. They were contemptuous of middle-class politicians and middle-class life-styles and had as their creed to "live dangerously" and seek no personal advantage for nationalist ends. Many lived in poverty. One of their big attractions was their rousing and fairly belligerent song, which later became the national anthem. Many read Marxist literature and turned their energy toward organizing groups of mill workers and oil company employees, but this was only partly fruitful, as very few industrial workers were Burmese, most being Indian. Nietzsche was also a popular inspiration. Some, including perhaps the more clever ones, became Communists, and both a Burma Communist Party and Burma Socialist Party were formed in the years before the war. They were noticed, but barely, by the British authorities, the more established political leaders, and the public at large. They were schoolboys playing politics, marching up and down the street, conspiring in smoky tea shops over a tasty Indian snack, and arguing late at night about John Strachey's *Theory and Practice of Socialism* in someone's dingy dorm room, all while British officials and their wives were enjoying a long drink at the Pegu Club or watching a cricket match on the verandah of the Gymkhana. Who would have thought, as late as 1941, that in seven years' time the Thakins would form Burma's first independent government?

Under the 1935 constitution, Burma had what looked a lot like a real government. This was an add-on to the 1935 India Act. As part of it Burma was separated from India, ending years of acrimonious debate, while being given as much home rule as any Indian province. There was a House of Representatives with 113 seats, including 12 reserved for ethnic Karen constituencies and 11 for business groups, mainly Scottish. There was also a 36-member Senate, designed as a conservative check, limited (through high-income eligibility rules) to well-to-do businessmen, professionals, landowners, and senior government officials. A cabinet headed by a prime minister was responsible to this new parliament. The governor retained authority over the Shan States and other hill areas as well as various emergency powers. This meant the British were still very much at the top, but there was reason to believe that influence and day-to-day decision making were finally shifting from a purely British officialdom to elected Burmese ministers.

One of the newer faces was an up-and-coming barrister named Dr. Ba Maw. The son of one of Thibaw's courtiers, Ba Maw was rumored to be of part-Armenian ancestry. A vain man who made showing off his good looks a lifelong pursuit, he designed his own clothes. Based on formal Burmese dress, they might be best described as retroconservative with a twist, as might Ba Maw's politics. He had gone up to Cambridge to read law at St. Catherine's College but was then unceremoniously sent down after his tutors discovered that he had been secretly studying for the bar in London as well. By now a committed Anglophobe, he made his way to France, where he struggled to master French and then completed, with some difficulty, a doctorate in literature at Bordeaux.

He had become well known in 1930 representing Saya San at his trial for sedition. It was a good opening for an aspiring nationalist politician, and Ba Maw was elected the first prime minister of Burma under the new constitution. His was to be a coalition government with a radical slant. His own party, the Sinyetha, or Poor Man's Party, had campaigned on a populist ticket. Mimicking the rhetoric of the day, Dr. Ba Maw called for a program of people's socialism, adapted to Burma's national needs, attacking capitalists and promising to lower taxes. But his majority was dependent on the support of business and other conservative groups in the new legislative chamber. There would be a big divide between rhetoric and reality.[16]

In this first Burmese experiment with democracy, politics was messy and violent. Because ultimate power was in the hands of the British governor and officialdom, the political parties inhabited a strange middle space between responsible government and theater. Over four years there were three coalition ministries, Ba Maw's being ousted in 1940. It was a sort of mimicry of what politics in an independent country might be like. Burma was still beset by growing economic and social problems. The economy was still in bad shape. Communal tensions flared up into violent riots, including new and bloody Muslim-Buddhist clashes in 1938. Crime rates remained severe. And the country's leadership, such as it was, was either consumed by jockeying for ministerial posts or single-mindedly focused on a seemingly distant dream of independence. To the extent anyone had a platform for what an independent Burmese government would actually do, it was the left and the Communists in particular that provided most of the answers. These years also saw the rise of private militias. Surprisingly tolerated by the British authorities, these so-called pocket armies of key political leaders (Ba Maw had his own) were modeled on the Brownshirts and other fascist thugs in Central Europe and paraded up and down the streets of Rangoon, in khaki shorts, brandishing batons and intimidating onlookers. In all this, Britain was of course still in charge and still responsible, and more creative British attention might have improved matters. But with events in Europe, the British had other things to worry about.

By 1938 an epidemic of school and university strikes had begun. And there was growing alignment between the younger Thakins and the All Burma Student Union. On 20 December students demanded the release of some imprisoned Thakin activists. The protest turned violent, and in the ensuing fighting, a policeman broke his club over the head of one of the demonstrators, who later died. The students had their first martyr. This led to more unrest, not just in Rangoon but elsewhere. In February 1939 troops at Mandalay opened fire to disperse thousands of students, Buddhist monks, and workers. Fourteen demonstrators were killed. A framework for Burmese politics for many decades was being set.

Writing in a Rangoon paper in 1939, thirty-year-old U Thant criticized the direction things were taking and his country's political immaturity, accusing his countrymen of being unable to think critically. "Burmese politics have no meaning save to keep Burmese newspapers busy," he wrote, adding, "We need not despair. Recognition of the causes of a malady are half the cure."[17] But time for a more nuanced debate was running out.

THE APPROACHING WAR

On 1 September 1939, fifty-six Wehrmacht divisions, including six panzer divisions, led by Colonel Generals Feder von Bock and Gerd von Rundstedt, crossed the border into Poland, and the British Empire declared war on Germany. Over the next eleven months much of Western Europe fell to the armies of Adolf Hitler. By June France had surrendered, and Britain was the only country left standing against what was then the strongest military power in the world. In the Battle of Britain that followed, London was bombed day and night, with as many as three thousand civilians killed on a single raid.

For a while Burma remained comfortably far away. Many on the Thakin side leaned to the left and were willing to see fascism as a threat. But others saw opportunity as well. Dr. Ba Maw now came back into the picture as the head of a new Freedom Bloc, which had three demands: (1) Britain's recognition of Burma's right to independence, (2) preparations for calling a constituent assembly, and (3) bringing all the special authorities of the governor immediately within the purview of the cabinet. Ba Maw was appointed the *anarshin* (the dictator or literally the "Master of Authority") of the new group. Aung San was appointed general secretary. Taking advantage of war to gain independence was the only goal.

There were differences of opinion about how to do this. Some like Ba Maw were inclined to seek out a secret alliance with the Japanese. Some were attracted to the idea of a partnership with the Chinese, and this faction included moderates like U Nu; a mission in late 1939 crossed the mountains to Nanking to see what might be possible.

Another politician now entered the picture: U Saw, who maneuvered his way to the prime ministership in 1939. Cunning and opportunistic, with little formal schooling and a virile dose of political ambition, he banned all militias and used London's 1941 Defense of

Burma Act to put in place severe restrictions on the press. He took over the once-respected *Sun* newspaper and turned it into his party's mouthpiece, stirring up ethnic divisions. Communists and Thakins and other political rivals were locked up. Ba Maw, U Nu, and dozens of others wound up in the Mandalay jail. U Saw toned down some of his own violent rhetoric, in part to cozy up to the British, but he still demanded home rule. In 1941 he flew to England to make Burma's case in person to Winston Churchill, only to be politely dismissed; determined to get something somewhere, he then made contact with Japanese agents in Lisbon, was found out by British intelligence, and was promptly arrested. But he would be back, with a special vengeance.

THE THUNDERBOLT

The Japanese had been stealthily gathering political and other intelligence in Burma for a few years, secretly paying for pro-Japanese articles in *The Sun* and *New Burma* newspapers. They had a modest intelligence network in the region, drawing on an expanding Japanese expatriate presence in the region: photographers, pimps and prostitutes, barbers, and chemists. At home, preparations were beginning for what some hoped would be war against the Americans and Europeans in Southeast Asia. Schools taught Burmese, Thai, Malay, and Indian languages, and young men made themselves ready for the coming battle through daily sumo wrestling and martial arts.[18] Skirmishes between China and Japan had already turned into all-out fighting; the entire Chinese seaboard was in Tokyo's hands, but early wins had not translated into quick victory. The Chinese fell back onto the inland city of Chungking, far up the Yangtze, and the British and the Americans were pulled into the conflict, providing support to the besieged Nationalist armies under Chiang Kai-shek. With war in Europe, war in the Pacific seemed increasingly inevitable. For some, the dream of a Japanese Empire across Southeast Asia was closer than ever.

Keiji Suzuki, nominally head of the Shipping Section in the General Staff Headquarters, was given the special and secret task of developing an offensive strategy in Asia and closing off the Burma Road. Like Lawrence of Arabia, he was tasked with cultivating a local cadre that could help his country's broader war aims. He was a graduate of the prestigious General Staff College, spoke English fluently, and had a lifelong passion for grand strategy. More recently he had established the Minami Kikan (meaning the "Southern Agency") as a covert operation run together with other creatively minded imperialists from the elite Nakano spy school in Tokyo.[19]

Also like Lawrence of Arabia, he came increasingly to identify with the cause of native nationalism. A photograph taken in Burma after the Japanese conquest shows him in full Burmese formal dress, and he encouraged rumors that he was secretly the long-lost son of the prince of Myingun, the elder half brother of Thibaw's, and the man considered by many in the 1880s the rightful claimant to the throne.

In May 1940 Suzuki and a colleague slipped into Rangoon and set up a secret office at 40 Judah Ezekiel Street, and were soon nurturing the networks that would form the basis of the Minami Kitan and help drive the British from Burma.[20] They made contact with the Thakins, hoping for future collaboration. Then, one day, word reached Suzuki that two of the Thakins, including the ex-student leader Aung San, had been found wandering the streets of Nippon-occupied Amoy, in China. This was exactly what Suzuki needed.

The 1930s were the formative years of Burmese politics. That this decade was dominated by extremist and militant agendas worldwide was something that left a lasting mark on the country. The debates of the Student Union and the meeting rooms of the young politicians would echo for a long time to come, abstract and ideological debates of the far left and the far right, about agitation and subversion, underground movements and mass demonstrations. There was never any room for pragmatism or compromise. The Great Depression had wiped out the savings of millions, and many in the up-and-coming generation were geared up for action. And colonial institutions had proved themselves singularly unable to manage the multiethnic and multicultural nature of British Burma; they had displaced the old hierarchies but were unable to offer anything convincing in return. There was only one ingredient left, war.

TEN

MAKING THE BATTLEFIELD

*The Second World War engulfs Burma, setting the stage for
the country's civil war; and the unlikely story of Aung San,
the young man who seemingly stood down the British Empire*

⊶⊷

Fifty-six years after Harry Prendergast's overthrow of King Thibaw, British rule in Burma collapsed like a house of cards, its soldiers and officials tossed out together with hundreds of thousands of panic-stricken refugees by the elegantly mustached lieutenant general Shojiro Iida and his Fifteenth Imperial Army. The Burmese had nothing to do with the war, but it destroyed their country.

For the Japanese, modernization and militarism had long gone hand in hand. The Tokugawa Shogunate was overthrown in 1868, and the new reform-minded and West-looking oligarchs were committed from the start to armed forces strong enough to bully their neighbors. At the turn of the century, war against China had led to decisive victory, and vast tracts of the Manchurian plain as well as the island of Taiwan were annexed to the infant Nippon Empire. By 1905 the Japanese were even able to defeat a major European power, Russia, sending shock waves through the West and leading to the revolution against Czar Nicholas that same year.

All these things buoyed up Japan's self-image as a global force on the same scale as Britain and France; and when the First World War ended, Tokyo resented deeply not being treated as an equal. An even more expansionist policy followed. In 1931 the remainder of Manchuria was swallowed up, and a puppet government was established under the last Qing emperor, Aisin Guoro, "Henry" Pu Yi. In 1937 Japan invaded China proper, and condemnation by the foundering League of Nations did little to prevent the blood-soaked aggression to follow. By this time on the other end of the Eurasian landmass the Spanish civil war was already in full swing, with Germany's Luftwaffe and the Condor Legion Fighter Group intervening in support of General Francisco Franco's fascist rebels. In less than two years all Europe would be at war.

War in Europe meant opportunity for Tokyo's schemers, who were increasingly drawn south to the tropical shores of Southeast Asia. One attraction was control over the raw materials of the region—rubber, tin, and oil—including the oil fields of middle Burma. And control of Burma had another, more important attraction: it would sever the overland access between China and the outside world over the famed Burma Road, a mountain path of a thousand hairpin turns that ultimately linked Rangoon's ports with the inland territories still controlled by Nationalist China. Cutting the road would be a deathblow to Nationalist Generalissimo Chiang Kai-shek and finish off the Japanese conquest of the Middle Kingdom. There was also a third, final reason. An occupation of Burma would place the men of Nippon at the very gates of India. Perhaps, they thought, from here an invasion of India would lead quickly to an insurrection in Bengal and an end to the British Empire.

But could they really pull it off? Not everyone was convinced the Imperial Army had what it took to bring down the British and their American friends in the East. What they needed was an opening gambit so audacious, so unexpected that it would buy them time, time to create their East Asia Co-Prosperity Sphere before the Allies had the chance to react. And so in late November 1941 a secret force of warships and planes assembled near the icy Kuril Islands and began creeping their way toward the Hawaiian coast.

THE LAST SUMMER

Just a few weeks before, during the height of the monsoon rains, Air Chief Marshal Sir Robert Brook-Popham, the commander in chief of the British Far Eastern Command, came up to Burma from Singapore and had a look around. A veteran of the Boer War and a former governor of Kenya, he was cool and confident. The Japanese were already entrenched in French Indochina, but the prevailing wisdom was that the economic impact of new U.S. and U.K. sanctions would make any further Japanese advance unlikely. Brook-Popham and his officers believed that any attack on British territory, if it came at all, would be from northern Siam into the Shan States. He placed most of the single Burma Division in that remote corner. Only one brigade would guard the beaches to the south, where the country bordered Malaya. There was, he informed his masters in London, no need for reinforcements.[1]

Prime Minister Sir Winston Churchill was not too sure, and sent his man Alfred Duff Cooper for a personal evaluation. Cooper, a Conservative politician and minister for information, found the whole British scene in Rangoon silly and stuffy but also didn't sense that a Japanese invasion was around the corner. Cooper may also not have taken his task particularly seriously, bringing along his wife, Lady Diana, together with her over one hundred pieces of luggage. He told the British officers he met that they were unlikely to see any fighting.

It was only in October that the alarm bells began to ring. Small and stocky, General A. P. Wavell was Britain's most distinguished general but had been driven straight across the North African desert by Field Marshal Erwin Rommel's Deutsche Afrika Korps. He was then commander in chief in India, an appointment intended, at least in part, to give him a chance to rest and take his mind off things. No one had reckoned an India posting would see much action. But the old soldier soon realized that prospects for war in his theater were far from a distant proposition and that Burma could well be overrun.[2] He recommended immediate reinforcements as well as the building of an all-weather road from Assam to Rangoon. The battle cruisers *Prince of Wales* and *Repulse* were ordered to Singapore. But it was almost too late.

When the Japanese onslaught came, it was as if a sudden storm after long days of blue skies had made it difficult to imagine anything other than a light rain. At dawn on 7 December the American Navy at Pearl Harbor was destroyed. Then one by one the Philippines, Hong Kong, and Malaya fell in rapid succession in a sort of reflection of the German conquests in Europe two years before. In Hong Kong twelve thousand British Empire troops were taken prisoner on Christmas Day. The same week Japanese troops entered Siam.

The British in Rangoon now finally saw the writing on the wall and urgently appealed for help. The nearest source of help was China, and

Chiang Kai-shek offered and sent two of his armies then in Yunnan down into the eastern hills. London also promised troops, including the Seventeenth Indian Division from Iraq and two brigades of African troops. But time was short.

On the morning of 23 December, as Bob Hope and Bing Crosby's *The Road to Zanzibar* was about to play at the New Excelsior Cinema, Rangoon was bombed for the first time. The city had no antiaircraft guns, only Claire Chennault's Flying Tigers, an American volunteer squadron with a reputation for throwing good parties. They were based out at Mingaladon airport and were paid a handsome bonus by Chiang Kai-shek for every Japanese plane they shot down. They now engaged the Nippon fliers but were unable to stop them from attacking the city. The streets that day were packed as usual, and all along the Strand Road and up and around Fraser and Merchant Streets thousands stopped to stare skyward and watch the dogfights overhead just as the first explosives careered down. Within minutes downtown Rangoon was littered with blown-apart and horribly maimed bodies. Nearly three thousand people lost their lives (out of four hundred thousand altogether in Rangoon). Uncontrolled fires broke out. People panicked, as no one had been prepared for this at all. The medical and other emergency services collapsed, and by the time a second attack came on Christmas Day, the road north out of Rangoon was crammed with refugees. Those who could, especially in the Indian population, scrambled onto every available ship bound for Calcutta or Madras.

The man at the center of the unfolding tragedy was Burma's governor, Sir Reginald Dorman-Smith. A former agriculture minister, he was, like so many British officials in Burma, from an Anglo-Irish family. Particularly proud of his Irish background, he had once happily startled his cabinet colleagues during a discussion of the possible internment of Irish citizens by revealing that he had remained a citizen of Eire. He was also a staunch proponent of traditional farming as opposed to "scientific farming" and had once helped lead a group best known for its passionate opposition to pasteurized milk. Harrow-educated and with slicked-back hair, Dorman-Smith also liked to present himself as someone who understood the anticolonial position. One day while he was enjoying a cup of tea in the badly lit cabinet office's basement canteen, he was asked whether he would consider becoming governor of Burma. "Irishmen should always take up challenges of this sort even though they seldom lead anywhere," he thought, and then accepted.[3]

When the first Japanese air raids were taking place, Dorman-Smith had been governor for barely six months. Neither he nor the army in Burma had much intelligence of what was going on, where the Japanese were, and what was likely to happen next. The extra troops that had been promised were now sent instead to Malaya, where a Japanese force had landed and was fast moving south toward Singapore. London thought that Singapore had to be defended to the end, come what may. Everyone knew that if Singapore fell to the Japanese, their navy would dominate the entire Indian Ocean from Australia to the Red Sea; Burma would have to accept that it was a lower priority. In the middle of January the coastal towns of Mergui and Tavoy were lost as Japanese forces scurried over the hills from Siam. The deputy commissioner in Mergui managed to escape but told Dorman-Smith: "I would rather have stayed and been taken prisoner . . . We will never be able to hold up our heads again." Dorman-Smith also wanted to do the right thing. He wired the Burma Office in London: "I hate the idea of deserting the local population. I would welcome your views, my own view is that we all should stay." Within a few weeks the mood had changed from cool optimism to acceptance of all-out defeat.

THE LONGEST RETREAT

Despite all the frenzied preparation (at the expense of Burma), the "impregnable fortress" of Singapore fell on 15 February, and Lieutenant General Arthur Percival, with knobby knees and in short khaki trousers, surrendered at the Ford motor factory to the much smaller force of General Tomoyuki Yamashita, the bull-necked "Tiger of Malaya." No fewer than seventy thousand imperial troops—British, Australians, and Indians—had been defeated by thirty thousand Japanese. Contrary to myth, the problem was not that Singapore's famous large-caliber stationary guns were unable to turn around from the sea and face the attacking force to the north. The problem was the guns had only armor-piercing shells, designed to penetrate the hulls of warships. Against foot soldiers coming down jungle roads they were of little use.

To the north the Japanese Thirty-third and Fifty-fifth Divisions seized

Moulmein, Burma's third-largest town, on the first day of February and were soon peering over the banks of the Salween River toward Rangoon and the heartlands of Burma on the other side. All this time the American pilots, led by John Van Kuren "Scarsdale Jack" Newkirk (who cut short his honeymoon to get back to Burma), did their best to beat off the waves of bombers. Though outnumbered, the Americans, joined by British, Canadian, Australian, and Indian airmen, managed to shoot down 122 enemy planes (including 25 for Scarsdale Jack) while losing only 5 of their own Tomahawk and Hurricane fighters.

In late February, Rangoon was readied for evacuation. Hospital patients and staff were sent to Mandalay, and the lunatics in the asylum were released together with all the common criminals in the Insein jail. The police were soon pulled out, and law and order predictably broke down as the poor of the city set fires and broke into shops and warehouses. In 1824 British soldiers had emptied the cellars of Rangoon on the very first night of occupation. In a fitting bookend to nearly 120 years of occupation, some emptied the cellars again under the pretense of denying comfort to the enemy.

Around the same time, the first tanks ever seen in Burma arrived together with the Seventh Armored Brigade from Egypt, but it was not enough to stanch the Japanese juggernaut. On 22 February the British blew up the bridge over the Sittang River (less than a hundred miles east of Rangoon), only to find that two brigades of the Seventeenth Indian Division were still left on the other side.

The situation was obviously becoming desperate, and at this point Churchill asked Prime Minister John Curtin of Australia to reroute the Australian Sixth and Seventh Divisions, which were then on their way home from the Middle East. Curtin refused, and though Churchill ordered the convoys to go to Burma anyway, he finally backed down in the face of Curtin's indignation. The Australian prime minister was worried about a Japanese landing in his own backyard. The one force that might have saved Burma now sailed by.

As the Japanese crossed the Sittang and moved west toward the Pegu road (which connects Rangoon northward to Mandalay), Dorman-Smith prepared for his last night in the capital. There was almost no one left at Government House, a great Victorian pile not far from the hilltop Shwedagon Pagoda. There was his aide-de-camp and son-in-law Eric Battersby, and his military liaison officer, Wally Richmond, and they and the governor and two war correspondents from London ate their last meal in the cavernous teak-paneled dining room. Out of 110 staff, only the head butler and cook were left, and the cook prepared mutton, a sheep that Dorman-Smith had become attached to after seeing it for several days grazing quietly outside his window. They also decided to drink all the remaining claret and port before merrily smashing up all the large portraits of Burma's prim and supercilious ex-governors hanging along the walls.[4]

Though there were few reinforcing battalions and divisions to be had, new generals were sent, like expert doctors to a dying patient. General Sir Harold Alexander, the future field marshal and the last commander off the beach at Dunkirk, flew in to take over Allied forces in the country, as did General "Vinegar Joe" Stilwell, President Roosevelt's choice to head up the Chinese armies in Burma in a special arrangement with Chiang Kai-shek. But they could do little to stop the tide, only to help manage what became the longest retreat in British history.

While many ordinary Burmese feared for the future, the Indians in the country were the ones who were perhaps the most afraid of what a non-British Burma would have in store. More than a hundred thousand Indians were now fleeing in the direction of Arakan, entire families on foot or by bullock cart, their possessions piled high, and dying by the thousands of hunger, disease, and exhaustion. Another hundred thousand were camped outside Mandalay and near Amarapura. British authorities permitted only five hundred a day to proceed up the road in order not to hold up the retreating British Army. No one knows how many died, but the number is likely in the tens of thousands. About two hundred thousand finally made it over the mountains into India.

Along the middle Irrawaddy, the river town of Prome fell, and then Toungoo, as both British and Chinese armies gave way to superior Japanese confidence, tactics, and fighting ability. Then the bombs rained over Mandalay. On 3 March the railway station was blown to bits together with the firehouse and the hospital. The remains of people and horses were scattered along dusty streets or were floating among the lilies in the old royal moat. Two-thirds of the town was then engulfed by fire, with huge flames whipping across Mindon and Thibaw's city in the intense hundred-degree Fahrenheit heat. Almost no trees or buildings were left intact. Telephone lines lay across the cratered streets, and a terrible smell blanketed what little was left of Mandalay.

More destruction would come. The oil wells that had provided fat profits over so many years to businessmen in Glasgow and London were now blown up by the retreating British, and great clouds of black smoke drifted over the nearby medieval ruins at Pagan. It was now early March, and Dorman-Smith was at Maymyo, the summer capital in the eastern hills. The Japanese had taken the entire southern half of the country and showed no signs of slowing down. General Alexander planned to take his army across the Irrawaddy westward toward India, leaving the Chinese to fend for themselves as best they could.

The Japanese would soon enter Maymyo. Everything at the governor's residence there had already disappeared to looters. There were no carpets left, or even spoons or forks. Dorman-Smith and his aides burned his papers only to find at lunchtime there was also nothing left to eat. When an old Burmese messenger appeared and Sir Reginald politely asked him for some food, he replied that he had only his own lunch, and this he would happily share. And so the king's representative ate a meal of rice and curry with his fingers. Not far in the distance, angry and humiliated Chinese soliders were hiking back to Yunnan, torching villages and butchering civilians along the way.

From Maymyo Dorman-Smith headed north into the Kachin hills. When he reached Myitkyina on 28 April, many of his personal staff and other officials were already there and waiting for him, as was his wife and their pet monkey, Miss Gibbs. The airfield there was the only one left in Burma that was still in British hands, and the highland town was choked with refugees, many of them Anglo-Indian or Anglo-Burmese government workers and their families, the most loyal citizens of the Raj, all of whom were now desperate to be flown out. Dorman-Smith was himself ill with dysentery but thought the noble thing would be to hide in the jungle and not to desert the Burmese entirely. At the very least he should share the hardships of the others and walk out. Calcutta said he must fly out at once, but even then he hesitated until ordered directly by Churchill. Lady Dorman-Smith and Miss Gibbs having left already, he was escorted out immediately by the Royal Air Force.[5]

Though that was the end of the story for now for Sir Reginald, his wife, and his monkey, for hundreds of thousands of others there were still hundreds of miles of torturous mountain tracks between the advancing Japanese and the relative safety of India, northwest through

dense rain forest and then pine-shrouded hills. Those who crossed
were mainly Indians, but there were also many others, Burmese and
European. At least two thousand who made the trek were already
wounded. What made everything much worse was that the monsoon
downpours were just beginning, thunderous sheets of water drenching
the men, women, and children to the bone, dragging them down in
knee-deep mud, with clouds of sandflies and mosquitoes buzzing all
around and leeches dropping off the trees, with many suffering from
malaria and dysentery and all hungry from a lack of proper food. Narrow, slippery paths wound their way around cliffs a thousand feet high.
People usually made their way in small groups and passed through
Kachin mountain villages, often deserted because of recent attacks by
renegade soldiers. Everywhere along the way were dead bodies. Only
once they had crossed the four-thousand-foot-high Pangsau Pass would
they be in Assam and on safe ground. Many were met on the other side
by the volunteers of the Indian Tea Association.

One man traveled another, more difficult way to India, over the
death-defying and ice-covered Diphu Pass, fourteen thousand feet up.
This was the world-renowned botanist and explorer Frank Kingdon
Ward, who had gone north from Fort Hertz and then walked two
months and four hundred miles alone along the Tibetan marches to
Assam. But as one Indian civil servant remarked, "He had done that
sort of thing all his life."[6]

THE THIRTY COMRADES

A little more than two years before, on 14 August 1940, just as the Luftwaffe was beginning its bombing raids over England, two young Burmese men smuggled themselves on board a Norwegian cargo ship
bound for the gritty port city of Amoy in China. One was Aung San, the
ex-student leader, who was on the run from the colonial police. It was
a slow and uncomfortable journey, the first long sea voyage for both
men, and was followed by weeks of wandering aimlessly in Amoy with
little money and no precise plan. They had apparently thought about
making contact with the Chinese Communists but eventually arranged
to be picked up by the Japanese and taken via Taiwan to Tokyo, arriving in the Japanese capital on the very day that the new Axis pact with

Germany was being signed and celebrated by giant flag-waving crowds.[7] Aung San was now part of Tokyo's grand plan to snatch away Britain's empire in the East.

For Colonel Keiji Suzuki, the Japanese "Lawrence of Arabia," Aung San's arrival in Tokyo was just what he was hoping for. His idea was to foment an anti-British rebellion inside Burma, to help pave the way for an eventual Japanese conquest. He did his homework well, traveling to the country (posing as a journalist) for long periods and making all the right contacts. And now he had Burma's most promising young politician in Tokyo.

Aung San spent the rest of 1940 in the Japanese capital, learning Japanese and apparently getting swept away in all the fascist euphoria surrounding him. "What we want is a strong state administration as exemplified in Germany and Japan. There shall be one nation, one state, one party, one leader . . . there shall be no nonsense of individualism. Everyone must submit to the state which is supreme over the individual . . . ," he wrote in those heady days of the Rising Sun.[8] He spoke Japanese, wore a kimono, and even took a Japanese name. He then sneaked back into Burma, landing secretly at Bassein. He changed into a *longyi* and then took the train unnoticed to Rangoon. He made contact with his old colleagues. Within weeks, in small batches and with the help of Suzuki's secret agents in Rangoon, Aung San and his new select team traveled by sea to the Japanese-controlled island of Hainan, in the South China Sea. There were thirty in all—the Thirty Comrades—and they would soon be immortalized in nationalist mythology.

Aung San at twenty-five was one of the three oldest. He took Teza meaning "Fire" as his nom de guerre. The other two took the names Setkya (A Magic Weapon) and Ne Win (the Bright Sun). All thirty prefixed their names with the title Bo. "Bo" meant an officer and had come to be the way all Europeans in Burma were referred to, signifying their ruling status. The Burmese were now to have their own "bo" for the first time since 1885. But six months of harsh Japanese military training still lay ahead. It wasn't easy, and at one point some of the younger men were close to calling it quits. Aung San, Setkya, and Ne Win received special training, as they were intended for senior positions. But all had to pass through the same grueling physical tests, saluting the Japanese flag and learning to sing Japanese songs. They heard tales of combat and listened to Suzuki boasting of how he had killed women and children in Siberia.[9] It was a bonding experience that would shape Burmese politics for decades to come.

In 1941, in the months before Pearl Harbor, they were moved to Bangkok, the riverside capital of Field Marshal Phibun Songkhram's pro-Axis dictatorship, and there they formed a Burma Independence Army (BIA) under Colonel Suzuki's enthusiastic supervision. Suzuki himself had taken the Burmese nom de guerre Bo Mogyo, meaning "the Thunderbolt," an astute choice that played on the (allegedly) old local prophecy that "the umbrella" (meaning "the British") would eventually be struck down by "the thunderbolt." Tokyo had yet to decide its Burma policy as both the Imperial Army and Navy jockeyed for influence and argued whether an amphibious or land offensive made most sense. But Suzuki's heart lay increasingly in Burma, and he encouraged the young men under him to themselves lead the fight for Burmese independence and move ahead of the emperor's forces. A rumor spread that Bo Mogyo was none other than a son of the prince of Myingun, Mindon's eldest son, who had rebelled against his father in 1866, then fled east to Saigon.

One night in a house in downtown Bangkok, not far from today's backpacker mecca at Khao San Road, the Thirty Comrades slit their fingers, pooled their blood, and swore oaths of loyalty, reenacting a ritual of Burma's extinct military aristocracy. Aung San's little band then trudged off to the front line, pushing eagerly behind the infantry and mountain regiments of the Japanese Fifteenth Army. Ne Win led a special unit that reached Rangoon early, and others soon fanned out across the delta and through the towns of the middle Irrawaddy, clashing here and there with the retreating British but leaving nearly all the real fighting to the Japanese. Within months their numbers had soared, as they were joined by their old fellow nationalists and other excited youngsters across the country. On 1 May 1942 they entered the blackened ruins of Mandalay. As Thibaw's ghost was being avenged, the Burmese civil war was also about to begin.

The bloodshed began in the western Irrawaddy Delta. Units of the Burma Independence Army, swollen with fresh recruits and patriotic pride, had just arrived alongside the black-booted Japanese and were beginning to disarm Karen soldiers as they were returning home. The soldiers were Christian Karens from this area who had been part of the colonial army, who had decided not to make the trek to India and instead to go home and try to protect their families. Everyone knew the potential for trouble ahead. The BIA was very much a nationalist ethnic Burmese force, and the sight of armed Burmese in uniform, after more than a lifetime of colonial occupation, had ignited strong passions. And the Karens feared what might lie ahead. An elder in the Karen community, Sir San C. Po, was working hard to diffuse tensions, and it was thanks to his efforts that violence had just been averted in the big port town of Bassein. For a while it looked as if violence might be avoided altogether. But then a group of Karens hatched a plot, aimed at attacking the town of Myaungmya, driving out the Burmese soldiers and rescuing the Karens living there, who they believed to be in mortal danger. But the plot was discovered by the Burmese, who immediately shot the local Karen leader, Saw Pe Tha, together with his Scottish wife and their children. Sir San C. Po managed to prevent an even greater tragedy by then persuading the Karens not to go ahead with their attack. But the genie had been let out of the bottle.

Over the next many weeks the BIA, thinking that its worst fears of Karen treachery were coming true, started daily executions of Karens suspected of disloyalty to the new order. Dozens, if not hundreds, were murdered. The Catholic Mission headquarters as well as an orphanage were burned to the ground. In retaliation, Karens in nearby villages attacked random Burmese villagers, and communal violence spread swiftly across the delta. Only the intervention of the Japanese Army weeks later finally stopped the killings. What began in those days would soon lead to a war that has yet to end.

END OF EMPIRE?

The Japanese conquest of Burma shocked the British in India and in London as well. This was now the spring of 1942, and the threat of a German landing on the British Isles had faded. Both the United States and the Soviet Union had joined the war. But with victory at Stalingrad and the first landings in North Africa still months away, India, with over two and a half million of its own men in uniform, was vital for success. The sudden loss of Hong Kong, Malaya, and Singapore meant that

British prestige in the East was at an all-time low. More to the point, India itself was now directly threatened.

In March the austere Socialist lawyer Sir Stafford Cripps arrived by propeller plane in Delhi, carrying with him the Churchill government's offer of future independence. The draft declaration he brought along stated that after the war an all-Indian constituent assembly would draw up a constitution for a new Indian union. Each province of India and each native state would be free to join or make separate arrangements. Both the Muslim League and the Congress Party rejected this and repeated their demands for immediate independence and a chance to fight in the war as equal members of the United Nations. Mahatma Gandhi called the offer "a post-dated check on a failing bank" and in July the Congress Party called on Britain to "Quit India." By August and September, as Japanese troops hovered along the Manipur and Arakan frontiers, violent nationwide protests, rebellions, and terrorist attacks across the subcontinent shook British rule to its foundations.

THE IMPORTANCE OF DRESSING UP

In the summer of 1943 Japan granted Burma formal independence. In many ways this was a completely sham independence, in the manner of the Vidkun Quisling government in Norway and the puppet regime of Emperor Henry Pu Yi in Manchuria. But the Burmese were a people who had once lived and breathed ritual and ceremony and who had for sixty years under British rule been starved of any sort of pride, pomp, or circumstance. The mere semblance of government—and by mid-1943 everyone knew it would only be a facsimile of independence—still had an impact, as if the form of statehood, with all the uniforms and flags and parades, made them want even more the real thing.[10]

The independence ceremony took place on 1 August 1943. Dr. Ba Maw, the prewar prime minister, became the *adipati*, or leader, in the manner of *der Führer*. The Japanese had thought of Aung San for the top job but found him too unimpressive in appearance and style and preferred the bigger and better-looking Ba Maw for their puppet. Being the emperor worshipers they were, they also considered restoring the monarchy and placing the septuagenarian prince of Pyinmana, a half

brother of Thibaw's, on the throne, and this had won a good measure
of Burmese support. But like the British in 1886, they really didn't want
to go to all the trouble and dropped the idea.

Aung San did, however, make it as the number two. As slender as
ever and now shaven-headed, he was to be the head of a smaller but
more professional Burmese army and minister for war. Many of the
thousands who had ballooned the ranks of the BIA and had caused so
much trouble in the delta and elsewhere were demobbed, and the remaining officers were sent to undergo intensive training by Japanese
instructors just outside Rangoon. These officers later dominated the
upper echelons of the armed forces until well into the 1970s.

It was to be a dictatorship along fashionable fascist lines. Ba Maw
made known his utter disdain for democratic principles and forms of
government, and the slogan of the new army under Aung San was
"One Blood, One Voice, One Command" (*ta-pyi, ta-than, ta-meint*),
still today the de facto slogan of the Burmese military. Ba Maw liked
the trappings of 1940s dictatorship, and his independence day ceremony was more like an ersatz coronation. Always a clotheshorse and a
man known for his sartorial creations, he now had a field day in design-
ing pseudoroyal outfits. The music was the music of Thibaw's court,
and a dwarf herald addressed the erstwhile St Catherine's College undergraduate as if he were a king. Manipuri Brahmins were hauled out
of long retirement and brought to Rangoon to bless the marriage of his
daughter Tinsa with one of the up-and-coming officers in the Burma
Independence Army.

Many soon tired of the show, especially when the Japanese, with
their interrogation centers and summary executions, their new sake
brewery at the Anglican Cathedral and their brothel at the Pegu Club,
their hair-raising torture techniques and sex slaves, made increasingly
clear who was actually in charge. Ba Maw and others went to Tokyo
for meetings of the East Asian Co-Prosperity Sphere, where they sat
around conference tables and posed for photographs with other real
and pseudonationalists. But at home, even within the group around
the *adipati*, there was a gnawing sense that history was about to favor a
different side.

WARTIME AT HOME

U Thant was one of those always wary of a Nippon-led liberation. In October 1941 he had sent an article entitled "From the Frying Pan into the Fire" to the editor of *New Burma*, warning against expecting much from the Axis powers. Though everything else he had sent in was promptly published, this article never appeared in print. A week later he received a handwritten note from Dr. Thein Maung, the publisher of the weekly, apologizing profusely for not publishing the piece but saying that the theme went entirely against prevailing opinion. Thant never wrote for the journal again. Thein Maung became Ba Maw's ambassador to Japan.

By March the Japanese had reached Pantanaw, and Thant came increasingly under suspicion, as a man with Anglophile and democratic leanings and as someone who would not always fall in line. He was, however, asked to take part in the new administration, mainly because he was in Aung San's good books and because his best friend, U Nu, was now the new "minister for foreign affairs." U Nu, aways ambivalent (at best) about the Japanese, remembered later that this was far from a real job and that most of the time at his fledgling Foreign Ministry was spent sending cables of congratulations to other Axis countries on their national holidays. Thant was asked to be secretary of the Burma Education Reorganization Committee; he thought it impossible to say no and accepted, moving for several months to a bomb-scared and half-deserted Rangoon.

Back in Pantanaw, he developed a fairly warm or at least collegial relationship with one of the several Japanese officers stationed in the town, a Lieutenant Oyama, who spoke and read English fluently. Oyama visited Thant's house from time to time in his mustard-colored uniform and peaked cap and even borrowed books, perhaps Po Hnit's Victorian novels or Thant's collections of Fabian essays. This relationship, however, did little to prevent the daily brutalities of life under occupation, and hundreds of young Burmese in neighboring towns were later found in mass graves, killed for suspicion of opposing the Japanese.

My grandfather remembered no one's being executed in Pantanaw itself for political reasons. Instead the Japanese policy toward the local people seemed to be one of "brutal disdain and condescension." He wrote:

A Japanese private, for instance, would slap a Burmese who looked disrespectful to him. As a result, the sense of intense fear and of utter helplessness was characteristic of the Burmese mood during the four-year Japanese regime . . . What amazed me was the fact that the Japanese people, who, in my experience, are among the most cultured, the most civilised and the most courteous of all people, could turn into the most arrogant and brutal masters.

For most Burmese, surprise at their self-styled liberators turned quietly into a desire for action.

JAPAN CONSIDERS ITS NEXT MOVE; THE BRITISH PLAN A COUNTERATTACK

For the British the winter of 1942–43 was a time to figure out what had gone wrong and plan for taking Burma back. For a while there was a stalemate, and along the front lines both sides tried to probe for each other's strengths and weaknesses. Feeling in need of a morale booster, General Wavell ordered an advance into Arakan, but it failed, lowering morale even further as the Japanese fought well and held their ground.

Into this grim picture leaped the Chindits. They were to be the largest of the Allied Special Forces anywhere in the world and took their name from the Burmese *chinthé*, or "lion." The Chindits were under the command of the diminutive and bearded brigadier Orde Wingate, the father of modern guerrilla warfare, who had trained the first Jewish commandos in Palestine and was known for his many eccentricities, such as wearing a raw onion on a string around his neck and occasionally biting into it as a snack. His Chindits parachuted deep behind enemy lines and lived and fought entirely cut off from bases in India, relying only on occasional supplies by air. There were two expeditions in all, and the second expedition, consisting of no fewer than twenty thousand British and other Allied soldiers, was the second-largest airborne assault in the war.

The Kachins, in the tribal mountains of the far north, also proved themselves excellent fighters. Thousands joined Detachment 101 of the American Office of Strategic Services, the forerunner of the Central Intelligence Agency. From a line of jungle outposts, Detachment 101 units mounted repeated attacks on Japanese supply lines, blowing up bridges and railroads, disrupting communications, and providing intelligence. During three years of jungle warfare they killed over five thousand Japanese and wounded perhaps twice that number. For the Japanese, the tenacious Kachin fighters were to be greatly feared, and the constant threat of ambush in the mountains sliced away at their self-confidence. For every Kachin casualty, they were able to inflict twenty-five on the enemy. These adept soldiers of proven loyalty naturally later expected loyalty from the British Raj in return. They also distrusted the Burmese whom they saw collaborating with the Japanese. This would be another volatile component in Burma's postindependence mix.

THE TURNING POINT IN IMPHAL

In Tokyo in September 1943 a meeting at the Japanese Imperial Headquarters was chaired by the emperor himself. A lot had happened over the past year, and now things weren't looking too good. The Americans were massing in the Pacific, in a long arc from the freezing waters off Alaska to the white sand beaches of Papua New Guinea. In Europe the Red Army was finally pushing their German allies back across the Ukraine. The assembled war chiefs in their gleaming boots and Prussian-style uniforms agreed their best hope was a knockout blow against both the Chinese and the British in India. This would allow them to concentrate on the coming threat from the Americans and be in a position, whatever happened to Germany, to negotiate the best peace settlement possible.[11] In March 1944 they would launch their last great offensive in Southeast Asia, from their bases northwest of Mandalay to Assam via the little hill towns of Imphal and Kohima.

For the Japanese and the British, these battles in early 1944 in the little principality of Manipur, three thousand feet up, were the turning point of the Burma campaign. Both sides knew it and gave it everything they had. The British brought up massive reinforcements and now assembled half a million soldiers with tens of thousands of additional laborers, fifty thousand vehicles, and every spare elephant in India, all along the wet and thickly jungled front. Against this the Japanese threw the two hundred thousand men they had under the command of General Renya Mutaguchi. When the fighting began, Lieutenant General Sir William Slim and his Fourteenth Army ensured that Imphal held out for three months against a ferocious Japanese onslaught, while Chindit forces hacked away at supply lines and the American and other Allied planes provided support from the air. The Japanese were stopped and when the attack was over, both at Imphal and at Kohima, more than eighty thousand Japanese and seventeen thousand Allied troops lay dead. What was left of Japanese forces fell back to the Chindwin River hundreds of miles to the east and then beyond, Orde Wingate's Chindits fast on their heels.

The tide had turned, and the Allies under Slim prepared for what had long been thought impossible, an overland reconquest of Burma. The British Fourteenth Army crossed first the Chindwin in November 1944 and then the Irrawaddy in January 1945, in the longest opposed river crossing anywhere in the world, meeting intense Japanese resistance every step of the way. Its front line in Burma was longer than either the eastern or western fronts in Europe. Despite its name, the Fourteenth Army was a multinational force, constituted primarily of units of the Indian Army as well as a large contingent of troops from East and West Africa. In March, Meiktila, the heart of the Japanese operation, was captured by the Seventeenth Indian Division after five days of fierce and close combat in the furnacelike spring heat. Only one huge leogryph survived; the rest of the town was obliterated. Less than three weeks later the Nineteenth Indian Division retook Mandalay, with the Fourth Gurkhas fighting their way up the north side of Mandalay Hill and reaching the summit just as the first sunlight illuminated the Shan hills in the distance. The Japanese tried to make a desperate last stand within the walls of the old royal city but eventually withdrew, the entire palace in flames. Nothing but the walls of the old city was left. By now British and Indian forces, joined by two West African divisions, had moved far into Arakan, taking Akyab in December 1944 and opening up a new front.

In a strange twist of fate, something the Burmese might call karma, Captain Basil Hamilton-Temple Blackwood was shot and killed by a stray bullet in March 1945 in front of the old palace walls. The old royal city of which the palace was a part was named Fort Dufferin, after the captain's grandfather the first Marquess of Dufferin and Ava.

Basil was the fourth marquess, an officer in the Royal Horse Guards, and a man Evelyn Waugh called the brightest mind of his generation, and he was killed at almost the exact spot where his ancestor had exiled Thibaw six decades before. It was six full days after the Nineteenth Indian Division had completed the capture of Mandalay and was as if Thibaw's ghost had decided to settle an old score with the erstwhile viceregal family.

The rains were only weeks away. The British were now racing to Rangoon.

By now things were not looking very bright for those who had thrown their lot in with the Japanese. Some Burmese politicians had never wanted to join forces with Tokyo, mainly the Communists, like Thakin Soe, who hid in the southern marshes to organize his men, and Thakin Thein Pe Myint, who walked out to India to make contact with British authorities. But by as early as 1944, when the battles at Imphal and Kohima were deciding the fate of the Japanese Fifteenth Army, many in the Rangoon puppet regime were also beginning to have their doubts. Dr. Ba Maw remained loyal to his sponsors to the end, fleeing to Japan and winding up in an American prison. But Aung San, Ne Win, and the rest decided that their only loyalty was to Burma's independence and began conspiring. Fascism wasn't quite all it was cracked up to be, and some, including Aung San, began shifting back toward their earlier left-wing inclinations. Messages were sent out to the Allies, offering to turn sides and help drive out the Japanese. An underground resistance movement was formed, called the Anti-Fascist People's Freedom League, with Aung San at the head. When to openly challenge the Japanese and launch an armed revolt? Every day in Rangoon under the Japanese thumb was a day that could lead to arrest, horrible tortures, and death. The word from India was to wait.

U Thant and his old Pantanaw friends retained a shortwave set, and every night at nine o'clock they went to a neighbor's house and listened upstairs while the family played records loudly below. They learned of the Soviet victory at Stalingrad and the Allied landings in North Africa and then at Normandy and suspected the days of occupation were numbered. They also learned about the Anti-Fascist People's Freedom League and prepared to do their part to help, secretly storing away rice for a future uprising. It was risky business for Thant, who was already being watched for refusing while at the Education Ministry in Rangoon to make Japanese-language instruction compulsory in schools. Then, one day in early 1945, Japanese soldiers came to Thant's house and took him to their nearby base. My grandmother and others felt sure they would never see him again. But when Thant arrived at the office of Lieutenant Oyama, he was surprised to find that Oyama wanted only to ask for his help. The Japanese officer had been living with a Burmese woman, and she had recently given birth to a little boy. He asked Thant to protect them as best as he could, and Thant agreed.

It seemed the Japanese retreat was beginning in earnest. But what was to come next? A new British occupation? That was hardly desired, but there was no clear alternative. Perhaps in the new world to come, the United Nations would ensure a good transition to self-determination. But in the marshlands and mangrove swamps around Pantanaw, there was already a more realistic intimation of the future, as underground Communist cells, ex-Karen soldiers, and demobbed Burma Independence Army recruits, all armed, all young, and for now all quiet, swirled around, waiting for their turn.

LORD LOUIS MOUNTBATTEN AND THE QUESTION OF THE BURMESE PARTISANS

Back in October 1943 Admiral Lord Louis "Dickie" Mountbatten, a cousin of the king's and later to be the last viceroy of India, was appointed the supreme Allied commander of the South-East Asia* Theatre, meaning that he was overall in charge of the recapture of Burma. A career naval officer and a favorite of Winston Churchill's, the forty-four-year-old Mountbatten brought an upper-class dislike of middle-class colonial prejudices and a desire to be and to seem to be on the right side of history. For many in the British Army, Aung San was a traitor, a Quisling, who needed to be brought to justice. But in February

---

*This is the origin of the term "Southeast Asia," meaning today Burma, Thailand, Laos, Cambodia, Vietnam, Malaysia, Singapore, Indonesia, Brunei, and the Philippines.

1945 Mountbatten chose to go against his own colonels and generals and won London's approval for arming Aung San's league. Mountbatten argued that Burmese partisans working behind Japanese lines could make a difference; he also saw Burmese nationalism in a kinder light than did some of his fellow officers.

For Aung San and his Thirty Comrades, knowing that they would have Allied support in turning on the Japanese must have been a relief. The future was still murky, but at least there might be a way ahead if they restyled themselves "antifascists," and presented the reconquering British with as much of a fait accompli as possible. Their demands would be the same as always—complete and unconditional independence—but this time they were not just students playing politics and jabbering away in the Student Union; they had guns, and they knew how to use them.

In a bit of daring theater, they decided first to hold a parade in Rangoon, near Government House, with Lieutenant General Hyotara Kimura, commander of the Burma Area Army, and other senior Japanese officers on the grandstand, saluting the somber marchers. Then, a few days later, on 27 March, a day now commemorated annually as Armed Forces Day, the young men in khaki drove out of the dusty city, saying they were off to meet the British enemy, but instead wheeling around and everywhere attacking their erstwhile masters.

Aung San had made his move just in time. On 3 May in soaking rain, two days after Adolf Hitler had shot himself dead in the Führerbunker, the Twenty-sixth Indian Division strode into Rangoon unopposed. Aung San could say that his forces had helped the British in their drive down the Sittang Valley toward the capital. Mopping-up operations continued, but the war in Burma was essentially over with the new focus on a planned amphibious assault on the coasts of Malaya (Operation Zipper).

On 16 May Aung San went to see General Slim, the top British general in the country. Aung San was still dressed in the uniform of a Japanese major general, complete with sword, and startled some of Slim's staff, who had not been warned of his coming. He then told Slim matter-of-factly that he was the minister of war of the Provisional Government of Burma set up by the Anti-Fascist League. The league wanted an alliance with Britain until all Japanese forces were driven from Burmese soil. Afterward Burma would be independent. It wasn't a demand, simply a statement of intent. Somewhat taken aback, Slim first thought Aung San was bluffing. He said he was in no position to discuss political matters but asked that Aung San incorporate his soldiers into the British-led forces. Aung San replied that as an ally he was happy to place his men under an Allied commander.

He had impressed Slim, who admired his boldness. When Slim said: "Don't you think you're taking considerable risks in coming here and adopting this attitude?" he had replied, "No." "Why not?" "Because you are a *British* officer." As Slim later wrote, Aung San scored heavily.[12]

THE WHITE PAPER: BRITAIN'S POLICY THROUGH 1946

Aung San may have scored heavily, but this did not affect the plans the mandarins in faraway London had approved for postwar Burma. A government-in-exile, headed by Governor Dorman-Smith and including a number of senior British as well as Burmese civil servants, had been living in Simla, the Himalayan station and summer capital of the Raj, for almost the entire war, brooding over the humiliating retreat, worrying about friends or family, and then busily imagining and writing about all the things that could be done to make up for the war, set things right, and build a better and more prosperous country.[13] Of course Burma would become self-governed, in good time, but not right away. Everything had to be sequenced properly. First would be reconstruction. The Burmese would have a say in everything, but for a few years only through a council appointed by the governor. When the economy was up and running and law and order had been restored, then there would be fresh elections, a new government along the lines of the 1935 constitution, and eventual home rule within a new British Commonwealth.

This was the vision, and it was laid out by London in an official White Paper in 1945.[14] The Burma Chamber of Commerce of mainly Scottish businessmen had also been busy lobbying and had strongly endorsed the focus on economic recovery, with British firms naturally playing a key role. Indian immigrants would be helped to return. Even the Chettyar moneylenders would have their lands restored. The United

States had advocated that Burma become a new trusteeship of the United Nations, but this suggestion was politely ignored.

For Sir Reginald and the men around him, it was a matter of making sure Burma had a bright future. But it was also a matter of doing the right thing for those who had stood by the British. Aung San and his league had their place, but so too did the older politicians who had refused to serve under the Japanese and had come out to Simla. There were also the Karens and the Kachins who had served with such distinction behind enemy lines, often at great cost to their own communities. Surely they had to be recognized and rewarded. Sir Reginald had a sense things had changed in Burma, even if London didn't, but he didn't realize how much.

In London few people were actually spending much time thinking about the future of Burma. In July 1945 a landslide election victory had returned the Labour Party to power and Clement Attlee became prime minister of a new Socialist government. And in the years that followed, the British people, exhausted from the war, concentrated on their own problems and their wish to create a modern welfare state. Transport and utilities industries were nationalized, and a national health service established. An estimated one-quarter of national wealth had been lost, and the national debt had tripled since 1939. And at this center of empire, food and coal were rationed. There wasn't even much energy to debate the great colonial issues of the day—the independence and partition of India and the creation of a Jewish state in Palestine—let alone a sideshow like Burma. And so the policy in the White Paper remained in place, until developments on the ground made London realize too late that it was courting disaster.

Burma in the autumn of 1945 bore little resemblance to the British Burma of four years before. The Military Administration's Handing Over Report said: "We do not think it any exaggeration to say that no British possession has suffered so much damage."[15] Rangoon was in shambles. Whole city blocks had been shelled into rubble. There was no electricity, and the harbor had been wiped out. Over five hundred trains and wagons had been blown up by the retreating Japanese, who had also destroyed everything from the Irish girls' school on Prome Road to the Yacht Club on Inya Lake. Rubbish and sewage were everywhere, and some streets were two feet deep in filth. Nearly everything of value had been looted. Soon the city was filled with tens of thousands of squatters living in squalid makeshift huts while other refugees crammed into apartments and houses abandoned by their owners. Disease and in particular sexually transmitted diseases were spreading fast, in large part because of the huge increase in prostitution during the war.[16] Only a special production of *Hamlet* with John Gielgud in the title role at the Jubilee Hall in February 1946, complete with Elizabethan costume, helped to lift the morale of the returning Raj.[17]

But if Rangoon suffered, it was nothing like the scene in other parts of the country. Mandalay was effectively gone. Not a single building had been left standing. Bodies and carcasses lay rotting on the city's streets and among the waterlilies in the old palace moat. Over 150,000 people had lost their homes. In many other cities and towns it was the same. Shwebo, Meiktila, Prome, and Bassein were simply wiped out, with nothing left of their handsome colonial buildings, manicured gardens, teak houses, and leafy boulevards. Mogaung in the far north, once a pleasant place with tree-lined streets and old wooden monasteries, was now a ghost town, covered in high grass and left to starving dogs. And everywhere were the corpses and makeshift graves of hundreds of thousands of Japanese, British, American, Indian, African, Chinese, Australian, and Burmese men and women.

The war ended on 14 August, with the atomic bombing of Hiroshima and Nagasaki and the unconditional surrender of the emperor Hirohito. Just days before, the Japanese Twenty-eighth Army in desperation had tried to fight its way out of the thickly forested Pegu mountain range and flee east across the monsoon-swollen Salween River. More than seventeen thousand died trying.

On 12 September, Lord Mountbatten accepted Japan's formal surrender in Singapore's city hall, later receiving his opposite number Field Marshal Count Hisaichi Terauchi's seven-hundred-year-old samurai sword. As the commander on the ground Mountbatten had already set a policy of working with the league, and London felt in no real position to complain. Toward the end of the month he invited the young officers of the league, including Aung San, to Kandy in the tea-growing highlands of Ceylon, in order to reach an agreement on a new Burma Army. They agreed that a new army would include forces from both the Japanese-trained army of Aung San and the existing British-trained Burma Army, roughly in equal numbers of about five thousand each. The British part was heavily comprised of ethnic minorities, mainly Karens, Kachins, and Chins from their own hills areas (there were only three British-trained ethnic Burmese officers), all fearful of life under a Burmese administration and with increasingly rosy memories of British rule.

The other part of the army brought a very different set of values and experience. They were largely former Thakin students, deeply devoted to the whole notion of anticolonialism and, after a nightmarish flirtation with fascism, politically of the left. They had learned from the Japanese a system of harsh punishments and strict loyalty to their superiors, never to act independently or to question authority, and always to place the army above all else. They were the generation of action, which would bring their country to independence after six decades of alien rule. They were confident and had no other life than politics and soldiering.

In a way, they were part of a new national mood, at least among the Burmese, one that believed that the future belonged to them and that whatever else, there could be no going back to the days when an all-white Pegu Club of linen-suited officials and businessmen ran their country behind closed doors.

DORMAN-SMITH TRIES TO IMPLEMENT THE WHITE PAPER, AND THE LEAGUE IS UNIMPRESSED

Shortly after the war's end, Reginald Dorman-Smith returned to Burma with the unenviable task of trying to implement the White Paper. He knew the league distrusted him and that the old conservative politicians—men he saw as friends, by and large—were tired and had nothing like the energy and determination of the up-and-coming generation. Before taking charge (from Mountbatten's military administration), he had met with many of them on board a warship, the HMS *Cumberland*, docked off Rangoon, where in their silk jackets and *pasos*, they had listened politely to his pleas that this time British rule would be different, helping themselves to several generous scoops of ice cream and wondering whether the British would really have the nerve to see this through.

After taking charge, Dorman-Smith addressed a reception inside the mildewed walls of Rangoon's City Hall, saying, "Burma will—no longer 'may'—take her place among the fully self-governing nations . . . Burma's battle for freedom is over." But they must first have an election. "Let us get on with this election job as quickly as we can." In the meantime he would appoint an advisory council and place it in charge of government departments. It would be a representative council, representative of the pre-1942 political spectrum with a special place for the league as the obvious main force on the ground.

Aung San saw the situation differently. For him there was only one problem in Burma, and that was the presence of the British; change that, and everything else would soon fall into place. The old politicians and the ethnic minorities could be accommodated as necessary, but these were secondary issues. For now the need was for unity and discipline under a single authority, the league, to force the British into recognizing that the cost of staying was much greater than the cost of leaving.

When Aung San read Dorman-Smith's offer of a new council and a special place for the league, he made a counteroffer he knew the governor could not accept: a majority of seats on the council for the league and the right to determine which league members would receive which departments, one of which had to be the Home Department, which controlled the police. It was meant to drive home the point that the league saw itself as the provincial government of Burma and could accept no other arrangement. It was a gamble, but Aung San was already used to making the toughest decisions with supreme confidence.

Whitehall ordered Dorman-Smith to stand firm. Aung San was being cocky and needed to be put in his place. The ex-BIA leader's demands were refused. The league then denounced Dorman-Smith as a fascist, and Aung San began hinting of an armed uprising. British troops in Burma were being drawn down fast, and Dorman-Smith knew (and perhaps Aung San knew as well) that there were not likely to be enough soldiers to fight a counterinsurgency war. The British military was uncomfortable with the way things were moving and wanted to rethink policy. But London insisted that the White Paper be implemented. The Burmese would have to learn to accept what was on offer. But in every town and village Aung San's men were making sure that would be impossible.

———

The next many months, from late autumn 1945 to the summer of 1946, were essentially a test of wills between the British and the league, as Aung San solidified his following and ratcheted up the pressure and as Dorman-Smith struggled in vain to implement the White Paper without provoking rebellion.[18]

Aung San had many of his top men inside the new Burma Army, as agreed to with Mountbatten at Kandy. But he needed something more, his own private army, and so he formed the People's Volunteer Organization. It was made up of tens of thousands of ex-soldiers, those who had served under him as part of the Japanese-backed army but who were now officially demobilized and not included in the new (British-commanded) armed forces. There were also fresh recruits. For the young men of 1946, all they had seen was war, and now, with the war over, they wanted to make sure they too had a piece of the action. At the same time, Aung San, gaunt in his rumpled khaki unform and speaking in clear, simple language, called for unity around a single demand, independence, and organized mass meetings in protest. He sometimes also railed against British economic recovery efforts, arguing that these would lead to profits for only the City of London. The demonstrations were always peaceful, but with the hint of violence lurking in the background, controlled to show who now had the upper hand. Those outside the league, the more moderate politicians, stayed silent, understanding the weight of popular feeling and the growing adoration of Aung San.

Before Christmas, Dorman-Smith recognized this as well, writing, "The whole strength of the League appears to depend on the personality of Aung San." He recommended that London invite him to visit. London ignored the suggestion. It was around then that the police opened fire and killed three people during a nationalist demonstration at Tantabin, a little town in the delta. The league decided there would be a public funeral and that Aung San himself would be there to speak. He met the governor beforehand, and the governor asked him whether or not he intended to start a rebellion and pleaded with him that working together would lead more quickly to freedom and greater future prosperity for Burma. Aung San wouldn't agree. He said that freedom would come faster through him. But he said he would tone down his speech and guarantee a peaceful funeral. It wasn't a threat but a veiled warning that London was running out of good choices.

The British had also to consider their obligations in the hill regions, the Scheduled Areas, which had been administered separately from Burma proper and whose people had fought so heroically for the Allied side throughout the war. The stated policy was not to abandon them and to include them in a future Rangoon government only if they wished. In the brilliant cool sunshine of early 1946 Dorman-Smith went up to Myitkyina, for the first time since he had flown out of that town with his wife and pet monkey nearly four years before. He noticed that one of the leading Kachin chiefs was wearing the handsome Savile Row dinner jacket he had left behind. He also noticed that the town was largely obliterated. The Kachins seemed nevertheless in high spirits, certain that the British would soon recognize their sacrifice and meet their promises of money and assistance, for schools and hospitals and a better life for their children.[19]

By now London was getting a little nervous. Why not early elections? Some of the old politicians and Burmese civil servants began regaining a bit of confidence, saying that Aung San would not win a majority. Some even suggested that an arrest of Aung San would help things along and that he would be quickly forgotten if detained. But for others, including British military analysts, the picture was very different. Aung San had his private army as well as the loyalty of his ex-officers in the Burma Army. Whatever the extent of his popular following, he could cause considerable trouble if he wanted to. And Indian troops would simply not be available to crush any Burmese uprising. There were two options. One was to somehow bring Aung San on board, whatever it took; the other was to use the non-Indian troops available — four British battalions, four Gurkha battalions, eleven thousand West African troops, and whichever Burmese remained loyal.[20] But the option to use force would be done in the face of a empty treasury at home and likely American displeasure at the new United Nations. It was not impossible to keep Aung San in check by force, but with growing headaches in Palestine and India, it was not an attractive proposition. Muddling on and leaving hard decisions for later seemed like the best thing to do.

For Aung San the calculation was different. He had remained as single-minded as ever; only independence mattered, come what may. There was nothing else to negotiate. And every day his single-mindedness and steely nature won him an ever-rising popularity, among all classes and all parts of society. He was drawing enormous crowds and had become a hero to his people. But he knew he was walking a tightrope. He was sitting at the top of a huge and unwieldy coalition, of Communists and Socialists, militia leaders and student-politicians, old and new colleagues, army officers and businessmen. How long could that continue? He had to play his hand sooner rather than later.

Around this time a strange sort of friendship developed between Aung San and Dorman-Smith. Aung San tended to become melancholy and sometimes turned to the Irish organic farmer to talk about his loneliness. He had no friends, he said, and found it difficult to make friends. Dorman-Smith asked him how he could say that "when you are the people's idol?" "I did not seek to be that," said Aung San, "but only to free my country. But now it is so lonely," and saying this, he wept. Dorman-Smith tried his best to comfort him, but it was no good. "How long do national heroes last? Not long in this country; they have too many enemies . . . I do not give myself more than another eighteen months of life."[21]

LONDON LOSES ITS NERVE

Then came the test. As a legislative council was meeting for its first session and speeches were being made by rival politicians against the league, one council member, a former Thakin and one of the Thirty Comrades who had trained with Aung San at Hainan Island, stood up and accused his former commander of murder. In the early months of the war he and Aung San had marched into the Tenasserim on the coattails of an advancing Japanese division. At a village near Moulmein they had found that the village headman, an Indian, had remained in contact with the British and was preparing to organize a local resistance. Aung San arranged for the man to be tried by a court-martial and sentenced to death. The battle novice Aung San then tried to personally carry out the sentence, striking the man with a sword, but, failing to kill him, ordered another soldier to finish the job.

The story was all over the London as well as the Rangoon press, and a formal police inquiry was automatically begun. On 27 March at a meeting at Government House, Dorman-Smith canvassed the opinions of his chief lieutenants, and they were divided. The chief secretary to the government, Sir John Wise, said that they would legally be obliged to arrest Aung San if a formal complaint was made, but the inspector general of police argued that this would lead to rebellion. He also reminded the governor that a pardon of all wartime offenses was being discussed. The commander in chief of Burma Command, the top British military officer in the country, said that an arrest of Aung San would lead not just to rebellion but to a mutiny from within the Burma Army and that there would be no Indian troops to deal with the consequences.

Aung San quickly heard of what was happening. He was not unhappy. This would force the issue and reveal once and for all whether the British were really going to try to stay. He saw what was going on in the world. Two weeks before, Ho Chi Minh, leader of the Vietminh guerrillas, had been elected the president of North Vietnam, and the Yugoslav partisan commander, Josef Broz Tito, was setting up his new government in Belgrade. The UN Security Council had held its first session, and Clement Attlee had just promised India independence as soon as a new constitution could be agreed on. History would forgive nothing but decisiveness.

The next morning Aung San walked into Sir Reginald's office and told him as politely but directly as he could that the story about the murder was correct and that he accepted full responsibility. The governor warned that he might have to arrest him. Two weeks later an order arrived from Whitehall telling him to do just that, and the police were instructed to comply. In the Dutch East Indies, thousands had already died in fighting between Indonesian nationalists and the returning Dutch regime. Burma seemed on the eve of a similar war, perhaps one that would eventually drag in the Chinese and the Americans as well. But then, just as policemen had gone out to serve the order, a new order arrived from London, canceling the first. Over those twenty-four hours London had lost its nerve.

Dorman-Smith then decided to press home the issue and wrote to his superiors that at this point nothing other than the establishment of a provisional government under Aung San would calm tensions. He recommended immediate elections for a constituent assembly that would pave the way for unconditional independence. The world had changed, and Aung San had positioned himself just right. Dorman-Smith was asked to come back to London and would be made the

scapegoat for a year of inattention by Clement Attlee and his government. He was soon replaced as governor by Sir Hubert Rance. The
British were getting ready to quit Burma.

By now political instability, the protests and strikes, the stillborn reconstruction, and the absence of any real law and order meant the country
was a mess. Banditry was a problem almost everywhere in a country
awash in guns and martial spirit and with a standard of living far below
that of the 1920s. Rice was in short supply, with government price ceil-
ings and diversion of part of the crop to famine-stricken India. The Irrawaddy Flotilla Company, the lifeline of many backwater towns, was
forced to discontinue service in the delta because of fears over security.
Armed guards had to be assigned to all trains, buses, and boats. On
8 June even *The New York Times* reported that revolution was imminent.

Against this backdrop, the British House of Commons held its first
proper debate on Burma, and the government's Burma policy was attacked from both sides. Erstwhile journalist and alleged Communist spy
Tom Driberg led calls from within the Labour Party in favor of working
with Aung San and the nationalists, blaming not Dorman-Smith but
the old Burma establishment at Government House and the Pegu Club,
who, he said, were simply incapable by their background and training
of understanding the new forces around them and of being anything
but patronizing in their attitude toward the Burmese. On the Conservative side, Captain Leonard Gammans said that the real mistake was
not having arrested Aung San sooner as a Japanese collaborator. Restore law and order, by force if necessary, and the Burmese would regain confidence in British rule. There was no real alternative; if the
British pulled out now, someone else would come in. The government,
while not quite taking Driberg's line, said that the best course forward
now was working with Aung San toward a speedy independence.

On 2 September, Pandit Nehru's provisional government took
power in New Delhi. As talks continued on possible partition, Nehru
made clear again that the Indian Army could play no role against Aung
San. Sir Hubert Rance had just arrived as the new and last governor
and was welcomed by a wave of strikes, including a police strike that
soon spread, first to all government workers and then to the railways
and oil industry. By late September all business and administration was

at a standstill. A giant demonstration in Rangoon denounced the White Paper. Aung San knew he was gaining ground and prepared for a national strike to underline his position.

Governor Rance acted fast to show the Burmese things had changed. He met with the league on 21 September, and within two weeks a deal was made. There would be a new executive council with himself as chair and Aung San as deputy chair as well as the member in charge of defense and external affairs. The league was well represented, but other political groupings, including those of minority groups, would also be there. Aung San would be the de facto prime minister of a provincial government.

A national strike was averted, but Aung San made certain he would now set the pace. On 10 November he issued a four-part demand, including elections in April 1947, the inclusion of the hill regions in the whole process, an agreement that Burma would be independent by 31 January 1948, and a relook at economic reconstruction issues and in particular the role of British companies. Having come this far, Aung San also knew that he now needed the British to see things through and hold the country together. An armed rebellion at this point would mean that everyone would lose. He also needed to reassure minority peoples—in particular the Karens—that he could be trusted and that there would be no discrimination in an independent Burma. The lessons of India were close at hand, where vicious communal rioting in Calcutta was soon overshadowed by partition, a million refugees, and tens of thousands more dead across Bengal and the Punjab. And Rangoon was volatile. Militia commanders declaring loyalty to Aung San threatened violence and local strikes, and demonstrations continued, including one that nearly invaded the Secretariat building. With Aung San's agreement, West African troops were sent in to patrol Rangoon, and this had good effect, but the situation was far from calm.

U AUNG SAN GOES TO LONDON

Prime Minister Attlee was now ready to accept anything, including full independence for Burma outside the new British Commonwealth. In a speech to Parliament just before Christmas holiday, he said: "We do not desire to retain within the Commonwealth and Empire any unwilling peoples. It is for the people of Burma to decide their own future . . . For the sake of the Burmese people, it is of the utmost importance that this should be an orderly—though rapid—progress." He proposed inviting Burmese representatives to London to discuss a new policy. Churchill, now the opposition leader and mindful of his father's legacy, replied that the government was throwing away "what has been gained by so many generations of toil and sacrifice . . . this undue haste that we should get out of Burma finally and forever." He hoped for delay and a chance for Britain's friends in Burma to regain the initiative. Attlee responded that both India and Ireland were examples of the British doing the right thing too late.[22]

Aung San and the other delegates arrived by air to a poorly heated London in the middle of a freezing cold January. For some like Tin Tut, educated at Dulwich and Cambridge, London was familiar territory, but for Aung San, wearing a greatcoat against the unfamiliar climate, it was his very first time in the West. Tin Tut, the brightest Burmese official of his generation, quickly found himself Aung San's deputy, and together they made speedy progress and were in a good mood. By 27 January there was an agreement. The interim government would be respected as a full dominion government (like Canada and Australia) and would control the Burma Army as soon as all Allied forces were withdrawn. A constituent assembly would be elected as soon as possible, and the final constitutional document would be presented to the British Parliament for approval. A portion of this assembly would become the provisional Burmese Parliament and would decide whether or not to remain in the Commonwealth after independence. Financial matters and the question of a future military alliance would be left to later talks. Britain would nominate Burma for membership in the United Nations.

The main problem for Aung San now was not with the British but with rivals at home. His closest colleague, Than Tun, left the league and as the leader of the Communist Party began warning of a sham independence, one that would leave the country to the mercy of British commercial interests and Anglo-American military domination. From the right, U Saw, the prewar prime minister, began making similar noises. A few months before, unknown assassins had tried to kill U Saw but only managed to blow out an eye. He blamed the league and began plotting his revenge.

On 29 January, a bitterly cold night, Aung San threw a reception at the Dorchester Hotel for the diplomatic corps and members of Parliament. The fountain outside was frozen, and small electric fires were scattered about the big drawing room to make up for the breakdown in central heating. It was the first Burmese diplomatic reception since the Kinwun's reception on a ship in the Thames in 1874, at the beginning of what were more than sixty years of European imperialism. He was wearing a pressed major general's uniform, and to those who knew him he seemed for the first time to be relaxed and happy. He received the visitors with politeness and assurance and was observed inquisitively by the assembled dignitaries as the young Asian man who had stood down the British Empire. They addressed him as Your Excellency. He was thirty-one years old.[23]

The most urgent challenge now for Aung San was to convince people in the hill areas to join in the new deal, all while keeping the Communists and other restless elements in check. At the little Shan town of Panglong, he gained an agreement with the Shan *sawbwas* that their states would be part of the new republic, while retaining a good deal of autonomy. They would also have the right to secede after ten years, in 1958; Burma would be the only British possession to gain independence with an option for a future breakup built into the constitution. The Karen leaders, though, would agree to nothing. The memories of bloodletting were too fresh, and their hope for British and American help was too strong. They insisted on a separate Karen state within the British Empire, looking perhaps to the example of Pakistan, and unperturbed by the fact that Burma's Karen minority, like India's Muslims, lived scattered across much of the country.

On 7 April, elections went ahead, but they were far from ideal. The Karens boycotted the entire process, and many of Aung San's enemies refused to take part. The league naturally won a huge majority, and all its candidates were returned. One of the first things the new league-dominated Parliament did was to withdraw from the British Commonwealth. It was not an easy decision and was a great blow to the British, but it was taken when staying in the Commonwealth seemed to mean remaining a dominion and keeping the British monarch as head of state. The Indian example of being a republic in the Commonwealth was in the future. At a time when the Communists and U Saw were attacking Aung San's "sham independence" deal, he could not afford to give them any further ammunition.

Aung San's Executive Council—the interim government—was made up of many, if not all, of the country's most promising new leaders. It did not include Than Tun and the Communists, many of whom were clever and capable, but it did include many other men on whom any bright future would depend, not only ethnic Burmese like Aung San and Tin Tut, but also the Karen leader Mahn Ba Khaing, whom Aung San had persuaded to join; Sao Hsam Htun,* one of the Shan chiefs; and Adul Razak, a Muslim leader of considerable standing from Mandalay. The Council normally met under Sir Hubert's chairmanship at Government House, but it decided to meet on the morning of 19 July at the Secretariat instead, as there was nothing in the agenda on that muggy and overcast day that would concern the governor's residual areas of responsibility.

The Secretariat is today surrounded by a high wall as well as an outer fence, with coils of barbed wire in between, but in 1947 there was no real protective barrier. In any case the car that sped in at just before half past ten in the light drizzle, through the front entrance off Dalhousie Street and into the central courtyard, was carrying men in army fatigues. They were unchallenged by the sentries on duty. Three of them, armed with Sten guns, then raced up one of the stairways, shot the single guard standing outside, and burst into the council chamber, where the meeting was taking place, opening fire immediately. Apparently having heard the gunshots outside, Aung San stood up as the doors were flung open and was shot first with a volley in the chest. The gunman then fired to Aung San's right and left, killing four other council members on the spot and mortally wounding two others. Only three of those in the room survived. Aung San was dead.[24]

There was now the danger of an uprising by the Communists or a coup. Rumors spread that the British were behind the killings. The only council member who was not present was U Nu; assassins had rushed to his house, but he had luckily been away. Governor Rance

---

*"Sao" is an honorific in Shan, usually reserved for members of princely families.

quickly asked him to take over and form a new council, which was sworn in the next day. But who had been responsible?

It soon emerged that U Saw, Aung San's bitter rival who had lost an eye, had been at the center of a plot that also involved British officers. To this day conspiracy theories abound, linking the assassination with the British government. But it seems certain that these British officers were acting on their own; Aung San was increasingly seen by London as an asset against a Communist takeover, and there would seem little reason for the Labour government in London at this point to want him dead. But an inquiry by Rance showed that in June and July arms and equipment from the (still British-controlled) Army Ordnance Depot had found its way (through forged documents) into the hands of U Saw's men and that U Saw had directly paid two British Army officers. Another British officer had reported to his superiors that U Saw himself admitted stealing the arms, and on reading this report, the senior officer simply filed it away, rather than tell the police. The senior officer, the chief of the Ordnance Depot, claims to have forgotten all about it until after the assassination. U Nu was told of this but decided not to reveal all the facts to a Burmese public that would have demanded retribution.[25] Instead U Saw, the man who actually organized the assassination, was tried before a Burmese court, denied an appeal to the House of Lords, and was hanged.

The drama surrounding the country's independence was part of many great changes occurring across an exhausted but fast-changing postwar world. Just as soon as the United Nations was up and running, a new cold war between the West and the Soviet Union was creeping up over the international landscape. In May 1947 President Harry S. Truman unveiled his Truman Doctrine, proclaiming that the United States would come to the aid of peoples threatened by Communist insurrection. Aid was delivered to anti-Communist forces in Turkey and Greece, and a forty-year policy of containment was begun.

World attention was elsewhere. In November 1947 the United Nations General Assembly had voted to partition Palestine between Jews and Arabs, and within months six Arab armies invaded the new state of Israel. Closer to home, the partition of India into independent India and Pakistan had left up to a million dead, made ten million refugees, and, in October, ignited the very first Indo-Pakistani War over the fate of Kashmir. The 30 January assassination of Mahatma Gandhi underscored the end of an era. Britain was in full retreat. Even more ominously, on 24 June, the Soviet Union began its blockade of Berlin, threatening to turn the cold war into a nuclear confrontation.

Independent Burma would very soon enter this world with several of its key leaders, including its nationalist hero, dead, its principal minority demanding an independent state, and another nationalist leader getting ready to lead a Communist rebellion. It was not to be an auspicious start.

ELEVEN

ALTERNATIVE UTOPIAS

Burma's newly independent government tries to be a progressive and responsible member of the international community, but insurgencies and foreign invasions lead to the buildup of a big military machine

~~~

T here are only a few days a year when a man can wear a suit in Rangoon and not feel uncomfortable, and this was one of those days. The last of the monsoon downpours had ended more than a fortnight before, and bright, sunny afternoons were followed unfailingly by cool and cloudless nights. And now it was the dead of night. Sir Hubert Rance, the last British governor of Burma, must have wondered what sort of people would choose such a time to begin the independence of their new state. The Burmese, all avid (if sometimes closet) believers in astrology, had taken the advice of learned *ponnas* and asked that the formal handover of power occur at this most auspicious time, fourtwenty in the morning on 4 January 1948. The British could only agree. And so Sir Hubert, a tall, slightly stooped man with a thick graying mustache, got up and dressed in his morning coat and striped trousers, put on his top hat, and then by car made his way through Rangoon's dimly lit avenues, the headlights illuminating the enormous and happy crowds in their best silk sarongs, blowing horns, munching on snacks, letting off firecrackers, and playing music. Few had slept at all. For many Burmese it was a moment of reflection as well as celebration, especially for the older generation, who had lived through so many years of foreign occupation, finally to reach a day hardly any had dared imagine would ever really come.

After a slow few miles across the outskirts of the town, past the Scott Market and the Holy Trinity Cathedral and the ancient Sule Pagoda,

Sir Hubert's Rolls-Royce (now with a collector in Baltimore, Maryland) finally turned into Fytche Square, where a small party of British and Burmese notables were already assembled expectantly against the charcoal sky. Speeches were given, the Union Jack was lowered for the last time, and the new flag of the Union of Burma was hauled up, the faces of the young Burmese politicians beaming with happiness. The governor shook hands with the republic's new president and prime minister while several of the Englishwomen, wives of senior officials, quietly wept.

A few hours later, after the morning sun had lit up the grimy dockyards along the the river, the last company of the King's Own Yorkshire Light Infantry trooped onto the waiting British cruiser, HMS *Birmingham*. A band played "Auld Lang Syne," and Sir Hubert, with his wife and aides-de-camp, like Thibaw sixty-two years before, walked across a narrow plank and sailed away never to come back. Burma was independent. The country was also already at civil war.

The Burmese civil war is the longest-running armed conflict in the world and has continued, in one form or another, from independence to the present day.[1] In a way Burma is a place where the Second World War never really stopped. Ever since the first Japanese bombers hummed overhead and dropped their payloads over downtown Rangoon, the country has never known peace. For a brief period, between August 1945 and independence in January 1948, there were no open hostilities. And since then, there have been times, like today, when fighting is sporadic, small encounters here and there, affecting only isolated areas. But the gun has never been taken away from Burmese politics. And no government has governed the entirety of Burma since 1941. Elections have never been held across the entire country, and no government has been able to conduct a proper census. Few border regions are even today free of rebel control. There has not been a succession of wars; rather the same war, the same rhetoric, and sometimes even the same old rifles have staggered on and on, with only minor changes to the cast and plot and a few new special effects. Some of the very same groups that first took up arms in the 1940s, when Mahatma Gandhi was languishing in a British jail and Joe Louis was heavyweight champion of the world, are still duking it out today. Perhaps a million dead, millions more displaced, an economy in ruins, and a robust military machine designed to fight the enemy within have been the main stuff of Burma's postindependence history.

When U Nu took over the reins of government from Rance (who went on to a cushier job as governor of Trinidad), the country was already saddled with two active, if minor, insurgencies. The first was the revolt of the so-called Red Flag Communists, hard-line Stalinists, loyal to their firebrand ex-schoolmaster party chairman, Thakin Soe. The other was the mujahideen Islamic insurgency in the north of Arakan. A much bigger problem than either was the huge militia, called the People's Volunteer Organization, made up of demobilized former soldiers of the Burma Independence Army, once loyal to Aung San and the cause of independence and since the death of Aung San without clear aims or leadership. They tended politically to the left and were ready to dive energetically into whatever fight was coming. The country was awash in weapons and full of young men who had never held proper jobs and had little reason to give up politics just as things were getting interesting. A generation had grown up watching the armies of Imperial Japan, the British Empire, China, and the United States battling it out in their own backyard and could imagine nothing more exciting than soldiering. And this was the generation that was coming of age.[2]

The next to revolt was the Communist Party of Burma under its boss, Thakin Than Tun. It was the most formidable of the government's foes, popular, well armed, and with the possibility of foreign backing. The Communists argued, to themselves and to anyone who would listen, that the Anti-Fascist People's Freedom League had become little more than a tool of British imperialism and that it was therefore necessary to overthrow it and establish a proper people's government. This was the thesis crafted by H. N. Goshal, the party's chief dogmatist, and was formally adopted by the Central Council a month after the British departure. Strikes were organized, and violence was stirred up. Last-minute attempts at compromise went nowhere. The militia groups, the various Communist factions, and the government considered and then rejected a peaceful solution. Prime Minister U Nu offered to stand down.

On the same day, before an enormous gathering in the center of

Rangoon, Than Tun ridiculed the weakness of the ruling league and called for a people's revolution. Then, knowing he would very soon be locked up, he and his top lieutenants hurried away that same night to their stronghold at Pyinmana (about halfway between Rangoon and Mandalay) and from there ordered their twenty thousand or so armed men to begin their campaign. Within weeks, up and down the Irrawaddy Valley, one town after another fell to the Communists. In April Communist units seized police stations, took over town centers, looted rice warehouses, and cut telephone and telegraph lines. The government fought back, and after a few weeks it looked as if the worst might be over. At this point U Nu tried to make yet another offer of reconciliation and announced his own "Leftist Unity" program. It called for state control of much of the economy and society and for a new league that would be devoted to Marxist doctrine and would be made up of Communists as well as Socialists. British and American journalists and intelligence analysts wrote that Burma was on the verge of being handed over lock, stock, and barrel to Than Tun and his puppet masters in the Kremlin.

Closer to summer, as increasingly humid heat gave way to welcome showers, parts of the regular army itself began to peel away from Rangoon's authority. At the time the Burma Army amounted only to around fifteen thousand men, organized into ten frontline battalions. Half the army was heavily politicized, ethnic Burmese battalions, often left-leaning or at least radical and full of derring-do. One of these battalions, the Sixth Burma Rifles, mutinied at Pegu on 16 June, and many of its officers and men immediately joined up with the Communists. Worse was to come. In July the entire People's Volunteer Organization, the umbrella for various militia groups, also went into revolt. Then two more army battalions mutinied: the First Burma Rifles at Thayetmyo and the Third Burma Rifles at the Mingaladon Air Base just outside the capital. Both were headed by former lieutenants of Aung San's. They attempted to link up and march on Rangoon, but their convoys were only just stopped by the Burma Air Force, led by the Anglo-Shan wing commander Tommy Clift, on 10 August. Then it was the turn of the Union Military Police, which declared itself on no side in particular but in opposition to the government all the same, taking reams of cash from government treasuries as well as arms and ammunition. Half the country was now in the hands of one rebel faction or another. Trains and steamers stopped running. In places a state of emergency was declared. Rumors circulated. Some said Indian troops had landed or that the British Fourteenth Army would soon be back. What was to come was no less fantastic.[3]

Up until this time the government was depending heavily on the support of the six battalions of Karen and Kachin Rifles inherited from the British Burma Army. These troops had helped retake the strategic town of Prome halfway up the Irrawaddy as well as Thayetmyo and the Pyinmana area in the first of what were to be fifty years of counterinsurgency operations. The commander in chief at the time was Lieutenant General Smith Dun, an ethnic Karen who was purportedly named after Jimmy Stewart's character in *Mr. Smith Goes to Washington*. His deputy and the head of the army was Major General Ne Win. For a while things seemed to be going in the right direction. In December the Communists were routed in a few targeted operations and driven from their Pyinmana headquarters. Three thousand other Communists surrendered at Toungoo. All of this was the work of loyal Karen and Kachin fighters, including Kachin units under the command of the dashing captain Naw Seng, a much-decorated anti-Japanese war hero.

Naturally enough, some of the Karen fighters began wondering whether they were doing the right thing in propping up the government and whether they shouldn't instead be thinking more of taking advantage of the situation and pushing their own demands. Some wanted to set up an independent Karen state in the east of the country. Around this time Moulmein, the third-largest city, was taken over by disgruntled Karens from the military police. More Karen rebellions seemed imminent. Some leaders in the Karen community, including former Ringling Bros. and Barnum & Bailey Circus performer San Po Thin, tried to negotiate some sort of deal with Rangoon. Moulmein was eventually handed back, and a new commission to look at autonomy issues was set up. It was a good and representative commission, but there were many, on both sides, who wanted no compromise. There were Burmese who hated the Karens and Karens who thought all-out independence was within their grasp—"like Laos," some said. British troublemakers egged them on, and at least two former members of Force 136, the wartime British Special Forces group, were caught smuggling arms into the country and expelled. The Karen National Union began building up its military wing, the Karen National Defense Organization, or KNDO. Rangoon responded by hastily raising thousands of extra militia to defend the capital. The Communists had been killing for a workers' paradise in the little pagoda towns of middle Burma. Now ethnic nationalists, both Burmese and Karen, were itching for their own war.

On Christmas Eve 1948 Burmese government soldiers massacred at least eight Karen civilians in eight different churches in and around the palm-shaded beach town of Mergui. A little later a Karen village north of Rangoon was attacked by police under the command of a leading Burmese politician. Over 150 Karens were killed, 30 shot down in cold blood. The KNDO then raided the armory at Insein (next to Rangoon), and the Fourth Burma Rifles (an ethnic Burmese battalion) burned to the ground the American Baptist Mission school at Maubin. In villages around the delta neighbors suddenly turned on one another. Karen pastors preached the need to lead their people from the hands of the unbelievers. The KNDO attacked the port city of Bassein only to be driven out after two days of heavy fighting. On 31 January clashes broke out on the outskirts of Rangoon itself.

The next day General Smith Dun, the loyal Karen head of the armed forces, was replaced by Japanese-groomed Major General (now General) Ne Win, a Burmese. Karen neighborhoods in the west of Rangoon were set on fire by angry mobs, and Karen civilians gunned down as they tried to escape from their homes. Just to the north of the city the KNDO seized the suburb of Insein as well as the sizable armory at Mingaladon. Incensed at what was happening to their kinsmen, three Karen battalions, arguably the best-trained third of the army, then went into full rebellion. If they had acted quickly, they might have combined forces and easily taken the capital. The U Nu government would have collapsed, and the whole history of postwar Burma would have been different. But they hesitated. They were angry, but they had no plan. Some of their units came within a few miles of the city center but did not break through the main government positions. On the other side, the hero of the day was General Ne Win, whose Fourth Burma Rifles, together with military police and some quickly raised Gurkha and Anglo-Burmese militiamen, were able to hold the line. Two of the Karen battalions came down the main roads leading to Rangoon but were held up near Tharrawaddy and then strafed by the blue and red–striped government Spitfires. A sort of front line emerged just outside Rangoon, and both sides set about digging in.

If that wasn't enough, government workers went on a general strike in protest against recent pay cuts. By mid-February all government offices were shut down, and civil administration everywhere ground to a halt. Rangoon itself was paralyzed by mass demonstrations, and an assortment of armed groups began parading up and down city streets, calling for the overthrow of U Nu. Then, to top it off, and suspiciously just before exam month, the students went on strike. But through all this Parliament continued to meet and even passed a few new laws. And for those looking for a fun time, the cinemas remained open, as well as the racetracks at the Rangoon Turf Club, where General Ne Win could be seen every weekend despite sounds of artillery not far away. For a few rupees it was even possible to ride a special bus to the front line and take a few potshots at the Karen soldiers lurking in the distance.

Elsewhere in the country things were not looking very good either. The Kachin commander Naw Seng raised his own flag of revolt, declared that his First Kachin Rifles were now in an alliance with the rebel Karens, and quickly overran a succession of towns in the hilly areas from Pyinmana to Maymyo. On 13 March, despite a fierce defense by local militia, Mandalay fell to the rebel side. At Pakkoku, to the west of the Irrawaddy, the commanding officer of an ethnic Chin battalion,* having received no orders for a while, came to the reasonable conclusion that all government had come to an end and simply marched his men back home to the hills. It was an incredibly confusing picture. In some places the Communists shared power with militia leaders whereas Mandalay came under the joint rule of the Karens and the Communist Party. In other places various strongmen with no particular affiliations emerged at the head of armed groups to take over admin-

---

*The Chins are an upland people living along the Burmese-Indian border. On the Indian side they are known as Mizos and today have their own state.

istration. Few had clear aims, and those that did had no desire to compromise. The lesson of World War II and Aung San's campaign against
the British seemed to be that stubbornness, coupled with as much force
as possible, was the best way to get ahead. All the young men clung to
their separate visions of a perfect Burma, and were happy to soldier on.

It was from this ignominious beginning that the Burmese military machine of today was built up, almost from scratch. The combined
strength of all the antigovernment forces was estimated at around thirty
thousand troops, and these were good troops, including whole battalions trained by the British. Against this, the General Ne Win had a pal-
try three thousand regular soldiers from some loyal companies, mainly
men of his own Fourth Burma Rifles, men who had served under him
and Aung San during the war and who included many trained by the
Japanese. From the scrap heaps left behind by General Slim's Fourteenth Army, Ne Win was able to cobble together two tanks. But as the
specter of anarchy or Communist takeover loomed large, valuable help
came from the British, who supplied arms and ammunition as well as
six Dakota airplanes that allowed the government side to maintain contact with disparate parts of the country and ferry troops around as necessary. These were flown by British pilots on civilian contracts. Ne
Win's men were also helped by Catalina flying boats, flown by American war veterans as well as by Burmese airmen, easy-to-land planes that
could wreak havoc on enemy troop concentrations with their nifty side
machine guns. Even the prime minister flew around in a Catalina (pi-
loted by Captain Chet Brown of the U.S.A.) to rally his people. Britain
also lent six million pounds to the beleaguered government, and
Britain, together with Australia, India, Ceylon, and the United States,
gave another eight million dollars in emergency aid. As British, Indian,
and other ambassadors tried to facilitate talks, there was speculation
that Burma, after a little more than a year away, might even rejoin the
Commonwealth.[4]

In April a column of two thousand troops led by the renegade
Kachin commander Naw Seng moved south in Willis jeeps and worn-
out trucks with the hope of taking Rangoon by 1 May but was stopped
less than a hundred miles from the capital. It was the last major attempt
of its kind, and the tide soon began to turn in earnest. Mandalay was re-

taken after ferocious fighting, and the civil service strike collapsed, the clerks in their sarongs and short cotton jackets creeping back to their desks. The Karens were defeated in a series of clashes around Rangoon and then driven across the river toward the onetime Portuguese settlement at Syriam. A few weeks later their stronghold at Toungoo was taken, and their leader, the former schoolteacher Saw Ba U Gyi, was assassinated in a Burmese army ambush. The Communists looked expectantly toward help from China and, in the early months of the Korean War, repositioned many of their forces up to Katha (George Orwell's old post) in the hope of linking up with Chinese forces in a new Pacific war. But Ne Win was able to move from strength to strength, and a spirited army operation soon overran the Communist headquarters ("the Sunflower Camp"), splintering the "People's Army" into less threatening guerrilla bands. After this cascade of government good fortune, the Communists and the Karens were divided on what to do next. Some pushed for terms with the government. It was not quite over, but slowly, town by town, village by village, the Burma Army began to assert its authority.

For the young republic, it had been a disastrous start, and on top of all the destruction of the Second World War, the recent fighting had cost the country an estimated 250 million pounds (or over 5 billion pounds, more than 9 billion U.S. dollars, in today's money) in material damage. There were two men who had pulled the country back from the brink and had averted a Communist takeover or an all-out disintegration of the country: Prime Minister U Nu and the armed forces commander in chief General Ne Win. Together, and in entirely different ways, they would shape the Burma of the next half century.

THE LIFE AND TIMES OF U NU

Mention U Nu, and most Burmese, especially those of a certain age, will light up and have a good thing to say. Handsome, charming, perhaps more than a little clownish, he gave the impression of an eternal schoolboy, always looking for answers to the big questions of life and never quite ready to grow up. I met him several times in the 1980s, first at a Burmese home in northern Virginia, during his final years of exile, and later at his little bungalow off Goodliffe Road in Rangoon. It was easy to see why he was such an effective politician. He always seemed cheerful even when making a serious point, and in old age this was still combined with a gentle but mischievous air. U Nu was the sort of person you wanted to go on an adventure with, because you knew it would be fun. In 1986 he had been persuaded to play the role of visiting scholar at Northern Illinois University, where a new Burma Studies Center was improbably being created amid the cornfields of Middle America. He had agreed to give talks on Buddhism. Every day an official from the center offered to walk him from his dormitory room to the lecture hall, and every day he declined, saying he would rather find his own way, and every day he got lost. The official would have to look for him, wandering the midwestern campus, and U Nu almost invariably arrived for class half an hour late.

U Nu was born in May 1907 in the hot and sticky delta town of Wakema, about fifty miles from Rangoon, an area that was mainly elephant- and tiger-filled jungle until just twenty years before. He was the eldest son, and his parents were well-to-do shopkeepers, part of a Burmese and Buddhist family that also owned quite a lot of land in this prosperous rice-growing region. His aunt was a particularly rich woman who had recently won a hefty sum in a British sweepstakes lottery.[5]

The man who would one day guide Burma through its early years of independence was in his youth, by his own account, "a devil-may-care fellow." He had developed early on a taste for drink and as a teenager constantly found himself in trouble. He was a good boxer and played football in school, and both women and politics were favorite pastimes. He also developed a fervent interest in Buddhism, and a strong religious spirit remained with him throughout his long life.

At Rangoon University in the late 1920s he was nicknamed Philosopher Nu and Don Quixote, dressed strangely, and attracted many friends. Though his English was not very good (he read history), his most heartfelt ambition was to become a great English writer. This was his passion. He wrote plays and sent them off to competitions in England. He even sent one to George Bernard Shaw and fancied himself the George Bernard Shaw of Burma. One vacation he built himself a little hut outside Rangoon so he could sit by himself the whole time and write undisturbed.

Nu was sometimes on the receiving end of his friends' practical jokes. He had gone to see a play at Jubilee Hall and found himself sitting next to an elegant and beautiful Parsee woman. Next to her was her sister, "also a beauty," and their elderly parents. Nu noticed that she was "tall and slender, with bewitching eyes," "obviously a person of refinement and an uninhibited and friendly type." As he was without a copy of the program, she gave him hers, saying she would share her sister's. When she asked him whether he knew the story of *The Admirable Crichton*, he confessed he did not, and she gave him a brief rundown. He was in love. But he found his English inadequate, "the Parsee girl's being so perfect." With nods and smiles he could only encourage her and found himself tongue tied and hoping the play would never stop. She bade him goodbye. "Wasn't *Crichton* perfectly admirable?"

Nu remembered that "still savoring her perfume," he stared after her car until it was out of sight. "Every fibre tingled at the thought of her, the curvature of her body, the expression in her eyes, the melody in her voice." He wrote her a sonnet. But where to send it? He didn't even know her name. He kept his feelings bottled up for a few days and finally confided in his friends. Rangoon was full of Parsees, they said. "You're a fool." He wandered around town, looking for her. The cinemas, the parks, Fytche Square. When the Gymkhana Club staged a revue at Jubilee Hall, he went two nights in a row, hoping she might be there. After a month a college friend brought an address for a "Miss Homasjee." He sent the sonnet. No reply. He was advised to persevere. Three more letters were sent at decent intervals. He decided to go in person. "Show me the way," he said, and his friends, laughing heartily, admitted that they had lifted the first Parsee name they could find in the phone book.[6]

After university, Nu moved to Pantanaw, a stone's throw from his hometown, where he was soon accepted for a post as the superintendent of the local private school. He taught English and history and enjoyed giving speeches condemning colonialism. His good friend from university days, U Thant, was already the headmaster of the school, and it was at Pantanaw that the friendship grew closer. Both men were then in their mid-twenties. It was also at Pantanaw that U Nu fell, again, in love.

Daw Mya Yi* was a quiet, devout Buddhist and the daughter of a mill owner who was the president of the school committee. Her father

---

*"Daw" is an honorific for women, equivalent to "U" for men.

thought Nu was not good enough for his daughter, but Mya Yi was also in love and agreed to elope, escaping through the dark jungle creeks in a motorboat (which some old people in Pantanaw claim was arranged by U Thant). They fled to Rangoon for a nervous honeymoon.

Nu could not return to Pantanaw and after some hesitation began work on a graduate degree in law. He immediately got caught up in nationalist politics. A natural politician, by 1936 he had been elected the president of the Student Union, having been persuaded to stand by Aung San and others keen on their group's capturing control of the organization. The Student Union was never the same again, and it was during Nu's tenure that the focus shifted suddenly from organizing social events and sporting competitions to politics.

Nu and Aung San were a team, and the students' strike of 1936 was precipitated by the expulsion of both young troublemakers from the Rangoon campus. The British authorities had offered Nu a scholarship to England, to get him out of the country, but he refused, traveling around up-country and giving fiery speeches to approving crowds, his voice often breaking with emotion. But like the other students and Thakins at the time, he wasn't always quite sure what he was campaigning for. At a speech in Henzada he rounded on the University Act, but when asked what was actually wrong with it, he couldn't reply. He said he did not know but would ask his colleague Raschid to answer, as Raschid "knew everything." Raschid complained about his frankness, but U Nu replied, "We must be honest!"

U Nu also became interested in communism. Some of his closest friends had begun considering themselves Communists, and in later years two of them (Than Tun and Soe) became his battlefield enemies as the twin leaders of the Communist insurgency. He once told Than Tun, "You'll be the Lenin of Burma and I'll be your Maxim Gorky." But Nu and many others could not really reconcile Marxism with their Buddhist beliefs and upbringing and preferred to call themselves Socialists.

U Nu lived an incredibly simple life even after becoming prime minister in 1947. His house was always modestly furnished with a few pictures of his family and of him with international statesmen. He spent the nights not in the big main house but in a small hut in the garden of his official residence. In 1948, though still happily married and now with several children, he took a vow of sexual abstinence. And when he left office in late 1958, he gave away of all his personal belongings except a few pieces of clothing.

When U Nu was in office, his personal devotion to Buddhism combined with politically more calculated efforts to strengthen Buddhism as a defense against communism. His was a somewhat eclectic brand of Buddhism, with a colorful dose of Burmese *nat* worship and astrology thrown in. Like Mindon a hundred years before, he was a personally religious man and tolerant of other faiths as a result of his religious beliefs. Many Burmese Buddhists believed that he had accumulated great merit, from this life and from past incarnations. My grandmother, afraid of flying, said that she would happily fly if U Nu was on board as well, confident that his good karma would ensure a safe trip. In 1954–56 U Nu organized a grand international Buddhist Synod, bringing together Buddhist monks and scholars from across Asia, and the U Nu period of the 1950s witnessed a remarkable renaissance of Buddhist teaching and practice, with new schools of meditation and the lavishing of funds on a reinvigorated *sangha*.

At all times U Nu remained a deeply charming and engaging man. "The most immediately impressive thing about Nu," said Jawaharlal Nehru, "is his radiant personality—it wins him friends wherever he goes."

BURMA'S DEMOCRATIC EXPERIMENT

There is a persistent myth among those who write about Burma that it is a "rich country gone wrong," a country that emerged from colonial rule in good shape, with a sound economy and all the attributes necessary for future prosperity. "It was much better off than South Korea!" they say. This view is usually part of a critique of present-day woes and not only a way of describing how far Burma has fallen but a way of suggesting lost opportunities and blaming successive military regimes. That successive military regimes have done little or nothing to better the economy is hard to dispute. But this does not mean that Burma in the years after independence was a promising young Asian star. The truth is that Burma in 1950, the year the civil war ebbed away, was in shambles, and war had been replaced, in many parts, by anarchy. Communications were down nearly everywhere, and the trains and steamers that operated did so only under heavily armed escort. The countryside was held by a patchwork of rebels and government loyalists, islands of government control in a sea of uncertain authority. As Home Minister Kyaw Nyein said in an interview with *Time* magazine, "three hundred armed men can take any place except Rangoon itself."[7] The mines and sawmills and oil wells of British times had largely shut down, and rice exports, once three million tons a year, had plummeted to less than a million tons. Everywhere life was tough.

In Pantanaw's neighboring town of Maubin, for example, its prewar population of nine thousand had swollen to over twenty thousand with an influx of refugees, most living in miserable grass and thatch huts along the riverbank. The fields were largely abandoned, and most people were trying to eke out a living doing menial labor or selling what they could. Before the war the district around Maubin had about a dozen civil police, but in 1949 an entire battalion of Chin Rifles, quartered in the former home of the deputy commissioner and district judge, was necessary to maintain a veneer of security. Outside the gates of the town was no-man's-land, with Karen rebels and an assortment of bandit gangs, always ready to shoot up a police post, loot a warehouse, or hijack a passing steamer. It was this situation that was repeated a hundred times across the country.

To deal with all this, Burma had U Nu, youthful at forty-four years old but a good deal older than many of his colleagues in government. U Nu's cabinet was made up of many from the old Student Union, the Thakin nationalists, and Japanese collaborators, some of whom were now inching into their thirties. Few had any real knowledge of government. In India power had been passed to Pandit Nehru and others, educated men who had been in positions of government responsibility since the mid-1930s. In Burma the political leaders of the 1930s, such as Dr. Ba Maw, were now in disgrace or had been pushed aside by a much younger generation.

The only really experienced hand in the government was U Tin Tut. A keen rugby player, educated at Dulwich College and Cambridge University, he had served in Mesopotamia in the First World War and was a lawyer who had been called to the English bar and had gone on to be the first Burmese to pass the Indian Civil Service examinations, serving for several years at the central Secretariat in New Delhi. At independence he became Burma's first foreign minister, and he would have been an important, perhaps critical adviser to U Nu, but he was killed when a grenade was lobbed into his car in broad daylight in September 1948, just nine months after independence. His assassins were never caught, and no one was ever charged with his murder.

It was around this time that U Nu asked my grandfather to work more closely with him. U Thant had left Pantanaw in 1947 under heavy pressure from both Aung San and U Nu to be the chief propagandist for the league. His job was to edit the weekly party journal and to act as spokesman, both to the local press and with visitors from overseas. He also wrote anonymous editorials in the Burmese papers and over the next several years would write nearly two thousand articles, anonymous to everyone but the paper's publishers and U Nu himself.

But U Nu wanted U Thant to be more than just his official and unofficial public relations man. He believed that Thant might have a talent for diplomacy, and in the worst days of 1949 he asked him to drive through the front lines and try to arrange a cease-fire. My grandmother was obviously concerned but stoical. Not so the wife of the driver, who became hysterical and threatened divorce. They managed to pass through the heavily fortified barricades and KNDO checkpoints, past the tired men in fatigues smoking green cheroots, explaining their mission, and finally driving on to the Karen headquarters. There Thant was happy to see his old Pantanaw friend Saw Hunter Tha Hmwe, now one of the Karen leaders, as well as the Karen chief and fellow school headmaster Saw Ba U Gyi. He was well received, and the two got on swimmingly, but in the end there was no breakthrough, though Thant did get his first real taste of diplomacy.

As a teenager Thant had dreamed of becoming a civil service mandarin but had been deterred by his family's sudden poverty and his need to look after his mother and younger brothers. Now, in an odd twist of fate, he was being pulled into the top echelons of the administration, rising swiftly and becoming, by 1950, the secretary for information and broadcasting. Being a secretary meant being the most senior civil servant in the ministry, just under the elected minister, who was a member of Parliament. All the other secretaries were members of the "heaven-born" Indian Civil Service or Burma Civil Service (First Class), before an exclusively European preserve and now the preserve of an embattled and tiny Anglicized Burmese elite. These were men who had been at Oxford or Cambridge or London, including extremely capable men like James Barringon, an Anglo-Burman, who had thrown in his lot with the new government and who went on to be a key architect of the country's foreign policy. But there was naturally some resentment voiced at Thant's appointment, of a man with only an intermediate degree from a Burmese university, over the heads of so many others.

In April 1953, Nu moved Thant to his own office as secretary to the prime minister. Together with the Foreign Office, the prime minister's office was housed in a set of former residential buildings just off the flame tree–lined Prome Road, once the haunt of British officials. There was a nicely done up office for the prime minister, but Nu never came to the office, preferring always to work from home. Next to his office was the office of the cabinet secretary, a very distinguished person, and his aides. Thant had no place to work, and Nu told him to just take his office.

When Thant moved into the office originally meant for the prime minister, there was more than grumblings among the senior civil servants. How could someone neither a civil servant nor an elected member of Parliament sit in the prime minister's office? Thant mentioned the brewing resentment to Nu. Nu was livid and demanded to know the names of those who protested. Thant changed the subject.

Every morning Nu and Thant took a long walk together around Windermere Court where the prime minister's official residence was located. They talked about the old days in Pantanaw and about friends and family. They were distantly related by marriage, had children the same age, and because of the Karen insurrection, practically all their relations had moved en masse to Rangoon. But they also discussed government policy: repairing the damage done by the war and the recent fighting and longer-term strategies to develop the country. Life was clearly much more difficult than it had been in the heyday of British rule. Now, with political freedom, they had to show that a better society and economy were possible. What was independence for? A couple of color photographs survive of those walks, and they show the two in their *longyis* with long-sleeved double-cuffed shirts and woolen waistcoats. With their walking sticks and genteel demeanors they give an air of authority drawn from hard experience, making it easy to forget that they were both only in their early forties.

The name U Nu gave to his plan for the future was *Pyidawtha,* which might roughly translate as the "Pleasant Land," *tha* meaning "pleasant" in a slightly understated way, as in a pleasing view or an agreeably furnished home. It was a social democratic vision of the future, of a welfare state and government-managed development within the framework of a parliamentary democracy. Nu and Thant complemented each other. Nu was much more the dreamer, impulsive and quixotic, Thant more reserved and pragmatic. Both men were committed democrats, and any other inclinations they may have had died a quick death under the Japanese occupation. They were also both sympathetic to Socialist arguments while at the same time suspicious of the Burmese left.

By 1950 U Nu had honed his political skills and had shown himself a worthy successor to Aung San. His league enjoyed a robust majority in Parliament. He was in many ways what Burma needed, a populist who was understanding of minority concerns and whose popularity allowed him to keep radical and militant views in check. His vision of progress in Burma had its flaws, but they were flaws common to much of the emerging postcolonial elite, not just in Burma but across Asia and Africa. It emphasized quick change, land reforms, industrialization, and heavy state involvement. There would be five-year plans and government planning committees and more than a hint of Soviet style. For a while this seemed not so impractical. The Korean War had driven up rice prices internationally, and the economy seemed to be heading in the right direction. But the Pleasant Land never materialized, for two principal reasons: one was a new war which few had foreseen, and the other was the military machine that had to be built to fight this war.

CHINA REDUX—THE INVASION OF 1950

On 1 October 1949 Mao Tse-tung, standing at the gates of the Forbidden City in Peking, formally proclaimed the establishment of the People's Republic of China. Thousands of miles to the southwest the beaten remnants of Chiang Kai-shek's Nationalist armies straggled across the barely demarcated border along the cloud-covered Wa hills and into the princely state of Kengtung in the far east of Burma. They were led by General Li Mi of the Chinese Eighth Army, and they headquartered themselves at the little frontier town of Tachilek on the road leading down to Thailand. At this point the Chinese Nationalists were still a proper army and did not molest the local population. Their strength was about twenty-five hundred.

Alarmed at the incursion, in July 1950, units of the Burmese army moved against them and retook Tachilek, swinging around troops from hard-pressed anti-insurgent operations in the center of the country. But the Chinese Nationalists only regrouped at nearby Mong Hsat and began enlisting local Shans and tribals to boost their strength. In an echo of the Ming invaders of the 1640s, their aim was never actually to stay in Burma but to use Burma as a base from which to regain their homeland.

But for now they were there to stay. By 1953 they had recruited over twelve thousand new troops, imposed local taxes, and built an airport at Mong Hsat with regular flights to their fellow Kuomintang (KMT) forces, which had fled in the opposite direction, to Taiwan. Huge quantities of arms and supplies were flown in together with secret American trainers and other government officials. Soon the KMT took over the whole region east of the Salween River, moving up toward the Kachin hills and down toward the upland areas controlled by the Karens, with whom they made a sort of tactical alliance. In March 1953 they were on the verge of taking all the Shan States and were within a day's march of the regional capital, Taunggyi.

From the Burmese point of view, this was nothing less than a combined Chinese Nationalist and American invasion, and nothing could be spared in meeting this unexpected threat. Three good brigades were placed under the command of the Anglo-Burmese brigadier Douglas Blake, who then drove the KMT east across the Salween as far as he could until he finally met with fierce resistance near Kengtung. Along the way his men discovered the bodies of three American men and letters with New York and Washington addresses.[8]

In April the Burmese lobbied for a resolution in the United Nations General Assembly, calling for negotiations and a withdrawal of the Chinese forces to Taiwan. After a series of meetings in Bangkok the Chinese finally agreed to evacuate two thousand troops; this did happen (with General Chennault's Air Transport Company flying the planes), but most of the two thousand were young boys, local recruits, and many noncombatants, and many of the arms surrendered were antiquated junk. The Burmese were not very satisfied. After so much expectation, they now believed they couldn't really depend on the UN and in the future would have to learn to defend themselves better. They needed a bigger and better army.

Over the 1950s the Burma Army turned itself from a small politicized and factionalized hybrid force, half British and half Japanese by training, into a more professional and more coherent military machine, loyal only to itself. Martial law in the Shan States, a result of the Chinese invasions, had meant that the army was dangerously overstretched, across multiple fronts and without a clear command and control structure. With everything going on, the War Office in Rangoon was too busy dealing with the day-to-day crises to think in the long term and gain a clear upper hand. General Ne Win was more than aware of the problems and the need for strategy and coordination. In 1951 he established his Military Planning Staff under a group of young colonels, saying that the country was nearly at full-scale war and could no longer wait to undertake the needed reforms. The young colonels quickly set to work.[9]

Their analysis was that China constituted the number one threat to Burma and that the Burmese army needed to be able to contain any aggression by Peking for at least three months, after which with a bit of luck, there would be intervention by the Americans under a UN flag. The KMT Nationalists were a problem because they could easily provoke this much bigger invasion. "U Nu thinks we can make friends with everyone . . . but we have got to have a big stick," said the young colonels. Or at least a reasonable-sized one. Reports describing armies around the world—the British, the American, the Indian, the Soviet, and the Australian—suggesting ideas and lessons to be drawn from each, soon circulated within the military. Study missions were sent abroad to learn firsthand what worked best, and shopping trips were organized to Commonwealth countries, Israel, Yugoslavia, and Western Europe, to buy the latest in military hardware. Israel provided inspiration for a civil defense plan, and a new Defense Academy at Maymyo was modeled on a combination of Sandhurst, West Point, St. Cyr in France, and Dehra Dun in India. In the context of the cold war, all sides were eager to lend the Burmese officers a hand and compete for as much influence as possible. A psychological warfare directorate was set up. The old War Office became a much more efficiently run Defense Ministry, with only the pretense of democratic control and a reality of airtight and closely guarded army autonomy.

The changes had a big impact. By 1954 the army was able to mount more complex and effective operations, against rebels and battlefield opponents of all stripes. The Chinese Nationalists were at first routed near the Mekong and survived only because they received fresh reinforcements from Taiwan. Another campaign targeted the Karens and forced the bulk of KNDO forces up into the heavily forested limestone hills along the Thai border. Smaller operations pushed back the Communists south of Mandalay as well as the Islamic insurgents in Arakan. Over the months nearly twenty-five thousand rebels surrendered. In October, U Nu was able to say that the civil war, "which at one time seemed likely to swallow Burma, is no longer a menace to the integrity of the State."[10] It was quite an achievement.

At the same time, personnel changes altered the balance of power within the army itself, as the group around General Ne Win removed anyone with any possible other loyalty. Those who had come into the armed forces under the British were quietly retired, and senior positions were increasingly reserved for men of the Fourth Burma Rifles, Ne Win's original (Japanese-trained) battalion. These same men also staffed the new Defense Services Institute, a sort of supercanteen that first catered to the needs of soldiers but then began running its own businesses at a profit. By the end of the 1950s it would be managing the Five Star Shipping Line freighter service, the Ava Bank, and major import-export operations like the old Rowe and Co. department store. This further strengthened the hand of the War Office, both over its commanders in the field and over the politicians and civil servants who would otherwise control the army's coffers. The army even began funding its own newspaper, the English-language *Guardian*, headed by one of the country's most respected journalists, Sein Win.

This was at a time when armies throughout newly independent Asia were coming into their own: in South Korea and Taiwan; in South Vietnam, where the army was being built under U.S. assistance; and in Indonesia, where right-wing officers in 1956 first formulated their *dwifungsi* doctrine. In Burma the army was stepping into a huge institutional vacuum, left behind by the collapse of old royal structures, incomplete or ineffective colonial state building, years of war, and then a sudden colonial withdrawal. And this military machine was slowly but surely coming under the control of just one man, General Ne Win.

NEUTRALISTS

In April 1955 representatives of twenty-nine Asian and African nations gathered in the relaxingly cool Indonesian hill station of Bandung in West Java. The aim was to promote cooperation among the newly in-dependent countries of the world and to resist being drawn into U.S. or Soviet global designs. All the great men of the non-Western world were there: Nehru of India, Sukarno of Indonesia, Nkrumah of Ghana, Nasser of Egypt, and Chou En-lai of China, as well as U Nu of Burma, who was seen as an equal of the others. Meeting in the Dutch-built art deco buildings of an earlier generation, the conference led, seven years later, to the founding of the Non-Aligned Movement, with Burma as a founding member. U Thant was the energetic secretary of the Ban-dung Conference.

That Burma was held in high esteem internationally in the 1950s is a little hard to imagine these days, given how low it has sunk in the opinions of so many. Even harder to imagine is that Burma was active on the world stage, promoting its views, engaging in interna-tional politics through the United Nations, sending soldiers on peace-keeping missions overseas, and trying to play the part of a good global citizen.[11]

A big part of Burma's image and role on the world stage was U Nu. U Nu and U Thant traveled widely together in the mid-1950s and in the process developed a foreign policy that was at once neutral in the cold war while on good terms with as many different countries as pos-sible. A hundred years after King Mindon schemed to enmesh Burma in a web of diplomatic ties as a guarantee of future freedom, U Nu was doing the same. He and Thant visited China and met with Mao Tse-tung and Chou En-lai in the Forbidden City and later went to Hanoi to visit Ho Chi Minh. They both were deeply committed to the cause of Indonesian independence from Dutch rule and even sent a plane-load of arms (at a time when Rangoon itself was under assault) to

Jakarta, accompanied by the home minister himself as a gesture of solidarity. At U Nu's suggestion, Thant organized in 1954 a meeting of Asian leaders in support of the new Indonesian government, which was attended by India, Pakistan, and Ceylon as well as the Burmese and Indonesians themselves. U Nu also had a soft spot for the new state of Israel, because of the Holocaust and because he saw similarities between his own political views and those of the ruling Israeli Labor Party. Burma became one of the first countries in the world to recognize Israel, and it was only because of opposition from others that Israel was not included in the various forums, like the Indonesia conference, that Thant was busy putting together.

Travels continued later to Israel itself, Yugoslavia, Great Britain, and the United States. In London the two met Winston Churchill, then eighty. "Let us bury our old animosities," said the son of Lord Randolph Churchill, Thibaw's vanquisher, as he offered a whiskey to the teetotaler U Nu. Impartially, they also went to see Nikita Khrushchev in Moscow. In all these trips it was U Nu's winning ways that helped cement Burma's relationship with key countries. But sometimes Thant had to make sure that Nu's honest and open style didn't go too far.

During the Moscow trip, for example, U Nu decided to take with him a letter from his friend Prime Minister Moshe Sharett of Israel to Soviet Premier Nikolai Bulganin. He was concerned about the plight of Jews in the Soviet Union and was determined to help. He didn't tell anyone in the Burmese Foreign Office because he knew they would come up with all kinds of objections. At the Kremlin, just as soon as formal courtesies had been exchanged, U Nu produced the Israeli letter and then blurted out that he understood that there were Jews in the Soviet Union, that they wished to emigrate to Israel, and that he hoped Bulganin would change his policies and let them go. In U Nu's own words, "the Soviets were speechless with surprise." It was politely pointed out that this was something for the Israeli embassy in Moscow. U Nu pressed the issue. Afterward the Burmese ambassador in Moscow reproached U Nu, telling him he should not have done what he had just done. "I know that," snapped U Nu, but the next day he continued to say what was on his mind. At a lunch with party first secretary Khrushchev, U Nu gave a speech on the history of the Communist rebellion in Burma, saying that "a certain foreign power" had caused the Communists to rebel and had almost brought the government to the point of collapse. "But we fought back . . . and the Communists are on the run!" he told the members of the Soviet Politburo. Back at their guesthouse, a peeved Thant asked, "Did you see Khrushchev's face during your speech?"

"Why do you ask that? Of course. I was looking at him all through lunch."

"Then you must have seen how his expression changed!"

"I don't believe I did that. He seemed very quiet."

The other Burmese officials chimed in to back Thant up. U Nu replied, "I can't help that. It was because of these Russians that our country was reduced to dust and ashes . . . I think these Russians should thank me for not coming right out and saying that they fomented the Communist rebellion in Burma."

The next day there was another speech, this time at a dinner hosted by the mayor of Moscow. U Nu continued with his anti-Communist theme. The next morning the Soviet ambassador to Burma, who was back in Moscow for the visit, called on Thant and explained, politely, that more similar speeches would not be very useful for Soviet-Burmese relations. Thant finally had a one-to-one meeting with his old Pantanaw friend. Afterward he missed all of the day's scheduled events, rewriting all of his old friend's speeches.[12]

The following summer U Nu and U Thant went on their first visit to America. It was the year Disneyland had opened its doors in Anaheim, Marlon Brando had won an Oscar for *On the Waterfront*, and *I Love Lucy* was enjoying its fifth fun-filled season. America was leading the world in practically everything, and the cold war was at its height. At his meeting with President Eisenhower Nu presented the erstwhile Allied commander a check for five thousand dollars for the families of U.S. soldiers killed in Burma during the Second World War.[13] "Burma and America are in the same boat—we fight the same evils," he said adroitly, and reminded his audiences in Washington of what he had said in Peking to Chairman Mao, that the Americans were a "brave and generous people." At the National Press Club, U Nu pressed forward his vision of friendly neutrality, quoting George Washington's Farewell Address on the need to steer clear of entangling foreign alliances, while also underlining Burma's and America's mutual commitment to a democratic way of life.

It was then on to the U.S. Naval Academy at Annapolis, Philadelphia and Independence Hall, and finally the far West. In Pasadena, California, he was treated to a performance of his own play, *The People Win Through*. Both he and my grandfather were more than impressed with what they saw of the new superpower. At a Ford factory they watched in wonder as a car was assembled for them in less than a minute, and in Knoxville, Tennessee, they listened awestruck as a waiter at a small hotel told them that he owned two cars, one for himself and one for his wife, and that his salary was more than that of the Burmese prime minister! Perhaps what impressed U Nu the most was what he saw of American charity. At San Francisco's Mark Hopkins Hotel the hotel barber told him that he had raised and donated sixty-five thouand dollars for his church. U Nu was so moved he gave a hundred dollars of his own money to the same church.

For the next many years Thant served as Nu's adviser and aide, writing many of his speeches, translating Burmese ones into English, meeting visiting dignitaries, and talking to foreign correspondents. Thant had taken a trip up-country early on and had successfully mediated between rival political factions; he had proved very good at intraparty diplomacy, and Nu asked him to do this more often. But he thought this was the work of politicians and declined. Other work piled on. He traveled more and more overseas, both with Nu and on his own. Nu even asked him to write a comprehensive history of the first few years of Burma's independence. Eventually the work became too much. Thant's health deteriorated, and despite daily walks and swims, he developed insomnia and lost weight. He asked Nu to be allowed to resign. But Nu would not let him go.

Then, on a baking hot Saturday afternoon in March 1957, Nu told Thant that he should consider moving to New York as Burma's permanent representative to the UN. It was a shock. Thant had been to New York before, in 1952, as part of the Burmese delegation. He had also kept a keen eye on the progress of the world body. If he thought about a diplomatic assignment, New York and the UN would certainly be his first choice. But he hesitated.

One reason he hesitated was that he assumed my grandmother would be against moving so far away. But she was, much to his surprise, more than willing to try for a new life in New York. She was equally unhappy with the pressures of his job and even more with the atmosphere surrounding recent divisions in the ruling league. Thant had managed to stay friends with both sides, but how much longer would this last? "Don't take a few days; Nu tends to be mercurial," she said. "Accept while the offer is there." The next morning Thant told Nu that he would go to the United Nations. Four years later he was elected the organization's third secretary-general, succeeding Dag Hammarskjöld. He served until 1971.

DEMOCRACY'S DYING DAYS

The 1950s are often looked back on as a golden age for the Burmese middle classes. To many these were the years of freedom and progress and at least a sense of hope for the future. They now occupied all the top civil service posts once the preserve of Europeans, lived in the pukka houses of Rangoon's Golden Valley and Windermere Park, and entered occasionally lucrative business ventures, sometimes on the coattails of their Indian and Chinese compatriots. These were also the days of an animated and unrestrained media, with hundreds of newspapers and magazines, like the lively *Nation* newspaper set up by Edward Law-Yone, the iconoclastic part-English grandson of a Yunnanese muleteer who had served with the Office of Strategic Services (the forerunner of the CIA) during the war.

There was also progress in education. As King Mindon had done exactly a hundred years before, U Nu's government sent hundreds of young men and women to universities abroad as state scholars. The majority went to the United Kingdom and other Commonwealth countries, but a good number went to the United States. My father, Tyn Myint-U (U Thant's future son-in-law), was one of these new America-bound students. Soon after the British takeover of Mandalay in 1885, his great-grandfather, who had been Thibaw's privy treasurer, had retired to their ancestral villages at Dabessway, next to Ava, together with his extended family, returning to the royal city only years later. As was the case for many of the old Court of Ava, the following years were a period of deep bitterness and ill feeling toward the Raj, combined with nostalgia and vain attempts to keep up the old ways.

Some mementos of the old court—the golden *salway* worn by the nobility, a fading photograph of my great-great-grandfather in court dress, now retouched with color—were kept, but very soon there would be little to distinguish my father's family from anybody else's. It was a big family. His father was the youngest of eleven children, including nine boys. In the 1920s one of his great-uncles, Mandalay Ba U, had set up a passionately nationalist as well as monarchist newspaper, the *Bahosi*, formed an ultraconservative party, and then won a seat in Parliament. For a short while he had been a minister in Dr. Ba Maw's 1937 government. My father grew up around that time and was old enough to remember the destruction of Mandalay and his family's panicked flight by bullock cart in early 1942 to a little village up north, where they waited out the Japanese occupation.

In the U Nu days, after a few years at Rangoon University, my father was among many of his generation eager to improve themselves in the bigger world, applying for and winning a prized state scholarship. He was first assigned to the Queen's University at Belfast, but believing he would be doomed to endless meals of fish and chips and hoping to be somewhere closer to Hollywood, he arranged to swap with another successful candidate and was eventually sent to study engineering at the University of Michigan in blustery Ann Arbor. He was one of many that year (1953), and his particular group left altogether for America, first by ship through the Suez Canal, then by plane from London (where he thought he was sitting next to Elizabeth Taylor), and finally by train from New York, over the Appalachians and through the Ohio Valley. It was all very far from Mandalay, but the scholarships of those years did much to produce a solid class of young professionals and civil servants. But sadly, with the changes in store, few would ever have the chance to help in their country's development.

When my grandfather left Burma in the summer of 1957, together with his wife and two children (my mother, Aye Aye Thant, and her younger brother, both teenagers), he was excited by the prospects of the new job and being part of the still-young UN. But he (and my grandmother) also wanted to leave the increasingly ugly political atmosphere in Rangoon. The rot began at the top. After a decade in power, and despite electoral success, the league had begun to fall apart by the mid-1950s. It had always been a hodgepodge of competing interests, ambitions, and loyalties, held together by the partnerships at the very peak, between U Nu and his chief lieutenants. Now these lieutenants, in particular Ministers U Ba Swe and U Kyaw Nyein, were becoming restive. There was no clear ideological divide or really even differences over policy. It was more the story of friends and colleagues who after twenty years living and working at close quarters, through war and peace, were getting tired of one another—and whose wives were getting tired of one another, with U Nu, Ba Swe, and Kyaw Nyein's wives barely, if at all, on speaking terms. With the wives having fallen out, people said it was only a matter of time before the league would come apart as well.[14]

The irony was that the league had succeeded well at the ballot box and still enjoyed a comfortable majority in Parliament. The formal split came on June 1958, a windy and rainy day, and everyone present knew that an era, which had begun in the Student Union in the mid-1930s, was now coming to a close. U Nu's own chief ministers had submitted a no-confidence motion against the government. There were rumors of coups and countercoups, and armored cars patrolled outside while U Nu and his rivals, all in their yellow or pink headdresses, gave their contending speeches in the cream-colored Chamber of Deputies, fans whirring overhead and a portrait of Aung San hanging directly behind them. U Nu survived the vote, but only just. The league was now only half its former self, and the government, to stay in power, depended on the support of hard-core leftists in Parliament. This frightened the military.

Everything now became very messy. U Nu's marriage of convenience with the "aboveground" Communists (as distinct from the Communist insurgents) unsettled the army, whose officers veered toward support for the prime minister's opponents. Even worse, the split at the very top of the league had begun to mirror the split in the countryside, politicians in each town and village breaking up into rival factions. Army commanders in the field complained about all this and the instability it was causing and accused U Nu's party loyalists of direct harassment. These field commanders, led by the northern commander Colonel Aung Shwe (later chairman of Aung San Suu Kyi's National League for Democracy), then began to conspire among themselves. More rumors circulated. Some said that units of the Union Military Police, loyal to U Nu's home minister, would soon take over Rangoon. Others said that the field commanders would move in with their troops and seize the capital.

On 22 September soldiers under the command of Colonel Kyi Maung (another future chairman of Aung San Suu Kyi's party), together with Special Forces directly under the War Office, surrounded key government offices as well as the Windermere compound that was home to most cabinet ministers and senior civil servants. U Nu was told in no uncertain terms that the field commanders were planning a coup, but that the War Office and the men around General Ne Win would protect him. It was, ostensibly, a "preemptive" coup by the War Office to protect the government from the disgruntled commanders in the field.

Four days later in September, U Nu spoke over Radio Rangoon and announced that he had invited General Ne Win "to assume the reins of government—in a 'Caretaker Government'—due to the prevailing situation regarding security and law and order," until fresh elections could be held. The army had taken over.

The army's caretaker government that followed was, by all accounts, the most effective and efficient in modern Burmese history. It was also high-handed and at times brutal. Corruption was exposed and rooted out, including at the highest levels of administration. The press and law courts were generally kept free and independent. Prices were kept stable, and technocrats were slotted into key ministerial positions.

Rangoon got a face-lift. Houses were ordered to be painted, the rubbish in the streets removed, and about 165,000 squatters, mainly people displaced from the civil war, were forced to move into new satellite towns outside the city. Prior to 1958 Rangoon had been filthy, with squalid squatters' camps and packs of pariah dogs. A can-do colonel took over the administration of the capital, and mobilizing a hundred thousand people every Sunday for twenty-five weeks, he collected over ten thousand tons of rubbish for disposal. For the middle classes this was a good thing, perhaps much less so for poor people, who now had to trek long distances to their work. In the countryside the reorganization of district law and order personnel under new "security councils" brought about a steep drop in violent crime. Gangsters and racketeers were arrested and locked up.

At the same time, the army had lost no time prosecuting the war. List after list was published of rebels who had been killed, wounded, or captured. In the early 1950s the back of the Communist threat had been broken; now the last Communist bases were overrun. Against other insurgencies as well, Rangoon went from strength to strength, and for the first time it looked as if Burma's civil war was actually nearing an end. A glossy publication *Is Trust Vindicated?* showcased the army's accomplishments.

The caretaker government lasted until December 1960, when it held promised elections. But all its efficiency failed to convince voters to elect the anti–U Nu faction it supported. Instead the charismatic, if less efficient, U Nu was returned by a landslide. General Ne Win himself was nonchalant and handed power back as promised. He gave the impression of never having enjoyed the extra responsibility and certainly of not wanting it back in the future if at all avoidable. He grumbled about his sinuses, took to the Rangoon party scene, and complained that as acting prime minister he had not had enough time for his golf.[15] He shunned publicity, and at the one press conference he held, he told newsmen to write whatever they wanted and then walked out. It was a studied disinterest. Even though the army stood down, it was still very much in the picture. In the countryside solidarity councils had been set up with the motto Lightning from the Sky, to circumvent party politics and provide a power base right down to the village level. And the military's own business empire grew by leaps and bounds, moving into everything from bookshops to fisheries to soft drinks. The army men believed they had acquitted themselves admirably and could run the country better than anyone else. They wanted another chance, this time without any electoral deadline looming overhead.

TOWARD THE COUP OF 1962

Soon after the invasion of Thibaw's kingdom, Sir George Scott (the man who introduced football to Burma) and other British representatives had met with all the various Shan chiefs in the eastern hills, a beautiful plateau of rolling highlands, lakes, and near-perfect weather, convincing or compelling them one by one to accept a fairly light version of colonial rule. There would be a British superintendent based at the hill station of Taunggyi and men of the Frontier Service would advise the chiefs as necessary, but in general they would be left to themselves and their hereditary rights would be honored. In 1922 a Council of Chiefs was set up with a British official as president, but no other reforms were introduced, and the hills remained happily uninvolved in the politics and problems of the plains. For more than a generation after the fall of the Court of Ava, the little Shan courts maintained many of the same traditions, giving a glimpse of what Upper Burma itself might have been like if the British had chosen to establish a protectorate rather than abolish the monarchy altogether.

By the 1950s the *sawbwas* were all men who had grown up under British rule. Nearly all had studied at a school in Taunggyi, set on a hilltop amid pleasant grassy fields and run in the manner of an English boarding school, complete with an imported headmaster and a rigorous schedule of games. Some had also gone on to school and university in England and America. At Hsipaw, for example, an ancient mountain valley town along the winding Namtu River, the local chief, Sao Kya Hseng, had an engineering degree from Colorado in the United States. His father, Sao On Kya, had studied at Rugby and Brasenose College, Oxford. Many were seen by the British as gentlemen who combined the best of Eastern and Western manners, and for a few decades the Shan States seemed to enjoy an almost idyllic peace and prosperity.[16]

Another leading chief was the *sawbwa* of the tea-producing statelet of Mongmit, Sao Hkun Hkio. He had met his wife, Mabel, when he was an undergraduate at Cambridge in the early fifties, when both happened to be walking their dogs on Parker's Piece. Her parents were modest townspeople, and when Sao Hkun Hkio proposed, they had no objection, though they couldn't have had an inkling of the life she would later lead. The couple were soon married, but when the young prince finally plucked up the courage to tell his father, the ruling *sawbwa* at the time, he was angrily told to return home at once or risk losing everything. Mabel was not acceptable. What could he do? He couldn't go home and leave his new bride, but he also had no money to stay in England. He thought about finding a job in Cambridge or London but decided in the end to face his father and hope for the best.

The father would not give way, even when told that Mabel had just had their first child, a son. Luckily for the young couple, the father soon died, and the son ascended the throne as the new *sawbwa* with Mabel as the *mahadevi*, or "great goddess," of Mongmit. There they lived for many years, with their children and dogs, four great Danes and a bloodhound, as the rulers of dozens of misty tea-growing villages all around. Mongmit itself was a small place, more like a sprawling village, pressed up along the China border and just past the ruby mines of Mogok. Sao Hkun Hkio would go on to a distinguished career in independent Burma, as foreign minister under U Nu and later as a deputy prime minister and head of the Shan States.

After the army took over in 1962, Hkun Hkio was imprisoned, like all the Shan chiefs (Sao Kya Hseng, the Colorado graduate, would never be seen again). When freed after a few years, he left the country, never to return. He and Mabel retraced their steps back to equally misty Cambridge, to a house not far from Parker's Piece. He had just died when I went up to Cambridge to begin work on a Ph.D. at Trinity College. This was in 1991, and unlike at the turn of the century, when there were dozens of Burmese students and a Cambridge Burmese Students Association, when I arrived I was the only Burmese there (as far as I knew), except for Pascal Khoo Thwe (later the author of *From the Land of Green Ghosts*[17]), who introduced me to the old *sawbwa*'s family. When I called on Mabel, she was still living in the unassuming semidetached house they shared, with a little sign on the door that said MONGMIT.

But that was years ahead. Back in the 1950s it was these chiefs of Mongmit and Hsipaw, both close to U Nu and the new Rangoon establishment, who dominated politics in the Shan States. The biggest problem was the invasion of the Chinese Nationalists and the resulting influx of often heavy-handed Burma Army troops. In many places they were the first and only ethnic Burmese the people of this part of the country had ever seen. Grievances arose. Areas of the Shan States were placed under military administration, and by the mid-1950s there were some who were agitating for Shan self-rule. U Nu argued against this, but many younger Shans began looking at the Karen example and thinking about their own insurgency. An embryonic Shan Army was formed in 1958 along the Thai border.

For the Chinese Nationalists and their backers this was a good thing. The KMT was still operating through Thai and Taiwanese support, and it was hoped that a Shan insurgency would provide a more legitimate facade. The Thais also wanted a buffer against their age-old enemies the Burmese. Everyone also wanted a piece of the opium trade. Iran and China—both once the biggest growers of opium in the world—had stopped production, and in their place had emerged the border areas of Burma, Thailand, and Laos, the so-called Golden Triangle.

Bangkok was now the international center for drug trafficking, and there was a lot of money at stake as well as an unseemly number of prominent people involved. Thai strongman and army commander Sarit Thanarat had taken power in a coup in 1957 and had promised President Eisenhower that he would turn his country "into the bulwark that the US needed to halt the communist advance in East Asia." Anything Thailand did to help Burmese rebels or facilitate the drug trade would be fine with Washington.[18]

Way up north, the Kachins were also growing unhappy with their lot in independent Burma. A border agreement with China had left three Kachin villages on the Chinese side, and U Nu's recent decision to make Buddhism the state religion had angered the mainly Christian Kachins. On 5 February 1961 a Kachin Independence Army, headed by war hero and U.S. Detachment 101 veteran Zau Seng, was founded in the hills not far from Hsenwi and Mongmit. As with the Shans, though the incipient rebel forces were tiny, there was now a clear indication that things might easily spiral in an even more violent direction.

Around the same time, twenty thousand troops of the Chinese People's Liberation Army crossed over the border into the Shan state of Kengtung, near Thailand. Their aim was to crush the KMT, and the KMT was forced south, where it was attacked by the Burmese army's Ninth Brigade. Several bases were captured, and large quantities of U.S.-made arms and ammunition were found.[19] Over the next many months many of the defeated Chinese Nationalists were airlifted to Taiwan, but many thousands of others remained, some on the Burma side, others in northern Thailand, and a few hundred in Laos, where they were recruited into the Royal Laotian Army to fight the rebel Pathet Lao.

There was an awareness that the country was at a crossroads. The economy was doing reasonably well, but after nearly fifteen years of independence, many of the hopes of Burma's development planners had not yet materialized. Neighboring Thailand enjoyed a slightly higher per capita GDP, and farther east newly independent Malaysia and Singapore were racing ahead. But the country's main problems were not economic; they were political. First there was the ethnic conflict, armed and violent in some places, simmering just below the surface in others. Colonial rule had left a legacy of distrust and the inability of many in the Burmese elite to see that Burma was home not just to the stereotypical Burmese Buddhist but to many different peoples and cultures. At best there was a genuflection to the notion that minorities and foreigners had their place. But few want to think of themselves as simply a minority or as foreigners in the land of their birth.

And then there were the repeated foreign interventions—by the Americans, the Thais, and the Chinese Nationalists, by the Soviets and the Chinese Communists—all adding fuel to the fire, making impossible any local solution to Burma's civil war. Finally there was the Burmese army itself, moving in, skillfully and successfully, to fill the vacuum left by the sudden British withdrawal and the near collapse of the government. The army built a shadow state, and soon this shadow state seemed all that was necessary to meet the challenges ahead.

In a way Burmese democracy had flourished under U Nu, with perhaps the freest and most lively press in Asia and basic respect for civil liberties, but the 1958 coup had left an indelible scar, one that signaled the rise of army power. Over the summer of 1961 Shan leaders met at Taunggyi to consider a new federal system of government as a solution to the country's ethnic dilemma. They had a constitutional right to secede, and though they promised not to use it, they wanted a new deal. U Nu was not unsympathetic and promised to work with the Shans and others. In early 1962 he convened a Nationalities Seminar in Rangoon to discuss these and related issues. But the armed forces under General Ne Win had other ideas.

TWELVE

THE TIGER'S TAIL

The soldiers take over and decide they know what's best:
expel the Indians, nationalize the economy,
and shut out the rest of the world

~~~

I n the already balmy early-morning hours of 2 March 1962, tanks and mechanized units of the Burmese army rolled into downtown Rangoon and took over the Government House, the Secretariat, the High Court, and other important places. Other army units swept across the leafy residential neighborhoods to the north of the Royal Lakes and arrested nearly all the top leaders: Prime Minister U Nu, five other government ministers, and the chief justice were taken into custody, together with thirty Shan and Karenni chiefs. The first president of the union, the hereditary *sawbwa* of Yawnghwe, Sao Shwe Thaik, was also detained by the army and would die later that year in prison. His seventeen-year-old son was shot dead attempting to protect him; he was the only casualty in an otherwise bloodless textbook coup d'état.

The night before, the army chief General Ne Win had attended a performance of a Chinese ballet company visiting Rangoon. The show finished late, and the general was seen afterward congratulating the leading ballerina before quietly slipping away. Whether he slept at all that night no one knows. But at 8:50 a.m. he went on the radio to announce that the armed forces had seized power because of "the greatly deteriorating conditions of the Union." The next day Parliament was disbanded, and the constitution officially suspended. A Revolutionary Council made up of Ne Win's senior lieutenants, mainly loyal men of the Fourth Burma Rifles, was to rule the country with no check or limitation. Ne Win himself was to be minister for defense, finance, and revenue as well as president of the republic. Local revolutionary councils, led by army officers, were established to take over local government and military tribunals, replacing the existing judicial courts. This time there was no promise of future elections. An entirely new course would be laid. Speaking to reporters later that week, the new dictator of Burma declared his belief in democracy, socialism, and "healthy politics." The following month a Burma press council was set up to muzzle the lively and multilingual press. Much worse would follow.

The ideology of the new regime was laid out in two confused, almost Orwellian documents, "The Burmese Way to Socialism" and the even more befuddled "System of Correlation of Man and His Environment." A generous interpretation would say that this was a good-faith attempt to marry the various streams in Burmese political life and to reconcile socialism and Buddhism. What seems more likely is that both were half-baked attempts by less than able scholars to provide window dressing for General Ne Win's own rising xenophobia and desire for uncontested power.

For those who had lived through the caretaker military government of 1958–60, what happened next was perplexing. The first military government had turned to technocrats—civil servants, senior academics, and others—to get the job done efficiently and effectively. This new military government was to be the exact opposite, intensely distrustful of the educated professional class. Scores of well-trained, well-educated bureaucrats, including the entire top echelon of officials schooled in the old colonial civil service, were sacked in the coming months. Many were men who would have been an asset to any bureaucracy and later went on to successful careers abroad. For a small developing country to suddenly discard them was a singularly harsh self-inflicted blow.

Also to go were the Western foreign aid agencies and advisers. The Ford Foundation and Asia Foundation were unceremoniously kicked out of the country, and the Fulbright and other state scholarship programs, which had sent hundreds of young Burmese to America and elsewhere, were stopped. The Johns Hopkins School of Advanced International Studies, today with campuses in Washington, Bologna, and Nanking, then had a campus in Rangoon; the teachers were told to pack up, and hopes for educating a new generation of world-class Burmese diplomats were ended. Even the English-language training centers, run by the British and the Americans, were shut down. The strong puritan streak in Burmese militarism also showed itself. Western-style dancing, horse racing, and beauty contests were banned, and Rangoon's few nightclubs were told to close. There was a strong message that the fun was over. By late 1963 even the Boy Scouts and the Automobile Association of Burma were nationalized. No more foreigners would be let in. Visas were restricted to just twenty-four hours. Until then Rangoon had been a hub for air traffic in the region. Pan Am, BOAC, Northwest, Air France, and KLM jets all flew well-heeled passengers direct from Europe and North America. Traveling to Thailand or even Singapore meant first a stopover in Rangoon. Now only a musty Union of Burma Airways propeller plane to Bangkok connected the country to the outside world.

Just as the world outside was embarking on an incredible decade of turmoil and creativity, Ne Win and his generals were hanging a big Do Not Disturb sign on the front door. The sixties would pass Burma by.

The Burmese army was certainly not alone in deciding that only the armed forces could run a country. In South Korea the dictatorship of General Park Chung Hee, destined to last twenty-six years, had also just begun (but with very different and economically much more benign consequences). In Pakistan (which then bordered Burma) the government of Field Marshal Ayub Khan was pushing through educational and land reforms and building a new capital near Rawalpindi. And next door in Thailand, Field Marshal Sarit Thanarat's government was one of a long line of military dictatorships with no end in sight. Indeed, democracy in the region was the exception, and not even a particularly admired exception at the time.

Any dissent was immediately crushed as the army showed that it meant business. On 7 July troops raided the Rangoon University campus as hundreds of students were meeting to demand a restoration of democratic government. Rioting then followed in parts of the city. The trigger was apparently an order by the new rulers that all students be confined to their dormitories every night after eight. But unease had been growing for weeks as the Revolutionary Council announced its intention to create a new one-party system. At least fifteen students were killed and many more wounded in what would be the start of a decades-long and unfinished struggle between Burma's educated youth and the men in uniform. The very next morning an explosives team marched up to the whitewashed Student Union building, an icon of anticolonialism since the 1920s and home to speeches by Aung San, U Nu, and U Thant, and blew it to pieces. Though there were many bloodier clashes to come, the scars of this particular incident lasted for a long time. In 1988, in his last public address, Ne Win went out of his way to deny responsibility for destroying the Student Union building.

More serious was what was happening to the economy. It was already in bad shape. Heavy floods the previous year had wiped out nearly a million acres of rice fields just as the U Nu government was about to launch an ambitious new development program. The first military government had worked closely with business leaders, and there were hopes for a repeat performance. But as in so many other things, policies under the Revolutionary Council took an entirely new direction. Ne Win's chief deputy, Brigadier General Aung Gyi, who was seen as close to business interests, was sacked. This was a big surprise as Aung Gyi had been viewed by many as an architect of the coup and Ne Win's heir apparent. Ne Win would also later blame him for dynamiting the Student Union. But he went quietly, retiring for a while to a remote Buddhist monastery and then running a successful chain of cake shops, reemerging in public life decades later as a leading politician in the 1988 uprising and the chairman of the new National League for Democracy (with Aung San Suu Kyi as the general secretary).

Within a week of Aung Gyi's ouster the government announced the nationalization of all major businesses and industries. No new private firms were to be allowed, and on one Saturday afternoon all twenty-four foreign and domestic banks were taken over by the state. The local branch of Lloyds Bank was renamed People's Bank No. 19. "The people's stores," painted army green and white, were set up around the country. Inasmuch as only state-run companies benefited from access to raw materials and protection against labor strikes, some private companies petitioned to be nationalized, only to find that the government then had no qualified managers to take charge. The impact on the economy and investor confidence was devastating. By August industrial production had fallen 40 percent, and unemployment in the cities soared. Twelve months later a demonetization of currency, apparently to put a brake on black-market activities, wiped out personal savings for hundreds of thousands of ordinary people.

With the racetrack shut, the beauty pageants over, jobs lost, scholarship opportunities gone, and only beer from the People's Brewery and Distillery left to drink, it was as if someone had just turned off the lights on a chaotic and often corrupt but nevertheless vibrant and competitive society. The aim was order and an orderly approach to development. The result would be a catastrophe for the country only fourteen years after independence and less than two decades after the ravages of World War II.[1]

The man who would lead Burma down the path of austerity and isolation was General Ne Win, playboy, tyrant, numerologist, and onetime post office clerk, a man who understood his countrymen's psyche well enough to wield nearly total power for the better part of thirty years. Ne Win was born in 1911, and like so many of the other political figures of his generation, he came from the new small-town middle class. His father was a minor civil servant in a town called Paungdale, and Ne Win was sent for his education to the National High School at nearby Prome. Prome sits at the end of the railway line north of Rangoon, where people and goods spend a few hours or a night before boarding a ship up the Irrawaddy to Mandalay. In the 1920s Prome was a pleasant place, with handsome streets and solid teak-roofed buildings, a fair-size European presence, and an air of constant movement and money being made.[2]

Ne Win did well enough in school to be accepted to University College, Rangoon, in June 1929 to read natural science. His hope was to become a doctor, and in a different world a Dr. Ne Win might never have considered politics or soldiering and instead gone on to a profitable practice back in his leafy hometown. But after two years he failed his intermediate exams, and the twenty-year-old dropout was forced to look for a job, just as the full weight of the Great Depression was hitting Burma and just as ethnic tensions and labor disputes were simmering over into violence. He first turned to coal. He knew there were coal deposits near Prome, that coal was much cheaper there than in Rangoon, and he knew that selling coal was a profitable trade. Working hard, he started a little business but was immediately cut down by the competition, all Indian, and soon realized he could never break the immigrants' collective grip over the retail market. It was a bitter lesson. One imagines the thoughts brewing in the head of a man later renowned for his bad temper as he saw his first business effort fail at the hands of the Tamil and Malwari merchants of Mughal Street.

He then drifted around for a while and eventually landed work at the post office. He also made friends. This was around the time Aung San was becoming active in Student Union politics. Ne Win shared a flat downtown with some aspiring young politicians and spent many evenings at the home of one of my great-uncles, then a writer and organizer of the Left Book Club. Many of his friends were self-declared Marxists, and Ne Win, presumably on days off from selling stamps, helped translate the *Communist Manifesto*.

Like so many other young men at the time, he had no attachments and was more than ready for excitement when Aung San led the way and made contact with the Japanese. Ne Win soon became one of Aung San's deputies, training with him on Hainan Island and then leading the Burma Independence Army across the hills from Siam. Ne Win had found his calling. And the ruthlessness of Nippon militarism proved a welcome tonic to years of postal work and endless student debates. His original name was Shu Maung, and Ne Win was actually his nom de guerre (it means "Bright Sun"). He proved himself a very capable soldier, and from the start of the civil war in 1948 to the coup in 1962 he was the unquestioned head of the army. The army machine that was built up, first to defend Rangoon and defeat the insurgencies, then to battle the Chinese in the remote reaches of the Salween River, was Ne Win's machine. There were many other talented and ambitious officers, but Ne Win proved shrewd enough to beat off any challenge. With the coup and the end of civilian government, there were no competitors left.

All this time his own political ambitions had been underestimated by others. While his colonels schemed and were seen to be scheming, Ne Win appeared above the fray. He looked more interested in other things. Though he was happily married in 1962 to Kitty Ba Than (the second of at least four wives in succession; no one knows exactly how many), he was well known as a charismatic man-about-town, fond of lavish parties and with a keen eye for the opposite sex. But now in 1962 this was all in the past. Not only had he personally moved on from evenings out in Rangoon, but he had shut down the nightclubs as well.

But how else to use power? Perhaps it was the soldier in him, but his early flirtations with communism seem to have left only a residual attraction to Leninist organization and notions of state control. What seemed to drive him most were two things: as a onetime (and perhaps longtime) devotee of Japanese militarism, he hated the messiness of party politics, and as a onetime young and hopeful entrepreneur whose coal business had been run into the ground, he had a deep and burning desire to rid the country of people he saw as foreigners, in particular immigrants from India.

The Indian communities in Burma had shrunk considerably since the early twentieth century. Many had died during the march out in 1942 or left either then or at independence and not returned. Rangoon, once more than two-thirds Indian, by the 1950s had a Burmese majority. But there certainly remained a strong Indian presence across the country, and Indians were still a big part of Rangoon's professional and commercial class. Beginning in 1964, however, under orders from Ne Win, hundreds of thousands, men, women, and children, were expelled from Burma and sent to India and Pakistan. The Indian government under the last year of Pandit Nehru's leadership accepted Ne Win's desire to send these people away, and special ships and planes were chartered on New Delhi's order to bring them "home." Only for some it wasn't a return home but the start of an entirely new life as refugees. A good portion had never lived outside Burma and were often from families that had been in Burma for generations. Some spoke only Burmese. They included doctors, lawyers, journalists, businessmen, and teachers as well as shopkeepers and ordinary workers. They all left penniless, with only their clothes on their back and no compensation whatsoever for a lifetime (or many generations) of work, for their homes and property, their businesses (including many of the biggest in the country), or even for their personal possessions.

Eight years later Idi Amin, the dictator of Uganda, similarly drove out sixty thousand Ugandan Asians, many of whom wound up in the United Kingdom. The expulsions in Burma—perhaps totaling four hundred thousand people—were no less tragic and were on a much greater scale but were much less well known.[3] As in Uganda, the forced departure of entire communities of people left the country permanently scarred and culturally poorer. In Malaysia, Indian and Chinese minorities became dynamic and integral parts of the postcolonial society, keys to growing success; in Burma there would be no attempt to try to include these communities in a new national identity.

Ne Win's other focus was the insurgency. There were still two sets of Communist rebels in the field: the main Communist Party of Burma and the more radical Red Flag Communists of Thakin Soe. Thakin Soe was the first to accept Ne Win's offer of talks, and in the summer of 1963 he emerged from his swampy hideout and traveled by government plane to Rangoon. He was a notorious womanizer and was always flanked — Muammar Gaddafi–style — by a team of attractive young women in beige uniforms. He angrily denounced Soviet Premier Khrushchev's "revisionist line" and demanded a cease-fire, a withdrawal of Burmese troops from his areas, and a meeting of all political groups to form a new government. Ne Win replied that Thakin Soe was "insincere" but nevertheless gave him seven days to get back safely to his jungle base.

The other, mainstream Communists arrived both from the jungle and from exile in China. One, Bo Zeya, was an old wartime colleague of Aung San and Ne Win's and had not seen his family in Rangoon since the civil war began in 1948. There were also representatives of the ethnic-based rebel groups. The Shans and the Kachins demanded autonomy and a federal system of government. An Arakanese Communist group demanded a separate Arakanese Republic. There was no meeting of minds and no real discussion. Whether the talks had been only for show or not, Ne Win was now committed to a military solution. Over a thousand alleged Communists and sympathizers were soon rounded up. With no civilian government to offer even a limited check to the Burmese military, the civil war would soon take a violent turn.[4]

THE WORLD OF JIMMY YANG

Far away in the frost- and forest-covered hilltops of Kokang, in the rough Yunnan border country, the Kokang Revolutionary Force of Jimmy Yang was preparing to combine forces with other Shan rebels against the new regime. The area had long been ruled by Jimmy Yang's forebears and was famous for its tea and its opium, regarded by connoisseurs as the best in Southeast Asia.

Originally from Nanking in central China, the Yang family had arrived in the area with other Ming loyalists in the later part of the seventeenth century. The founder of the clan had first settled at Dali in Yunnan and married the daughter of a prosperous local tea merchant before moving to Kokang itself. They were of military stock and, according to family lore, made their mark by protecting local folk and freeing villages from the terror of bandits and freebooters. Bit by bit the Chinese clan extended its control, negotiating valuable marriages and waging little wars on surrounding chiefs. In the late 1700s the Yangs assumed the hereditary title of *heng*. When Thibaw lost his throne a hundred years later and the British and the Chinese sought to demarcate the border, Kokang was placed within the borders of British Burma as a substate of Hsenwi, with the *heng* of Kokang subordinate to the grander *sawbwa* of Hsenwi.[5]

During the Second World War the Yang family proved their loyalty to the Allies, and as a reward Kokang was created as a separate principality just on the eve of Burma's independence. The ruler became a *sawbwa*, and Kokang a constituent part of the Shan States and the Union of Burma. The first *sawbwa* had six daughters and nine sons, one of whom, Sao Yang Kyein Tsai (also known as Edward Yang), succeeded him in 1949. The Yangs straddled several worlds. Jimmy Yang, Edward's brother, was educated at the mock-English Shan Chiefs School at Taunggyi as well as Rangoon University. But he was also educated in China and commissioned a captain in the Chinese Nationalist Army during the war. In the U Nu years he was a member of Parliament for Kokang, before becoming an insurgent and then the manager of the Rincome Hotel in northern Thailand. After ten years of further exile in France he eventually returned to Burma under a general amnesty in 1981 and settled in Rangoon.

His half sister was Yang Lyin Hsui, the bisexual warlady also known as Olive Yang. Born in 1927 and educated at the Guardian Angel's Convent School at Lashio in the northern Shan States, she developed an early reputation for toughness and an attraction to the violent life. Rumored to have carried a revolver in her handbag even at convent school, she later became a familiar figure in Burma's civil war. When the Chinese Nationalist forces crossed into Kokang in 1951, they enlisted her support, and she was eager for a piece of the action, raising her own militia and taking to wearing a stylish gray uniform with a Belgian Army pistol on each hip.

Olive would wind up in a Burmese prison. In the mid-1960s Jimmy Yang's militia joined up with other budding rebel armies in the Shan hills to try to offer more effective resistance to Ne Win. Rangoon, with its fifty thousand soldiers already overstretched, responded by encouraging and aiding rival militias in the hills, including one headed by the warlord Lo Hsing-Han, a former retainer in the Yang family and now its archenemy. As allies of the government Lo and others like him were free to deal in the opium trade, and this opening soon made these militia chiefs the most notorious and powerful men in the international drug trade.

Adding to the problem, by the mid-1960s the Burmese Communists had begun receiving open support from China. And farther to the north the recently formed Kachin Independence Army was quickly seizing control over nearly all the northern highlands.

The government of Thailand was also getting in on the act. The army there was waging its own war against Communist and other left-wing dissidents, and its Communist Suppression Operations Command was happy to help the Karens and other insurgents along the Burmese border, so long as they were anti-Communist. A paramilitary force was created under General Sudsai "The Red Bull" Hasdin, and this force, together with the Border Patrol Police, began what would be a decades-long policy of support for Burmese rebels. The families of insurgent leaders were allowed to live in Thailand, and insurgent armies (other than the Communists) were free to buy arms, ammunition, and other supplies. Even for Burmese less than sympathetic to the Rangoon regime, Thailand's active encouragement of the civil war would stain perceptions of Bangkok for a very long time.

> He admitted that he didn't know anything about economics. But he said every economist he talked to told him something different, and he didn't know what to do.
>
> —Former U.S. Ambassador Henry Byroade,
> recalling a conversation with General Ne Win[6]

By Christmas 1965 even General Ne Win had to admit that things were not proceeding very well. He had established his Burma Socialist

Program Party as the only legal political party in the country. It was made up mainly of army men and ex-army men together with a few civilian left-wingers he felt he could trust. They were the guardians of his Burmese Way to Socialism, and he told them candidly at their annual party seminar that after everything in sight had been nationalized, the economy was a mess. "If Burma were not a country with an abundance of food, we would all be starving," said the self-appointed Revolutionary Council chairman.[7] One reason food was still available was that agriculture had remained in private hands and recent rice harvests had been decent. Everything else, including essentials like salt and cooking oil, was now rationed through the people's stores, which had replaced Indian-owned shops. In Rangoon people waited in long queues from before first light, flimsy ration cards in hand, hoping to be able to buy a little rice, soap, or cloth for a *longyi*. Rationing in turn had led to a booming black market. On the rivers more than a third of the boats of the Irrawaddy Flotilla Company were laid up for lack of spare parts. But what to do? The obvious thing would be to resign, admit his mistakes, and allow a new civilian government to take over. But that was probably the last thing on the general's mind.

He saw enemies everywhere. Singapore's Prime Minister Lee Kuan Yew visited around this time and happily agreed to play a round of golf with his fellow Southeast Asian leader. But he noticed that the general was always surrounded by men with guns, even right on the course, and wore a steel helmet except when swinging his club. "To prevent assassination," the general said. Ne Win was nervous, but when he was nervous, he always pushed ahead.[8]

Ne Win explained to journalists that his policies had not worked but that "it was like having caught hold of a tiger's tail" and "there was nothing else to do but hang on to it." He could see no alternative. At least, he may have thought, there was a degree of law and order. The insurgencies would have worsened anyway, and now that the army was in charge there was no chance that ill-informed civilians could interfere in military affairs and divide the officer corps. More important, with the Indians kicked out and the foreign advisers and aid workers packed up and gone, the Burmese would have to learn to do things for themselves. It might take longer, but British rule had made the Burmese weak and lazy and ill disciplined. They had to change, the hard way, if necessary. Even more important, with an increasingly unpredictable China next door and the war in Vietnam growing fiercer by the month, turning inward perhaps had other benefits as well. By 1968 there would be seven hundred thousand American combat troops in Southeast Asia. It wasn't hard to see Burma going the way of its neighbors to the east.

The Do Not Disturb sign would remain hanging for a while longer.

MR. NE WIN GOES TO WASHINGTON

All this time Ne Win had been keeping the Americans at arm's length. While several Soviet aid programs had been allowed to continue, the American ones had largely ended in 1962. He had taken pride in signing the Sino-Burmese border agreement of 1960 and placed a good relationship with Communist China quite high on his list of priorities. Some said this was because he was partly of Chinese descent himself, but it was more likely based on his awareness that in the postcolonial age, Burma's and China's futures were again intimately linked. But what of the Americans? Ne Win was worried that the Americans would see his policies as a turn too far to the left and not the attempt to outflank the Communists that it was meant to be. He feared the Americans. In November 1963, South Vietnamese President Ngo Dinh Diem had been killed after being overthrown in a U.S.-backed coup. In March 1970 another U.S.-backed coup would replace Prince Norodom Sihanouk with General Lon Nol. And the CIA's support for Chinese Nationalist forces in the eastern Shan States had not been that long ago. He was not entirely wrong to wear a steel helmet on the golf course. But it seems the Americans actually had no intention to intervene. Instead they were looking to win him over.

The U.S. ambassador at the time was Henry Byroade, a career diplomat who had served in Burma during the war. Ne Win liked him. His predecessors had all denied U.S. involvement in arming the Chinese Nationalists in the early 1950s, but Byroade was different: he didn't deny what had happened, and his straight talk appealed to Ne Win, who prided himself as a straight talker. Both sides were beginning to realize a good relationship could be useful.

In 1966 the general was invited to make a state visit in America, and on a warm September afternoon he arrived by helicopter on the South

Lawn of the White House to be greeted by a Marine honor guard, a brass band, and a smiling President Lyndon Baines Johnson. These occasions are normally chock-full of rhetoric and fancy speeches. Not so for the Burmese strongman. In what may have been the shortest lunch toast ever on a state occasion, Ne Win raised his glass only to say, "I hope that these contacts will afford better understanding."[9] The Americans didn't mind. Their aim was to make Ne Win feel at ease and for him and Johnson to get to know each other. They had already come to the conclusion that strict Burmese neutrality, however disastrous the domestic politics that went with it, was in Washington's best interests.

After a couple of days of talks, including an hour alone with Johnson, Ne Win slipped out of Washington without any press conference or fanfare, first for a short stop in New York to visit U Thant at the United Nations and then for an eleven-day tour of the rest of America. Though this was his first state visit, Ne Win had been to the United States five times before, and his previous trip had not gone very well. The Americans knew that Ne Win was still sensitive about the treatment he had received that time (it was an official visit in 1960) and were keen not to repeat any problems. That time U.S. customs had searched his bags, the general had been kept waiting for an appointment at the Pentagon, and Madame Ne Win had apparently overheard a disparaging remark made about her by then first lady Mamie Eisenhower. This time, whatever Ne Win wanted, Ne Win would get. And so when the chairman of the Burmese Revolutionary Council said, "Look, I don't want to go to any factories or anything like that. Let's go to Maui and play golf," it was off to the links in the Aloha State for the rest of the stay.[10]

The growing U.S.-Burma friendship was well timed. Ne Win's hopes for a comfortable relationship with China would soon sour.

THE RED GUARDS COME TO BURMA

Throughout history the ups and downs of Chinese politics have inevitably shaped the fortunes of China's little neighbors to the southwest. It was the Mongol desire to encircle the Sung that sent Kublai Khan's Turkish-led cavalry into the Irrawaddy Valley in the 1200s, and it was the convulsions following the fall of the Ming that ravaged the countryside four hundred years later. The Qing invasions in the 1700s might have overthrown the new Konbaung dynasty, and it was this resistance against the Qing that did so much to bolster Burmese self-confidence and launch it on its collision course with British India. Even the Japanese invasion, in part an attempt to use the country as a bridgehead into India, was even more a Japanese move to cut off supplies to Chungking. Most recently, the Chinese Communist Revolution had given hope and inspiration to fellow Communists in Burma, igniting the civil war. Now its radical turn would deepen Burma's already considerable problems.

In the late 1950s the Great Leap Forward, a ludicrous attempt at instant industrialization, had thrown China into economic disaster. As many as twenty million people died during the ensuing famine. For a few years in the early 1960s more pragmatic leaders like Liu Xiaoqi and Deng Xiaoping had briefly gained in influence, but by the summer of 1966 a new cycle of radicalism and upheaval, the Great Proletarian Cultural Revolution, was in full swing. Led by the so-called Gang of Four and by hundreds of thousands of fanatical civilian Red Guards, ten years of confusion and chaotic violence followed. Millions marched in support of anarchy. Many in the top Communist leadership were purged, and Liu himself died of starvation while in detention in 1967. A cult of personality around Mao quickly developed, and the portly chairman was raised to near-godlike status. Even the People's Liberation Army was at times unable to contain the disorder being let loose across the giant country.

Throughout the world 1968 was a year of historic upheaval. It was the year Martin Luther King, Jr., and Robert F. Kennedy were killed by assassins and student demonstrators took over campuses across the United States; Warsaw Pact tanks invaded Czechoslovakia to end the Prague Spring; students and workers rocked the French Republic; and President Johnson himself decided not to seek reelection against the background of mounting anti–Vietnam War protests. But even by the standards of that remarkable year, the chaos in China was of a different order. And a wave of that massive unrest would flow directly south, to Burma.

A couple of years before, the expulsion orders that had driven so many ethnic Indians out of the country had not touched the sizable, though

smaller communities of ethnic Chinese. Like so many Chinese overseas, many came from a single county, Taishan, a collection of towns
and villages along the southeast coast not far from Hong Kong. Incredibly, this little strip of land was home to more than half of all the Chinese who had immigrated to America before 1965, and to a similar
percentage of those in Burma's cities and towns. Most of the rest came
from Fujian, opposite Taiwan. All were part of the same diaspora with
links across Southeast Asia.

Until 1962 they had their own schools, and though these were nationalized, Chinese children were still taught by Chinese teachers in
Rangoon and elsewhere. It was a politically divided community, but
the majority were probably more sympathetic to the Communist government in Peking than to the old Nationalists in Taiwan. When the
Cultural Revolution began to excite passions across their homeland,
many were also swept up in the excitement, wearing Mao badges,
shouting Cultural Revolution slogans, and marching up and down the
streets. There was tacit encouragement from the Chinese embassy. The
problem for these would-be Maoist fanatics was that they were not in
dusty Xi'an or icy Harbin with millions of flag-waving comrades for
company. They were in the middle of Burmese, Buddhist, military-ruled
Rangoon. With the economy at an all-time low, no jobs to show up for,
and many fewer Indian shops to attack, the earnest young Chinese protesters were an attractive target. The Burmese decided they were fed up
with the Maoists in their midst.

On 26 June 1967 big crowds surrounded two Chinese schools, and
the next day Chinese businesses were looted and smashed all around
Rangoon. Dozens of ethnic Chinese were beaten up and killed in a
frenzy of fairly one-sided communal violence. The police did little to
intervene, and after several more days of rioting, a mob attacked the
Chinese embassy itself and burned down the Chinese Teachers Feder-
ation building.

Part of the reason the police did not intervene may have been the
government's reckoning that a bout of communal rioting might help
deflect anger from the worsening economic picture. But the government itself was also angry at the Chinese—not so much the Chinese
in Rangoon, the innocent victims of the violence, as the Chinese in
China who had begun to step up aid to the Communist Party of
Burma. After their glory days in the late 1940s the Burmese Communist insurgents had become a bit of a spent force. Many of their leaders

had sought refuge in China, and others were holed up in the densely forested Pegu mountain range, which runs parallel to the Irrawaddy River. The army believed it had the upper hand and had no desire to see the Communists balloon up again into a threatening force. But this is precisely what happened.

In July 1967, only days after China had detonated its first hydrogen bomb in the marshlands of the Tarim Basin, Peking Radio began to call openly for a "people's revolt" against the Ne Win "fascist regime" and encouraged the Burmese people to fight on until the "Chiang Kai-shek of Burma" was dead. Newly aroused by the prospect of more help from Chairman Mao, the Burmese Communists (who then numbered about five thousand men under arms) took the offensive, attacking and holding for a few days a string of towns north of Rangoon. In October they blew up a train bound for Mandalay, killing over thirty people. But there was a limit to how successful a new Communist offensive in the Pegu mountain area could be. It was too close to Rangoon; there was no direct contact with China, no way to regularly funnel in arms and ammunition.

Masterminding China's Burma policy was Kang Sheng, the sinister and bespectacled driving force in the Peking politics of the day, and later an ardent supporter of Pol Pot and the Khmer Rouge. Rumored to be a lover of Madame Mao's, Kang decided that a major ratcheting up of support for the Communist Party of Burma would be a good thing for the Cultural Revolution. His plan was to first seize control of a slice of Burmese territory bordering China. And for this the Chinese needed the help of the local peoples—Shans, Kachins, and others—who straddled the border. Luckily for them they already had an ace in their pocket, Kachin war hero Naw Seng, the former British-trained commander of the Kachin Rifles. This World War II hero had defected to the rebels in 1949 and then fled to China, with hundreds of his men, and had lived there anonymously these past twenty years. On Kang Sheng's orders Naw Seng was now resurrected, an appropriately mixed force of Chinese, border minorities, and Burmese Communists would be set up, and the first step to a Burmese People's Republic would soon be reality.

Early in the morning of 1 January 1968, the very same morning that the Tet offensive nearly overwhelmed Saigon, hundreds of Chinese and

Chinese-backed Communist troops forded the shallow river that sepa-
rates Burma from China and attacked the Burmese army garrison at
the misty border hamlet of Mongko. A New Year's party had been in
full swing, and Mongko's mixed population was enjoying its rice wine
and loud music in the cold mountain air. The local garrison had a couple of dozen guns among them and was no match for the heavily
armed force that stormed in.[11]

Within days other Communist forces crossed the frontier into
Kokang, home of the Yang family and Jimmy Yang's militia. Many
were Red Guard volunteers as well as trainers from the People's Liberation Army. Local resistance was soon crushed, even in the rugged surrounding hills, and government forces were in full retreat. In February
a third invasion column entered the valley of the Shweli River. Fighting spread across the area; when Burmese army reinforcements finally
arrived, they were ambushed and swept aside by well-equipped Communist units. Bridges heading south into the lowlands were blown up,
and encircled companies of government soldiers were wiped out. By the
summer the Communists controlled three thousand square kilometers
of territory. The Burmese army's nightmare scenario of a Chinese-
backed insurgency along the border was coming true.

Ne Win and his colonels were shocked. Their biggest worry now
was a linkup between the invading force and the Communist bases in
the Pegu Mountains north of Rangoon. At an emergency Commanding Officers' Conference in Rangoon, Ne Win gave an impassioned
call to resistance. The general also abandoned any pretense at strict
neutrality and began to more actively seek help from wherever he
could find it. A Soviet mission was welcomed and discussed the possibility of aid. Japanese Prime Minister Eisaku Sato and German Chancellor Kurt Kiesinger also visited, and both were asked for economic
assistance. More significantly, the trickle of American military support
now quietly grew to include shipments of weapons and other equipment, together with some American trainers for the feeble Burma Air
Force.

Tactically on the ground the Burmese army decided to deal first
with the weaker enemy in central Burma (in the Pegu Mountains) and
only then to confront the new forces in the north. A couple of days after the Commanding Officers' Conference, a covert intelligence officer who had infiltrated the Communist headquarters in the Pegu

Mountains managed to assassinate the party chairman, Thakin Than Tun, as the old man, once a chief lieutenant of Aung San's, was leaving his jungle house. Soon the camp itself was overrun by the army's crack Seventy-seventh Light Infantry Division.

Up in the Shan States these blitzkrieg tactics were not possible, and Ne Win decided that there his best bet was to reinforce friendly militia. He reactivated his support for the opium warlords Lo Hsing-Han and Khun Sa, both of whom had long-standing ties to remaining Chinese Nationalist forces and to the Kuomintang government in Taiwan. Long mule caravans, manned by the Panthays of Panglong, descendants of refugees from the 1876 massacre of Muslims at Dali, carried stores of U.S. M-16 rifles, M-60 rocket launchers, and 57 and 75 mm recoilless rifles from Thailand.

Soon in the remote hills of northeastern Burma there would be little replays of the Communist–Nationalist Chinese civil war, more than twenty years after the war's end, on a miniscale, with Red Guards and their Burmese comrades battling it out against the Nationalist troops of General Li Mi and their drug-trafficking allies.

For a long time it was the Communists that tended to win. By 1971 they had taken over much of the Wa hills and were moving south and west toward the major towns in the northern Shan States. Only a huge effort by Ne Win and his men stopped them from marching down the old Burma Road and seizing Maymyo, the old British hill station overlooking Mandalay. Farther south, a Communist force several thousand strong, led in part by the half-Welsh, half-Shan warlord Mike Davies, overran the strategic garrison at Mongyang and threatened the large town of Kengtung, which sits close to the border of both Laos and Thailand. Burmese forces in the area were under the command of Lieutenant Colonel Tun Yi, short and bald and nicknamed Napoleon, and it took twenty battalions of Napoleon's men to defend Kengtung and dislodge the invaders from Mongyang.[12] But in the surrounding highlands over the Mekong and elsewhere, the Communists were there to stay, entrenched in a swath of territory across much of the eastern Shan States, until the strange events of 1989.

THE NEVER-ENDING WAR

Complicating this already barely comprehensible patchwork of armies and militia was yet another new insurgent group, backed by Thailand and led by none other than ousted Prime Minister U Nu.

U Nu had been released from prison in 1966. Two years later, around the time of the Chinese invasion when Ne Win was looking around for friends, he invited U Nu and many of the other old politicians to advise him on the way ahead. For months this group discussed various options, and the majority came down on the side of returning to a parliamentary democracy. Ne Win, after apparently some honest reflection, rejected the advice. In April 1968 U Nu asked that he be allowed to leave the country for medical reasons, and Ne Win agreed. Once out, Nu quickly traveled to London and announced that he was establishing a new movement to oust the Revolutionary Council regime by force. His adviser and cheerleader in all this was Edward Law-Yone, the forceful and articulate former editor of *The Nation* newspaper.

The idea was to establish a base in Thailand and win American or other Western support for an armed revolt inside Burma. By this time Ne Win's regime had alienated practically all of the old postindependence elite, and many now found their way to Law-Yone's rented house near Bangkok's Lumpini Park. It was almost a who's who of the 1950s, including four of the original Thirty Comrades and former senior figures in the armed forces like Air Commodore Tommy Clift, the Anglo-Shan who had been head of the air force until 1963. Jimmy Yang of Kokang was also there, as was the *mahadevi* of Yawnghwe, wife of the former president and now leader of the rebel Shan State Army.[13]

Thai intelligence provided help and connected the Burmese exiles with the Karen and Mon rebel bosses already under Thai sponsorship. But no real help, from the Americans or anyone else, ever came. A Canadian oil company gave a few million dollars in return for future and exclusive exploration rights, but that was all. A fledgling army was formed but never got more than a few miles inside the country. An audacious air raid over Rangoon dropped thousands of leaflets calling for an uprising, but then nothing happened. Ne Win's flirtations with Washington had helped. And the rising Communist threat convinced Western military analysts that support now for U Nu would only destabilize Rangoon and play into the hands of Peking. Even more important, the Burmese people, impoverished and without opportunity, had little energy left for politics.

Everyone was stuck with the Burmese Way to Socialism for a while longer. Ne Win had thought about change but then retreated in the face of new pressures. The Chinese invasion and the friendly sounds from the United States might have helped him make up his mind. In 1974 the Revolutionary Council was formally abolished, and a new constitution adopted. It enshrined the Burmese Socialist Program Party as the only legal party in the country and set up a cumbersome system of people's councils and committees. But in the end it was General Ne Win who called the shots, now more than ever. Aged sixty-three, he wasn't about to change his ways.

For the people of the Shan, Karen, and Kachin hills, the continuation of war brought only misery and increasing brutality. The Burmese army had adopted its four cuts strategy, designed to deny armed opposition groups access to food, money, information, and recruits. In a distant echo of the British pacification of the 1880s and the more recent American-led strategic hamlets campaign in South Vietnam, the government counted on mass relocations and the destruction of whole communities in their attempt to dislodge and isolate rebel groups. A generation of army officers rose through the ranks during this time and would achieve prominence in the years after the 1988 uprising. Unlike the earlier generation around Ne Win, men who had joined the army during the independence movement and had first served under an elected government, for this younger generation their formative experience was not anticolonial politics but counterinsurgency, a vicious jungle campaign in which enemies were all around. An army that prided itself on being the savior of the nation seemed bound to lose its way.

THE DEATH OF U THANT

It was around this time that I first went to Burma. I was eight and had lived up until that time with my parents and grandparents, including my grandfather U Thant, in New York. Exhausted after ten years at the head of the organization and suffering from stomach ulcers and other stress-related ailments, U Thant had retired from the UN at the end of two terms in 1971. His first term had won him many accolades, especially for his role in helping defuse the Cuban missile crisis, overseeing an end to the war in the Congo, and launching much of the UN's now-familiar humanitarian, development, and environmental work. He and his team quietly mediated peace agreements in Yemen, Bahrain, and elsewhere. His experiences in Burma shaped who he was, even during this time. He remained passionately anticolonialist and appreciative of the monumental challenges facing new nations in Asia and Africa. He was a staunch and vocal opponent of apartheid. As U Nu's former press secretary he prided himself on his relations with the media and remains the only secretary-general ever to hold weekly press conferences. But he must have had moments of surprise, surprise that a headmaster from Pantanaw had come this far only twelve years after leaving by steamer up the muddy creeks to Rangoon.

His second term had not been a happy one. He had spoken out very early on against the U.S. war in Vietnam, and this had alienated him from his erstwhile supporters in Washington. And he was scapegoated for the outbreak of the 1967 Arab-Israeli War, blamed for agreeing to an Egyptian demand to pull out UN peacekeepers from the Sinai when in fact two of the key countries that had sent the troops, India and Yugoslavia, had already decided themselves on a withdrawal *and* when Egyptian tanks and armored cars were already streaming past the small and isolated UN outposts. The big powers on the Security Council did nothing. His lonely visit to Cairo, to see President Gamal Abdul Nasser on the eve of the war, was a failure. He was the only one who had tried to mediate but was blamed nonetheless. All this weakened him, and within two years of leaving office he was ill with cancer, cancer from the Burmese cigars he kept in a little humidor (a gift from Fidel Castro) in the corner of his office.

I remember very well that the day he died was a Thursday because every Thursday I had an afternoon violin class. In the middle of the lesson a secretary from the headmaster's office came in and told me that a car was waiting to take me home early. It was my grandfather's car, a black Cadillac, with his driver, William Eagan, in the front and my little sister, eating a banana, in the back. At home there was a lot of commotion, and after seeing my parents, I tried to keep myself out of the way of the many Burmese men and women milling around downstairs. The next morning the stack of papers my grandfather normally read lay in a pile by a rocking chair, a *New York Times* on the top with the headline "U Thant Dead of Cancer at 65."

That day or the next day it was decided that I would go with my parents to bury my grandfather in Burma. It was my grandmother's wish that I go, she being too unwell to travel. I don't think anyone had a good idea of what lay ahead. At the root of it was General Ne Win's smoldering hatred of U Thant.

To some extent, the full force of the animosity goes back only to 1969, when U Nu, then in the early days of his attempts to overthrow the Ne Win government, visited New York as part of an international tour to drum up support. My grandfather was then on a mission in Africa and was unable to see him, but arranged instead for my father to meet his old friend on arrival at the airport. But entirely unknown to anyone in my family, U Nu had made arrangements with the UN press corps to speak at its club (inside the UN building), where he launched a vitriolic attack on the Rangoon regime and called for revolution. Never before had a call for the overthrow of a UN member state government been made from inside the UN. My grandfather later phoned U Nu and told him his action had been inappropriate; U Nu apologized for his indiscretion.

But General Ne Win was upset and became sure that U Thant was now conniving with U Nu. He told his men to consider Thant an enemy of the state. When he went home on a personal visit the following year, Ne Win refused to see him, and later Thant had difficulty renewing his passport. But even before 1969 the two men had probably never cared much for each other, being very different in character and my grandfather being the only senior member of the U Nu government never arrested after the 1962 coup. The idea that U Thant would be accorded any special honors in death was likely very far from the old general's mind.

For a day his coffin was set just inside the entrance to the UN's General Assembly building, in front of a beautiful stained glass by Marc Chagall, while assembled diplomats and then Secretary-General Kurt Waldheim filtered past. I remember all this vividly, the UN security men in their light and dark blue uniforms lifting the coffin and the tall, stooping figure of Waldheim coming over to say hello.

On 29 November my parents and I, accompanied by the UN's protocol chief, set off from John F. Kennedy Airport's WorldPort terminal on a Pan American flight bound for Bangkok. Those were the days when a New York–Bangkok flight (now a nonstop nineteen-hour marathon) still made nearly half a dozen landings along the way and when first class meant a lot of space, especially for an eight-year-old. From Bangkok a special charter plane, empty except for the four of us and the cabin crew, flew us to Rangoon.

My first view of Burma was of the quiltlike rice fields, green and brown, as the plane flew over the south coast and then touched down at Mingaladon Airfield. From inside the propeller plane I could see soldiers marching past against a low line of trees in the near distance.

A crowd of people were waiting just off the tarmac. They included dozens of my relatives, almost all of whom I was meeting for the very first time. One took my hand and led me away. But there were no government representatives and not even an official vehicle to transport the shiny oak coffin, only a slightly battered Volkswagen van belonging to the local Red Cross. U Thant's body was then driven to the Maidan, where the old racetrack was, to give ordinary people a chance to pay their respects before the burial.

Ne Win's position was made crystal clear to anyone who might have had dissenting thoughts. The deputy education minister, U Aung Tin, was a former student of my grandfather's and in a gesture of personal loyalty had come out to the airport. He also suggested at a cabinet meeting that day that the actual day of U Thant's funeral should be made a holiday. He was immediately sacked. Others were frightened enough that one floral wreath placed in front of the casket at the racetrack was simply signed "Seventeen necessarily anonymous public servants."

At the old racetrack, I remember the crush of people filing past the coffin under what seemed to me a huge tent. There was a small mountain of flowers and wreaths in front, together with his framed portrait. I sat for a long time on a wooden stool nearby, the sun setting, mosquitoes buzzing around, with the floodlit Shwedagon Pagoda gleaming under the evening sky.

The next day Ne Win's ire took him a step further, and the state media claimed that my family had broken the law in bringing U Thant's body back without sanction and said legal action might follow. While we waited for official clearance for burial (which for anyone in Burma meant negotiating a bureaucratic labyrinth), my grandfather's casket remained on the unkempt grass in the middle of the racetrack, where ever-larger crowds of people in colorful *longyis* and velvet slippers gathered every day. Finally permission came, not for burial in any special place but in a small private cemetery. A little disappointed, my family agreed.

There were hints of trouble ahead, and my parents decided not to take me to the funeral, leaving me instead at the home of my great-uncle to play with my cousins in the big backyard. The Buddhist funeral service itself went as planned, but then, as the motorcade began driving toward the cemetery, a big throng of students stopped the hearse carrying the coffin. They had been arriving all day long in the thousands, with thousands more onlookers cheering them on. Through loudspeakers mounted on jeeps they declared: "We are on our way to pay our tribute and accompany our beloved U Thant, architect of peace, on his last journey." One of my grandfather's younger brothers pleaded with them to let the family bury him quietly and to take up other issues later, but to no avail. The coffin was seized and sped away on a truck to Rangoon University. Their intentions were clearly in sympathy with my grandfather, but their actions left my family shaken.

At the university the casket was placed on a dais in the middle of the dilapidated Convocation Hall, ceiling fans whirring overhead in the stifling heat. Buddhist monks chanted prayers, and students kept a vigil night and day. Soon the campus was filled with an enormous number of ordinary people. But now a political mood was also in the air. Speeches were made condemning the government and calling for change. The next day the student organizers sent a letter to the authorities demanding a proper state funeral and said that if the government did not agree, they would hold their own funeral, one befitting a Burmese hero. For the location of their planned mausoleum, they chose the site of the old Student Union, where U Nu had first tried his hand at public speaking, where Aung San had been president in the 1930s, and which Ne Win had blown up in 1962. More speeches followed as crowds grew and demands became more strident.

On 7 December the government offered a compromise. U Thant would be buried at a mausoleum to be built at the foot of the Shwedagon Pagoda, but there would be no state funeral. The students were inclined to say no immediately, but my father and my great-uncles counseled them not to reject anything out of hand; after all, a public funeral in many ways would be more fitting than a state funeral organized by a military regime. There were also concerns for the students themselves and their fate and whether an amnesty for their actions would be guaranteed. At a meeting among my family, student representatives, and Buddhist monks, the majority agreed to accept the government's offer.

And so the next day a second attempt to bury my grandfather was made. His coffin was first lifted and placed temporarily at the site of the old Student Union, as a gesture toward the students who had wished him interred there. My family prostrated themselves on the ground before the casket, together with the many young men and women nearby. What seemed like all Rangoon was lined up along the broad avenues from the campus to the Shwedagon Pagoda a couple of miles away. But it was all not to be. At the last moment the more radical student faction seized the coffin yet again with the intent of burying U Thant at the Student Union site, no matter what.

For three days it went on. No one knew what to do next. Students were still camped out at the university, and my grandfather's body remained at the makeshift "Peace Mausoleum" erected by the protesters. Then, at two in the morning on 11 December, approximately fifteen platoons of riot police backed by over a thousand soldiers stormed the university grounds. The students and monks who had been on watch near the coffin put up a brief struggle, pleading with the soldiers to join them in defying Ne Win. Within an hour the army was in full control. Some reports say dozens of students were killed, some trying to guard the coffin to the very end, though no one really knows how many might have died. Many hundreds were rounded up and arrested. Some would serve long years in prison. Flanked on all sides by armored vehicles and automatic weapons just unleashed on unarmed men and women, the body of the former schoolteacher and UN secretary-general was hurried to his final resting place. Riots broke out around Rangoon. An angry crowd of several thousand destroyed a police station, and both a government ministry and several cinemas were wrecked. Troops opened fire, and more people were killed. The hospital was said to be filled with wounded. Martial law was imposed, and soldiers in full combat gear lined the main streets.

At about six that morning we were woken up at our hotel by a phone call from downstairs. The caller, who identified himself as a government agent, said that U Thant's body had been retrieved from the university and was now at the Cantonment Garden near the Shwedagon Pagoda. They said there had been no violence and that only tear gas had been used. My family was allowed to pay their last respects. We were asked to leave the country and about a week later headed back to New York. Only much later did we realize the full magnitude of what had happened that day.

Being eight, I took only some of this in. I remember the feeling of having missed more than three weeks of school as well as Christmas. I didn't see any of the violence myself, but I did see the faces of the crowds at the university as they pressed around our car and the young, often scrawny soldiers in their ill-fitting uniforms with their bayonets and shiny boots. I also met my great-grandmother, U Thant's mother, then in her early nineties, and in playing with my cousins learned a little about all the fun things childhood in Burma could mean, colors and sounds and flavors far away from suburban New York. I also remember their excitement at eating vanilla ice cream and fairly tasteless sandwiches at our Soviet-built hotel, the only place where Western snacks could be bought. I saw Rangoon at the height of Ne Win's road to socialism, with barely a car on the street and the old colonial buildings quietly crumbling, musty shops without much to sell, a city even a child could understand had seen happier days.

One day during this trip, I don't know when, my parents were having lunch at the home of friends, a retired air force officer and his wife, and I was outside with their daughter and her nanny. It was a posh residential neighborhood, and a solitary military policeman in white gloves was checking his motorcycle along the empty tree-lined street. Then suddenly he stood to attention, and a black limousine preceded by two outriders whizzed past us. In the backseat of the limousine, waving as we waved, was a smiling general Ne Win.

There were other challenges to the status quo in the mid-1970s, including an abortive coup by some mid-level officers that led to their arrest and execution and to the imprisonment of the army chief of staff General Tin Oo. Tin Oo, who later emerged as Aung San Suu Kyi's closest colleague and chairman of her party, had remained loyally in charge of the army during the U Thant demonstrations but was now accused of knowing about the assassination plot against Ne Win and of not doing anything to stop it.

After this, and from the late 1970s to the 1988 uprising, the country settled into a low groove. There was little unrest; the economy after its darkest days had started to pick up a bit, there was new aid from the West and from the United Nations, and the civil war, still sputtering on, was largely confined to the border areas. Ne Win was getting old, and everyone looked forward to better times ahead.

Some regimes manage to offset economic difficulties with an appeal to patriotism or some sort of political excitement. Ne Win offered nothing of the sort. He rarely appeared in public and certainly was not one for making speeches or holding flashy parades. In the 1960s he had traveled regularly to Vienna to consult the well-known psychiatrist Dr. Hans Hoff, usually in between shopping trips to London and Geneva. The secrets of what the Burmese dictator said on the couch remained locked in an Austrian office, but whatever was troubling Ne Win, he stopped receiving therapy in the mid-1970s. Around the same time his wife died, and this, it seems, affected him deeply. Soon after, he married Yadana Nat Mai, aka June Rose Bellamy, the daughter of a Burmese princess and an Australian bookie, but the marriage ended acrimoniously, and the general withdrew into deeper seclusion. Few, if anyone, outside his immediate family knew much about his personal life, but stories that emerged pointed to two things, a bad temper and a growing irrationality.

That Ne Win was temperamental was always well known and probably was part of his success as a strong military leader. In 1976 the resident diplomatic community got to see a bit of it as well. It was New Year's Eve, and the general was apparently upset with the loud music drifting from the Inya Lake Hotel across the lake to his own villa. Rowing himself across (according to one version of the story), he crashed the party, kicked in the drums, manhandled the drummer, and then punched a Norwegian aid official who happened to be standing nearby. Other stories focused on his passion for numerology and more generally for magic and in particular on his fixation with the number nine. No one knows the truth about Ne Win's beliefs, but one thing is factual: in 1986, Burmese currency notes were replaced with those divisible by nine. There were no more ten-, fifty-, and hundred-kyat notes—only nine-, forty-five-, and ninety-kyat notes. Shopping suddenly meant becoming much better at math.

There was no bread, but there was also little circus. For a brief and shining moment Burma had dominated Asian soccer, and from 1965 to 1973 it had won the biennial Southeast Asian Games an unprecedented five times and the Asian Games twice, in 1966 and 1970. But then the decline set in, and by the late 1970s there wasn't even much of a sports team, in any field, to cheer on. Then a big change happened: television and videos.

Television was first introduced in 1979 to a population starved for entertainment. The cinema had always been popular, but for a long time very few Western films were being shown, for financial reasons as much as anything else. One exception was James Bond, who always packed them in, and a generation of young Rangoonites were at least able to make the transition from Sean Connery to Roger Moore in step with the rest of the world. But now there was TV as well. There was only one channel, and this channel offered a mix of tightly controlled news, staid Burmese music performances, and old local films. It was on the air only a few hours a day but ushered in a quiet revolution in expectations. First, it did broadcast, usually in the early evenings, an episode of some American television series, and for a while *The Love Boat* captivated Burmese audiences, showing people an admittedly strange and warped but still not an entirely inaccurate vision of rich and prosperous life in the West.

Then there was the arrival by the early 1980s of videocassette recorders (VCRs) and bootleg videotapes smuggled over the Tenasserim hills from Thailand. I remember in the mid-1980s (when I often spent the summer holidays in Rangoon) visiting the corner video shop, usually a little wooden hut where the selection was decent (especially if one's tastes tended toward B movie action thrillers with lots of blood and gore). It wasn't just in Rangoon. Though the relatively well-to-do had televisions and VCRs in their homes, others even in up-country towns could still watch films at tea shops. All in all, a sizable section of the population was seeing for the first time and in living color what they were missing under their nativist and puritanical regime.

THE KACHIN HILLS

In the cold weather of 1991–92 I traveled across western Yunnan, first from Dali southeast to the old Burma Road crossing at Shweli and then north by truck along the valley of the Salween River and into the Kachin hills. It was an illegal trip. At that time foreigners were not allowed in that part of Yunnan, and I was guided all along the way by representatives of the Kachin Independence Organization (KIO), the political wing of the rebel Kachin Independence Army. We crossed some of the most spectacular scenery in the world, a landscape of rolling green hills, empty except for a few small villages and ponies munching on the fresh grass, interspersed by deep gorges and towering snow-covered mountains. Three of the world's great rivers—the Yangtze, the Mekong, and the Brahmaputra—come within a hundred miles of one another here, in nearly parallel lines, before setting off for thousands more miles in different ways and meeting the sea at Shanghai, Saigon, and Calcutta. The area had once been the heartland of the ninth-century Nanzhao Empire and was the home of the Burmese language. Today much of the hills, on both sides of the border, were the home of the Kachins, a mix of different peoples, with distinct cultures but speaking languages kindred to Burmese and Tibetan.

The Kachins, who had been in rebellion for the better part of a quarter century, would continue the fight for a few more years until agreeing to a cease-fire with Rangoon in 1994. Their headquarters were at Pajau, a sprawling army base of bamboo and thatch huts, nestled along the largely denuded mountains and looking a little like a cross between *M*A*S*H* and *Gilligan's Island*. It wasn't a guerrilla war. After having taken control of a vast arc of highlands, but never being able to capture and hold the major lowland towns, the Kachins settled into a defensive position, administering their territories and keeping Rangoon's forces at bay. The cost had been enormous: thousands killed, villages razed, and tens, perhaps hundreds of thousands of people displaced from their homes, out of a total Kachin population of well under a million.

Almost everyone wore an army green Chinese overcoat, and I had bought the smartest one I could find at a market in southwestern Yunnan along the way. Though the days were sunny with temperatures in the fifties and a brilliant blue sky overhead, by late evening it was biting cold, well below freezing. Sleeping in a thatch hut like everyone else (I had the clean and spacious "guest hut"), I had to decide whether to keep a small fire going and have a smoky room or instead wake up in a very frosty bed. Early on, Kachin officials had tried to impress on me their commitment to ending opium cultivation in their area, saying that they were encouraging their farmers to grow potatoes instead. It was to impress this point that they served up a big dish of French fries and, finding that I liked them, served French fries for almost every meal.

It didn't really feel like a war zone. Pajau in those days seemed quite settled, even though the front lines were only twenty or so miles away. It was all very orderly, with huts for various parts of the Kachin Independence Organization and even a special hut where shortwave radio broadcasts of the BBC, Voice of America, and All-India Radio were regularly monitored. There were little children everywhere in brightly colored knits and padded jackets, as well as a kindergarten and school, and all this was built very neatly along the slope of a great mountain, with China to one side and the headwaters of the Irrawaddy somewhere down below.

I spoke to some of the new recruits, young men in their late teens and early twenties who had volunteered straight out of high school in Myitkyina and Bhamo, both government-held towns. In asking them why they had joined, I had thought they might respond with words of Kachin nationalism, but instead they all gave me a reasoned and sad commentary about what they saw as their lowly place in the world and their desire to improve the basic lot of their people. They criticized the education system they had grown up with, the health care system, and even sanitation in their hometowns, comparing it with what they saw as global standards and saying that they were fighting for equal rights and a better life for the Kachins more than anything else.

I was there over Christmas, and the Kachins were all Christians, a mix of Baptists, Anglicans, and Roman Catholics. In a fairly novel explanation, one of my hosts told me that earlier in the century, his ancestors, believing that to be modern, they needed to trade in their traditional animism for either Christianity or Buddhism, chose Christianity because, being avid hunters, they "enjoyed killing animals." They invited me to a big Christmas feast and a play, in the Jingpaw language of most Kachins, with the plump uniformed officer in the seat next to me translating matter-of-factly as if I had never heard the story before ("the woman will have a baby . . . they are now in a new town and have to sleep in a manger . . ."). There was also quite a lot of caroling, with the local choir going from hut to hut and ending each song with an energetic "Merry Christmas!"

Some of the caroling was done by a small group of ethnic Burmese university students, most from Mandalay, who had fled to Pajau following the end of the uprising in 1988. Some were eager to return home; others were determined to train as soldiers and take up some sort of armed fight against the military government. But with their Christmas cheer they didn't seem quite the hardened revolutionaries they wanted to be. They followed with enthusiasm the recent news that Aung San Suu Kyi had won the Nobel Peace Prize, though more than one ex-student, in talking about the award, kept referring to it as the Oscar, the other, perhaps better-known prize, even at the edge of the Kachin hills.

By 1988 a somewhat better economy, a rising level of foreign aid, and a generally more relaxed government mood had fed a sense of growing expectations. Many exiles, including U Nu, had returned, and many other political opponents were released from prison. And Ne Win himself was getting old. Surely things would change soon, people thought. The desire, first and foremost in those days, was for a return to normalcy, a reintegration of the country with the world. Then Ne Win gave his speech calling for a return to democracy, and thousands took to the streets, demanding an end to military rule. And in the distant hills, an equally profound shift in Burmese politics was taking shape.

THIRTEEN

PALIMPSEST

Luther and Johnny Htoo were the illiterate and lice-ridden twelve-year-old twin warlords of the self-styled "God's Army," a nominally Christian force of perhaps two hundred Karen hill tribesmen nestled along the Burma-Thailand border. Together they lived in a bamboo and grass-thatched village at Kersay Doh ("God's Mountain") in the malarial rain forests of the Dawna Range, about a day's drive along the motorway from Bangkok and a world away from twenty-first-century civilization. There was no running water or electricity on God's Mountain, and their followers worshiped the not quite teenage militants as messiahs. Then, one day in early 2000, ten of their fighters left the bush and took hostage over five hundred doctors, nurses, and patients at the provincial Ratchaburi General Hospital in Thailand. Their apparent aim was to protest a recent shelling of their village by the Thai Army. Outraged and determined to look tough, the Thai government quickly ordered its commandos to storm the hospital. The medical workers were soon freed, and the ten soldiers of the little messiahs were gunned down or executed.[1]

Three years before, when Karen outposts were being overrun by the Burmese army, this small band of guerrillas, mainly teenagers, had managed to fight their way out of a Burmese encirclement. According to local lore, the cheroot-smoking twins had inspired them to stand and fight, and an army of spirits had joined the battle. From then on, their following grew, and the group broke off from the main Karen force with Luther and Johnny in charge. Some said that the twins were invulnerable to bullets and that they were able to step on land mines without fear. The twins laid down the law in their village: no pork, eggs, or alcohol. But in some ways they were still children, playing with dogs and cats and climbing trees. A shadowy dwarf known only as Mr. David became their chief adviser, and he was said to wield considerable influence behind the scenes. They claimed to be Baptists, and guests at the Kersay Doh Christmas feast in 1998 were treated to a giant lizard, monkey, and deer, as well as a selection of wild vegetables. There was singing and dancing all night.

But after the hospital takeover, the pressure on God's Army was stepped up, and eventually Johnny and Luther decided to lay down their assault weapons and surrender to the Thai Army. In Thailand they found a new life. Luther soon fell in love and married an older woman (she's nineteen) and is now a father. Both he and Johnny also learned to play the guitar, and playing the guitar has become their passion. They say they are still committed to a better life for the Karen people. But what they now hope for most is a music scholarship.

For many people outside the country the Burmese civil war, to the extent they have heard of it at all, remains confusingly and hopelessly exotic, with passing images of opium merchants and child soldiers and Vietnam-like jungles, a war without a clear beginning or end, a natural part of a faraway corner, and a sideshow to the more understandable duel between Aung San Suu Kyi and the military junta. The story of Johnny and Luther Htoo was virtually the only story about the fighting in Burma that has been covered in the international press over the past several years, underlining an impression that whatever armed conflict there may be in that country, it is of a different and perhaps less serious kind than, say, the wars in Afghanistan or the heart of Africa. Some may have heard of the Karen rebels, helped by the proximity of that long-standing rebellion to the air-conditioned comforts of Bangkok and the small industry of largely Western aid workers who for years have helped Karen refugees along the border. But it is not that the rest of the civil war went away. Instead, because of a strange turn, barely reported and away from the television cameras, nearly all the guns have at least temporarily gone quiet and the longest-running armed conflict in the world has come tantalizingly close to ending.

———————

In March 1989, way up in the blue green Kokang mountains, where early-spring mornings are still cold and frost covers the ground, ethnic Chinese soldiers under their commander, Pheung Kya-shin, openly challenged the leadership of the Communist Party of Burma. Since the late sixties the Communists had been in control of Kokang, and Pheung's men were part of the multiethnic Communist army. Their timing had been right. Within days the revolt spread quickly to the other Communist bases strung along the thickly forested hills, and one by one, Communist army units overthrew the party that they had been set up to serve. On 16 April mutineers from the Twelfth Brigade stormed the headquarters at Pangsang, smashing portraits of Marx, Engels, and Lenin and seizing arms and ammunition. The aging party officials, who had for a lifetime dreamed of a tropical proletarian paradise, now sped off into Yunnan and into the dustbin of history. The Burmese Communist insurgency, almost exactly four decades old, suddenly collapsed, defeated in the end not by special American weaponry or shrewd Burmese army tactics but by the weariness of the local people, who had for so long been carrying the burden of the leftist struggle.[2]

For ten years Deng Xiaoping had kept open China's doors to the outside world, improving relations to the West and setting the stage for unprecedented economic growth. China would soon end its support to the Khmer Rouge and had already worked to strengthen ties with Ne Win. But the septuagenarian Marxist intellectuals from Rangoon had showed no signs of wanting to give up the people's war and remained as keen as ever on using local villagers as cannon fodder for a revolution that would never happen. Now the local villagers were finally free of the party masters, but they were still armed to the teeth. The question for the mutineers was: What next?

Few, if any, of the mutineers were Burmese in the sense of being from the Burmese-speaking Buddhist majority. Several of the officers were ethnic Chinese, either from across the border or from Kokang, including more than a few former Red Guards from the days of the Cultural Revolution. The vast majority were Was, the little-known but fairly numerous hill people of the region. It was these Was who had died in droves time and again in Maoist-style wave attacks against Burmese army positions. They were dirt poor, but at least now they could protect their own interests. In the weeks that followed, the Communist force quickly and fairly amicably broke up along ethnic lines, and the new United Wa State Army became the main successor army of the once-feared Communist force.

The heartland of the Wa people is an awe-inspiring series of north-south mountain ranges that drop down steep slopes into valleys four or five thousand feet below. There are about seven hundred thousand Was in Burma and another three hundred thousand in China, and many live in this compact area, stretching about a hundred miles along the wild Salween River and about fifty miles east toward the Mekong. Their little villages are often set along the sides of these mountains and were once considered impregnable, with earthen ramparts surrounding them and the only entrances through long tunnels. Until the first American Baptist missionaries arrived a hundred years ago and converted some to Christianity, the Was were almost all animist. They claimed to have been an indigenous people, present in the Wa hills since the beginning of time and to have evolved from tadpoles on a mysterious mountain lake.[3] But their main reputation was as headhunters.

> Outside every village, there is a grove of trees, usually stretching along the ridge. It is usually fairly broad and is made up of huge trees, with heavy un-dergrowth, strips of the forest which, years and years ago, covered the whole country. From a distance it looks like an avenue, sometimes little over one hundred yards long, sometimes stretching for long distances from village to village. This is the avenue of skulls . . .[4]

The early British officials who reached this area said that many villages had dozens of heads set along rows of wooden posts but that some had hundreds of skulls in varying states of preservation. They were safe-guards against evil spirits, and the idea was that the ghost of the dead man would protect the area, not because of any concern for the vil-lagers but because of a dislike of any vagrant spirits entering his patch. The Burmese and Shans claimed that the Was were cannibals as well, but the Was themselves denied this, saying that a good skull or two would ensure all the maize and dog and good liquor (strong rice wine) they needed to be happy. Dog was a big part of the Wa table.

They also had a particular attraction for unusual heads and for the heads of eminent people, and though they were following what one colonial observer described as an "eclectic and dilettante" style of head-hunting, there were certain rules, with the legitimate head-hunting season opening in March and lasting through the last week in April. As late as the 1930s (and perhaps much later) the Was remained true to their tradition, and in the 1930s a touring Sikh physician, resplendent in beard and turban, became too mouthwatering a prize and had to be escorted out of the area under heavy guard. Their reputation was not helped by their dress, which in hot weather consisted of nothing at all, for both men and women.[5]

In 1989 it was these tough and self-reliant men who inherited the main part of the Communist military machine, armed to the teeth with fairly up-to-date Chinese weapons, peering out from behind their mountain strongholds and wondering who their friends and who their enemies would be.

An obvious choice for the Was and the other ex-Communist fighters would have been to team up with the existing ethnic insurgencies and present, for the very first time, a united front against Rangoon. The Kachin insurgency in the hills just to the north was still going strong, as were a variety of ethnic insurgencies farther south. In the early weeks after the mutiny, some talks did take place with representatives of the Karen National Union and other groups along the Thai border. But the Burmese army was quick to step in and fill the breach. Rangoon realized what was at stake. Either it could neutralize its longtime battle-field foes once and for all, or it could see the ex-Communist army mutate into an even graver threat, this time in league with all the various ethnic-based armies. It had only been months since the 1988 uprising, and an even more threatening possibility (to the Burmese military) was that all these groups would in turn ally themselves with the prodemocracy movement in the cities. A deal would have to be struck.

That the Burmese army was willing to negotiate under these conditions was perhaps not surprising but was unprecedented nevertheless. Its policy had always been to seek a military solution. But with a democracy movement still simmering in the cities and an ethnic insurgency that still carried some punch, an important strategic decision was made. By negotiating an armistice with the ex-Communist soldiers, the Burmese army would be free to focus its attention elsewhere. An end to nearly half a century of civil war was suddenly in sight.

And so during the autumn of 1989 a trio of unlikely visitors made their way to Pangsang to make friends with their former enemies. The old militia leader Lo Hsing-Han was dusted off and sent to talk to the insurgents, and he was followed by both the aging warlady Olive Yang and former Brigadier General Aung Gyi, a leader in the just-crushed uprising and an erstwhile colleague of Aung San Suu Kyi's. But the man who designed and cemented the deal was the intelligence czar Khin Nyunt. Flying by helicopter to the secluded mountain base, he invited Wa leaders to a meeting with the top brass of the Burmese military. The offer was accepted, and at the meeting Rangoon promised a development scheme with roads and bridges and schools as well as food and other aid to this poorest part of a very poor country. More important, the Was would be allowed to keep their weapons and would enjoy de facto autonomy in the area they controlled, pending a final peace agreement. They would also be allowed, even encouraged, to do what they and many other insurgents in the area had long been doing, which was profit from the opium trade, only now they would be able to use government roads and invest their proceeds in a soon-to-be-freed-up economy. The Wa chiefs and other former Communist officers were feted in the official press as great leaders of "the national races."

Between March 1989 and the end of 1990, General Khin Nyunt reached cease-fire agreements with the leaders of all the successor armies to the Communist Party. The Kokang Chinese formed the Myanmar National Democratic Alliance Army to rule their highland fastness. Along the opium-rich middle reaches of the Mekong in what had been the Communist 815 War Zone a new National Democracy Alliance Army was set up by former Cultural Revolution Red Guards. And the most important of all was the United Wa State Army, headquartered in the former Communist base at Pangsang, ambitious and twenty thousand strong.

The new alphabet soup of militia lost no time in making money from the main moneymaking business in eastern Burma, narcotic drugs. The Communists had allowed growing and trading in opium as assistance from Peking dried up, and a local tax on opium helped keep the coffers reasonably full. But now it was time to make big bucks, and the Was and others moved up the production ladder and into heroin, setting up twenty-three refineries in the Kokang area alone between 1989 and 1991. The old Yang clan jumped into the game as well, and it was only the personal intervention of Khin Nyunt in 1992 that stopped a small war from breaking out between the Yangs and their rivals.

In the Wa country, heroin dealing was mainly in the hands of ethnic Chinese, some tied to the remnants of the old Chinese Nationalist forces in or near Thailand. By the early 1990s the Was were building refineries for themselves. More recently, opium production has waned considerably, and they have diversified into methamphetamines, flooding the Thai market with millions of pills of what the Thais call *yaba*, the crazy drug.

But drugs weren't the only way to make money. As the Burmese Road to Socialism was jettisoned out the window, the new Burmese Road to Capitalism offered quick riches for those well connected. And the Was were the newly well connected. Foreign exchange policies were liberalized. More important, banks were allowed to take deposits of "uncertain" origin, so long as a tax to the government was paid. Funds poured in. And by 1994 house prices in Rangoon and Mandalay had skyrocketed, with a four-bedroom in a nice neighborhood fetching as much as a million U.S. dollars, cash. Around the same time, the Was set up shop in Rangoon, investing in real estate, mining, hotels and tourism, food processing, and transportation and establishing branch offices in Thailand, Hong Kong, and elsewhere overseas. They wanted to establish a bank as well, but heroin warlords with a bank were too much even for the Burmese authorities, and permission was quietly denied. The erstwhile headhunters (or at least their Chinese fellow travelers) were now Burma's most successful entrepreneurs. The Kokang Chinese also were having their day, owning everything from the Mitsubishi Electric's Burmese franchise to producing and selling Myanmar Rum and Myanmar Dry Gin. Other warlords like Lo Hsing-Han (now with his own *Asia World* business empire) and Khun Sa (once the powerful head of the rebel Mong Tai Army) also joined the ranks of the new and somewhat shady business elite.

All this was happening within the context of a much wider liberalization, one aimed at unraveling nearly thirty years of self-imposed isolation and economic stagnation.[6] In 1988 the Burmese army officer corps wanted a freeing up of the economy as much as anyone. Some seemed to have in their minds a sort of market-based military authoritarian government along the lines of neighboring Thailand with the armed forces keeping a comfortable slice of an increasingly prosperous pie. I remember that a year before the uprising an army captain told me, over a cup of weak coffee at the then paint-peeling Strand Hotel, of the need for change, saying that no one was happy with Ne Win's so-called Burmese socialism. "What we really want," he said hopefully, "is to change from being an isolated left-wing military dictatorship to a pro-American right-wing military dictatorship." He looked around at the stained carpets and rickety chairs and rolled his eyes. Now they had their chance.

In the weeks after the uprising, in the last months of 1988, foreign exchange reserves fell to nearly nothing. Simply to keep the army afloat, the government needed hard cash to buy petrol and spare parts and ammunition from overseas. Foreign debt, at six billion dollars, needed over two hundred million dollars a year just to service. Western aid had been worth about five hundred million dollars a year, but this was now almost entirely cut. West Germany, Japan, and the United States together provided the country with 90 percent of its foreign exchange income.[7] It looked as if the government were on its knees and that the financial crisis alone might force a more compromising position.

But in stepped the Thai army commander in chief, General Chao-valit Yongchaiyudh, looking plump and cheerful in his tight brown uniform, who flew to Rangoon in December 1988 and came back with a handsome line of business deals, including several lucrative logging concessions. Favored Thai firms would get rich, the Burmese army would receive just enough money to survive, and huge areas of forest would be cut down at an unprecedented rate.[8] A year later there was a hundred million dollars in the bank. After logging, the government turned to oil, and contracts for oil exploration were signed with a number of companies eager for a foot inside one of the world's last oil frontiers. Easiest of all was the sale of part of the Burmese embassy property in Tokyo. Tokyo real estate prices and the value of the yen had reached astronomical heights in the late eighties. A part of Burma's embassy garden—a gift of the Japanese government during the Ba Maw years of the Second World War—was sold for $200 million.[9]

But the new government wasn't interested just in money to stay afloat. It genuinely wanted to move away from the autarkic policies of the past. The officers in charge were no democrats, but many were keen to see economic progress and an end to the disastrous isolation of the last quarter century. But how to do this? Nobody in the government had the appropriate training or experience to oversee an overhaul of the economy. And now, with Western sanctions, the foreign advisers and the international banks and the extra aid and loans that might have helped were gone. The ruling generals and colonels were also afraid. Having come that close to a successful popular revolution, one that could have seen each and every one of them arrested, imprisoned, or worse, they would make sure any reform was tentative, with the possibility of rollback kept securely in the back pocket.

Over the early 1990s there was a big freeing up of social and cultural life. Before, one needed a permit even to travel within the country; this was abolished. And obtaining a passport to travel abroad was made much easier. Burmese exiles were welcomed back. Tourism was encouraged, and visas made easy; whereas before, foreigners had been largely limited to Rangoon, Mandalay, Pagan and the Inle Lake area, now they were allowed to venture off into dozens of towns and villages that hadn't seen Westerners for more than a generation. Sports were newly emphasized, and soon there were over six hundred football clubs with nearly twenty thousand players. And a hint of Rangoon's more free-wheeling days were revived, with nightclubs and karaoke bars, some offering more than just karaoke, and rock concerts, hosting bands with names like Empire and Iron Cross, were allowed to dazzle the crowds.

Central Rangoon was transformed. Private business was encouraged for the first time in thirty years, and there was a wholehearted push for foreign investment. Dozens of four-star and five-star hotels, with luxury spas and inviting swimming pools, sprouted up around town. The Strand Hotel was bought up by international hoteliers and remade into a jet-set oasis. Crumbling colonial-era mansions were fashioned into boutiques and trendy restaurants offering everything from Korean to Italian cuisine. Nationalized firms were sold off. There was talk of a stock market. There were new cars, new traffic jams, new cinemas, and new things to buy. Burma's first shopping malls finally offered teenagers wearing hundred-dollar Levi's 501s a place to hang out. The social pages of the foreign-managed *Myanmar Times* cheerfully reported on cocktail parties and fashion shows. And there was satellite television, with MTV and CNN, and the very beginnings of Internet access. For many life eked on as before. For some of the urban poor it was worse, with rising prices and new developments forcing them out of the city center. But for thousands of people in the middle class there was a bittersweet taste of what had been missing and a cautious air of possibility.

For the government, development primarily meant roads, bridges, airports, and dams, and dozens of infrastructural works were begun and completed with all the enthusiasm of a well-laid battle plan. Just south of Ava an enormous new airport, capable of handling a fleet of 747s, was built, and every day in *The New Light of Myanmar* were pictures of severe-looking generals and colonels inspecting new irrigation works or giving instructions for the completion of a new port. For the generals a better life also meant better golf courses, a legacy of British Burma's strong Scottish influence; the Burma Golf Club was spruced up, and new, swankier courses popped up around Rangoon and around the country. There were even daily articles covering the game, the no-nonsense government-run paper, for example, cheerfully reporting on 29 April 2005 that "U Nyunt Aye scored a hole-in-one while he was playing together with his partners U Sein Than and U Thein Toe at the City Golf Resort. He drove the ball with wood 3 Callaway stick to the 16th hole from 167 yards away."

But sustainable (not to mention equitable) economic progress was elusive. There seemed no willingness to make tough decisions. Corruption was rife. Foreigners were allowed to own businesses, but in practice they needed a local partner, and better yet, a local partner well connected with the powers-that-be. The government also maintained a monopoly on rice, teak, and mineral exports. Agricultural production, nearly half the economy, was hardly free. And though the foreign exchange market had been liberalized, the government still maintained a complex system, with an official rate that stood at a tiny fraction of the market rate. Education and health care remained starved of funds and expert attention. Most fundamentally, this was still an economy run by soldiers deeply suspicious of technocrats, and there were, as always, few, if any, in the top leadership with even a rudimentary knowledge of economics. By the late 1990s, with new American sanctions, foreign investment dwindling, and no help from international financial institutions on the horizon, the wheels of development had slowed yet again.

Where there *was* change was within the armed forces, which over the 1990s dramatically increased their size and strength. The number of military personnel, almost entirely in the army, jumped from approximately 180,000 before 1988 to over 400,000 in 1996. At the same time, hundreds of millions of dollars were spent on buying new airplanes, ships, tanks, and armored personnel carriers. New factories to supply arms and ammunition were set up, and services for soldiers and their families were improved.[10]

And with this bigger and better-equipped army, the balance of power firmly shifted to Rangoon. With the ex-Communist cease-fires in place, the Burmese army was able to pressure or cajole nearly all the various ethnic-based insurgencies to agree to similar accords. Seventeen in all agreed to stop fighting, including the formidable Kachin Independence Organization, which had been in revolt since the early 1960s. Those that didn't came under withering attack, like the Karen National Union, losing all its bases along the Thai border and then finally entering talks at the end of the decade. By the mid-1990s the fighting had, at least temporarily, stopped, bringing for millions of people in the uplands the first feeling of day-to-day security, however faltering and incomplete, in nearly a lifetime.

At the same time, the former Communist forces, the Was and the others, moved ever more firmly in a money-oriented direction. Burma and China had opened up their border to trade. Until then poverty-stricken little mountain villages in Communist-held areas had a closed-off Cultural Revolution–wrecked Maoist China to their backs. In the 1990s they became gateways to the wheeling-dealing superpower of the future. These same mountain villages became, virtually overnight, vibrant international cities, with big-wheeled trucks lumbering past, carrying Burma's natural inheritance in one direction and the goods of the Chinese Industrial Revolution in the other. At Ruili, opposite Kokang, banks and restaurants now stay open well into the night, and discos, once an unheard-of thing, keep the clients coming until well after sunrise. At another town, Mongla, a special transvestite cabaret attracts coachloads of gawking tourists from far into the People's Republic and even South Korea, the "ladyboys" of Mongla being at the most innocuous end of a ever-expanding sex and entertainment trade, with prostitutes from as far away as Russia and the Ukraine. Criminal gangs, many from Fujian Province, opposite Taiwan, have inevitably become active and entrenched, offering up a new heyday for Chinese mobsters, perhaps their best since the 1930s, when the godfather Du Yuesheng and his Green Gang ruled the Shanghai Bund.[11]

But from the outside world, there have been no words of congratulation or encouragement for the cease-fires, no real offers of mediation, or even an insistence that both sides keep on a road to peace. No apparent interest in ending the world's longest-running conflict or concern that the whole thing could still unravel. No thought as to how this tentative peace and move toward a market economy could be made irreversible. Only deafening silence. Instead, for the outside world, there was really only one story in Burma in the 1990s, the story of Aung San Suu Kyi and her struggle against the ruling generals.

AUNG SAN'S DAUGHTER

On a sweltering April morning in 1989 Aung San Suu Kyi and a group of her party activists set off on a trip to the Irrawaddy Delta. Their aim was to mobilize support and also to test the army's limits in the Gandhian tradition of nonviolent resistance. It was on the second day of this tour that they arrived by boat at the town of Danubyu. Danubyu was already famous in Burmese history, as the place where Thado Maha Bandula, driven from Rangoon, had made what was to be his last stand against the rockets and steamships of General Archibald Campbell during the First Anglo-Burmese War. Now it was to be famous again, for a very different resistance. As Aung San Suu Kyi and her young followers walked along the street and toward the local National League for Democracy office, they found their way blocked by a small company of soldiers, kneeling and with automatic weapons pointed toward them. Aung San Suu Kyi told her people to keep moving. The captain in charge threatened to shoot. She spoke calmly and asked that they be allowed to pass, all the while moving forward. Just then a superior officer rushed to the scene and ordered his men to stand down. Courage had triumphed over repression. Aung San Suu Kyi's fame soon spread.

She hoped, perhaps, that something like this would happen all around the country and that the "second struggle for independence," as she called it, would play out along similar lines. Peaceful but determined, the National League for Democracy would stand firm, and the army would somehow magically give way. Sadly, though, nothing of the sort has happened. Instead over the seventeen years since this incident the NLD has been largely decimated, its leadership almost entirely in prison or under house arrest. Democracy is no nearer today than it was in Danubyu that hot spring day. What went wrong? And what else could have been done?

Aung San Suu Kyi was born on 19 June 1945, the third child of General Aung San and his wife, Daw Khin Kyi. These were the chaotic weeks after the British Sixteenth Army had retaken Rangoon and Lord Mountbatten was about to begin talks with the brash young leadership of the self-styled Burmese Anti-Fascist League. Her eldest brother would soon die in a tragic drowning accident, and her other brother would become an engineer and settle in San Diego, California. She was just two when her father was assassinated.

At age fourteen, when her mother, once a nurse, was appointed by U Nu as Burma's ambassador to India, Aung San Suu Kyi left the country, not to return to live for nearly thirty years. She went to school in New Delhi and then went on to read philosophy, politics, and economics at St. Hugh's College, Oxford. Through mutual friends, she soon met her future husband, Michael Aris, an expert on Tibetan language and literature and a gentle and selfless man, who quickly fell in love with the beautiful and exotic student from Burma.

Before settling down to married life, she first had a spell in New York. This was in 1969, but Aung San Suu Kyi seems to have had no attraction at all to the great goings-on of the Swinging Sixties. No Woodstock or Vietnam protests, no experimentation of any kind. Instead she found a very proper job on the staff of the UN's Advisory Committee on Administrative and Budgetary Questions (in real life no less dreadful than it sounds) and, choosing not to live alone, shared an apartment with Daw Than E, a much older Burmese woman (her "emergency aunt," she would call her), who had been a famous singer in Rangoon in the 1930s and 1940s. No parties or concerts but instead evenings and weekends volunteering at a local hospital or an occasional visit to our house in Riverdale.

All the while she kept up an active correspondence with Michael

Aris. When she finally agreed to marry him, they moved together to the Himalayan kingdom of Bhutan, where he worked on his Ph.D. and served as a tutor to the royal family, including the future king, Jigme Wangchuk. Aung San Suu Kyi worked in the little Foreign Ministry, which was being established.

She had a feeling that some national calling would one day compel her to sacrifice her family life. In one of her nearly two hundred letters to her future husband around this time, she made it clear that she might one day have to return to Burma. "Should my people need me, you would help me to do my duty by them." But for now the young couple were busy with two children, both sons, and after several bliss-ful years in Asia returned together to Oxford, where Michael Aris pur-sued his scholarship and she began her own research, on her father and on Burmese history. I visited them in the summer of 1984 at their town house off Banbury Road. It was sunny and warm, and their brick-walled garden was full of flowers. Daw Than E (her emergency aunt) was there too, and the conversation soon turned to films about the British Empire, Merchant Ivory's *Heat and Dust* and David Lean's *A Passage to India* having shown recently in Oxford's cinemas. Michael sat contentedly and quietly smoking his pipe, their kids playing in the room nearby. In her always polite and somewhat schoolmarmish way, she encouraged me to come to England for a Ph.D. and to work on Burmese history as well. In later years I felt I had a sense of the happy life both she and Michael had given up.

It was only by chance that Aung San Suu Kyi was in Burma when the 1988 protests nearly toppled the regime. Her mother had been hos-pitalized with a severe stroke, and she had gone back to Rangoon to live at her family's sprawling lakeside house and look after her. "I had a premonition," Aris wrote in the introduction to a collection of essays about his wife, "that our lives would change forever."[12]

During the uprising itself she had been besieged by university stu-dents and others, asking her to join in. And she had been deeply moved by the sight of thousands carrying her father's portrait, some as they were gunned down. After a few weeks she gave in and her maiden speech in late August excited the country. She turned to her father's rhetoric and called repeatedly for "unity" and "discipline."

In the days after the uprising was crushed, she banded together with several former army officers to form the National League for Democ-

racy. Brigadier General Aung Gyi, the man who had led the 1962
takeover with Ne Win, would be its first chairman. The vice-chairman
was General Tin Oo, army chief of staff in the 1970s who was jailed for
his alleged role in the abortive 1975 coup. Others included Colonel
Kyi Maung, a member of Ne Win's Revolutionary Council in 1962,
and Brigadier Aung Shwe, a man who had almost led his own coup
against U Nu in 1958. All had been in the Japanese-trained Burma Independence Army under Aung San, and all had served in the Fourth
Burma Rifles under Ne Win, rising to senior positions in the 1950s.
Then they had fallen out with the top man, and now, in the central
irony of recent Burmese history, they were heading the opposition, together with Aung San's daughter.

Aung San Suu Kyi was placed under house arrest on 20 July 1989 while
many other party members were imprisoned. The army had allowed
the NLD to form and organize but decided to crack down when Aung
San Suu Kyi's popularity and determination quickly showed itself. She
kept up a strict regime, meditating, listening to the news on the radio,
exercising, and reading. Her husband was allowed to visit from time to
time. The State Law and Order Restoration Council (SLORC) accused the NLD both of being in cahoots with the Communist Party of
Burma and of being part of a conspiracy with foreign "right-wing"
forces, producing their arguments in the wonderfully titled *The Conspiracy of Treasonous Minions within the Myanmar naing-ngan and
Their Traitorous Cohorts Abroad.*

Despite the crackdown and the arrest, the government went ahead
and in May 1990 did what no one expected and what no once since has
really been able to explain: it held reasonably free and fair multiparty
elections. There were problems, of course: The campaigning itself had
been very restricted, and many parts of the country, the hill areas in
particular, were in no position to take part because of the ongoing insurgency. But the balloting itself was fine, with less irregularity than
any of the elections in the late 1940s or 1950s. The outcome, though,
was a shock for the men in uniform, returning a clear victory for the
NLD. With around two-thirds of eligible voters casting their ballots,
the NLD won just under 60 percent of the vote and 392 out of 492
seats in the new Assembly. The military's proxy was the National Unity

Party, the rebranded Burma Socialist Program Party of the ostensibly retired strongman General Ne Win. But the National Unity Party trailed far behind with only 21 percent of the vote and 10 seats, the rest going to a medley of mainly ethnic-based parties. The military had seriously miscalculated the mood of the people.

What next? The army was schizophrenic. On the one hand, it appeared to have in mind its glory year of 1959–60, when it ran a highly competent, if ruthless, government and then handed power back to an elected government, pleased with itself for having done so and congratulated by admirers both at home and abroad. It had tried to do the same now, with 1959 as the template, right down to the slum clearings and the newly paved roads. On the other hand, it knew that 1960 brought problems and then a new army coup in 1962; it thought this time needed to be different, not just a handover to elected officials but something that would more clearly preserve its legacy and its authority. And in Aung San Suu Kyi, the passion and anger of the uprising behind her, it sensed a danger, to its institution and to itself personally that had had no equivalent in 1960. On 28 July the NLD met at Gandhi Hall in Rangoon and adopted a resolution calling on the SLORC to stand down and hand over power to a government based on the results of the elections—in other words, to the NLD. There was talk of trials for "crimes against humanity." The whole world called on the Burmese officers to give up. They dithered and then rolled back on their promises, making things up as they went along.

Aung San Suu Kyi was freed six years later in July 1995, though she was able to travel outside Rangoon only with permission. Every Saturday afternoon at four she stood up on a little box and spoke from behind the gates of her house, and hundreds of people came to listen and ask questions. But few democratic reforms were in sight. There were some talks with the government, but the two sides were far apart, and no agreement was reached. Resorting to nonviolence tactics, she tried to provoke the government and test its limits through her speeches and through her attempts to ignore its restrictions on her movement. But she wasn't facing the Raj of the 1930s or the Johnson administration of the 1960s. These were tough men who played a very different game. In 2000, Aung San Suu Kyi was again placed under house arrest, this time for a little more than two years.

She was disliked by many in the military, partly because of her perceived foreignness. For all her time abroad, however, she was first and foremost her father's daughter. For Aung San, a no-nonsense, straight-talking approach coupled with courage and an iron will seemed a winning combination. And it was these same qualities that did much to win her popular adoration. But to believe that it was this single-mindedness that won independence is to misread the lessons of the 1940s. Britain's withdrawal from Burma was part of its withdrawal from India; the question was one of the nature and timing of the postcolonial transition. Unlike the British, Burma's generals were never ready to quit Burma. It wasn't a matter of forcing the pace. They were considering going in a different direction altogether.

By the late 1990s, beneath the talk of democracy and dictatorship, Burmese society was changing fast. The population was surging ahead and by 2006 had reached roughly fifty-three million people, a very young population, the majority having been born *after* the 1988 uprising. Towns and cities became more crowded, with fewer and fewer qualified teachers and doctors or any sort of infrastructure (including electricity) to meet expanding needs; and in the countryside, where most of the people still lived, an ever-increasing number of farmers squeezed out a livelihood on the same little plots of land. Many moved north in search of new opportunities, or simply to survive, to the jade mines and the bustling Chinese border towns, or across the Tenasserim Range into Thailand, where hundreds of thousands of Burmese today toil away, illegally and for little money, in construction jobs, performing menial labor, and in the sex industry. HIV/AIDS spread rapidly, in a society with increased narcotics use and where family planning had been virtually nonexistent during the Ne Win years. Some began to warn of an impending (or present) humanitarian crisis, in which millions of the country's poorest, their savings finally gone, were finding it impossible to meet their most basic needs, to feed themselves and their children or obtain even the most essential health care.

There was political change as well. The military government convened a National Convention to discuss and draw up a new constitution, one of its committees chaired for a while by the mischievously named U James Bond. The convention was the government's response to the elections in 1991 and its refusal to hand over power to the National League for Democracy. It initially included the NLD and other parties that had won seats in the polls, but it also included representatives of the ethnic insurgent armies and handpicked hundreds of others. It was clear from the start that this wouldn't be a freewheeling debate on the future of the country, and the aim was fairly plain: find some constitutional formula that would include a paramount role for the army. The military may have been thinking about constitutions in nearby Thailand or Indonesia, both of which, in the recent past, ensured army autonomy as well as a certain number of seats in Parliament for the armed forces. Or it may have looked to its own colonial past (without admitting it), to the constitutions of the 1920s and 1930s that allowed British mandarins only very slowly to hand over government responsibility to elected politicians, while retaining for themselves a range of emergency powers, undiminished authority over the highlands, and an unambiguous sense of who was ultimately in charge.

For most in the National League for Democracy this was an unacceptable process. They pleaded for an amendment in the convention's working procedures and in particular asked for a repeal of the rule that made a felony any criticism of the military during the convention debates. This was refused. For two rainy days in November 1995 the NLD's eighty-six delegates boycotted the convention, and on the third day they were formally expelled. The convention soon went into a long recess.

For a while things simply plodded on. But then, in 2000, there was again a new energy, a new momentum. The National Convention was reconvened, and the adoption of a new constitution was to be followed by fresh elections and a civilian government. A somewhat more hurried round of talks began between the Burmese military and the insurgents, maps were examined, and options for local self-government were weighed. In 2003 a new government was formed and placed under the prime ministership of intelligence chief General Khin Nyunt. A seven-step Road Map to Democracy was unveiled. There were also signs of greater openness. The International Committee of the Red Cross was allowed for the very first time to visit prisons on a regular basis. The government admitted to a serious HIV/AIDS problem after years of denials and asked for international assistance. More than a hundred political prisoners were released. And talks were held between Aung San Suu Kyi and government representatives, at first secretly and then

openly. International negotiators scurried between the two sides, hopeful for a long-awaited breakthrough.

Was there now a way forward? And whatever happened to General
Ne Win?

THE LONG ROAD FROM HAINAN

For many years those who wanted reform in Burma waited, very pa-
tiently, for General Ne Win to leave the scene. He had been born in
1911 and by the 1988 uprising was already an old man. In that year he
had officially retired and then rarely appeared in public, but few suspected he had relinquished any real power. He lived, as always, in a
heavily guarded compound on Ady Road, on the opposite side of the
big swampy Inya Lake (on the outskirts of Rangoon) from Aung San
Suu Kyi. He must still be calling all the shots, people said. All the while
there was still the sense, a quarter-century-old optimism, that things
would change when he died.

Then he died, quietly, peacefully, in bed, in December 2002, aged
ninety-one. And nothing happened. It seems that he had in fact left political life a while ago, not immediately after the uprising in 1988 but a
few years later, intervening now and then to settle disputes within the
senior brass, but then fading away entirely to his own private world.
When dictators die while still in power, regimes tend to crumble at the
same time, but Ne Win had stepped back while still very much alive
and allowed a transition to consolidate itself while he was still around.
And then he apparently lost interest. Singapore's former prime minister Lee Kuan Yew saw him a couple of times in the nineties. In 1994
Ne Win, looking haggard and unwell, told him that after the uprising
had been crushed, he had been in torment, "fretting and worrying"
about what to do. But then he had discovered meditation, and meditation began to calm him. When Lee met him again in 1997, he said the
old soldier looked much better. Ne Win wanted only to talk about
meditation, giving Lee advice and saying that he himself spent many
hours, mornings and afternoons, in silent concentration. He no longer
worried about anything, friends, family, or the country. When his generals came for advice, he said, he sent them away.[13]

When he died, the man who had led his country to isolation and poverty was virtually unmourned. In his final few months his protégés in the army had moved against his family, locking up his son-in-law and grandsons and placing his daughter under house arrest, more to shut down their crooked business dealings than anything else. The Ne Win era was over, but a whole new Burmese army had already come to the fore.

And this army that had come to the fore was a generation or more removed from its founding, in the rain-drenched Japanese training camps on Hainan Island, where the importance of unquestioning obedience and unwavering loyalty, not to any higher authority but to the army itself, had first been programmed into the minds of eager young nationalists. Since then the army had gone through a lot and had battled incessantly for six decades against dozens of enemies, from the marshlands along the Bengal border to the foothills of the Himalayas. Along the way it had changed, from a few lightly armed (and nearly overwhelmed) infantry battalions to one of the biggest armed forces in the world and one that was involved in every aspect of the country's economy and administration. The Burmese military dictatorship is the longest-lasting military dictatorship in the world, and it is also its purest. It is not an army regime sitting on top of an otherwise civilian state. In Burma by the 1990s the military *was* the state. Army officers did everything. Normal government had withered away.

When the men in uniform looked to the past, they saw a country that tended to fall apart into little pieces and that had always needed to be melded together by force. They saw themselves in a long line of national unifiers and saw their task as unfinished. The Communists—always their biggest enemies—had collapsed, and nearly all their other battlefield foes were at most shadows of their former selves. The soldiers were on top for the first time. And in their imagination there remained the challenge of nation building, of creating and promoting a new *Myanmar* identity, based on Buddhism and what was perceived as correct and traditional Burmese culture, unmuddied by the humiliating days of colonial rule, something plain and simple and straightforward, like the army itself. These were men, for the most part, who knew no other life, had joined the armed forces as teenagers and never left, had fought in the mountains and forests for years, killing and seeing their fellow soldiers killed, living entirely apart from the rest of Burmese society. They had created a sort of military fantasy world, where everything was about making enemies and making war and everyone else had a supporting role, like camp followers in a Mongol horde. Perhaps to some, democracy sounded like a good thing, a worthy goal, but for many, imagining democracy was as hard as imagining a more democratic barracks. It just didn't fit in with the rest of the picture.

There were certainly those in the regime who wanted less isolation, who believed that some contact and some communication with the wider world were for the better, that Burma had fallen too far behind its old neighbors—the Chinese and the Indians and the Thais—and needed to catch up. The Asian economic miracle was all around. General Ne Win's Burmese socialism had been an economic catastrophe, and in these new times a new economic approach was needed. But how to do this? No one knew. And there were even those in the armed forces who thought that some sort of accommodation was possible with Aung San Suu Kyi as well as with the insurgent groups in the hills. In 2000 serious reforms had started. In 2003, Aung San Suu Kyi and a convoy of her supporters had been attacked on a dirt road by government-backed thugs. But even then talks continued, and there was an air of urgency. A new understanding seemed close at hand. But then things turned around yet again. A much expected release of Aung San Suu Kyi in the spring of 2004 never happened. And in October of that year, the prime minister, General Khin Nyunt, the man behind the talks, was himself sacked and detained, together with dozens of his aides.

The top general, Than Shwe, and many other combat-hardened army chiefs had felt there were too many risks involved in any compromise. The memory of 1988, when the country had come so close to revolution, the fear of retribution, was still fresh on their minds. There was also an impression that the outside world was out to get them no matter what. When the talks with the NLD and the ethnic insurgents were still progressing, Washington had imposed new, debilitating sanctions. Many felt that turning inward again was safer, more secure. There were venal motives as well, but the deeper source of today's conservatism is the contentment of too many in the officer corps with what they see, who admire the military state and military-led society, or at least who could not easily dream up anything much better.

This was the result of long years of isolation since 1962. It was not an ideology but a mentality that had grown up and become dominant. Isolation had placed anyone with a more progressive mind-set at a a disadvantage, and had fueled the attitudes that entrenched the status quo. And yet the response of the West was to isolate the country further.

In the years since the uprising, interest in Burma's plight has mushroomed. Many have now heard of Aung San Suu Kyi and are vaguely aware of the reluctance of the ruling generals to give up power. Almost no one, though, is aware of the civil war or the reasons why Burma's military machine developed and the country became so isolated in the first place. The paradigm is one of regime change, and the assumption is that sanctions, boycotts, more isolation will somehow pressure those in charge to mend their ways. The assumption is that Burma's military government couldn't survive further isolation when precisely the opposite is true: Much more than any other part of Burmese society, the army will weather another forty years of isolation just fine.

The award of the Nobel Peace Prize to Aung San Suu Kyi in 1991 raised her profile enormously around the world and has been a great boost to a growing confederacy of Burma activists in London, Washington, and elsewhere. A few of these Burma activists were older Burmese exiles, people who had stolen away during the ironfisted days of General Ne Win, including many from the ranks of the U Nu government, and their children. But many more were from the much younger generation of the 1988 uprising, university students and others who had taken to the streets that summer and then decided to leave the country illegally, winding up in Thailand and India and then eventually emigrating to other countries, like Australia and the United States.

Little communities grew up. In America, the biggest concentrations of Burmese expatriates were to be found in New York, Washington, and Southern California, but many hard-core activists wound up in places like Fort Wayne, Indiana, today an unlikely hotbed of Burmese exile action. Boasting Glenbrook Square ("the largest shopping center in Indiana") and Jefferson Point (with "trendy eateries and Mediterranean atmosphere"), this midwestern town of two hundred thousand is also now home to over three thousand refugees—Burmese, Mons, and Karens. There are no less than four Buddhist temples as well as services in Burmese at both the Lutheran and Baptist churches. Little Burma on South Lafayette Street sells a range of familiar groceries, from pickled tea leaves to sticky rice.

Like activists everywhere, by the late 1990s they were aggressively using the Internet, which soon sprouted hundreds of specialized Burmese political sites, chat rooms, newspapers, and message boards. They were joined by many non-Burmese, Americans, Australians, British, Scandinavians, and others who have often worked selflessly and with great dedication; together with the exiles, a formidable Burma lobby has slowly taken shape. As in any activist group, there are differences of opinion, on strategy and tactics, but the Burma lobby, with growing celebrity and high-level political support, has managed to largely stay on message: the military government is bad, Aung San Suu Kyi is good, and the international community needs to apply pressure on Rangoon and pressure means no aid, trade sanctions, and more isolation.

Most aid had been suspended since 1988, but by the late 1990s many private companies, who had rushed into Burma earlier in the decade, began to pull out, at least in part because of activist pressure. From the United States, Wal-Mart, Kenneth Cole, Tommy Hilfiger, Jones New York, and Federated Department Stores (owners of Macy's and Bloomingdale's), Pepsi Cola, Amoco, Levi Strauss & Co., Liz Claiborne, and Eddie Bauer ended their Burma operations. And in 1998 the U.S. government imposed a ban on new American investment in Burma. Campaigns to boycott tourism to Burma were also ratcheted up, and government attempts to attract more visitors have been only marginally successful. Tour companies began to shy away from business in the country, and many of the hotels, inns, and little guesthouses that had been built expectantly in the early 1990s remained largely empty. Other contacts were shunned. Visa bans were imposed so that officials of the government would not be able to visit the West, and scholarships and academic exchanges have remained virtually nonexistent. More damaging for the already poverty-stricken economy, assistance by the World Bank and other international financial institutions and aid agencies was largely prohibited, with even attempts to provide emergency humanitarian aid sometimes drawing censure.

In 2004 a new sanctions law was enacted by Washington, restricting Burmese imports into the United States and prohibiting almost any payments into the country. The already struggling textile industry was crippled. Those in Rangoon who argued that recent reforms would lead to an easing, rather than toughening, of sanctions quickly lost ground. Burma was labeled an "outpost of tyranny," bundled together with North Korea and Iran.

And in 2005, even the Global Fund (which fights the spread of HIV/AIDS, tuberculosis, and malaria) withdrew under heavy political pressure from pro-democracy activists.

In the inner meeting rooms of Rangoon's War Office, the hardliners saw their paranoia justified and their intransigence easier to defend. While the Americans and the European Union cut off aid and imposed sanctions, the government started to benefit from new economic opportunities. For a while, there was investment from the region, but this largely dried up, partly as a result of the Asian financial crisis of the late 1990s, but mainly the result of a still poor business environment. But by the late 1990s, discoveries of huge offshore natural gas fields, valued in the tens of billions of dollars, suddenly meant a steady supply of hard currency, more than enough to keep the military machine going. Voices that had called for free-market reform quieted down. The economy that was evolving under sanctions was exactly the opposite of one that could create a strong middle class and pave the way for progressive change.

In almost every way, this policy of isolating one of the most isolated countries in the world—where the military regime isolated itself for the better part of thirty years, and which indeed has grown up and evolved well in isolation—is both counterproductive and dangerous.

That a democratic government for Burma should be the aim is not in doubt. Especially for a country as diverse as Burma, with so many different peoples, languages, and cultures, only a free and liberal society can provide a lasting stability and lead to real prosperity. What needs to be asked is: What sort of transition to democracy is possible, what are the actual obstacles, and what international policy will work best?

Any transition to democracy is always difficult. In many places around the world, attempts to transform dictatorships into democracies have led to many new problems, including interethnic violence and civil war. Burma's transition will be especially difficult. This is a country that has *already* been at civil war for sixty years and where that civil war is not yet concluded; where there are hundreds of different ethnic and linguistic groups, many inhabiting remote mountain areas; where poverty is endemic and where a humanitarian crisis is looming; where there are hundreds of thousands of people displaced by the fighting and tens of thousands more who are refugees; and where there is a resilient narcotics industry and where some of the richest businessmen (always the most likely to be influential in a democracy) are tied to the drugs trade. And there are two especially difficult factors, legacies of Burmese history.

The first is the long history of failed state building. The nineteenth-century kings Mindon and Thibaw attempted to remake traditional institutions and create new ones to deal with the fast-changing world, but these initiatives in the end went nowhere because of the steady approach of British imperialism. The traditional order collapsed entirely. The British Raj then tried, as in other parts of its Indian domain, to transplant familiar institutions—a civil service, a judiciary, a professional police force and army, and eventually an elected legislature—but these remained largely alien institutions, unwedded to local society, and the abrupt end of colonial rule meant that they didn't long survive the British withdrawal. Then there was the attempt in the U Nu days to fashion a democratic state, but these efforts were crippled from the start by the civil war, the Chinese invasions of the 1950s, and the steady growth of General Ne Win's military machine. Today the military machine is all there is, with only the shadow of other institutions remaining. In Burma it's not simply getting the military out of the business of government. It's creating the state institutions that can replace the military state that exists.

The second factor is more in the realm of ideas. In the way that Burma's royal institutions collapsed in the wake of Thibaw's exile, the onset of colonial rule meant the fast disappearance of many earlier notions of kingship and the relationship between government and society. An entire tradition of learning, subtle and complex, based on centuries of court and monastic scholarship, ended almost overnight. In its place a militant nationalism came forward, merging at different times with different visions of the future. There is also a strong utopian streak, going back to the Student Union days of the 1930s, a proclivity for abstract debates, on communism, socialism, democracy, endless conversations about diverse constitutional models and long-term political schemes, which never see the light of day. What is altogether missing is a history of pragmatic and rigorous policy debate, on economics, finance, health care, or education as well as a more imaginative and empathetic discussion of minority rights and shared identities in modern Burmese society.

Of course some things could change overnight for the better. Political prisoners (there are estimated to be more than a thousand) could be released, restrictions on the media relaxed; there could even be fresh elections leading to a new civilian government. But what then? All these things could be overturned, also overnight, in a new coup, as in 1962. The army would still be there, lurking in the wings. There is a tendency to see Burma as a failed Eastern European–style revolution, where all it will take are new crowds to take to the streets, when a more apt comparison is with similarly war-torn societies like Cambodia or Afghanistan, where only a multifaceted path of institution building, social change, and economic development can lift the country from a long history of ills. And in the case of Burma this can only begin with breaking down Burma's isolation, reviving connections with the outside world, bringing in new ideas, providing fresh air to a stale political environment and—in the process—changing long-festering mentalities.

If Burma were a country where those in charge wanted to engage with the wider world or had much to lose by being isolated, then a policy of sanctions might make sense. If the ruling caste in Burma were actually committed to the benefits that more trade and interaction with the West could bring, then sanctions might be seen as a type of pressure. But this is not the case. Since 1988 and the first attempts to liberalize the economy and climb out of isolation, the officer corps had been at best halfhearted in its desire to actually open up and engage with the world. Many would prefer to keep the West at arm's length and deal only with China and perhaps a few other neighbors, worried of the dangers to the status quo inherent in allowing foreign businesses and foreign tourists to descend in large numbers and (to borrow a phrase from a different conflict) create new facts on the ground.

What is sometimes hard to perceive from the outside is just how damaging forty years of isolation—in particular, isolation from the West and the international scene—has been to those trapped inside. Trade with China and a few other (still developing) economies is no substitute for renewed contacts with people and places around the world. It is this isolation that has kept Burma in poverty; isolation that fuels a negative, almost xenophobic nationalism; isolation that makes the Burmese army see everything as a zero-sum game and any change as filled with peril; isolation that has made any conclusion to the war so elusive, hardening differences; and isolation that has weakened in-stitutions—the ones on which any transition to democracy would de-pend—to the point of collapse. Without isolation, the status quo will be impossible to sustain. This is not to say that problems will disappear overnight, but rather that solutions, so elusive today, will become more apparent and easier to reach.

In isolation, though, the army will simply and quite confidently push forward its agenda. A new military-dominated constitution will be adopted. And a new military-dominated government put in place. More statues of long-dead generals will go up, and the opposition will be largely decimated, the armed groups in the hills being forced to give up their arms and accept a new order. But of course that wouldn't be the end. Grievances would only fester underneath. Some might try their hand at terrorist tactics, something that has thus far remained nearly absent from the political scene. And all the while whatever gov-erning institutions outside the army still exist will become even more enfeebled, as the last generation educated abroad reaches retirement age or dies.

When General Ne Win came to power in 1962, there were military regimes everywhere in Asia. The difference between the Burmese mil-itary regime and its counterparts in South Korea, Thailand, and In-donesia is not that the Burmese regime has been any more repressive, but that the others trusted the advice of technocrats, presided over long periods of economic growth, and allowed for the development of civil society. All these things were possible because these countries were not isolated from the international community, and because trade and tourism strengthened rather than weakened the hand of those who eventually demanded political change. If Thailand and Indonesia had been under U.S. and European sanctions the past twenty years, they would not be democracies today. Would China be better off today if it had been kept poor and isolated since the demonstrations of 1989?

This is not to say that every type of interaction with the outside world is a good one or that there should not be ethical standards for trade and investment. But to say that companies should not tarnish themselves by doing business in a politically repressive country is very different from saying that sanctions on business will actually effect positive change.

So what of the future? There are no easy options, no quick fixes, no grand strategies that will create democracy in Burma overnight or even over several years. If Burma were less isolated, if there were more trade, more engagement—more tourism in particular—and if this were coupled with a desire by the government for greater economic reform, a rebuilding of state institutions, and a slow opening up of space for civil society, then perhaps the conditions for political change would emerge over the next decade or two. Though not a particularly encouraging scenario, it is a realistic one, however much it might lack the punch of more revolutionary approaches.

There is a second and much worse possible scenario—that Burma's international isolation will only deepen through an unholy alliance between those outside who favor sanctions and inside hard-liners who advocate a retreat from the global community, that this isolation will further undermine institutions of government, that a new generation will grow up less educated and in worse health, and that a decade or two from now, the world will be staring at another failed state, without any prospect of democratic change and with the military no longer holding things together. There would be a return to anarchy and the conditions of 1948, only this time with more guns, more people, and strong, confident neighbors unlikely to idly stand by. If that were to come to pass, the remaining years of this century would not be enough time for Burma to recover.

NOTES

~~~~

1: THE FALL OF THE KINGDOM

1. Henry Yule, *A Narrative of the Mission to the Court of Ava in 1855* (Kuala Lumpur: Oxford University Press, 1968), 139.
2. A. T. Q. Stewart, *The Pagoda War: Lord Dufferin and the Fall of the Kingdom of Ava, 1885–6* (London: Faber and Faber, 1972), 76–79.
3. H. Maxim, *My Life* (London: Methuen & Co., 1915).
4. Archibald Colquhoun, *English Policy in the Far East: Being* The Times *Special Correspondence* (London: Field & Tuer, The Leadenhall Press, 1885), and *Burma and the Burmans: Or, "The Best Unopened Market in the World"* (London: Field & Tuer, The Leadenhall Press, 1885).
5. On Churchill and Burma, see Htin Aung, *Lord Randolph Churchill and the Dancing Peacock: British Conquest of Burma 1885* (New Delhi: Manohar, 1990).
6. Mike Davis, *Late Victorian Holocausts: El Niño Famines and the Making of the Third World* (New York: Verso, 2001).
7. For a fictionalized version of the story, drawn in part from interviews in the early twentieth century, see F. Tennyson Jesse, *The Lacquer Lady* (London: W. Heinemann, 1929). See also Htin Aung, *Lord Randolph Churchill*, chapter 12.
8. Htin Aung, *Lord Randolph Churchill*, 171–72.
9. On the war, I have drawn largely on Stewart, *The Pagoda War;* see also Tin, *The Royal Administration of Burma*, trans. L. E. Bagshawe (Bangkok: Ava Publishing House, 2001), 276; Tin, *Konbaungzet Maha Yazawindaw-gyi* (repr., Rangoon, 1968), 707–27; as well as my own *The Making of Modern Burma* (Cambridge: Cambridge University Press, 2001).
10. Maung Maung Tin, *Kinwun Mingyi Thamaing* (Rangoon: Burma Research Society Text Series No. 38, n.d. [1930s?]), 123–39; I am grateful to L. E. Bagshawe for bringing this to my attention and providing me a copy.
11. Stewart, *The Pagoda War*, 94–95.
12. Ibid., 96.
13. Ibid., 97.
14. Secretary for Upper Burma to the Chief Commissioner to the Secretary to Gov-

ernment of India, Home Department, 19 October 1886, quoted in *History of the Third Burmese War (1885, 1886, 1887), Period One* (Calcutta, 1887).

15. Stewart, *The Pagoda War*, 21–22.

16. Quoted in Ni Ni Myint, *Burma's Struggle Against British Imperialism, 1885–1895* (Rangoon: Universities Press, 1983), 42.

17. Ibid., 33–68.

18. Stewart, *The Pagoda War*, 132–39.

19. Charles Crosthwaite, *The Pacification of Burma* (London: E. Arnold, 1912).

20. On the impact of the resistance and pacification on Burmese society, see Myint-U, *The Making of Modern Burma*, chapter 8.

2: DEBATING BURMA

1. On the uprising, see Bertil Lintner, *Outrage: Burma's Struggle for Democracy* (Hong Kong, 1989); Maung Maung, *The 1988 Uprising in Burma* (New Haven: Yale University Southeast Asia Studies, 1999).

3: FOUNDATIONS

1. Pe Maung Tin, *The Glass Palace Chronicle of the Burmese Kings*, G. H. Luce, trans. (Rangoon: Rangoon University Press, 1960).

2. Aldous Huxley, *Jesting Pilate: The Diary of a Journey* (London: Flamingo, 1999), 118–20.

3. Bob Hudson, "A Pyu Homeland in the Samon Valley: A New Theory of the Origins of Myanmar's Early Urban System," *Proceedings of the Myanmar Historical Commission Golden Jubilee International Conference*, January 2005; Bob Hudson, "Thoughts on Some Chronological Markers of Myanmar Archaeology in the Preurban Period," *Journal of the Yangon University Archaeology Department*, Rangoon. On Bronze Age Southeast Asia, see Charles Higham, *The Bronze Age of Southeast Asia* (Cambridge: Cambridge University Press, 1996).

4. Fan Chuo, *Manshu: Book of the Southern Barbarians*, trans. Gordon Luce. Cornell Data Paper Number 44, Southeast Asia Program, Department of Far Eastern Studies, Cornell University (Ithaca, N.Y., December 1961), 90–91.

5. Bo Wen et al., "Analyses of Genetic Structure of Tibeto-Burman Populations Reveals Sex-Biased Admixture in Southern Tibeto Burmans," *American Journal of Human Genetics* 74:856–65 (2004).

6. Jacques Gernet, *A History of Chinese Civilization* (Cambridge: Cambridge University Press, 1999), 119–20; Nicola di Cosmo, *Ancient China and Its Enemies: The Rise of Nomadic Power in East Asian History* (Cambridge: Cambridge University Press, 2004), 197–98.

7. Bin Yang, "Horses, Silver, and Cowries: Yunnan in Global Perspective," *Journal of World History* 15:3 (September 2004).

8. G. H. Luce, "The Tan (A.D. 97–132) and the Ngai-lao," *Journal of the Burma Research Society* 14:2, 100–103.

9. Romila Thapar, *Early India: From Origins to A.D. 1300* (Berkeley: University of California Press, 2004), 174–84.

10. On the history of Buddhism, see especially Richard H. Robinson and Willard L.

Johnson, *The Buddhist Religion: A Historical Introduction* (Belmont, Calif.: Wadsworth, 1997).

11. Janice Stargardt, *The Ancient Pyu of Burma*, vol. 1, *Early Pyu Cities in a Man-Made Landscape* (Cambridge: PACSEA, Cambridge, in association with the Institute of Southeast Asian Studies, Singapore, 1990), chapter 7. See also Burton Stein, *A History of India* (Oxford: Blackwell, 1998) 100–104, 127–28.

12. Tansen Sen, *Buddhism, Diplomacy, and Trade* (Honolulu: University of Hawai'i Press, 2003), 150–51, 174.

13. From the Old Tang History quoted in Luce, "The Ancient Pyu," *Journal of the Burma Research Society* 27:3 (1937).

14. G. H. Luce, *Phases of Pre-Pagan Burma: Languages and History*, 2 vols. (Oxford: Oxford University Press, 1985); Stargardt, *The Ancient Pyu of Burma*, vol. 1.

15. On Nanzhao, see Charles Backus, *The Nan-chao Kingdom and T'ang China's Southwestern Frontier* (Cambridge: Cambridge University Press, 1981); see also Christopher Beckwith, *The Tibetan Empire in Central Asia* (Princeton: Princeton University Press, 1987), especially chapter 6.

16. Fan Chuo, *Manshu*, 28.

17. Beckwith, *The Tibetan Empire*, 157.

18. Fan Chuo, *Manshu*, 91.

19. Michael Aung-Thwin, *Pagan: The Origins of Modern Burma* (Honolulu: University of Hawai'i Press, 1985); Htin Aung, *Burmese History Before 1287: A Defense of the Chronicles* (Oxford: Akoka Society, 1970).

20. Bob Hudson, "The King of 'Free Rabbit' Island: A G.I.S.-Based Archeological Approach to Myanmar's Medieval Capital, Bagan," *Proceedings of the Myanmar Two Millennia Conference, 15–17 December 1999* (Rangoon, 2000).

21. On Aniruddha, see G. E. Harvey, *History of Burma: from the Earliest Times to 10 March 1824—The Beginning of the English Conquest* (1925; repr., New York: Octagon Books, 1967), 18–36; G. H. Luce, *Old Burma Early Pagan*, 3 vols. (Locust Valley, N.Y.: Artibus Asiae, 1969); Tin, *The Glass Palace Chronicle*, 64–71. On Pagan in general see also Michael Aung-Thwin, *Pagan: The Origins of Modern Burma* and Victor Lieberman, *Strange Parallels: Southeast Asia in Global Context c. 800–1830* (Cambridge: Cambridge University Press, 2003), 85–123.

22. The Sung History, chapter 489, quoted in Luce, *Old Burma Early Pagan*, 58–59.

23. Harvey, *History of Burma*, 48.

24. Paul Bennett, "The 'Fall of Pagan': Continunity and Change in 14th-Century Burma," in *Conference Under the Tamarind Tree: Three Essays in Burmese History*, ed. Paul Bennett (New Haven: Yale University Southeast Asia Studies, 1971).

25. On the Mongol campaigns in Burma see Aung-Thwin, *Myth and History in the Historiography of Early Burma: Paradigms, Primary Sources, and Prejudices* (Singapore: Institute of Southeast Asian Studies, 1998); Harvey, *History of Burma*, 64–70; Htin Aung, *History of Burma* (New York: Columbia University Press, 1967), 69–83.

4: PIRATES AND PRINCES ALONG THE BAY OF BENGAL

1. Caesar Frederick of Venice, *Account of Venice*, trans. Master Thomas Hickock, reproduced in *SOAS Bulletin of Burma Research* 2:2 (Autumn 2004).

2. For perspectives on Bayinnaung, see Sunait Chutinaranond, "King Bayinnaung as Historical Hero in Thai Perspective," *Comparative Studies on Literature and History of Thailand and Myanmar* (Bangkok: Institute of Asian Studies, Chulalongkorn University, 1997); Kyaw Win, "King Bayinnaung as a Historical Hero in Myanmar Perspective," ibid., 1–7.

3. Than Tun, "History of Burma, a.d. 1300–1400," *Journal of the Burma Research Society* 42:2 (1959), 135–91; Than Hla Thaw, "History of Burma, a.d. 1400–1500," *Journal of the Burma Research Society* 42:2 (1959), 135–51.

4. On the early modern trading world in the Bay of Bengal, see Om Prakash, "Coastal Burma and the Trading World of the Bay of Bengal, 1500–1680," in Jos Gommans and Jacques Leider, eds., *The Maritime Frontier of Burma: Exploring Political, Cultural, and Commercial Interaction in the Indian Ocean World, 1200–1800* (Leiden: KITLV Press, 2002).

5. Jon Fernquist, "Min-gyi-nyo, the Shan Invasions of Ava (1524–27), and the Beginnings of Expansionary Warfare in Toungoo Burma: 1486–1539," *SOAS Bulletin of Burma Research* 3 (Autumn 2005).

6. John King Fairbank, *China: A New History* (Cambridge, Mass.: Harvard University Press, 1992), 128–40.

7. Louise Levathes, *When China Ruled the Seas: The Treasure Fleet of the Dragon Throne* (New York: Oxford University Press, 1994).

8. On Bayinnaung's conquests, see Htin Aung, *History of Burma*, 102–27; Victor Lieberman, *Burmese Administrative Cycles: Anarchy and Conquest, c. 1580–1760* (Princeton: Princeton University Press, 1984); see also Harvey, *History of Burma*, 162–79; and Lieberman, *Strange Parallels*, 123–67.

9. Sanjay Subrahmanyam, *The Portugese Empire in Asia: A Political and Economic History* (London: Longman, 1993), chapter 4.

10. Harvey, *History of Burma*, 160–62.

11. On Arakan's history, see Michael Charney, "Arakan, Min Yazagyi and the Portuguese: The Relationship Between the Growth of Arakanese Imperial Power and Portuguese Mercenaries on the Fringe of Southeast Asia," *SOAS Bulletin of Burma Research* 3:2 (2005); Richard Eaton, "Locating Arakan and Time, Space and Historical Scholarship," in Gommans and Leider, *The Maritime Frontier of Burma*; Harvey, *History of Burma*, 137–49; Pamela Gutman, *Burma's Lost Kingdoms: Splendours of Arakan* (Bangkok: Orchid Press, 2001); Sanjay Subrahmanyam, "And a River Runs Through It: The Mrauk-U Kingdom and Its Bay of Bengal Context," in Gommans and Leider, *The Maritime Frontier of Burma*.

12. Father A. Farinha, "Journey of Father A. Farinha, S.J., from Diego to Arakan, 1639–40," in Sebastião Manrique, *Travels of Fray Sebastien Manrique, 1629–1643* (Oxford: Printed for Hakluyt Society, 1927), 172–75.

13. G. E. Harvey, "Bayinnaung's Living Descendent: The Magh Bohmong," *Journal of the Burma Research Society* 44:1 (1961), 35–42.

14. Duarte Barbosa, *A Description of the Coasts of East Africa and Malabar in the Beginning of the Sixteenth Century*, trans. from an early Spanish manuscript by Henry E. J. Stanley (1866; repr., New Delhi: Asian Educational Services, 1995), 182–83.

15. François Bernier, *Travels in the Mogul Empire* (London: W. Pickering, 1826), 175.

16. D. G. E. Hall, "Studies in Dutch Relations with Arakan," *Journal of the Burma Research Society* 26 (1936), 1–31.

17. ARA, Letter from Governor-General Coen and Council at Batavia to Andries Soury and Abraham van Uffelen at Masulipatam, 8 May 1622, VOC 1076, ff. 76–78, quoted in Om Prakash, "Coastal Burma and the Trading World," in Gommans and Leider, *The Maritime Frontier of Burma*, 98.

18. Alexander Hamilton, *New Account of the East Indies* (Edinburgh: J. Mosman, 1727), quoted in Henry Yule, *Narrative of the Mission to the Court of Ava in 1855* (repr., London: Oxford University Press, 1968), 110.

19. On de Brito's career, see Harvey, *History of Burma*, 185–89; Htin Aung, *A History of Burma*, 134–44.

20. Harvey, *History of Burma*, 187.

21. Htin Aung, *A History of Burma*, 137.

22. Ibid., 140.

23. Paul Ambroise Bigandet, *An Outline of the History of the Catholic Burmese Mission from the Year 1720 to 1887* (Rangoon: Hanthawaddy Press, 1887), 11.

24. G. E. Harvey, "The Fate of Shah Shuja 1661," *Journal of the Burma Research Society* 12 (1922), 107–15.

25. Harvey, *History of Burma*, 146–48.

26. Jonathan D. Spence, *The Search for Modern China* (New York: W. W. Norton, 1990), 26–48.

27. Ibid., 37.

28. Fernquist, "Min-gyi-nyo, the Shan Invasions of Ava."

29. Harvey, *History of Burma*, 196–201, 352–53.

30. For a comprehensive account of Burmese state formation up to the early nineteenth century, see Lieberman, *Strange Parallels*, chapter 2.

5: THE CONSEQUENCES OF PATRIOTISM

1. *Burma Gazetteer—Shwebo District*, vol. A (Rangoon: Supt., Govt. Print. and Stationery, 1929), 1–10.

2. On the early Konbaung dynasty, see Htin Aung, *History of Burma*, 157–93; William J. Koenig, *The Burmese Polity, 1752–1819: Politics, Administration, and Social Organization in the Early Konbaung Period* (Ann Arbor: Center for South and Southeast Asian Studies, University of Michigan, 1990); Harvey, *History of Burma*, 219–305.

3. Proceedings of an Embassy to the King of Ava, Pegu & in 1757, Alexander Dalrymple, *Oriental Repertory* (London: W. Ballintine, 1808), quoted in *SOAS Bulletin of Burma Research* 3:1 (Spring 2005).

4. Robert Lester, "Proceedings of an Embassy to the King of Ava, Pegu, &C. in 1757"; *SOAS Bulletin of Burma Research* 3:1 (2005).

5. Though it was arguably not an ethnic Burmese v. ethnic Mon conflict, see Victor Lieberman, "Ethnic Politics in Eighteenth Century Burma," *Modern Asian Studies* 12:3 (1978).

6. D. G. E. Hall, *Europe and Burma* (London: Oxford University Press, 1945), 66–67.

7. Negrais was later overrun and the English there massacred. See J. S. Furnivall, "The Tragedy of Negrais," *Journal of the Burma Research Society* 21:3 (1931), 1–133.

8. Harvey, *History of Burma*, 229–31.
9. Sayadaw Athwa III, 148, quoted in Harvey, *History of Burma*, 235.
10. Tin, *Konbaungzet Maha Yazawindaw-gyi*, vol. 1, 182.
11. Spence, *The Search for Modern China*, 90–116.
12. On the Qing invasions of the 1760s, I've relied on Yingcong Dai's seminal study "A Disguised Defeat: The Myanmar Campaign of the Qing Dynasty," *Modern Asian Studies* 38:1 (2004), 145–89; see also Harvey, *History of Burma*, 253–58, 355–56; Htin Aung, A *History of Burma*, 175–83.
13. Quoted in Yingcong Dai, "A Disguised Defeat," 157.
14. Ibid., 166.
15. On Bodawpaya's reign, see Myint-U, *The Making of Modern Burma*, 13–17.

6: WAR

1. Myint-U, *The Making of Modern Burma*, 13–15.
2. On the Manipur and Assam campaigns, see Gangmumei Kabui, *History of Manipur*, vol. 1, *Precolonial Period* (New Delhi, 1991), 194–291; S. L. Baruah, A *Comprehensive History of Assam* (New Delhi: Munshiram Manoharlal Publishers, 1985), 220–369.
3. Quoted in Dorothy Woodman, *The Making of Burma* (London: Cresset Press, 1962), 64.
4. Political and Secret Correspondence with India, Bengal: Secret and Political (341), India Office Records, the British Library, 5 August 1826.
5. On the First Anglo-Burmese War, see especially J. J. Snodgrass, *The Burmese War* (London: J. Murray, 1827); see also Anna Allott, *The End of the First Anglo-Burmese War: The Burmese Chronicle Account of How the 1826 Treaty of Yandabo Was Negotiated* (Bangkok: Chulalongkorn University Press, 1994); George Ludgate Bruce, *The Burma Wars 1824–1884* (London: Hart Davis, MacGibbon, 1973); W. S. Desai, "Events at the Court and Capital of Ava During the First Anglo-Burmese War," *Journal of the Burma Research Society* 27:1 (1937), 1–14; C. M. Enriquez, "Bandula—A Burmese Soldier," *Journal of the Burma Research Society* 11 (1921), 158–62.
6. Chris Bayly, *Empire and Information: Intelligence Gathering and Social Communication in India, 1780–1870* (Cambridge: Cambridge University Press, 1997), chapter 3.
7. Snodgrass, *The Burmese War*, 16.
8. Ibid., 102–103.
9. Maj. Enriquez, "Bandula—A Burmese Soldier," 158–62.
10. *The Lonely Planet Guide to Myanmar (Burma)* (Victoria, Australia: Lonely Planet Publications, 2002), 245.
11. Yule, *Narrative of the Mission to the Court of Ava*, 151. He was referring to Amarapura a few years later, but as the entire population was moved from Ava to the new royal city, the Muslim population, which he estimated at around nine thousand in Amarapura, must have been generally the same.
12. V. C. Scott O'Connor, *Mandalay and Other Cities of the Past in Burma* (London: Hutchinson & Co., 1907), 110.

7: MANDALAY

1. Aung Myint, *Ancient Myanmar Cities in Aerial Photos* (Rangoon: Ministry of Culture, 1999).

2. Thaung Blackmore, "The Founding of the City of Mandalay by King Mindon," *Journal of Oriental Studies* 5 (1959–60), 82–97.

3. Oliver Pollak, "A Mid-Victorian Coverup: The Case of the 'Combustible Commodore' and the Second Anglo-Burmese War," *Albion* X (1978), 171–83.

4. Henry Burney, "On the Population of the Burman Empire," *Journal of the Burma Research Society* 31 (1941), 155.

5. Ibid., 97–98.

6. On Mindon and his reign, see Williams Barretto, *King Mindon* (Rangoon: New Light of Burma Press, 1935); Kyan, "King Mindon's Councillors," *Journal of the Burma Research Society* 44 (1961), 43–60; Myo Myint, "The Politics of Survival in Burma: Diplomacy and Statecraft in the Reign of King Mindon 1853–1878," unpublished Ph.D. dissertation, Cornell University, 1987; Oliver B. Pollak, *Empires in Collision: Anglo-Burmese Relations in the Mid-Nineteenth Century* (Westport, Conn.: Greenwood Press, 1979); Thaung, "Burmese Kingship in Theory and Practice Under the Reign of King Mindon," *Journal of the Burma Research Society* 42 (1959), 171–84.

7. On Mindon's reforms, see Myint-U, *The Making of Modern Burma*, chapters 5 and 6.

8. Langham Carter, "The Burmese Army," *Journal of the Burma Research Society* 27 (1937), 254–76.

9. Yule, *Narrative to the Mission to the Court of Ava*, xxxvii.

10. Ibid., 111.

11. Ibid., 107.

12. James Lee, "Food Supply and Population Growth in Southwest China, 1250–1850," *Journal of Asian Studies* 41:4 (1982), 729.

13. On the Panthay rebellion I have drawn mainly on David Atwill, "Blinkered Visions: Islamic Identity, Hui Ethnicity, and the Panthay Rebellion in Southwest China, 1856–1873," *Journal of Asian Studies* 62:4 (2003); see also C. Pat Giersch, "A Motley Throng, Social Change on Southwest China's Early Modern Frontier, 1700–1880," *Journal of Asian Studies* 60:1 (2001).

14. Spence, *The Search for Modern China*, chapter 8.

15. On this trip and Anglo-Burmese relations during this period more generally, see Htin Aung, *The Stricken Peacock: Anglo-Burmese Relations, 1752–1948* (The Hague: M. Nijhoff, 1965); Htin Aung, "First Burmese Mission to the Court of St. James: Kinwun Mingyi's Diaries 1872–1874," *Journal of the Burma Research Society* (December 1974). I have not, unfortunately, been able to consult the more recent translation by L. E. Bagshawe, *Kinwun Mingyi's London Diary: The First Mission of a Burmese Minister in Britain, 1872* (Bangkok: Oxford Press, 2006).

16. Htin Aung, "First Burmese Mission," 4–13.

17. Ibid., 76–77.

18. Tin, *The Royal Administration of Burma*, 251.

19. Paul Bennett, "The Conference Under the Tamarind Tree: Burmese Politics and the Ascension of King Thibaw, 1878–1882," in Bennett, *Conference Under the Tamarind Tree*.

20. John Ebenezer Marks, *Forty Years in Burma* (London: Hutchinson and Co., 1917), chapters 15 and 18.
21. On the Thibaw government and the reforms, see Myint-U, *The Making of Modern Burma*, chapter 7.
22. Po Hlaing, the lord of Yaw, "Rajadhammasangaha," *SOAS Bulletin of Burma Research* 2:2 (2004).
23. On Yanaung, see Tin, *The Royal Administration of Burma*, 250–76.
24. Ibid., 271.
25. Ibid.
26. Htin Aung, *Lord Randolph Churchill*, 65–73.

8: TRANSITIONS
1. Paul Edmonds, *Peacocks and Pagodas* (London: George Routledge and Sons, 1924), 96–100.
2. On U Thant, I have relied largely on family oral history as well as an unpublished autobiographical paper written shortly before his death in 1974; see also Thant, *View from the UN: The Memoirs of U Thant* (1978; repr., Englewood Cliffs, N.J.: Prentice Hall, 2005); as well as June Bingham, *U Thant: The Search for Peace* (New York: Knopf, 1966); Ramses Nassif, *U Thant in New York 1961–71: A Portrait of the Third UN Secretary-General* (New York: St. Martin's Press, 1988); Kaba Sein Tin, *Nyeinchanyay Bithuka U Thant* (Rangoon: Tagaung Press, 1967); Brian Urquhart, *A Life in War and Peace* (New York: Harper & Row, 1987), chapters 15 and 16.
3. *Imperial Gazetteer of India* 19 (Oxford: Clarendon Press, 1908), 403.
4. Michael Adas, *The Burma Delta: Economic Development and Social Change on an Asian Rice Frontier*, 1852–1941 (Madison: University of Wisconsin Press, 1974).
5. There is no accepted way of determining today's value of old money; different methods will arrive at different conclusions, in this case from just over three million pounds to more than twenty-three million pounds. See Lawrence H. Officer, "What Is Its Relative Value in UK Pounds?" *Economic History Services*, 30 October 2004, http://www.eh.net.
6. *Rangoon Times*, 3 January 1928; Pantanaw U Thant, "We Burmans," *New Burma*, 8 September 1939.
7. J. S. Furnivall, *Colonial Policy and Practice: A Comparative Study of Burma and Netherlands India* (Cambridge: Cambridge University Press, 1948).
8. Harvey, *History of Burma*, 85–86.
9. On Thibaw in exile, see W. S. Desai, *Deposed King Thibaw of Burma in India, 1885–1916* (Bombay: Bharatiya Vidya Bhavan, 1967).
10. Norman Lewis, *Golden Earth: Travels in Burma* (London: Cape, 1952), 100.
11. Kaung, "A Survey of the History of Education in Burma Before the British Conquest and After," *Journal of the Burma Research Society* 46:2 (1963), 1–124.
12. N. R. Chakravarti, *The Indian Minority in Burma* (London: Oxford University Press for the Institute of Race Relations, 1971).
13. Sean Turnell, "The Chettiars in Burma," *Macquarie Economics Research Papers*, no. 12/2005 (July 2005).

14. Rudyard Kipling, *From Sea to Sea and Other Sketches: Letters of Travel* (1889), vol. 1, no. 2 (New York: Doubleday, 1914).

15. John Cady, *A History of Modern Burma* (Ithaca, N.Y.: Cornell University Press, 1958); F. S. V. Donnison, *Public Administration in Burma: A Study of Development During the British Connexion* (London: Royal Institute of International Affairs, 1953); G. E. Harvey, *British Rule in Burma, 1824–42* (London: Faber and Faber, 1946); A. Ireland, *The Province of Burma*, 2 vols. (Boston: Houghton, Mifflin and Company, 1907).

16. Bernard Crick, *George Orwell: A Life* (London: Secker & Warburg, 1980), chapter 5.

17. On the life of British civil servants in the later colonial period, see especially Maurice Collis, *Trials in Burma* (London: Faber, 1938) and Leslie Glass, *The Changing of the Kings: Memories of Burma 1934–1949* (London: Owen, 1985).

18. Alister McCrae, *Scots in Burma: Golden Times in a Golden Land* (Edinburgh: Kiscadale, 1990).

19. On British life in Burma in colonial times, see B. R. Pearn, *A History of Rangoon* (Rangoon: American Baptist Mission Press, 1939); James George Scott, *Burma, A Handbook of Practical Information* (London: Daniel O'Conner, 1906).

20. Noel F. Singer, *Old Rangoon: City of the Shwedagon* (Gartmore, Scotland: Kiscadale, 1995), 109.

21. Maung Htin Aung, "George Orwell and Burma," in *The World of George Orwell*, ed. Miriam Gross (London: Weidenfeld and Nicolson, 1971), 26–27.

22. H. Fielding Hall, *A People at School* (London: Macmillan, 1906), 22–23.

23. Joseph Dautremer, *Burma Under British Rule*, trans. George Scott (London: T. F. Unwin, 1913), 78.

24. Herbert Thirkell White, *A Civil Servant in Burma* (London: E. Arnold, 1913), 129.

25. H. H. Risely and E. A. Gait, Census of India 1901, vol. 1, part 1 (General Report) (Calcutta: Government of India, 1903).

26. Scott, *Burma: A Handbook of Practical Information*, 61–62.

9: STUDYING IN THE AGE OF EXTREMISM

1. Harvey, *British Rule in Burma*, 28.

2. Joint Committee on Indian Constitutional Reform, 22 April 1918, quoted in Cady, *A History of Modern Burma*, 201.

3. Ba U, *My Burma: The Autobiography of a President* (New York: Taplinger, 1958).

4. U May Oung, "The Modern Burman," *Rangoon Gazette*, 10 August 1908.

5. On the nationalist movement from the First World War to independence, see Maung Maung, *Burmese Nationalist Movements 1940–48* (Honolulu: University of Hawai'i Press, 1989); Maung Maung Pye, *Burma in the Crucible* (Rangoon: Khittaya, 1951); Josef Silverstein, *Burmese Politics: The Dilemma of National Unity* (New Brunswick, N.J.: Rutgers University Press, 1980).

6. George Brown, *Burma as I Saw It, 1889–1917* (New York: Frederick A. Stokes, 1925).

7. Donald M. Goldstein and Katherine V. Dillon, *Amelia: A Life of the Aviation Legend* (Dulles, Va.: Potomac Books, 1999), 210.

8. S. R. Chakravorty, "Bengal Revolutionaries in Burma," *Quarterly Review of Historical Studies* 19:1–2 (1979–80), 42–49.
9. Quoted in Cady, *A History of Modern Burma*, 290.
10. Ian Brown, *A Colonial Economy in Crisis: Burma's Rice Cultivators and the World Depression of the 1930s* (London: RoutledgeCurzon, 2005).
11. Bertie Reginald Pearn, *Judson of Burma* (London: Edinburgh House, 1962).
12. On Aung San, see Aung San Suu Kyi, *Aung San* (St. Lucia, Queensland, Australia: University of Queensland Press, 1984); Maung Maung, *Aung San of Burma* (The Hague: M. Nijhoff, 1962).
13. Maung, *Aung San of Burma*.
14. Bingham, *U Thant: The Search for Peace*, 128–29.
15. Khin Yi, *The Dobama Movement in Burma (1930–1938)* (Ithaca, N.Y.: Southeast Asia Program, Cornell University, 1988).
16. For Ba Maw's account of this period and the war, see Ba Maw, *Breakthrough in Burma: Memoirs of a Revolution 1939–46* (New Haven: Yale University Press, 1967).
17. Pantanaw U Thant, "We Burmans."
18. Chris Bayly and Tim Harper, *Forgotten Armies: The Fall of British Asia 1941–45* (Cambridge, Mass.: Belknap Press of Harvard University Press, 2005), 4.
19. Stephen Mercado, *Shadow Warriors of Nakano: A History of the Imperial Japanese Army's Elite Intelligence School* (Washington, D.C.: Brassey's, 2003).
20. For the best account of wartime and immediate postwar Burmese politics, see Bayly and Harper, *Forgotten Armies*.

10: MAKING THE BATTLEFIELD

1. On the war, I've drawn mainly on Louis Allen, *Burma, the Longest War, 1941–45* (London: J. M. Dent & Sons, 1984); Maurice Collis, *Last and First in Burma* (London: Faber and Faber, 1956); and Viscount William Slim, *Defeat into Victory* (London: Cassell, 1956).
2. Collis, *Last and First in Burma*, 40–42.
3. Bayly and Harper, *Forgotten Armies*, 86.
4. Collis, *Last and First in Burma*, 104–105.
5. Ibid., 158–67.
6. Ibid., 178.
7. Donald M. Seekins, "Burma's Japanese Interlude, 1941–45: Did Japan Liberate Burma?," Japan Policy Research Institute Working Paper No. 87 (August 2002); on Aung San's political views, see also Clive Christie, *Ideology and Revolution in Southeast Asia, 1900–1975* (London: RoutledgeCurzon, 2000), 102–104.
8. Quoted in Ba Maw, *Breakthrough in Burma*, 127.
9. Mercado, *Shadow Warriors of Nakano*, 238.
10. On life in the Ba Maw government, see Thakin Nu, *Burma Under the Japanese* (London: Macmillan, 1954).
11. Bayly and Harper, *Forgotten Armies*, 360.
12. Slim, *Defeat into Victory*, 517–19.
13. On the views of conservative Burmese officials, see Kyaw Min, *The Burma We Love* (Calcutta: Bharati Bhavan, 1945).

14. For all the key official documents of the period, see Hugh Tinker, ed., *Burma: The Struggle for Independence 1944–48*, 2 vols. (London: HM Stationery Office, 1983).
15. Quoted in Collis, *Last and First in Burma*, 253B.
16. Bayly and Harper, *Forgotten Armies*, 438.
17. Phillip Plumb in Derek Brooke-Wavell, ed., *Lines from a Shining Land* (London: Britain-Burma Society, 1998), 153–54.
18. On Dorman-Smith during this period, see especially Collis, *Last and First in Burma*, 261–82; see also Cady, *A History of Modern Burma*, 522–35; Maung Maung Pye, *Burma in the Crucible*, 88–145.
19. Collis, *Last and First in Burma*, 270–71.
20. On the military balance, see J. H. McEnery, *Epilogue in Burma, 1945–48: The Military Dimension of British Withdrawal* (Tunbridge Wells: Spellmount, 1990).
21. Collis, *Last and First in Burma*, 270.
22. Cady, *A History of Modern Burma*, 539–41.
23. Ibid., 287.
24. Kin Oung, *Who Killed Aung San?* (Bangkok: White Lotus, 1993); Maung Maung, *A Trial in Burma: The Assassination of Aung San* (The Hague: M. Nijhoff, 1962).
25. *Memoirs of the Earl of Listowel*, chapter 10. Available at www.redrice.com/listowel/index.html.

11: ALTERNATIVE UTOPIAS

1. Human Security Centre, *The Human Security Report 2005* (Vancouver: The Liu Institute for Global Issues, 2005).
2. J. S. Furnivall, "Independence and After," *Pacific Affairs* (June 1949).
3. On the early years of the civil war, see Hugh Tinker, *The Union of Burma: A Study of the First Years of Independence* (London: Oxford University Press, 1961); Frank Trager, *Burma from Kingdom to Republic: A Historical and Political Analysis* (London: Pall Mall, 1966); Cady, *A History of Modern Burma*, 528–624.
4. Cady, *A History of Modern Burma*, 598–99.
5. On U Nu, see Richard Butwell, *U Nu of Burma* (Stanford: Stanford University Press, 1963), as well as his own autobiography: *U Nu, Saturday's Son*, trans. Law-Yone Nu, ed. Kyaw Win (New Haven: Yale University Press, 1975).
6. Nu, *U Nu, Saturday's Son*, 37–38.
7. "Burma's Mess and Ne Win's Plans for an Anti-Guerrilla Army," *Time*, 7 November 1949.
8. Bertil Lintner, *Burma in Revolt: Opium and Insurgency Since 1948* (Boulder, Colo.: Westview Press, 1944), 113. On U.S. support for the KMT, see also Robert H. Taylor, *Foreign and Domestic Consequences of the KMT Intervention in Burma* (Ithaca, N.Y.: Southeast Asia Program, Dept. of Asian Studies, Cornell University, 1973).
9. On the development of the Burmese army in the first fifteen years after independence, I have relied on Mary Callahan's seminal work, *Making Enemies: War and State-building in Burma* (Ithaca, N.Y.: Cornell University Press, 2003), chapters 6 and 7.
10. Callahan, *Making Enemies*, 162.
11. On Burma's foreign policy in the 1950s, see William C. Johnstone, *Burma's Foreign Policy: A Study in Neutralism* (Cambridge: Harvard University Press, 1963).

12. Nu, *U Nu, Saturday's Son*, 276–78.
13. "U Nu Visits Eisenhower," *Time*, 11 July 1955; "U Nu in America," *Time*, 8 August 1955.
14. On Burmese politics in the 1950s, see Cady, *A History of Modern Burma*, 625–42; Tinker, *The Union of Burma*, 34–128, 379–88; Trager, *Burma from Kingdom to Republic*, part 2.
15. "The Caretaker Government and the 1960 Elections," *Time*, 15 February 1960.
16. On the life of the Shan princes, see Maurice Collis, *Lords of the Sunset* (Faber, 1938); C. Y. Lee, *The Sawbwa and His Secretary: My Burmese Reminiscences* (New York: Farrar, Straus and Cudahy, 1958); and Inge Sargent, *Twilight over Burma: My Life as a Shan Princess* (Honolulu: University of Hawai'i Press, 1994).
17. Pascal Khoo Thwe, *From the Land of Green Ghosts: A Burmese Odyssey* (New York: HarperCollins, 2002).
18. Lintner, *Burma in Revolt*, 157.
19. Josef Silverstein, *Burma: Military Rule and the Politics of Stagnation* (Ithaca, N.Y.: Cornell University Press, 1977), 175; Lintner, *Burma in Revolt*, 165.

12: THE TIGER'S TAIL

1. On the Socialist period, see David Steinberg, *Burma: A Socialist Nation of Southeast Asia* (Boulder, Colo.: Westview Press, 1982); Robert H. Taylor, *The State in Burma* (London: C. Hurst & Co., 1987).
2. On Ne Win, see Maung Maung, *Burma and General Ne Win* (London: Asia Publishing House, 1969). On the Ne Win period generally, see Silverstein, *Burma: Military Rule and the Politics of Stagnation*; David Steinberg, *Burma's Road Toward Development: Growth and Ideology Under Military Rule* (Boulder, Colo.: Westview Press, 1981); Robert H. Taylor, *The State in Burma* (London: C. Hurst & Co., 1987).
3. For a personal story of expulsion, see the memoirs of the former Pegu commissioner Balwant Singh, *Burma's Democratic Decade 1952–62: Prelude to Dictatorship* (Tempe, Ariz.: Arizona State University Program for Southeast Asian Studies Monograph Series Press, 2001). See also Mira Kamdar, *Motiba's Tattoos* (New York: PublicAffairs, 2000).
4. On the civil war in the Ne Win years, I have drawn largely on Bertil Lintner, *The Rise and Fall of the Communist Party of Burma (CPB)* (Ithaca, N.Y.: Southeast Asia Program, Cornell University, 1990); Lintner, *Burma in Revolt*; and Martin Smith, *Burma: Insurgency and the Politics of Ethnicity* (London: Zed Books, 1991).
5. *Chiefs and Leading Families of the Shan States and Karenni*, 2nd ed. (Rangoon: Govt. of Burma, 1919); Jackie Yang Li, *The House of Yang, Guardians of an Unknown Frontier* (Sydney: Bookpress, 1997). On the Yang family genealogy, see Christopher Buyers's Yang Dynasty page at www.4dw.net/royalark/Burma/kokang2.htm.
6. Oral history interview with Henry Byroade, Potomac, Maryland, 19 and 21 September 1988, by M. Johnson, Truman Library.
7. "Grinding to a Halt," *Time*, 24 December 1965.
8. Lee Kuan Yew, *From Third World to First: The Singapore Story, 1965–2000* (New York: HarperCollins, 2000), 321.

9. "The 200% Neutral," *Time*, 16 September 1966.
10. Recounted in oral history interview with Henry Byroade.
11. Lintner, *Burma in Revolt*, 201–209; Smith, *Burma: Insurgency and the Politics of Ethnicity*, 219–46.
12. Lintner, *Burma in Revolt*, 211–34.
13. Ibid., 209–10.

13: PALIMPSEST
1. Terry McCarthy, "The Twin Terrors," *Time Asia*, 7 February 2000.
2. Lintner, *The Rise and Fall of the Communist Party of Burma*, 39–46.
3. James George Scott, *Gazetteer of Upper Burma and the Shan States*, vol. 1 (Rangoon: Printed by the Superintendent, Government Printing, Burma, 1900), part 1, 496.
4. Ibid., 499–500.
5. Ibid., 500.
6. For an overview of Burma in the 1990s, see David Steinberg, *The Future of Burma: Crisis and Choice in Myanmar* (New York: Asia Society, 1990).
7. *Financial Times*, 9 November 1989, 6; *Far Eastern Economic Review*, 21 December 1989, 22.
8. *Financial Times*, 21 June 1990, 6.
9. *Far Eastern Economic Review*, 21 December 1989, 22; *Financial Times*, 19 May 1990, sec. 2, 1, and 25 May 1990, 6.
10. Andrew Selth, *Burma's Order of Battle: An Interim Assessment* (Canberra, Australia: Strategic and Defence Studies Centre, Australian National University, 2000).
11. Anthony Davis, "Law and Disorder: A Growing Torrent of Guns and Narcotics Overwhelms China," *Asiaweek*, 25 August 1995.
12. Aung San Suu Kyi, *Freedom from Fear and Other Writings*, ed. Michael Aris (New York: Penguin Books, 1991).
13. Yew, *From Third World to First*, 323.

ACKNOWLEDGMENTS

I am very grateful to Jane Elias, Kevin Doughten, Cara Spitalewitz, and their colleagues at Farrar, Straus and Giroux for their first-rate work and all their assistance this past year. I'd like to thank Walter Donohue at Faber and Faber for his insightful suggestions, as well as Sofia Busch and David Harland, both of whom read early drafts of several chapters and gave me their thoughtful and incisive comments.

I'd also like to say thank you to my parents, Dr. and Mrs. Tyn Myint-U, and other relatives and friends in Burma who shared with me their stories and the stories of my family's past, some of which I have tried to include faithfully in this book.

My special thanks go first to my agent, Clare Alexander, without whom I would never have started writing *The River of Lost Footsteps* and whose encouragement and astute counsel I have valued greatly. And a special thank-you to my editor, Paul Elie; Paul's patient attention, guidance, and steady hand have made this a much better book than it would otherwise have been.